Marie-Antoinette

Marie-Antoinette

Writings on the Body of a Queen

edited by

Dena Goodman

ROUTLEDGE
New York & London

Published in 2003 by
Routledge
29 West 35th Street
New York, NY 10001
www.routledge-ny.com

Published in Great Britain by
Routledge
11 New Fetter Lane
London EC4P 4EE
www.routledge.co.uk

Routledge is an imprint of the Taylor & Francis Group.
Printed in the United States of America on acid-free paper.

10 9 8 7 6 5 4 3 2 1

Library of Congress Cataloging-in-Publication data
Marie-Antoinette : writing on the body of a queen / edited by Dena Goodman.
    p. cm.
Includes bibliographical references and index.
ISBN 0-415-93394-3—ISBN 0-415-93395-1 (pbk.)
    1. Marie Antoinette, Queen, consort of Louis XVI, King of France, 1755–1793.
2. Queens—France—Biography.   3. France—History—Louis XVI, 1774–1793.
I. Goodman, Dena, 1952–

DC137.1 .M375 2003
944'.035'092—dc21
[B]
                                            2002032980

Contents

*Illustrations are gathered in a photo
insert between pages 138 and 139.*

Credits

"A Select Chronology of Marie Antoinette's Life," reprinted from Chantal Thomas, *The Wicked Queen: The Origins of the Myth of Marie-Antoinette*, translated by Julie Rose (Zone Books, 2001), 165–68. With permission of Zone Books.

Larry Wolff, "Hapsburg Letters: The Disciplinary Dynamics of Epistolary Narrative in the Correspondence of Maria Theresa and Marie-Antoinette," reprinted from Ann Fehn, Ingeborg Hoesterey, and Maria Tatar, eds., *Neverending Stories: Toward a Critical Narratology* (Princeton University Press, 1992), 70–86. With permission of Princeton University Press.

Mary D. Sheriff, "The Portrait of the Queen," condensed from chapter 5 of *The Exceptional Woman: Elisabeth Vigée-Lebrun and the Cultural Politics of Art* (University of Chicago Press, 1996), 143–79. With permission of the University of Chicago Press.

Sarah Maza, "The Diamond Necklace Affair Revisited (1785–1786): The Case of the Missing Queen," reprinted from Lynn Hunt, ed., *Eroticism and the Body Politic* (Johns Hopkins University Press, 1991), 63–89. With permission of the Johns Hopkins University Press.

Chantal Thomas, "The Heroine of the Crime: Marie-Antoinette in Pamphlets," translated from "L'Héroïne du crime: Marie-Antoinette dans les pamphlets," in Jean-Claude Bonnet, ed., *La Carmagnole des muses: L'homme de lettres et l'artiste dans la Révolution* (Armand Colin, 1988), 245–60. With permission of Vivendi International.

Lynn Hunt, "The Many Bodies of Marie-Antoinette: Political Pornography and the Problem of the Feminine in the French Revolution," reprinted from Lynn Hunt, ed., *Eroticism and the Body Politic* (Johns Hopkins University Press, 1991), 108–30. With permission of The Johns Hopkins University Press.

Elizabeth Colwill, "Pass as a Woman, Act Like a Man: Marie-Antoinette as Tribade in the Pornography of the French Revolution," reprinted from Jeffrey Merrick and Bryant T. Ragan Jr., eds., *Homosexuality in Modern France* (Oxford University Press, 1996), 54–79. With permission of Oxford University Press.

Terry Castle, "Marie-Antoinette Obsession," reprinted from *Representations* 38 (spring 1992): 1–38. With permission of the Regents of the University of California.

Laura Mason, " 'We're Just Little People, Louis': Marie-Antoinette on Film," reprinted from *Film-Historia* 4, no. 3 (1994): 210–22. With permission of *Film-Historia*.

Pierre Saint-Amand, "Terrorizing Marie-Antoinette," reprinted from *Critical Inquiry* 20 (spring 1994): 379–400. With permission of the University of Chicago Press.

Acknowledgments

It seemed a simple matter to bring together a collection of essays on Marie-Antoinette that had already been published in journals and other volumes. But it turned out to be a much longer and more difficult task. I would not have been able to accomplish it without the help of many people and the encouragement of many more. I am grateful first, and most obviously, to the authors of the essays, all of whom have been enthusiastic about the project from the beginning and have given me the opportunity to bask in their reflected glory. Among them, Mary Sheriff, Pierre Saint-Amand, Larry Wolff, Tom Kaiser, and Susan Lanser have been collaborators and advisors on the project at various times; each of them deserves particular thanks. I am especially grateful to Tom and Susan for allowing me to include in this volume work that has not been previously published. Their essays add new perspectives on this rich scholarship and demonstrate the vitality of a field that continues to generate exciting new work.

Editing this volume has been made easier by the generosity of my two homes at the University of Michigan, the Department of History and the Women's Studies Program, both of which provided financial assistance for the final stages of the editing process. I am also grateful for the able assistance of Sean Takats, who drafted the biographical sketches included in the volume, and of Megan Moore, who helped with the translation of Chantal Thomas' essay, which appears here in English for the first time. Lora Guma provided invaluable library assistance early on, and Casey Carr saved me an enormous amount of work by typing all the essays so that they could be edited from disk.

At Routledge, Karen Wolny has made getting a manuscript from prospectus to contract seem like a piece of cake. I am grateful for her patience as well as for her efficiency and unflagging support. Darline Levy went well beyond her responsibilities as a reviewer of this project, not only giving invaluable advice for its improvement, but also acting as its advocate. I am grateful to her and to the many other colleagues whose enthusiasm for *Marie-Antoinette: Writings on the Body of a Queen* has brought it from just another good idea to happy reality.

Dena Goodman
Ann Arbor, July 2002

Introduction: Not Another Biography of Marie-Antoinette!

Dena Goodman

In the two hundred years since Marie-Antoinette's life ended at the guillotine, many biographies have been written, and all have fascinated the reading public.[1] This volume, however, is not another biography of Marie-Antoinette. The authors of the essays presented here do not claim to tell her life story, nor do they aim to pass judgment on her. Unlike biographers, they have not tried to make sense of her life by making a narrative of it.[2] Rather, they show us Marie-Antoinette at certain moments crucial in her life and in the life of the French monarchy and the French nation. At each of these moments we see not a woman so much as a struggle over the identity of a woman and the control of her life, her actions, her image, her self. What or who is that self? At least from the moment that a marriage was arranged between the daughter of the Hapsburg ruler Maria Theresa and the heir to the French throne, this question—who Marie-Antoinette ought to be, how she ought to act, what precisely it meant to be a woman and a queen—were questions that mattered to many people.

To resist making Marie-Antoinette's life into a story, however, does not mean to place her outside history. I suggest we view her as the historian Joan Scott has recently presented a group of nineteenth-century feminists: "as sites—historical locations or markers—where crucial political and cultural contests are enacted and can be examined in some detail."[3] Such contests were enacted, as the title of this volume suggests, on the very body of the queen, but also on the complex identity of Marie-Antoinette—as queen, as woman, as mother, as wife, as foreigner; as an individual, a member of a fam-

1

ily, and the representative of a monarchy and an entire social system identified by the French revolutionaries of 1789 as the "Old Regime."

As Scott makes sure to emphasize, to think of particular women as "sites" does not mean to rob them of their individuality or humanity. Rather, "to figure a person—in this case, a woman—as a place or location . . . is . . . to recognize the many factors that constitute her agency, the complex and multiple ways in which she is constructed as a historical actor."[4] The relationship between individuals and history summed up by Karl Marx's famous assertion that "men make their own history, but they do not make it just as they please" is even more acute in the case of women.[5] To present them as mere subjects of larger forces is to reinforce the notion of women as powerless victims; to present them as autonomous agents who make history as they please, however, is to grant them through words precisely that for which, through history, they continue to struggle: political agency and personal autonomy. Marie-Antoinette was no feminist campaigner, but she was a woman whose life more than others was woven into the fabric of history not only because of her prominence, but because she represented the contradictions in the social, political, and gender systems of her day. To examine her as a set of sites of contestation is thus not to minimize her importance as an individual, but to reconfigure the relationship between the (female) individual and history and to examine how each constituted the other. It is to reveal the various ways in which Marie-Antoinette and the history of France shaped each other in the struggle to define themselves in a time of great social change.

The problem of establishing some fixed identity is one with which modern women struggle throughout their lives. And, as historian Jo Burr Margadant reminds us, "no one 'invents' a self apart from cultural notions available to them in a particular historical setting."[6] Of course, very few of us have the curse or the privilege of carrying out this personal struggle on the public stage Marie-Antoinette inhabited throughout her life. It is because Marie-Antoinette was a public figure that her struggle was not simply her own, not simply a matter of personal psychology or family dynamics. Marie-Antoinette's status as a member of the French royal family—wife to the king and mother to the heir to the throne—meant that she could never retreat from the public arena to the private realm of the family. Who Marie-Antoinette was, and what her role and responsibilities to her family were, were never simply private matters. And although the same might be said of all queens, Marie-Antoinette was the first in France to live at a time when pamphlets and newspapers and other forms of print publicity were ready to put the spotlight on public figures—to manufacture news if necessary to satisfy an avid reading public newly introduced to the thrills of court scandals and revolutionary politics, and constantly flattered with the importance of its own opinions.[7] From the moment she arrived in France, Marie-Antoinette found herself treading a fine line that crossed two competing spheres of public life: the court at Versailles, the center and epitome of the Old Regime of formality, privilege, show, and duty; and a new public sphere of press and public opinion.[8]

For Marie-Antoinette, the struggle for agency and personal autonomy—the ability to be herself and to act according to her own will and desires—was carried out on the public stage and within a set of dynamic forces, within what we might call history itself. She was constantly being identified, constructed, presented, and represented. Her body was the site of controversy and power struggles; its image was central to those struggles. From her arrival in France for her marriage to the dauphin in 1770, Marie-Antoinette could not call her body her own. As she crossed the river that marked the boundary of French territory, she was stripped of her "Austrian" clothes and, thus, symbolically, of her attachment to the family and nation of her birth. She arrived in France naked, like a baby. There she received a set of French clothes and a French hairstyle, and thus reborn and reclad, she was brought to Versailles for the elaborate wedding ceremony that would present her to the French court and nation in a series of nuptial rituals, parties, and public celebrations. Everyone seems to have been charmed by her youth, her beauty, and her grace. Her first responsibility, however, was to produce an heir to the French throne, and that turned out to be no easy task. For reasons that have since become clear—Louis was afflicted with phimosis—but were not always so to the young couple, their worried parents, or the public at large, the marriage of Louis and Marie-Antoinette could not be consummated until 1777.[9] By the time her first child was born in 1778, doubts about the king's virility and the queen's sexuality and fidelity were firmly planted in the public mind, to be nurtured and exploited to the political advantage of disgruntled courtiers, rival factions, revolutionaries, and republicans alike.

Royal marriages had always been arranged in order to enhance the power of the state in one way or another, but Marie-Antoinette's marriage to Louis backfired in these terms almost from the start. Her mother, it should be remembered, was the ruler of one of the "superpowers" of the eighteenth century, and her husband would become king of its major rival on the European continent. The second half of the eighteenth century, moreover, was an era in which French political culture was shaped by a combination of old dynastic rule and a new sense of nationalism.[10] Rather than strengthening the bond between France and Austria, the presence of a "foreign queen" connected to France's greatest continental rival would become an irritant in the body politic and an endless source of suspicion. If the king was simply "France"—the name by which he was usually referred to —then who was the queen, if not, as her enemies constantly reminded their readers, the *Autrichienne,* "the Austrian"?

Until October 1789, when Parisian market women brought the royal family back to the capital with wagonloads of bread to feed their families, Marie-Antoinette lived in the insular world of Versailles. This was a world defined by court politics—by intrigue and influence and secret deals. Like other consorts of French kings— both queens and royal mistresses—Marie-Antoinette was a player in these traditional politics of secrecy and favoritism, in which reputations and careers rose and fell at the pleasure of anyone who could get the ear of the king. Her position, however, was complicated by several factors. First, while her marriage was supposed to cement an alliance between France and Austria, tensions and suspicions between the two powers put her in an awkward position between them. In court politics, her every move was scrutinized. Second, court politics itself—politics conducted behind closed doors and based on proximity to the king—no longer went unquestioned. A new political culture that condemned secrecy and demanded public accountability in the name of public opinion had developed in the eighteenth century. By the time Louis XVI took the throne in 1774, openness was demanded by an array of critics, from Enlightenment men of letters and journalists to aristocratic opponents of royal absolutism. For them, politics beyond closed doors was epitomized by a politics of the bedroom. In such a political climate, it was difficult to imagine any legitimate *political* role for the queen.[11]

And yet, if the politics of the court was seen as secretive, the daily life of those who inhabited the palace of Versailles was extremely public. By the time Marie-Antoinette was queen, ordinary citizens could take a Sunday drive from Paris to watch her engage in the most ordinary of daily activities. Here is an excerpt from one visitor's account of his outing to Versailles with a few friends in the summer of 1785:

> We stayed to wait for the queen, who was also supposed to attend the mass. There is a crowd on Sundays. Some come to Versailles out of curiosity, others for an audience with the ministers. The king's chapel was full today. I could see well because I'm tall, but lots of people couldn't see a thing. As far as I could tell, very few people listened to the mass, everyone was busy looking at the king. It's fun to see some people up on their tiptoes, craning their necks, others looking for some daylight in the crowd. . . .
>
> After having waited a little while, we saw the queen, who appeared, followed by her ladies, by Madame [her sister-in-law] and Madame the comtesse d'Artois [another sister-in-law]. Same ceremony as when the king passed by. She sat where the king had sat, Madame where Monsieur [the comte de Provence] had sat, and Madame d'Artois in her husband's place. After the mass, she left with the same ceremony as the king. We saw her pass by a second time.
>
> After having again examined the apartments and the crowd, we went to watch the king and queen dine. She was on the king's left. She didn't eat, but the king ate with a very good appetite, watching everybody, talking very little, but always with a happy air and an air of goodness that is satisfying to a subject. . . .
>
> I was really close to the king's table. There was no one in front of me. As soon as I saw that someone wanted to pass, I moved forward. Thus I found myself very close to the king. The queen spoke to a gentleman who was actually touching my right side; he had the air of being a member of the court. There was an incredible crowd there to see the king dine. The guard who was at the door sent lots of people away. Some duchesses were seated off to the side of the table on stools. The queen spoke to them a few times. To respond, they rose and then sat down again. Everything was done with considerable etiquette. The king's servants who carried in the dishes were forced to part the crowd in order to pass through.[12]

When the visitors strolled out to the Trianon, where the queen was known to enjoy herself in the company of a small group of women friends, however, they were told they could not see the interior of the château, only the gardens. In the public world of Versailles, where tourists jostled courtiers for a better view of the king and queen, the Trianon was for Marie-Antoinette a space of privacy and friendship. Not surprisingly, what the public could not see, they tried to imagine—or others imagined for them. The privacy of the Trianon, like the secrecy of court politics, became a site for the play of the political and the erotic imagination. It was a popular subject of books and pamphlets and of the rumor and gossip that circulated around the cafés, salons, taverns, and streets of Paris.[13]

Like other women, Marie-Antoinette was not born a queen, but unlike most other queens she did not die one: in 1792, as a result of the French Revolution, the French monarchy was abolished, and Queen Marie-Antoinette was reduced to "just another citizen."[14] The identity of Marie-Antoinette with queen of France was thus of fixed duration and enclosed within a before and an after. She had had to learn to be a queen, and now she had to learn how *not* to be one—how to be a person after having been a queen. But categories such as "citizen" and "woman" are as constructed as that of "queen," and each of these roles and identities could be learned or rejected, inhabited or contested, performed or struggled over in many different ways. Marie-Antoinette grew to womanhood at a time when gender was a very unstable category and debates about women's human potential and proper social role were hotly contested.[15] Running through the stream of words and images in which the queen was represented to the public was an anxiety caused by the contemporary perception that, in the words of historian Gary Kates, "traditional gender roles were topsy-turvy."[16] Marie-Antoinette had to learn how to be a woman (or at least how to perform femininity) long before she was deprived of her throne. Those who would be, were, and had been her subjects contributed to this educational project, challenging the queen's authority over her own identity. When Marie-Antoinette asserted her own taste by appearing publicly in the latest fashions or championing new music, they reminded her that it was not within the power of the queen to define her role, her place, her self. The question is thus raised: What was within the power of the queen? What is within the power of a woman? We might ask further: When is the exercise of power by women considered legitimate, and when is it considered usurpation or violation? Who determines not only where power lies, but when its exercise is legitimate?

Because Marie-Antoinette was not only a queen but a sister, a daughter, a wife, and a mother, the representations of the queen—from royal portraits to political pornography—also reveal and play upon the contradictions of her social position, her gender roles, and her place within the family. Her body became a playground for the representation of these contradictions. When France fell into revolution in 1789, Marie-Antoinette found herself caught more than ever in the web of conflicting loyalties and general suspicion. Her marital fidelity to her husband put her increasingly at odds with the revolutionaries, while loyalty to her birth family, the Austrian Hapsburgs, now headed by her brother, Leopold II, would make her an enemy of the French nation.

The period from the beginning of the revolution until the queen's execution in October 1793 was the heyday of the vicious play of representation. As the king wavered, always trying to resist the pressure of change before giving in to it reluctantly, the attacks on the queen became bolder and more frequent. The question not only remained but became more acute—if the king was weak or seemed to oppose the good and the will of the people, was it perhaps the queen's doing? How else to explain the widening gap between France the nation and France the king if not through the secret doings of the *Autrichienne*? If it was the king's brothers who were gathering support abroad for a counterrevolution and invasion, it was the queen's brother who was heading up the alliance of foreign powers amassing troops at France's borders. It was toward Austria that the royal family fled on the night of 20 June 1791, only to be captured in the French town of Varennes and returned under guard to Paris five days later, where they would remain imprisoned until their separate deaths. A year later, in July 1792, it was the queen's brother, along with the Prussian king, who threatened revenge on Paris if the royal family should be harmed—was it his fellow monarch he was most concerned about, or his sister? As the mythical bond between the king and his people weakened, the anomalous position of the queen became the central site of political contestation. After the trial and execution of the king in January 1793, one might have expected the pressure to be off and the queen to be left alone to live out her life as a simple widow, no longer holding any meaning or value for the republic, no longer even worth attacking. Instead, the queen herself was put on trial later that year, for crimes not only against the French nation but against nature itself: she was accused not only of treason and conspiracy but of incest with her son, who had already been removed from her care for his own safety. On 16 October 1793, after a three-day trial, crowds lined the streets as Marie-Antoinette was carried from her prison rooms in the Temple to be executed by guillotine in the center of Paris. She was thirty-seven years old.

The execution of Marie-Antoinette, who had already lost all of her titles—of queen, of wife, and of mother—has given her life,

begun as a romance, the character of tragedy in the hands of her biographers. The essays gathered here try to make sense of this death
without, however, letting it define the meaning of the life. This is not
another biography.

In the pages of this book, we first encounter Marie-Antoinette in the
letters she exchanged with her mother upon her arrival in France.
Between these two women—one the most powerful of her day on
the stage of global politics, and the other a fourteen-year-old just
learning how to assume her new role as future queen of France—
letters were themselves a form of power. Through a close reading of
their correspondence, Larry Wolff shows the mother to be a "mistress of epistolary discipline," who tries through the regularity of letter writing to impose order on her daughter's life, while the young
Marie-Antoinette spreads her wings in the pleasure fair that was the
court at Versailles. What the philosopher Michel Foucault has called
the "microphysics of power" here comes up against the will of a
young woman nourished by both royal status and the excitement of
Europe's most fashionable capital. And at issue, more than anything
else, is the young woman's body—how to portray it and how to regulate it so that her queenship will be made secure by motherhood.

    Art historian Mary Sheriff turns our attention to the portraits
painted of Marie-Antoinette over the course of her reign, and in
particular to Elisabeth Vigée-Lebrun's 1783 painting known as the
portrait *en chemise*. Vigée-Lebrun's portrait of the queen wearing a
fashionable but radically simple dress (the *chemise*) provoked such a
hostile reaction that the painting was withdrawn from public display. This public rejection provokes Sheriff to ask: how does "a portrait of the queen serve the aims of the state? What relations of representation, power, and imagination are at work in the queen's
portrait?" In the end, she finds in this and the many other portraits
of the queen painted by Vigée-Lebrun failed attempts by Marie-
Antoinette to assert herself not as a queen but as a woman against
established norms of gender and power. Indeed, it was because
Marie-Antoinette was queen of France that she and her painter were
unable to accomplish the most basic task of portraiture—to represent the subject.

    These first essays suggest how wary we must be of representa-
tions of Marie-Antoinette. Wolff reminds us that the letters exchanged between the young princess and her mother, which have

fascinated historians and readers since the nineteenth century, cannot be read as transparent documents. And Sheriff shows us how the many official portraits painted of Marie-Antoinette are documents of political struggles over her proper representation as both a woman and a queen, rather than simple likenesses. If these seemingly innocent, disinterested representations require the delicate analytic tools of literary and art criticism, with what greater care must we consider the waves of pornography, in word and image, that were hurled against the queen in the 1780s and '90s? To understand these disturbing portrayals occupies many of the authors here, for in the very crudeness of their representations of the queen they challenge us to sort through complex ideas about the relationships among bodies, gender, and power that they inscribe upon her.

As Sarah Maza notes in her essay, historians have long agreed that what came to be called the Diamond Necklace Affair marked the end of France's honeymoon with its young and attractive queen. In 1785, two years after Vigée-Lebrun's portrait of the queen in her too-fashionable dress was withdrawn from public view, a young streetwalker named Nicole Le Guay was sent out into the Bois de Boulogne to impersonate the queen in a dress very much like the one in the infamous portrait. There she met Cardinal de Rohan in a tryst arranged by one Jeanne de La Motte, the mastermind of an elaborate plot that had the cardinal buying an extremely expensive piece of jewelry, ostensibly for the queen, whose favor he sought. That night he handed the necklace over to Nicole *en chemise,* who in turn passed it on to La Motte and her husband, who promptly started selling the diamonds on the black market. La Motte and Le Guay were eventually arrested for their roles in the scheme, but what interests Maza is why a plot in which Marie-Antoinette was unwittingly impersonated should have brought *her* down. Why, she asks, did an adventuress and thief have more credibility than the queen? Why do historians still tend to blame the queen even as they acknowledge her innocence?[17] To answer these questions, Maza looks at the political culture of the Old Regime through the lens of gender. She finds that those characteristics then associated with women's nature—"deceit, seduction, and selfish pursuit of private interest"—were antithetical to the new values of a public sphere seen as transparent, open, and rational. It was the queen's "femininity" that damned her in the press, throwing her in the same basket with royal mistresses and common prostitutes.

While there were no daily papers in France before 1789, the pamphlet press had a field day with Marie-Antoinette, growing more and more virulent as the Old Regime gave way to revolution. In her essay, Chantal Thomas shows how the very ephemerality of the pamphlets, their brevity, and their integration into the oral culture of street and tavern constantly undermined the permanence of the monarchy and dragged the queen in particular down to their level—even though many of them originated in court circles. If the Diamond Necklace Affair placed the queen in the harsh light of publicity, the pamphlets ripped off her *chemise* and subjected her body to the pornographer's gaze. Thomas shows how pornography and politics were interwoven, culminating in an indictment for conspiracy, treason, and incest drawn from the discourse of the pamphlets.

Lynn Hunt also tries to unravel the web of pornography and politics in her essay on the queen's trial. She asks what the queen, and in particular the queen's sexualized body, represented in the French political imaginary before and during the Revolution. As the king was thought to have two bodies—one corporeal and the other mystical—the queen, she argues, had many bodies, each of them posing a threat to republican notions of manhood and virility. Hunt thus finds in the pornographic attacks on Marie-Antoinette that escalated after 1789 a fundamental anxiety among the revolutionaries over the masculinity of their new republican brotherhood. She finds the punishment of Marie-Antoinette to be part of a larger pattern of expelling women from the political public sphere of the Revolution, in which many had eagerly and actively participated since the Bastille fell in 1789.

One of the ways in which the anxiety of male republicans manifested itself was in the persistent representation of the queen as a tribade or lesbian. Elizabeth Colwill looks at the pornographic attacks on Marie-Antoinette as tribade not simply in the context of French political discourse or the emergent republican culture of the Revolution, but within a larger history of lesbianism. In this context, Colwill finds that "the pornography directed against Marie-Antoinette is suggestive precisely because her libidinal excesses marked the emergent boundaries of female desire in the modern period." The pamphlets' association of the queen with either a "threatening virility" or a "deviant femininity" carves out the narrow space of sexuality and gender that, Colwill argues, all modern women are expected to inhabit.

The analysis of the slanders hurled against the queen helps us to understand how women who had little sympathy for the monarchy came to Marie-Antoinette's defense when she stood on trial for conspiracy, treason, and incest. "They go awfully low to undermine the respect which the queen must inspire, by the use of the genre of calumny with which it is so easy to weaken all women," declared the writer Germaine de Staël in a passage quoted by Chantal Thomas. And Lynn Hunt suggests that Marie-Antoinette was not the only woman sent to the guillotine on the accusation of having violated the natural order of sex and gender—prominent republicans Manon Roland and Olympe de Gouges also paid with their lives.

Where Marie-Antoinette did stand apart from these other women was in her status as a queen and a foreigner. Thomas Kaiser brings us back to the matter of Marie-Antoinette's gender, rather than her sex or sexuality, by focusing attention on the identity of the queen as foreign other to the king's French self. Marie-Antoinette's chief problem, Kaiser argues, was that "she was suspected of not having sufficiently exchanged national identities as required by the marital 'traffic in women' that sealed alliances and treaties under the Old Regime." The revolutionaries, who rejected the identification of France with the king, were only too happy to pillory the queen as the head of a secret "Austrian committee" whose aim was to bring down the nation. We are left to ask what power exercised by the queen could have been seen as legitimate. In an age of dynastic rivalry, emergent nationalism, and family sentiment, what place was there for a foreign-born queen, the daughter, furthermore, of foreign female power incarnate, Maria Theresa? We might even wonder if the predicament of the queen became the predicament of all French women when France was transformed from monarchy to nation, and they from subjects to wives of citizens. As all Frenchmen claimed the king's place as "France" itself, Frenchwomen were cast in the role vacated by the queen.[18]

Through these essays, we can chart Marie-Antoinette's course from her arrival in France through a set of situations and scandals in which she is figured and refigured: from the Affair of the Minuet, a seemingly petty matter of court protocol at her wedding ball, through the Diamond Necklace Affair, and finally to the trial that ended in the queen's execution. Since that time, Marie-Antoinette has continued to figure not only in French history but in popular culture and in the history of women and lesbians. As a site of struggle and contestation, Marie-Antoinette is not bounded even by death. We thus follow her beyond her life, beyond her death, first into modern lesbian culture. There, Terry Castle argues, we find the Marie-Antoinette of the eighteenth-century political pornography—the tribade examined by Elizabeth Colwill—appropriated as a lesbian role model. Marie-Antoinette's relationships with the duchesse de Polignac and the princesse de Lamballe, which had been sexualized and made the basis of moral condemnation in the queen's own lifetime, Castle argues, were idealized by nineteenth-century biographers as models of true but chaste female friendship. "The very fiction of Marie-Antoinette's innocence," she concludes, "so feverishly adumbrated in the biographies, facilitated the subversive workings of lesbian romance. It opened up a space for erotic fantasy." Through these twists and turns, Marie-Antoinette became a lesbian icon for the twentieth century.

Laura Mason turns our attention to how Marie-Antoinette has been represented by Hollywood. In a close reading of the 1938 MGM blockbuster *Marie Antoinette,* Mason shows how American filmmakers used the life of the French queen to assert contemporary American values. "Unable to conceive of a world in which women actively shaped politics and culture," she writes, "they painted a picture of Old Regime society that suffered bitterly from the absence of bourgeois marriages and households headed by men." Marie-Antoinette's tragedy, they suggested, was that she was unable to realize the domestic ideal of twentieth-century America. And odd as this interpretation might seem, Mason reminds us that in its concern with masculine impotence and illegitimate female power, twentieth-century Hollywood had not a little in common with the pornographers and republicans who assaulted Marie-Antoinette in the 1780s and '90s.

In the 1990s an often hostile and sometimes even virulent American press focused its gaze on Hillary Clinton, another woman who challenged gender norms and was seen to exercise unauthorized power. Pierre Saint-Amand compares Marie-Antoinette's predicament with the struggles of the last American First Lady of the twentieth century to suggest the continuing problems posed by gender and power that examination of the life of Marie-Antoinette can help to illuminate. Most strikingly, what American First Ladies and French queens have in common is their proximity to power through marriage and their exclusion from any legitimate exercise of public power through law, custom, and the gender system of their day. Saint-Amand focuses specifically on how the bodies of these powerless powerful women become the focus of collective fears and anxieties. His concern, he writes, is to show "how ineluctably the body is invested in the political domain, how the entire system of politics is articulated by using the body." And he reminds us that both Hillary Clinton and Marie-Antoinette were victims of a backlash against women competing with men in the public sphere of press, politics, and power. In closing, Saint-Amand asks us to think about what we can learn from the public condemnation and scapegoating of these women who represent in some way the possibilities of female liberation.

To conclude this volume, feminist literary scholar Susan Lanser reflects on the body of writings that have been inscribed on that of Marie-Antoinette over the course of the last two hundred years—including those presented here. And she reminds us that whatever power the queen may have had in he r lifetime, her image continues to resonate powerfully in ours. Why, she asks, are so many popular Web sites devoted to a veritable worship of the queen, while she has effectively been erased from academic histories of the French Revolution? Why has "Let them eat cake!" come to be so commonly used and understood in our political discourse? If, as she suggests, "it is precisely what Marie-Antoinette *didn't* say that tells the people who she was," then we still have a lot to learn from the ways in which anger as well as political ideals can be displaced upon the body of a queen who was also, of course, just a woman.

To examine the life of Marie-Antoinette as it was represented and constructed by her contemporaries in politics, the arts, literature, and journalism is to study the contests that marked the end of the Old Regime in France and the revolution that created and destroyed it—from its early days through the Jacobin Terror. To study the afterlife of Marie-Antoinette in the modern imaginary is to turn the critical lens upon ourselves. The essays presented here do both these things and in so doing invite you, the reader, to consider issues of gender, sexuality, publicity, identity, and power in both past and present. Most of all, however, you are invited to think about Marie-Antoinette and the layers upon layers of representations of her that make her at least as fascinating today as she has been for the past two centuries.

Notes

1. Three new biographies have appeared since 2000: Evelyne Lever, *Marie Antoinette: The Last Queen of France,* trans. Catherine Temerson (New York: Farrar, Straus and Giroux, 2000); Antonia Fraser, *Marie Antoinette: The Journey* (New York: Doubleday, 2001); and Hortense Dufour, *Marie-Antoinette, la mal-aimée* (Paris: Flammarion, 2001). The complete list of biographies written since the death of Marie-Antoinette is too long to present here, but many of them are discussed in the essays that follow.

2. Feminist and postmodernist scholars in particular have challenged the possibility of writing biography on the grounds that it assumes both a unified, autonomous subject and the naturalness of its unfolding in narrative. Indeed, as William Epstein has pointed out, biography has contributed significantly to the belief in the modern understanding of the self as autonomous, driven by the force of its own will, passion, intellect, and interests, and of history as its creation. See William H. Epstein, "Introduction: Contesting the Subject," in Epstein, ed., *Contesting the Subject: Essays in the Postmodern Theory and Practice of Biography and Biographical Criticism* (West Lafayette, Ind.: Purdue University Press, 1991), 2. On the feminist critique of biography see, in the same volume, Sharon O'Brien, "Feminist Theory and Literary Biography," 123–33; and Jo Burr Margadant, "Introduction," in Margadant, ed., *The New Biography: Performing Femininity in Nineteenth-Century France* (Berkeley: University of California Press, 2000), 1–32.

3. Joan Wallach Scott, *Only Paradoxes to Offer: French Feminists and the Rights of Man* (Cambridge, Mass.: Harvard University Press, 1996), 16.

4. Ibid.

5. Karl Marx, *The Eighteenth Brumaire of Louis Bonaparte,* in *The Marx-Engels Reader,* ed. Robert C. Tucker, 2d ed. (New York: Norton, 1978), 595.

6. Margadant, "Introduction," 2.

7. On scandals and the reading public, see Sarah Maza, *Private Lives and Public Affairs: The Causes Célèbres of Prerevolutionary France* (Berkeley: University of California Press, 1993); Dena Goodman, "The Hume-Rousseau Affair: From Private *Querelle* to Public *Procès,*" *Eighteenth-Century Studies* 25 (winter 1991–92): 171–201.

8. The German sociologist Jürgen Habermas has been influential in helping contemporary scholars, including many represented in this volume, to consider the relationship between these two "public spheres" and the emergence of the modern world in the transformation from one to the other. See Habermas, *The Structural Transformation of the Public Sphere: An Inquiry into a Category of Bourgeois Society,* trans. Thomas Burger with the assistance of Frederick Lawrence (Cambridge, Mass.: MIT Press, 1989).

9. Louis' ailment, diagnosed around 1774, was not corrected with surgery until after a visit to Versailles by Marie-Antoinette's brother, two years later.

10. See David A. Bell, *The Cult of the Nation: Inventing Nationalism, 1680–1800* (Cambridge, Mass.: Harvard University Press, 2001).

11. In fact, queens had been precluded from having an official political role in France since the fourteenth-century invention of the Salic Law, which decreed that the throne could not pass to a woman or through the female line. Thereafter, French women could not rule in their own name, and the succession

could pass only through their sons. See the articles by Mary Sheriff and Lynn Hunt in this volume for discussion of the Salic Law and its implications for Marie-Antoinette.

12. Henri-Paulin Panon-Desbassayns, *Petit journal des époques pour servir à ma mémoire (1784–1786),* ed. Annie Lafforgue with the assistance of Christelle de Villele and Jean Barbier (Saint-Gilles-les-Hauts: Musée Historique, 1990), 61–67. Panon-Desbassayns was visiting France from his home in the Indian Ocean colony of the Île Bourbon; this is an account of his trip.

13. See Arlette Farge, *Subversive Words: Public Opinion in Eighteenth-Century France,* trans. Rosemary Morris (University Park, Penn.: Pennsylvania State University Press, 1994); Robert Darnton, *The Forbidden Best-sellers of Pre-revolutionary France* (New York: Norton, 1995).

14. Elizabeth Colwill, "Just Another *Citoyenne?* Marie-Antoinette on Trial, 1790–1793," *History Workshop Journal* 28 (1989): 63–87.

15. See, e.g., Lieselotte Steinbrügge, *The Moral Sex: Woman's Nature in the French Enlightenment,* trans. Pamela E. Selwyn (New York: Oxford University Press, 1992); Dena Goodman, "Women and the Enlightenment," in Renate Bridenthal et al., eds., *Becoming Visible: Women in European History,* 3d ed. (Boston: Houghton-Mifflin, 1998), 233–62.

16. Gary Kates, *Monsieur d'Eon Is a Woman: A Tale of Political Intrigue and Sexual Masquerade* (New York: Basic Books, 1995), xxi.

17. Indeed, the question of credibility has returned with a vengeance in a recent American film that retells the tale, ostensibly from Jeanne de La Motte's perspective. Here is how the film's Web site describes the story: "*Affair of the Necklace* is a romantic drama based on the controversial true story of Jeanne De La Motte Valois, a countess whose name was stripped from her by the Royal Family during the late 18th Century. The story of her fight to restore her name and proper place in society is filled with mystery, intrigue and desire, with an infamous diamond necklace at the center of it all." See http://affairoftheneck lace.warnerbros.com/.

18. In addition to the essays in this volume, discussions of the relationship between women and citizenship in and after the French Revolution include: Joan B. Landes, *Women and the Public Sphere in the Age of the French Revolution* (Ithaca: Cornell University Press, 1988); Dorinda Outram, *The Body and the French Revolution: Sex, Class, and Political Culture* (New Haven: Yale University Press, 1989); Scott, *Only Paradoxes to Offer;* Jennifer Heuer, "Foreigners, Families, and Citizens: Contradictions of National Citizenship in France, 1789–1830," Ph.D. dissertation, University of Chicago, 1998.

A SELECT CHRONOLOGY OF MARIE-ANTOINETTE'S LIFE

November 1755   Maria-Antonia Josepha Johanna, archduchess of Austria, is born in Vienna, the daughter of Empress Maria Theresa of Austria and of Francis I, duke of Lorraine, emperor of Germany. Her birth was preceded by those of Joseph (1741), Maria Christina (1742), Maria Elisabeth (1743), Charles Joseph (1745), Maria Amelia (1746), Pierre Leopold (1747), Jeanne-Gabrielle (1750), Maria Joseph (1751), Maria Caroline (1752), and Ferdinand (1754). It was followed by that of Maximilien Franz (1756).

1765   Death of Francis I, to whom little Maria-Antonia was very attached.

1768   The abbé de Vermond becomes Maria-Antonia's preceptor.

1770   Marriage of Maria-Antonia, from now on known as Marie-Antoinette, to the dauphin of France, Louis-Auguste, grandson of Louis XV (**16 May**). This union expressed Maria Theresa's political desire to reinforce the alliance and "diplomatic revolution" of 1756 between France and Austria, until then France's hereditary enemy.

The abbé de Vermond is named Marie-Antoinette's personal advisor. He remains her confidant and her sole link to childhood.

Beginning of the correspondence between Maria Theresa and Marie-Antoinette.

The comte de Mercy-Argenteau, Austrian ambassador to France, regularly dispatches secret reports to Maria Theresa on her daughter.

1773   Disgrace and fall of the duc de Choiseul, the major broker in the marriage between Louis-Auguste and Marie-Antoinette.

1774   Death of Louis XV (**10 May**). Beginning of Louis XVI's reign. Louis XVI offers Marie-Antoinette the Petit Trianon as a present.

The queen's extravagant hairdos and her passion for dress cause a scandal.

Beginning of the friendship with the princesse de Lamballe, who is named *surintendante* of the queen's household.

1777   Visit of her elder brother, now Joseph II.

Friendship with Madame de Polignac begins.

1778   A daughter is born and baptized Marie-Thérèse (**December 20**).

1778–1779   War of Succession in Bavaria. Maria Theresa of Austria pressures Marie-Antoinette to influence the king in her favor.

1780   France enters the American War of Independence.

Death of Maria Theresa of Austria.

1781   Birth of a son, Louis-Josèphe, heir to the throne (**22 October**). The king's brothers, the comte de Provence and the comte d'Artois, are forced to renounce their dreams of succession.

Madame de Polignac is named governess of the children of France. Her family is showered with favors.

1785 Birth of a second son, who receives the title of duc de Normandie.

1785–1786 The Diamond Necklace Affair. The queen is accused of using Cardinal de Rohan to purchase a diamond necklace for which she then refused to pay. On 31 May 1786, the *parlement* declares Cardinal de Rohan innocent and condemns Jeanne de La Motte, seen as the instigator in the affair, to be branded. In the eyes of the deliriously happy public, the queen is *the* guilty party.

1786 Birth of Sophie-Hélène-Béatrice, who dies at the age of one. The health of the dauphin, Louis-Josèphe, begins to be of grave concern.

4 May 1789 The meeting of the Estates General gets under way at Versailles.

14 June 1789 Death of Louis-Josèphe.

11 July 1789 The minister of finance, Jacques Necker, is dismissed at the height of his popularity.

14 July 1789 The storming of the Bastille.

16 July 1789 Necker is reinstated. Soon thereafter, the comte d'Artois and most of the courtiers leave Versailles, the Polignac family among them.

5–6 October 1789 A crowd of market women march to Versailles to demand "bread and the king." The royal family leaves the palace. They are driven to Paris and set up in the Tuileries. Without any consistent policy, the queen wildly forms the most disparate alliances. Her only consistent line: to get help from abroad for the royalists.

20 June 1791 The royal family surreptitiously leaves the Tuileries in an effort to join counterrevolutionary forces in Germany, but are stopped by a pro-revolutionary postman in the town of Varennes near the border and forced to return to Paris.

11 July 1792 Brunswick Manifesto issued by leader of allied forces (Prussia and Austria), threatening to hold Paris responsible if any harm comes to the royal family.

10 August 1792 A Parisian crowd storms the Tuileries; Louis XVI and Marie-Antoinette are placed under the protection of the National Assembly and are transferred to the Temple prison.

2–6 September 1792 Massacres in the jails. The princesse de Lamballe is assassinated.

22 September 1792 Abolition of the monarchy. First French Republic is declared.

21 January 1793 Execution of Louis XVI.

10 March 1793 A Revolutionary Tribunal is created.

13 July 1793 Charlotte Corday assassinates revolutionary leader Jean-Paul Marat.

August 1793 Marie-Antoinette is separated from her children and locked up in the Conciergerie.

14–16 October 1793 Marie-Antoinette is put on trial. She is guillotined the morning of 16 October.

BIOGRAPHICAL SKETCHES OF PRINCIPAL FIGURES IN THE LIFE OF MARIE-ANTOINETTE

Artois, Charles-Philippe, comte de (1757–1836; r. 1824–1830 as Charles X)
The youngest brother of Louis XVI, before the Revolution Artois was distinguished primarily for his gambling, debts, affairs with women, and generally dissolute life. Rumors linking him with Marie-Antoinette abounded. In 1787 and 1788 he was a spokesman for the conservative forces that doomed the Assemblies of Notables to failure. It is therefore not surprising that he became the first and most prominent émigré when he fled France just two days after the fall of the Bastille for the Austrian Netherlands. He became a leader of the royalist cause and the Counterrevolution. He returned to France only when the monarchy was restored and his older brother, the comte de Provence, was placed on the throne. When Louis XVIII died in 1824, Artois, then the leader of the Ultraroyalist Party, ascended the throne as Charles X. He was overthrown in the Revolution of 1830 and fled to Austria, where he died six years later.

Breteuil, Louis-Charles-Alexandre le Tonnelier, baron de (1730–1807)
At age twenty-eight, Breteuil was appointed ambassador to the elector of Cologne. He later served in St. Petersburg, Stockholm, Naples, and Vienna. In 1783, Louis XVI recalled Breteuil from his diplomatic career to serve as minister of the king's household, a post whose duties included the administration of the city of Paris. Both his humanitarian reforms of penal institutions and hospitals and his opposition to the *parlements* were evidence of his strong belief in the monarchy. Breteuil became a close friend of Marie-Antoinette and took charge of having Cardinal de Rohan arrested for his part in the Diamond Necklace Affair. Called upon by Louis XVI to take over as chief minister upon Necker's dismissal in July 1789, he was forced to relinquish that post after the fall of the Bastille and join the émigrés. From Switzerland, he was one of those who urged the royal family to flee France and seek support from the other European monarchs. Armed with a letter from Louis XVI giving him the authority to negotiate with foreign courts on behalf of the monarchy, he was a leader of the royalist cause until 1792, when the comte de Provence successfully challenged him for that position. Breteuil returned to Paris in 1802 and died there quietly.

Calonne, Charles-Alexandre de (1734–1802)
The son of the first president of the *parlement* of Flanders, Calonne made his own career in royal administration, including seventeen years of service as a royal intendant. Called in by Louis XV to resolve a crisis of authority with the *parlement* of Brittany in 1765, he drew the wrath of the nobility, whose resentment continued to plague him throughout his career. A protégé of the comte d'Artois, Vergennes, and Marie-Antoinette, Calonne was tapped to replace Necker as controller general and chief minister in 1783 after publicly disputing the validity of Necker's published account of the royal finances. During the Diamond Necklace Affair, Calonne championed Cardinal de Rohan. By 1786, convinced that France's financial problems could only be solved by political reform, Calonne persuaded Louis XVI to convene an Assembly of Notables to develop a plan of political and economic restructuring.

When they proved resistant to change, Calonne appealed to the public, who rewarded him with the epithet "Monsieur Déficit"—thereby pairing him with "Madame Déficit" (Marie-Antoinette) and blaming them both for France's financial crisis. In 1787 he was replaced by one of his chief critics, Loménie de Brienne. Calonne then left for England and, in 1790, joined the émigré cause on the continent, serving in the shadow government until 1795. Known for his expensive taste before the Revolution and associated in the public mind with the ruinous luxury of Marie-Antoinette and the court, in 1802 he returned to Paris an impoverished man and died shortly thereafter.

Choiseul, Etienne-François, duc de (1719–1785)

Although Choiseul distinguished himself in the French army serving against Austria during the War of the Austrian Succession, he later became the chief defender of France's new alliance with Austria. A favorite of Louis XV's mistress Madame de Pompadour, Choiseul began his diplomatic career with an appointment to the Vatican in 1752. In 1757, he was appointed ambassador to Austria and was charged with strengthening the alliance between France and its traditional continental enemy. The following year, Choiseul was called back to France to serve as secretary of state for foreign affairs; he was later appointed minister of the navy (1761–1766) and minister of war (1766–70). When Choiseul pressed for war against Britain, however, he rapidly fell from favor. He was exiled from Paris in December 1770 and did not return until after Louis XV's death in 1774.

du Barry, Jeanne Bécu, comtesse (1743–1793)

Born out of wedlock to working-class parents, Marie-Jeanne Bécu was educated in a convent. While working as a shop assistant, she became the mistress of Jean du Barry, a Gascon nobleman and war contractor. Bécu attracted the attentions of Louis XV, and a marriage was arranged in 1769 between Bécu and du Barry's brother Guillaume in order to provide Bécu with the requisite noble status to become a royal *maîtresse en titre*. As royal mistress, du Barry was involved in court politics. Most notably, she belonged to the faction that promoted the ministers Maupeou, Terray, and d'Aiguillon at the expense of her predecessor's protégé, the duc de Choiseul.

The diamond necklace that would plague Marie-Antoinette was originally intended for du Barry but never purchased. After Louis XV's death in 1774, du Barry retired to a château in the country. Between 1791 and 1793 she made frequent trips between France and England, ostensibly to follow the course of a trial of thieves said to have stolen her jewels in France and reappeared with them in London. The implausibility of this story, as well as its parallel to the Diamond Necklace Affair, supports the contention that she was a royalist agent. In 1793, she was arrested for counterrevolutionary activities, and in December of that year she was guillotined.

Fersen, Hans Axel von (1755–1810)

Born into high Swedish nobility, Fersen pursued a military career with the French army. He distinguished himself in the American Revolution at the siege of Yorktown (1781). After the war, Fersen returned to Versailles, where his close friendship with Marie-Antoinette stimulated rumors of being her lover. Fersen returned to the Swedish court in 1784 to serve in his home country's diplomatic corps but was sent back to Versailles in 1788. He remained a close friend of the queen during the monarchy's crisis. It was he who organized the royal family's failed attempt to escape France, driving the carriage for the first leg of the journey. Even after their capture at Varennes, he continued his efforts to save the royal family from his safe haven in Brussels, lobbying for a European coalition against revolutionary France. In 1792 he commissioned the drafting of the Brunswick Manifesto, in which a coalition of European forces threatened to invade France if the royal family was harmed. In 1810, Fersen met his own end at the hands of a Swedish mob who acted on unfounded rumors that he had murdered the crown prince.

Gouges, Olympe de (1748–1793)

Around 1770, Marie Gouzes left Montauban, the town of her birth, for Paris; with the intention of becoming a writer, she changed her name to Olympe de Gouges. She had been married in 1765, had a child within a year, and was now (perhaps) widowed. Her parentage was always questioned, but she claimed the butcher who raised her as her father. Her first literary success was *Zamour and Myrza, or the Happy Shipwreck*, a play produced by the Comédie Française in 1785. In 1788, she joined the prerevolutionary chorus of calls for economic reform with her *Letter to the People, Project for a Patriotic Fund*. A prolific writer of plays and novels, de Gouges is known primarily for her political activism on behalf of women and slaves, but she was equally committed to the monarchy. She dedicated her most famous work, *Declaration of the Rights of Woman and Citizen* (1791), to the queen. In 1793, de Gouges was guillotined because of her defense of the monarchy, her Girondinist associations, and, some historians argue, her sex.

Hébert, Jacques René (1757–1794)

Hébert's father, a goldsmith, died when the boy was only nine, but his mother made sure he received a proper classical education at the local Jesuit *collège*. The young man left Normandy for Paris in 1780 as the result of a scandal and lived a life of poverty there until the Revolution provided him the opportunity to make his name as a journalist and political leader. His newspaper, *Le Père Duchesne,* was as notable for its profanity and bloodlust as for its radical patriotism. After the flight of the royal family in 1791 Hébert was an outspoken republican. *Le Père Duchesne* was a leader in the defamation of Marie-Antoinette and was instrumental in building the charges that led her to the guillotine. But as the most prominent spokesman for the Parisian *sans-culottes,* Hébert posed a significant threat from the left to Robespierre and the Committee of Public Safety, who had him and his followers executed after a show trial at the height of the Terror, in 1794.

Joseph II (1741–1790; r. 1765–1790)

The eldest son of Maria Theresa and Francis Stephen of Lorraine, Joseph II was officially crowned holy Roman emperor, king of Hungary, and archduke of Austria upon his father's death in 1765, although his mother continued to reign as co-regent. After Maria Theresa died in 1780, Joseph became emperor in fact as well as in name. He added to his mother's significant domestic reforms a dramatic series of his own, most notably an edict of religious toleration (1781), the abolition of serfdom (1785), and reform of taxes and the penal system. These reforms met with a great deal of domestic opposition, however, and he was forced to repeal many of them. Joseph's attempts at expanding his empire antagonized Austria's neighbors to both the east and the west. France's "Austrian policy" became increasingly difficult to sustain in the light of these attempts at expansion, and Marie-Antoinette's position was increasingly compromised by it. Joseph lost two wives to smallpox in the space of just seven years and left no child to succeed him. Upon his death in 1790, Joseph's brother took the throne as Leopold II, just as their sister, Marie-Antoinette, began to lose hers.

Lamballe, Marie-Thérèse-Louise de Savoie-Carignan, princesse de (1749–1792)
Widowed at the age of eighteen, the princesse de Lamballe came to Versailles as a companion to Marie-Antoinette shortly after her marriage. After Marie-Antoinette took the throne in 1774, Lamballe was appointed superintendent of the queen's household and became her close friend and confidante. She followed the royal family during their forced move to Paris in October 1789, but fled toward England two years later, when they made their escape eastward. Learning of the capture of the royal family at Varennes, she returned to Paris to serve her queen and was imprisoned along with her. In 1792, Lamballe became the most prominent victim of the September Massacres, as the Parisian mob taunted the queen by parading her friend's severed head before the window of her prison cell.

Louis XV (1710–1774; r. 1723–1774)
The great-grandson of Louis XIV became dauphin as a very young child, after his parents and elder brother died of disease in 1712; he became king of France three years later. The duc d'Orléans acted as regent for Louis XV from 1715 until he reached his majority in 1723. Louis XV ruled France for more than fifty years, during which time the political culture of the nation changed markedly, from the barely challenged absolutism of Louis XIV to the open contestation that would lead to the Revolution. Political confrontations with nobles and intellectual challenges associated with the Enlightenment were facilitated by an era of relative peace: Louis XV's reign was noteworthy for minimal warfare (in contrast to that of Louis XIV), and none within France itself. However, the Seven Years' War (1756–1763) was a disaster which resulted in France losing most of its colonial territories to the British. Noteworthy also were Louis XV's mistresses, all of whom drew fire from an increasingly critical press, often manipulated by court factions. In 1770, Louis XV married his grandson and heir to Marie-Antoinette, the daughter of the Austrian empress Maria Theresa, thereby securing a diplomatic realignment with Austria. The end of his reign was marked by an attempt to thwart the growing power of the nobility by abolishing the *parlements* and instituting royal law courts. Louis XV died of smallpox in 1774.

Louis XVI (1754–1793; r. 1774–1792)
The grandson of Louis XV was married to the Austrian archduchess Marie-Antoinette in 1770 in a match designed to strengthen France's alliance with Austria. In 1774, he inherited both the throne and public distrust of the monarchy. Early attempts at economic reform ended in failure, as a succession of royal ministers were fired under public pressure and their initiatives reversed. The highly popular Amer-

ican Revolution contributed to the state's economic woes. In 1788, facing the financial collapse of the state, Louis XVI convoked the Estates General, which had not met since 1614. This attempt at consultation provoked enormous political debate that engaged the entire nation. The gathering of the elected representatives in Versailles in the spring of 1789, however, led directly to the French Revolution. The king continued to rule, although under stringent constitutional limits, until the royal family's attempt to join the Austrian troops at France's eastern border in the summer of 1791 undermined the king's remaining credibility in the eyes of the nation. He and his family were put under house arrest upon their return to Paris, but the monarchy was not formally abolished until September 1792. In December of that year the king was put on trial for treason; in January 1793 he was found guilty and sentenced to immediate execution.

Maria Theresa (1717–1780; r. 1740–1780)

Born in Vienna, Maria Theresa was the eldest daughter of Holy Roman Emperor Charles VI. The so-called Pragmatic Sanction elevated Maria Theresa to the position of heir to the Hapsburg lands after the death of her only brother, making her empress of Austria and queen of Hungary and Bohemia upon her father's death in 1740. She withstood a major challenge to her claim to the throne and to Austria itself mounted by the new king of Prussia, Frederick II. Although France had sided with Prussia in the War of the Austrian Succession (1740–1748), Maria Theresa later achieved a realignment of Austria away from its traditional ally, Britain, in favor of France; she also instituted a broad range of domestic reforms.

At age eighteen, Maria Theresa married Francis Stephen of Lorraine. Together, they had sixteen children, ten of whom survived to adulthood. After Francis Stephen's death in 1765, Maria Theresa continued to rule as co-regent with her eldest son, now nominally Emperor Joseph II. Maria Theresa cemented Austria's new alliance with France through the marriage of her daughter Marie-Antoinette to the French dauphin in 1770. Maria Theresa died in 1780.

Mercy-Argenteau, Florimund-Claude, comte de (1727–1794)

Born in the Austrian Netherlands, Mercy-Argenteau began his diplomatic career in 1756 as a member of the Austrian team that negotiated the Franco-Austrian alliance. Prior to his appointment as ambassador to Versailles ten years later, he was posted to Turin and St. Petersburg. Mercy-Argenteau was the duc de Choiseul's counterpart in the implementation of the alliance between France and Austria. In particular, he served as liaison between the Viennese court and Versailles in arranging and supervising the marriage of Marie-Antoinette and the French dauphin. In a voluminous correspondence with Maria Theresa, he provided detailed reports of Marie-Antoinette's doings, and in return received equally detailed advice to be conveyed to her daughter. Even after the fall of Choiseul, Mercy-Argenteau remained influential in French court politics, supporting first Loménie de Brienne and then Necker. He was recalled to Vienna by Emperor Leopold II in 1790 but continued to correspond with an increasingly worried Marie-Antoinette. After the capture of the royal family at Varennes in 1791, Mercy became a steadfast opponent of the Revolution and staunch supporter of the royal family, supporting the Brunswick Manifesto (1792) and becoming involved in various plans to rescue them. In July 1794,

Mercy-Argenteau went to London as Austrian ambassador extraordinary and died shortly thereafter.

Necker, Jacques (1732–1804)

A Geneva-born banker, Necker moved to Paris as a young man and made both his fortune and his reputation for financial genius and integrity there. Necker was appointed Geneva's resident minister in Paris and became a director of the French East India Company. Despite being both Protestant and a foreigner, Necker was appointed director of the royal treasury (1776) and later director general of finances (1777) after his essay in praise of Louis XIV's minister Colbert (1773) and his attack on the current minister Turgot's grain policies, *Essay on the Legislation and Commerce of Grains* (1775), attracted the attention of the court. When he later published an accounting of the royal finances (1781), Necker was dismissed from office, but this act earned him a reputation for honesty with the public and integrity with France's creditors. In August 1788, Necker was recalled to royal service and took charge of the convocation of the Estates General. On 11 July 1789, rumors that Necker was to be dismissed yet again precipitated the crisis that led to the storming of the Bastille three days later. Brought back to Versailles, he continued to be a central figure in the monarchy's attempt to negotiate with the Revolutionaries until his resignation in September 1790. He retired to a château in Switzerland with his wife, the salonnière Suzanne Curchod Necker, and their daughter, the writer Germaine de Staël (1766–1817). He died there in 1804.

Polignac, Yolande-Martine-Gabrielle de Polastron, duchesse de (1749–1793)

At age seventeen, Mademoiselle de Polastron married the comte de Polignac. She was one of the young women with whom Marie-Antoinette surrounded herself at Versailles and was reputed to be her closest friend. Through the influence of the queen, Polignac's husband was elevated to a dukedom in 1780, and she received the title of duchess. Polignac was subsequently appointed royal governess in 1782. At the urging of the queen, the Polignacs were among the first émigrés to leave France, in July 1789. The duchesse de Polignac died in Vienna in 1793, not long after her queen and friend.

Pompadour, Jeanne-Antoinette Poisson, marquise de (1721–1764)

Poisson and her brother were raised by a wealthy tax farmer, Le Normant d'Étioles. In 1741, Poisson married Le Normant's nephew, but this match was to be short-lived. Following the death of Louis XV's mistress, the duchesse de Châteauroux, in 1744, Poisson legally separated from her husband and was made the king's *maîtresse en titre*. In the process, she also received the title marquise de Pompadour. The most long-standing of Louis' mistresses, Pompadour earned a reputation as a patron of the arts and learning, and of the decorative arts in particular. She was associated with the growth of Paris as a center of the luxury trades, through her personal extravagance and her furnishing of various royal châteaux. Pompadour was also a major player in court politics. Notably, she was a patron of the duc de Choiseul, who was charged with implementing the Austrian policy. For all these reasons, Marie-Antoinette was often criticized for acting more like a royal mistress in the style of Madame de Pompadour than a queen. Pompadour died in 1764.

Rohan-Guémenée, Louis-René-Édouard, prince de (1734–1803)

Born into one of France's most ancient and wealthy noble families, Rohan held various high offices, including bishop of Strasbourg, ambassador to Vienna, grand almoner, and cardinal. Cardinal de Rohan was one of the key figures in the Diamond Necklace Affair (1785–86) but was acquitted at trial for his role. Released from the Bastille, he returned to his diocese in Alsace. In 1789, he was elected to the Estates General. When the Civil Constitution of the Clergy was enacted in 1790, he refused to take the constitutional oath and left France for the German portion of his see, where he remained until his death in 1803.

Vigée-Lebrun, Marie-Louise-Élisabeth (1755–1842)

The daughter of a minor portraitist, Elisabeth Vigée studied painting with Gabriel Briard, a history painter and member of the Royal Academy of Painting. She was later mentored by Jean-Baptiste Greuze and Joseph Vernet. In 1776, she married the art dealer Jean-Baptiste-Pierre Lebrun. Her portraits and landscapes gained her early renown and brought her to the attention of the young queen, her contemporary. She painted her first portrait of Marie-Antoinette in 1779 and went on to paint at least two dozen more as the queen's official painter. With Marie-Antoinette's intervention, Vigée-Lebrun was elected to the Royal Academy in 1783, one of only two women to receive that honor. In October 1789, already the target of attacks for her association with the queen, she fled France for Rome, beginning a twelve-year period of exile that would include Vienna and St. Petersburg. She continued to paint portraits in exile, and in 1800 was allowed to return to France in response to a petition signed by over two hundred of her fellow artists. She returned to Paris permanently in 1809, after a productive sojourn in London. She published her memoirs in 1835.

Hapsburg Letters: The Disciplinary Dynamics of Epistolary Narrative in the Correspondence of Maria Theresa and Marie-Antoinette

Larry Wolff

On 19 April 1770, the fourteen-year-old Hapsburg archduchess, Marie-Antoinette, was married in Vienna by proxy to the faraway Bourbon dauphin, the future Louis XVI. Two days later, Marie-Antoinette left Vienna forever, setting off to join her new husband in France, and taking leave of her mother, Empress Maria Theresa, whom she would never see again. That date—"21 April, the day of departure"—headed the first letter in the ten-year correspondence that then ensued between mother and daughter. It is a correspondence that has exercised a certain historical fascination since its first publication in 1864, especially inasmuch as the empress addressed herself to her daughter's "frivolity" and "dissipation," precisely the qualities that were making Marie-Antoinette into an emblem of decadence for the ancien régime on the brink of the French Revolution. The unmitigated separation of the two correspondents leaves their letters as the substance of their direct relations during these ten years until the death of the empress, no personal encounter intervening. This integrity of the epistolary relation offers a model for analysis of correspondence as a narrative form, since in this case it need never be interpreted as a secondary and subordinate epiphenomenon of a more immediate personal relation. This condition, furthermore, encourages the application of literary and textual techniques to the historical correspondence, inasmuch as the historical actors, Maria Theresa and Marie-Antoinette, could come to exist for each other as narrative constructs, more and more with each passing year of separation.

Theoretical approaches to epistolary issues are largely based on epistolary fiction of the eighteenth century, in which correspondents are, by definition, the literary constructs of the author, while any personal encounter between corresponding characters must be read as a secondary construct of the fictional letters themselves, located within the crevices of the correspondence. Historical letters, on the other hand, may be read in terms of a literary relation subordinate to an authentic connection, serving the historian as a textual means of trying to achieve historical truth. The historian must penetrate and pass through such letters, while the reader of epistolary fiction must find literary meaning, however deeply embedded, in the text itself. Historical and fictional letters suggest reciprocal perspectives on the relation between correspondence and encounter: the primary "authenticity" of history mirrored in the secondary "artifice" of fiction. This opposition rests on the historian's professional faith that history itself is something more than a scholarly construct. In fact, from a purely formal point of view, epistolary fiction and nonfiction are very close indeed, and it is telling that some of the most famous correspondences have not been definitively categorized as one or the other. The seventeenth-century *Lettres portugaises,* the love letters of a Portuguese nun, remain to this day of ambiguous historical authenticity, while even the twelfth-century letters of Abelard and Héloïse have been called into question under the hypothesis that Abelard fictionally wrote her side of the correspondence as well as his own. The eighteenth century was unquestionably the golden age of letters, both fictional and nonfictional, and in examining the letters of Maria Theresa and Marie-Antoinette, the application of literary methods to historical texts may suggest some of the particular significances of epistolary narrative in both history and literature.

The first publication of these letters in 1864 was the work of Alfred von Arneth, the great nineteenth-century archivist and historian.[1] He was director of the Hapsburg archives in Vienna and the author of a ten-volume work on Maria Theresa. Arneth and M. A. Geffroy published in 1874 a new edition that presented the letters of Maria Theresa and Marie-Antoinette together with the even longer and highly relevant correspondence between the Hapsburg empress and her ambassador to France, Florimond Mercy-Argenteau. Arneth and Geffroy, though they filled three volumes, nevertheless edited with very particular Victorian discretion all material in the letters that referred to the unfortunate sex life of Marie-Antoinette and Louis XVI. This important aspect of the correspondence became known in 1932, when Stefan Zweig published his biography of Marie-Antoinette, and Georges Girard edited an unexpurgated edition of the letters in 1933.[2] By that time, the sexual details of the correspondence not only could be frankly included, but could even form the Freudian foundation for Zweig's historical argument: he argued that Marie-Antoinette's notorious frivolity grew out of the sexual frustration of her unconsummated marriage. In 1951, G. P. Gooch published a long biographical essay that focused on Marie-Antoinette, "to depict her fortunes during the first decade of her public life with the aid of a series of letters unique in historical literature."[3] In 1985 Oliver Bernier published an English edition of the correspondence as *Secrets of Marie-Antoinette.*[4]

The "secrets" of that title need not refer to the letters' unerotic sexual details, for every correspondence, fictional or nonfictional, whatever its thematic concerns, forces its readers into voyeurism by allowing them to read letters addressed to someone else. That same perspective, however, allows the reader the most direct observation of the forces and relations at play in epistolary narrative. Though the letters of Maria Theresa and Marie-Antoinette may indeed, in certain respects, be "unique in historical literature," they are letters nevertheless, and the text holds as yet unappreciated secrets that may emerge in formal epistolary analysis.

Maria Theresa's first letter of 21 April was, strictly speaking, neither a letter nor simply sequentially the first item of the correspondence. In fact, it was probably presented to Marie-Antoinette on her departure from Vienna, rather than posted to her in France. Lacking both salutation and formal closing, the document described itself in the heading "Regulation [*règlement*] to read every month."[5] Stripped of the personal salutation that signals a letter as a letter, this self-styled "regulation" revealed all the more clearly the very nature of epistolary writing as the narrative of power—that is, the literary articulation of the relation of power existing between two subjects. The regulation here prescribed for Marie-Antoinette, while nominally concealing its epistolary nature, in fact suggests the essential characterization of a narrative form that reaches out from within its own text to affect (to entertain, to engage, to inform, to enlighten, to regulate) its designated reader. This capacity for designation is in itself one of the principal powers of the letter. Every narrative, of course, must affect its readers, but it is only the letter that specifically names its reader and focuses its narrative forces on that chosen object. For this reason, every reader except Marie-Antoinette—the "nondesignated" readers who have examined Maria Theresa's letters with historical interest since their first publication in 1864—is placed in an illicit triangular relation with the two correspondents. This triangle is essential to epistolary fiction, in which the nondesignated readers are taken for granted as the text's conventional audience.

The historian's false reading relation to Maria Theresa's *Règlement* is immediately indicated in the stipulation "to read every month." No editor will reprint this regulation 120 times over the ten years' collected correspondence, and no historian will refer constantly back to the opening document for a fresh reading. Indeed, it seems hardly likely that Marie-Antoinette herself dutifully cooperated for many months, but a letter, as a textual expression of power, exists independent of its consequences, of whether it "fails" or "succeeds" outside the world of the text. Though the *Règlement* may be the first letter Maria Theresa wrote, and the first Marie-Antoinette read, the historian who accepts it as simply "the first letter" will have failed to appreciate the way that power was expressed here in epistolary form. This letter designated not only its reader but its time of reading, and became not an introduction but the recurrent key to the entire correspondence, governing its style, structure, and purpose as a coherent literary entity. Maria Theresa may have had second thoughts about the imprecision of that heading, for in the next letter, dated 4 May 1770, she specified that the *Règlement* was to be read regularly on the twenty-first day of each month.[6] The heading "Regulation to read every month" suggests that one of the principal powers of the letter as a narrative form is its revision, reordering, and regulation of time itself.

It is obviously fundamental to the nature of a letter that it breaks down geographical space, functioning economically as a postal commodity that may be produced in one place (Vienna, for instance) and then carried across Europe to be consumed in another place (Versailles, perhaps). The space between collapses as the correspondents send and receive their letters. The gap, however, is both temporal and geographical, and the letter breaks down time as well as space. The text must be written at one time and read at another—thus bringing those two times together as surely as it does the two associated places. Indeed, the text may be read any number of times (every month, for instance), each time bringing the past moment of writing into immediate conjunction with the present moment of reading. The temporality of the letter is so essential to its nature that the letter generally dates itself, usually recording its time of origin just before designating its reader in the salutation.

For the historian, this dating of the document is of the greatest importance for interpretation, so much so that the time of reception and reading, often more difficult to pinpoint, may not be so carefully considered. Similarly, in epistolary fiction, less strict standards of dating may make it still harder to bear in mind that each letter joins two points in time. It is, however, precisely this dual temporality, this capacity to take hold of time at more than one point, that enables the letter to compress time or stretch it, to order or deform, to liberate or regulate. Maria Theresa began her *Règlement* thus:

> When you wake up, you will immediately upon arising go through your morning prayers on your knees and read some religious text, even if it is only for six or seven minutes [*ne fût-ce même que d'un seul demi-quart d'heure*] without concerning yourself about anything else or speaking to anyone. All depends on the right beginning for the day and the intention with which you begin it, for it may change even indifferent actions into praiseworthy ones. You must be very strict [*très exacte*] about this, for it depends on you alone, and your temporal and spiritual happiness [*votre bonheur spirituel et temporel*] may depend upon it.[7]

The conventional figurative linking of "temporal and spiritual" seems exceptionally apt, inasmuch as the spirit of Marie-Antoinette was treated as a problem of time and temporality. Clearly, however, that linkage was far less an issue of her happiness than an aspect of her mother's power, while that power, at once spiritual and temporal, found appropriate expression in epistolary form.

It was not simply that the letter of the empress crossed time and space to address her daughter at each reading, but also that the narrative form allowed the writer an imperialistic assault on broader domains of future time that are mapped out and colonized from afar and before. The future tense was boldly employed from the first sentence, and the prescribed monthly readings of the letter were revealed as a mere framework for the prescription of daily readings and prayers. This breaking down of time into months and days did not preclude an interest in still smaller units, as evidenced in the empress's recommended minimum for morning devotions: "un seul demi-quart d'heure." The concept of the "half quarter hour" does not exist in English, but the more graceful translation of "six or seven minutes," though arithmetically plausible, loses the very essence of Maria Theresa's epistolary approach to time. The function of her letter was to exercise power over her daughter's spiritual life by analyzing it into its fractional temporal components: years into months into days, hours into quarters into half quarters.

Michel Foucault attributes to the Age of Enlightenment a "microphysics of power" based on "techniques of discipline."[8] Maria Theresa, an enlightened absolutist who exercised power both as an empress and as a mother, found in her correspondence with her daughter a narrative form ideally suited to weaving a disciplinary web across time and space. The fractional analysis of time, and indeed the very notion of the "half quarter hour," revealed a mind attuned to the refinements of "microphysics." Foucault particularly cites "the time-table" as a disciplinary mechanism, and Marie-Antoinette, after all, was expected to be "très exacte."[9] In one of her first letters to her mother from France, dated 12 July 1770, she elaborately responded to her mother's request for a daily schedule, including hairdressing at eleven, mass at noon, harpsichord and singing at five, cards at six, supper at nine. She promised that in a future letter she would account for Sundays and holidays.[10]

Six years later, on 31 October 1776, concerned about her daughter's "life of constant dissipation," Maria Theresa took her own name day, the feast of St. Theresa, as an occasion to state explicitly the terms of her temporal analysis: "Your excuses about forgetting my name day are accepted without rancor; but, my dear daughter, it is not once a year that I wish you to think of me, but every month, every week, and every day [tous les mois, semaines et jours], so that you forget neither my love nor my advice and the examples I give you."[11] The name day could serve as an annual marker, but in the *Règlement* of 1770, the empress was even bolder in her claims on the empire of time, reaching beyond her own death without letting go of her daughter's future: "Never forget the anniversary of your late dear father's death, and mine in its time: in the meantime you can use my birthday as the date on which to pray for me."[12] Her birthday and name day were both useful markers, but already, ten years be-

fore her death, Maria Theresa was putting the anniversary of that future date on the calendar of Marie-Antoinette.

The prescribed monthly reading of the *Règlement* provided the
perfect temporal framework for what was to become the most urgent occasion on the calendar cycle in the whole correspondence:
the monthly menstrual period of Marie-Antoinette, initially designated in the letters as "la générale." This aspect of the correspondence
remained generally unknown before the twentieth century. When
Arneth first published the correspondence in 1864, the letter of 12
July 1770, addressed to Maria Theresa in the formal third person,
showed Marie-Antoinette responding thus to the temporal monitoring of her religious life: "Regarding what you asked about my devotions, I will say that I have only taken communion one time."[13]
Arneth had neatly and discreetly edited out half the agenda, as history discovered when Girard published his edition in 1933: "Regarding what you asked about my devotions and my period [*la générale*],
I will say that I have only taken communion one time. . . . As for my
period, this is the fourth month that it has not come, without there
being any good reason."[14] The absence of "good reason" reflected the
absence of consummation in the marriage and the impossibility of
pregnancy. If the fourteen-year-old girl did not have her period for
four months, it might be attributed to the stress of royal marriage
and leaving home, but it definitely did not mean she was pregnant.

The unexpurgated passage indicates the dual religious and gynecological monitoring imposed by maternal discipline in the correspondence, a supervisory interest in devotions and periods, envision-
ing a future of regular communion and intercourse. The continued
postponement of the latter (for seven years) was distressing to Maria
Theresa, perhaps as much as to Marie-Antoinette. The empress naturally wanted her daughter's marriage to be consummated in order to
produce an heir to the French throne. Furthermore, Maria Theresa
saw in the sexual union of the young couple, after 1774 the king and
queen of France, the guarantee of the Bourbon-Hapsburg alliance, as
well as a key to Hapsburg influence on Louis XVI. The correspondence followed the monthly menstrual cycle, ultimately because sex
was an issue of public and political power for both France and Austria, but also because through sexual supervision the empress could
express her personal power over her daughter's private life.

Even with the marriage unconsummated, gynecological monitoring remained important, for menstruation could serve as an indi-

cator of the young woman's general physical and spiritual condition. After a year in France, on 16 April 1771, Marie-Antoinette began a letter to her mother with a careful account of herself: "Madame my very dear mother, I am delighted that Lent has not damaged your health. Mine is still rather good—I have the *générale* quite regularly [*assez régulièrement*]; this time it was nine days early."[15] Here the menstrual cycle was superimposed on the Lenten calendar, and Maria Theresa was informed very exactly that the cycle was nine days early. The phrase "assez régulièrement" showed how well Marie-Antoinette understood the nature of her mother's disciplinary concerns. Those concerns may also be interpreted in the light of Foucault's discussion of the "docile body" as an eighteenth-century disciplinary object. Foucault identifies the "analyzable" body with the "manipulable" body, and argues that this was the age that "discovered the body as an object and target of power."[16]

After the long-delayed consummation of the marriage in 1777, the delicate subject of menstruation acquired a fresh urgency in the correspondence. On 15 January 1778, Marie-Antoinette began her letter by writing, "I am quite ashamed and distressed to be obliged to inform my dear *maman* that my period [*mes règles*] came yesterday morning."[17] Maria Theresa immediately registered this information with displeasure, and began her reply of 1 February with the following remark: "Your letter of the 15th gave me no pleasure because of the return of your period."[18] The sense of being "obliged to inform my dear *maman*" summed up the disciplinary dynamic of the whole correspondence, while the juxtaposition of the daughter's shame with the mother's displeasure clearly represented the emotional relation that Maria Theresa had sought to cultivate in her letters as an aspect of that dynamic. The substitution of the more conventional expression "règles" for "générale" was also convenient in its suggestion of gynecological discipline, and the attention to the monthly "règles" of Marie-Antoinette, now queen of France, may still have called to mind the *Règlement*—to be read every month—that she had received eight years before when she first went to France as the dauphine.

The immediacy with which epistolary writing juxtaposes separate points in time and space is a function of its particular narrative nature. Just as a letter may be simply said to join two people, an epistolary narrative may be said, theoretically, to join two narrative per-

sons: the first person and the second person. In the *Règlement* of
1770, Maria Theresa introduced the second person from the very
beginning, with four instances in the opening phrase: "When *you*
wake up, *you* will immediately upon arising go through *your* morning prayers on *your* knees" [*À votre réveil vous ferez tout de suite, en
vous levant, vos prières du matin à genoux*].[19] One could say that the
employment of the second person here brought Marie-Antoinette to
her knees, for it was that narrative construction that made the document a letter, and at the same time made the letter an expression of
power. The presence of the second person identifies an epistolary
narrative—or rather the combination of first and second persons,
for the "you" implies an "I" who is writing, even when, as above, it
does not immediately advertise itself. The second person, of course,
also existed in eighteenth-century writing outside letters: "It is
enough to tell you, that as some of my worst comrades . . . knew me
by the name of Moll Flanders, so you may give me leave to speak of
myself under that name." The "you" to whom Moll Flanders ad-
dresses herself is all of us who read her story, whereas the distinction
of the epistolary "you" is its exclusion of all of us by the singling out
of the designated reader. Yet, paradoxically, though its narrative
form emphatically excludes us, the letter also allows us the most immediate observation of the balance between the two narrative persons, for the narrator who ignores us cannot authorially mediate
our reading of the text.

"You" and "I"—locked into their own relationship—offer the
nondesignated reader a narratively unmediated field for observing
and analyzing the microphysics of power. The *Règlement* of Maria
Theresa, opening with the second person alone, very quickly goes on
to choreograph the relation between the narrative persons:

> You will always write me and tell me which book you are using. [*Vous me
> marquerez toujours de quel livre vous vous servez.*] You will pray [*vous vous
> recueillerez*] during the day as often as you can, especially during the cel-
> ebration of Holy Mass. I hope you will attend it [*j'espère que vous l'enten-
> drez*] every day in the proper spirit, and twice on Sunday and holidays.[20]

The most obvious concern was still temporal calendar discipline,
mass every day, twice on Sundays. The pronouns of person, however, embedded in the epistolary text, reveal a more subtly conceived
disciplinary strategy. In the first sentence, the "you" deceptively proclaims itself the subject, though the intent is clearly to subordinate it

to the second-person object—"vous me marquerez"—so that the grammatical subject becomes an object of disciplinary surveillance. It is always the writer of the epistolary narrative who defines the relation of power between its two persons, reserving the option of assuming either subject or object status. In the second sentence Maria Theresa allows the "you" to enjoy both statuses in reflexive relation—"vous vous recueillerez"—so that surveillance gives way to self-discipline. Again, the discipline is only deceptively self-imposed by the second person (as it is only deceptively self-proclaimed in the first sentence), for the writer is always present in the epistolary text even without the advertisement of her own pronoun. On the other hand, to translate this sentence without the reflexive—"you will pray during the day as often as you can"—is to miss the self-disciplinary implications of the narrative strategy. For that, one must more awkwardly and less religiously render "vous vous recueillerez" as "you will collect yourself." It is not until the third sentence that the pronouns honestly proclaim their true epistolary relation—"j'espère que vous l'entendrez"—with the "I" as a hoping subject and the "you" itself the subject of a subordinate clause. Here the subordination in grammar perfectly reflects the formulated balance of power between the narrative persons.

These grammatical and narratological relations correspond to important issues of eighteenth-century cultural history. Both surveillance and self-discipline are crucial concepts in Foucault's formulation of the disciplinary revolution of the Enlightenment, which he traces from the spectacle of naked power and royal authority in public execution to the enclosed and unostentatious disciplinary surveillance in Bentham's vision of the Panopticon.[21] Maria Theresa's employment of the reflexive may be placed in the context of an eighteenth-century cultural trajectory. Already in 1693 Locke heralded a revolutionary rethinking of child rearing and education, deploring the brutality of excessive corporal punishment and advocating instead the disciplinary inculcation of feelings of shame and disgrace. Locke explained his preference in reflexive terms: "Every man must some time or other be trusted to himself."[22] One century later, Tuke could consummate this development and revolutionize mental health care by allowing self-discipline even to the insane at his York Retreat asylum. The madman too could be controlled reflexively: "He promised to restrain himself."[23] The echo of Locke's educational precepts in Maria Theresa's reflexive verbs reminds one that the correspondence (and balance of power) was between mother and daughter. Maria Theresa, one of the most powerful people in the world in 1770, was far from unversed in the articulation of authority, and she could assume the expressions and techniques of an enlightened mother as well as an enlightened empress. The letters reveal precisely how little she felt that the fourteen-year-old Marie-Antoinette could, in fact, be trusted to herself, but the transition to reflexive formulation, like the previewing of calendar anniversaries beyond her own death, recognizes the regrettable inevitability of independence. Just as epistolary narrative, by joining points in time, allows the writer to reach out beyond the moment of reception to broader temporal horizons, so the relation between "I" and "you," joining two persons, allows the writer boldly to manipulate the reflexive relation of the second person to herself.

In the most audacious line in the *Règlement,* Maria Theresa effaced herself completely, the better to warn her daughter that people will be watching her when she goes to church: "All eyes will be fixed on you [*tous les yeux seront fixés sur vous*], so do not give any cause for scandal."[24] The absent mother (pronominally absent from the sentence, as well as geographically distant in Vienna) could conjure up guardian eyes of surveillance lest Marie-Antoinette too fully embrace her independence. It was a sort of inverted Panopticon: instead of one eye on all the prisoners, all eyes on the one dauphine. In fact, Maria Theresa, keeping herself fully informed about her daughter through the dispatches of Mercy, the Austrian ambassador to Versailles, always tried to imply to her daughter that reports reached her in Vienna by way of general European gossip—the witnessed testimony of all those eyes. Thus, the warning was both cunningly false and at the same time politically prophetic. Already during her mother's lifetime, Marie-Antoinette would begin to cause scandal and would start on the path to being a public emblem of royal decadence.[25] Eyes would remain fixed on her with an ever-growing intensity until the ultimate moment when she ascended the guillotine in 1793. Thus, the narrative strategy of eighteenth-century discipline shows itself to be structurally related to the cultural strategy of eighteenth-century political mythology; the eyes that stand in for the concerned mother and empress meet the eyes of the outraged pornographers, philosophers, and revolutionaries.

In 1776, thirteen years before the revolution, nine years before the Diamond Necklace Affair that would ruin the reputation of

Marie-Antoinette beyond repair, Maria Theresa was already elaborating epistolary constructs that called into play the formal and thematic elements of revolutionary mythology. She wrote on 2 September, supposedly in response to the anonymous eyes and tongues that
constituted "the news from Paris":

> All the news from Paris announces [*toutes les nouvelles de Paris annon-
> cent*] that you have made a purchase of bracelets for 250,000 livres, that
> to that effect you have upset your finances and gone into debt, and that
> to remedy this you have given up some of your diamonds at a very low
> price, and that it is supposed [*qu'on suppose*] now that you lead the king
> astray [*que vous entraînez le roi*] into so many useless profusions, which
> have been mounting again for some time and putting the state in the dis-
> tress where it finds itself. I believe these articles to be exaggerated, but
> loving you so tenderly, I believe it was necessary that you be informed of
> the rumors [*des bruits qui courent*]. These kinds of anecdotes pierce my
> heart, especially for the future.[26]

One sees immediately that the thematic concerns anticipated the
coming of the revolution with startling clairvoyance, especially the
mythological association of the queen's extravagance with the state's
financial crisis. On closer examination, one sees that Maria Theresa
organized her concerns within a particular narrative strategy that
isolated Marie-Antoinette as the object of anonymous critical surveillance. In the whole first sentence the second person stands alone,
acting in subordinate clauses that are governed anonymously by "all
the news from Paris." In the second half of the sentence the "you" is
even more punishingly isolated by the interposition of an interme-
diary subordinate clause—"qu'on suppose"—between the news of
Paris and the culpable "you" who is leading the king astray. That is:
"Les nouvelles de Paris annoncent / qu'on suppose / que vous en-
traînez le roi."

Not until the following sentence did Maria Theresa permit herself to enter the narrative in the first person with a self-effacing "je
crois." Then she subtly cast herself as the twin victim of the same
anonymous forces of rumor—"des bruits qui courent"—that were
assaulting Marie-Antoinette. That is, "These kinds of anecdotes
pierce my heart." It was a narrative performance of strategic con-
cealment, first, because Maria Theresa received full reports on her
daughter from Mercy, and second, because, as the letter writer, she
always controlled completely the formal construction of the text. Interestingly, the enlightened absolutism of the empress seemed to an-

nounce itself in the further juxtaposition of her own victimized position—pierced to the heart—and that of "the state," not even her own, in "distress."

In the letters, as the purely grammatical relation between the "I" and the "you" moves toward the construction of the more culturally interpretable relation between the "eye" and the "you," epistolary narrative yields historical meaning. Paradoxically it is the most formal aspects of the narrative that illustrate the most historically complex issues of power, authority, and discipline. For this reason the theoretical treatment of epistolary form, though usually devoted to fiction, points the way toward a convergence of historical analysis and literary criticism. In 1962, Jean Rousset wrote about the epistolary novel as a literary form, and observed that such novels could resemble journals in their intimacy (as in *Pamela* or *Werther*), or alternatively could resemble works of theater in their immediacy, offering speech, action, and relation to the unmediated observation of the audience.[27] Rousset stresses the importance of a letter's recipient, even in the *Portuguese letters,* where the officer's actual absence and unresponsiveness make him no less an urgent presence in the nun's narrative.[28] In discussing *Les Liaisons dangereuses,* which critics of the genre tend to find most facinating and most rewarding of analysis, Rousset remarks that "each letter is so well addressed to someone, so much composed according to the measure of its addressee [*destinataire*], that this addressee is in the letter he receives as much as in that which he writes."[29] This consciousness of the narrative balance points to a conclusion about the world of the epistolary novel that would carry equal validity for letters in the historical world: "The world is a tissue of relations that diversify and intermingle."[30]

François Jost, writing in 1966 about narrative technique and the eighteenth-century epistolary novel, emphasized the distinction between a passive, static, confidential correspondence and an active, dynamic, dramatic correspondence.[31] *Les Liaisons dangereuses* provides Jost with his finest specimen of the latter, and again the critical vocabulary indicates those issues of power that might interest the historian. In 1967, Tzvetan Todorov published a study of *Les Liaisons dangereuses,* exploring "the signification of letters in general, and not only as a novelistic procedure."[32] Todorov observes the "temporal deformations" that may emerge from the epistolary form, and also identifies the "two opposite poles" of that form as the chronicle of impersonal events versus the drama of corresponding characters. The marquise de Merteuil serves as Todorov's "formal" heroine, insofar as her letters realize more than anyone else's the dramatic potential of the form. Just as she instructs Cécile that "when you write to someone, it is for him and not for you," so in her own letter writing the marquise is unique among the characters: according to Todorov, "she is the only one to aim [*viser*], in all her letters at the reaction of her interlocutor."[33] It is she who appreciates, as Maria Theresa did, the special potential of the epistolary form for the microphysics of power, and the letters of the fictional eighteenth-century marquise, like those of the historical empress, offer a model for the maximal manipulation and exploitation of epistolary narrative. Both women are mistresses of epistolary discipline—for discipline, as Foucault defines it, is "a type of power, a modality for its exercise, comprising a whole set of instruments, techniques, procedures, levels of application, targets."[34]

In 1982 Janet Altman published a book, *Epistolarity,* whose title underlines the importance of defining the unique qualities of the form. Altman notes the special literary triangle created by the letter writer, its internal reader or recipient, and the external reader or audience.[35] She stresses the designation of the reader as a "particularity of the I-you." She emphasizes the immediacy of the present tense, and points to the "temporal polyvalence" whereby "any given epistolary statement is relative to innumerable moments."[36] Altman identifies the "paradox of epistolarity" in its navigation of "polar consistencies."[37] The polar dimensions of the form include, for instance, "I/you, here/there, now/then," the specifications of person, place, and time.[38] She finally proposes three "registers" of epistolarity: one of reported events, one of the letter-writer, and one of the recipient reader.[39]

The scrupulousness of Altman's formal approach makes her observations on epistolarity as relevant to historical as to fictional letters. At the same time, her thoroughness in cataloguing the competing "polarities" of the form tends to avoid any highlighting of extreme, emphatic, essential epistolarity, the ideal type, as implied in Todorov's special fascination with the marquise de Merteuil. For while letters may vary tremendously and occupy a diversity of points on any graph of polar dimensions, it is precisely those letters that exploit the fullest combination of polarities that illustrate the fullest qualities of epistolarity. Plenty of letters, for instance, do not trespass far beyond the home turf of the first-person writer and the present time of writing. These are letters nonetheless, but one might argue that they demonstrate a less emphatic epistolarity than those that break out boldly from the circumscription of their origin. The marquise de Merteuil or the empress Maria Theresa, as they simultaneously embrace and assault the second person, the correspondent, the *destinataire,* exhibit a whole other level of epistolarity. Thus for Rousset, epistolary narrative may resemble either journal or theater; for Jost it may exhibit either static passivity or active dynamism; for Todorov it may rise from chronicle to drama. It is these latter qualities of extreme epistolarity that invite the historian to analyze and interpret letters as "instruments, techniques, procedures" in the evolving forms of disciplinary power.

Altman's triple register offers an approach not only to analyzing the letters as literary texts, but also to understanding the different ways historians make use of letters as historical documents. Any letter may involve all three registers—reported events, the sentiments of the writer, and the "aim" at the recipient—and these registers also generally correspond to the employment of three different narrative persons: third, first, and second. Todorov observes that the letter may resemble a third-person chronicle, and Rousset that it may resemble a first-person journal; for the historian, both chronicles and journals are valuable documents, and letters are often exploited just as if they were one or the other. For instance, the correspondence of Madame de Sévigné is an invaluable source of reported information about elite society in Paris and at Versailles in the age of Louis XIV. Consider the following reports:

> M. de Langlée has given Mme de Montespan a dress of gold on gold, all embroidered with gold, all edged with gold, and on top of that a sort of gold pile stitched with gold mixed with a certain gold, which makes the most divine stuff ever imagined. (6 November 1676)[40]

> The King wants to go to Versailles on Saturday, but it seems that God is not willing because it will be impossible for the buildings to be in a fit state to receive him and because of the enormous mortality of workmen of whom, as from the Hospital, they take away cartloads of dead every night. (12 October 1678)[41]

Such reports find their place in various historical treatments of the age, but it is important to observe that, taken thus as useful fragments, they exhibit no epistolary qualities, and may be employed by the historian without reference to their occurrence in letters. The correspondence of Madame de Sévigné may be treated as if it were, for all intents and purposes, the same sort of source as the memoirs of the duc de Saint-Simon.

Although the literary theory of epistolarity has especially focused on the eighteenth century, when the epistolary novel became such an important literary form, the formal analysis of letters is certainly also relevant to other centuries. Madame de Sévigné, the great epistolary genius of the seventeenth century, may inspire this sort of attention from scholars of French history and literature alike. On the other hand, looking forward to the correspondences of the nineteenth and twentieth centuries, when letters may assume a less self-consciously literary form, one sometimes further underestimates the significance of their formal epistolary qualities. For instance, the Freud-Fliess correspondence, which is so fundamental for modern intellectual historians, offers up as its most spectacular treasures the sentiments of the letter writer, Sigmund Freud himself.

> For the last four days my self-analysis, which I consider indispensable for the clarification of the whole problem, has continued in dreams and has presented me with the most valuable elucidations and clues. (3 October 1897)[42]

> I have found, in my own case too, being in love with my mother and jealous of my father, and I now consider it a universal event in early childhood. (15 October 1897)[43]

Here again the nuggets of gold may be mined without reference to their epistolary context. Just as Madame de Sévigné is invaluable for her third-person reports, so Sigmund Freud is for his first-person sentiments. The Freud-Fliess correspondence, in spite of its special narrative form, may be handled historically as if it were formally little different from the autobiography of John Stuart Mill or the diaries of Virginia Woolf.

At the same time, historians cannot help recognizing that the letters of Madame de Sévigné to Madame de Grignan reveal something important about relations between mother and daughter in the seventeenth century, and that the Freud-Fliess correspondence illustrates the odd collaborative origin of a cultural revolution. The second person cannot be ignored in these examples of correspondence, any more than in that of Maria Theresa and Marie-Antoinette.

And what do you think I am doing, my poor dear? Loving you, thinking of you, giving way to emotion at every turn more than I would like, concerning myself with your affairs, worrying about what you think, feeling your sufferings and pains, wanting to suffer them for you if possible, removing anything unpleasant from your heart as I used to clear your room of any tiresome people. (1 April 1671)[44]

Your happiness can vanish all too fast, and you may be plunged, by your own doing, into the greatest calamities. That is the result of your terrible dissipation, which prevents your being assiduous about anything serious. What have you read? (30 July 1775)[45]

You said nothing about my interpretation of *Oedipus Rex* and *Hamlet*. Since I have not told it to anyone else, because I can well imagine in advance the bewildered rejection, I should like to have a short comment on it from you. (5 November 1897)[46]

The historian's challenge must be to remain always aware of the narrative nature of the documents, to analyze them in their epistolary context. Literary theory offers an approach to epistolary form that may be used to historical advantage. Thus, the historian who appreciates the importance of the second person, the correspondent, in the letters of Madame de Sévigné, Maria Theresa, or Sigmund Freud will discover in their relations and liaisons the fundamental dynamics of social, political, and cultural history. It is Maria Theresa herself who reminds us that our critical eyes must be fixed on the "you."

Notes

1. Alfred von Arneth, ed., *Maria Theresia und Marie Antoinette: Ihr Briefwechsel während der Jahre 1770–1780* (Paris and Vienna: E. Jung–Treuttel, 1865); A. d'Arneth and M.A. Geffroy, eds., *Correspondance secrète entre Marie Thérèse et le comte de Mercy-Argenteau* (Paris: Firmin-Didot, 1874–1875).

2. Georges Girard, ed., *Correspondance entre Marie-Thérèse et Marie-Antoinette* (Paris: Éditions Bernard Grasset, 1933); Stefan Zweig, *Marie Antoinette: The Portrait of an Average Woman*, trans. Eden and Cedar Paul (Garden City, N.Y.: Garden City Publishing, 1933).

3. G. P. Gooch, "Maria Theresa and Marie Antoinette," in *Maria Theresa and Other Studies* (1951; reprint, Hamden, Conn.: Archon Books, 1965), 119.

4. Oliver Bernier, ed., *Secrets of Marie Antoinette: A Collection of Letters* (New York: Fromm, 1986).

5. Girard, *Correspondance*, letter of Maria Theresa, 21 April 1770, 21. All translations are mine except as otherwise noted.

6. Ibid., letter of Maria Theresa, 4 May 1770, 26.

7. Ibid., letter of Maria Theresa, 21 April 1770, 21; the translation is from Bernier, *Secrets*, 31.

8. Michel Foucault, *Discipline and Punish*, trans. Alan Sheridan (New York: Vintage, 1979), 139.

9. Ibid., 149.

10. Girard, *Correspondance*, letter of Marie-Antoinette, 12 July 1770, 30.

11. Ibid., letter of Maria Theresa, 31 October 1776, 192; the translation is from Bernier, *Secrets*, 203.

12. Girard, *Correspondance*, letter of Maria Theresa, 21 April 1770, 23; the translation is from Bernier, *Secrets*, 32.

13. Arneth, *Maria Theresa*, letter of Marie-Antoinette, 12 July 1770, 5.

14. Girard, *Correspondance*, letter of Marie-Antoinette, 12 July 1770, 29.

15. Ibid., letter of Marie-Antoinette, 16 April 1771, 40; the translation is from Bernier, *Secrets*, 61.

16. Foucault, *Discipline and Punish*, 136.

17. Girard, *Correspondance*, letter of Marie-Antoinette, 15 January 1778, 229.

18. Ibid., letter of Maria Theresa, 1 February 1778, 231.

19. Ibid., letter of Maria Theresa, 21 April 1770, 21; the translation is from Bernier, *Secrets*, 31 (emphasis added).

20. Girard, *Correspondance*, letter of Maria Theresa, 21 April 1770, 21; the translation is from Bernier, *Secrets*, 31.

21. Foucault, *Discipline and Punish*, pt. 3, chap. 3, "Panopticism," 195–228.

22. John Locke, "Some Thoughts Concerning Education" (1693), in Peter Gay, ed., *The Enlightenment: A Comprehensive Anthology* (New York: Touchstone, 1973), 91.

23. Michel Foucault, *Madness and Civilization* (1961; reprint, New York: Vintage, 1973), 246.

24. Girard, *Correspondance*, letter of Maria Theresa, 21 April 1770, 22.

25. Simon Schama, *Citizens: A Chronicle of the French Revolution* (New York: Knopf, 1989); on Marie-Antoinette, see chap. 6, "Body Politics," section i, "Uterine Furies and Dynastic Obstructions," 203–27.

26. Girard, *Correspondance*, letter of Maria Theresa, 2 September 1776, 185–86.

27. Jean Rousset, "Une forme littéraire: Le roman par les lettres," in Rousset, *Forme et signification* (Paris: Librairie José Corti, 1962), 67.

28. Ibid., 72.

29. Ibid., 95.

30. Ibid., 85

31. François Jost, "L'évolution d'un genre: le roman épistolaire dans les lettres occidentales," in Jost, *Essais de littérature comparée*, vol. 2, Europaeana, first series (Urbana: University of Illinois Press and Fribourg: Éditions Universitaires Fribourg Suisse, 1968), 124.

32. Tzvetan Todorov, *Littérature et signification* (Paris: Librairie Larousse, 1967), 13.

33. Ibid., 36–37.

34. Foucault, *Discipline and Punish*, 215.

35. Janet Gurkin Altman, *Epistolarity: Approaches to a Form* (Columbus: Ohio State University Press, 1982), 111.

36. Ibid., 117–18.

37. Ibid., 190.

38. Ibid., 186–87.

39. Ibid., 207–8.

40. Madame de Sévigné, letter of 6 November 1676, in Sévigné, *Selected Letters*, ed. and trans. Leonard Tancock (New York: Penguin, 1982), 215.

41. Ibid., letter of 12 October 1678, 226.

42. Sigmund Freud, letter of 3 October 1897, in *The Complete Letters of Sigmund Freud to Wilhelm Fliess*, trans. Jeffrey Moussaieff Masson (Cambridge, Mass.: Harvard University Press, 1985), 268.

43. Ibid., letter of 15 October 1897, 272.

44. Sévigné, *Selected Letters*, letter of 1 April 1671, 84.

45. Girard, *Correspondance*, letter of Maria Theresa, 30 July 1775, 156; the translation is from Bernier, *Secrets*, 172.

46. Freud, *Complete Letters*, letter of 5 November 1897, 277.

The Portrait of the Queen

Mary D. Sheriff

The Queen's New Clothes

Imagine yourself a visitor to the Salon exhibition of 1783 gazing on the portrait of Marie-Antoinette painted by Elisabeth Vigée-Lebrun (see photo insert). You see the queen sporting a straw hat and dressed fashionably in a simple gown of white muslin tied with a sash at the waist. How are you responding to the image? What narrative are you generating from the portrait? Ah, but you cannot have a response, you cannot generate a narrative until I tell you just what sort of visitor, even which particular visitor, you are. Marie-Antoinette appears at the Salon, but for whom, and as whom, is she appearing?

Vigée-Lebrun's portrait especially raises these questions because the public descried it, even forced Vigée-Lebrun to remove it from the Salon. Why did this portrait disturb? What of queenship was or was not represented there? The immediate answer isolates the unsuitability of the costume *en lévite* or *en chemise* for public appearance. Imported from England in the 1780s, and adapted by the famous dressmaker Rose Bertin, the *robe en chemise* was made from sheer white muslin, fastened down the back, and caught at the waist with a sash. The underskirt and corset, which ordinarily showed through the transparent muslin, were often of blue or pink silk. A soft fichu, usually of linen gauze, and a straw hat completed the look. The style was immensely popular in England, where it made a fashion statement for the "natural woman," suggesting simplicity and honest sentiment. In France, however, the formalities of court made these simple styles less acceptable; for public appearances the *robe en chemise* was considered immodest, even though it revealed far less of the body than traditional court dresses with deeply scooped necklines. On the other hand, the *robe en chemise* was included in the *Cabinet des modes* of 1786 under informal wear. When worn outside the boudoir or private chambers, such dress was usually reserved for walks in the park, for picnics, or for playing milkmaid with a few friends. Because this dress became closely associated with Marie-Antoinette, many called it the *chemise à la reine.*[1]

The *Correspondance littéraire* suggests that some Salon visitors were shocked by the impropriety—the immodesty—of the queen appearing publicly in such attire: "Earlier one noticed among the portraits of this amiable artist that of the queen *en lévite,* but because the public seemed to disapprove of a costume unworthy of Her Majesty, [Vigée-Lebrun] was pressed to substitute for it another with an attire more analogous to the dignity of the throne."[2] Pamphleteers were more clever in their criticism. In *La Morte de trois mille ans au Salon de 1783,* for example, comments about the queen's attire *en chemise* were indirect but nonetheless censorious. Simultaneously reporting and commenting on the reactions of the Greek maiden Dibutadis visiting the sculpture court, the narrator tells his reader that

> although it was an ancient practice, she found the fierce Achilles a bit too familiar for appearing nude before the ladies. He draws his sword undoubtedly to frighten those who would disapprove of his nudity. At least his attitude pleases. The ladies who appear in public *en chemise* cannot be overly critical of his attire. Their own contrasts with the noble simplicity that was the adornment of the beautiful Greek maiden.[3]

Seen in public and in mixed company, a woman garbed *en chemise* is as inappropriate as a nude man—and much less pleasing. Her dress is no more modest than his nakedness, and it stands in pointed contrast to the Greek maiden's "noble simplicity." Armed with his sword, Achilles can fend off all critics, but the woman *en chemise* is defenseless; she cannot even point a finger at the warrior's undress.

Years later Vigée-Lebrun described the controversy surrounding this portrait of Marie-Antoinette. Writing in her *Souvenirs* of the many images she made of the queen, she focused her attention on this one: "One among the others represented her donning a straw hat and garbed in a dress of white muslin with sleeves folded up, but quite orderly; when it was shown at the Salon, the malicious did not refrain from saying that the queen was represented in her underwear."[4] These reports of negative responses, however, contrast with other recorded ones, underlining the obvious point that reaction to the queen's portrait depended on who was looking when and where.

The queen herself apparently admired the work; she sent three versions of it to close women relatives and in 1786 judged it as the most resembling of all her portraits.[5]

Although the divergence of these responses leads to the obvious question of what these audiences saw when they looked at the queen's portrait, a more fundamental question might be, what did they expect to see in a publicly exhibited portrait of the queen? How does a portrait of the queen serve the aims of the state? What relations of representation, power, and imagination are at work in the queen's portrait?

Salic/Phallic Law

It should surprise no one that the French monarchy depended on the suppression of women's claims to the scepter. Indeed, one could suggest three sentences that characterize this gendered side of absolutist aesthetics. The first comes from Antoine Loisel's maxims (1607) and condenses the Salic Law: "The kingdom cannot fall to the distaff side."[6] The second, drawn from Bignon's *De l'excellence des roys et du royaume de France* (1610), justifies that law: "This is not a written law but one that was born with us that we have not invented but drawn from nature itself."[7] And the third, from Guy Coquille, *Institution du droit de François* (1588), separates the queen from the body of the king and hence from state power: "The king is monarch and has no companion in his royal majesty. External honors can be communicated to the wives of kings, but that which is of his majesty, representing his power and dignity, resides inextricably in his person alone."[8]

The Salic Law determined kingship by the right of succession and excluded from succession females and males descended in the female line. The queen of France signified the wife of the king, and "queen" had no meaning except in relation to "king." The Salic Law was considered first among the fundamental laws of France, which were laws perceived as anterior to all other laws and hence constitutional of the nation. Although by 1610 the Salic Law seemed to the French "born with us," it was not "drawn from nature itself" but manufactured in the early 1300s by Philippe V during a disputed succession.[9] Although the sacredness of monarchy and its mystical character was widely challenged in the Enlightenment—at least in philosophical circles—part of the Salic Law and its seventeenth-century justifications fit well with thinking on women that crossed political boundaries during the ancien régime and Revolution. Jurists such as Le Bret in his *Traité de la souveraineté du roi* justified the exclusion of women on the basis of natural law. The Salic Law, he argued, conformed

> to the law of nature which, having decreed woman imperfect, weak, and debilitated, as much in body as in mind, has submitted her to the power of man, whom she [nature] has . . . enriched with a stronger judgment, more assured courage, and a stronger physical force. Also we see that divine law wants a wife to recognize and render obedience to her husband as to her master and to her king.[10]

The fundamental law of France, the Salic Law, is thus justified along the same lines as those laws that prescribed a wife's *état* as one of subservience to her husband.[11]

When in the eighteenth century some public representations of monarchy were calculated to characterize the king as a benevolent father rather than Roman paterfamilias, the queen's position did not change. She had long been the first of the king's subjects, owing him obedience as husband and ruler. The image of the benevolent father visible in royal monuments, however, was not particularly evident in official state portraits, which continued to represent kingliness and majesty.[12] State portraits of kings remained fairly constant in type from Louis XIV to Louis XVI, and the same is true of the queen's official portraits. A queen is a wife, and an official portrait of the queen shows the wife of the king; it is always a (possible) companion piece to the king's portrait.

Carle Van Loo's portrait of Queen Marie Leszczynska, commissioned for the royal collection and shown in the Salon of 1747 (see photo insert), represents the type for the queen's public portrait. The painting is large-scale and shows the full-length standing figure; the pose, although formal, is not stiff, and the attitude suggests regal bearing in its straight lines and stability. Indeed, the portraitist establishes a virtual line that runs the center length of the body through the boned bodice. Thus centered, the queen becomes one of three strong verticals that define the picture; she is as solid as the columns to her right and left. In what is something of a tour de force, Van Loo manages to associate the queen, standing before us in her elaborate and frilled court dress, with these strong verticals, more than with the ornately carved rococo table leg curving prominently in the left foreground of the composition. We imagine her not as serpentine and seductive, but as standing straight and erect underneath the mounds of costume. The overall shape of her dressed body, moreover, tends toward a stable triangle, with the curve of her waist more or less straightened out by the fall of her cape. Comparing this type of queen's portrait to state portraits of the king—say, Van Loo's *Louis XV* (Versailles, Musée du Château)—shows a gendered contrast also at work. Kings look active and queens immobile. Kings partake of the energy encoded in the agitated drapery that swirls around them, and their taut leg muscles, visibly protruding, suggest the force attributed to the male body.

As is typical in official portraits, the queen, Marie Leszczynska, is displayed in elaborate court costume. Her dress bedecked with ribbons, lace, and gold embroidery, and the gold tonalities in the dress and furnishings suggest an opulence likewise marked in her jeweled hair, neck, and arms. The room is as ornamented as the queen, with inlaid marble floors, marble-top table elaborately trimmed in gilt rocaille, and other furnishings. Louis Marin has suggested that to be elegant is to show that a great number of people have worked to produce the effect. Hair, embroidery, ribbons, and the like are in the people's eyes effects of force—signs of work at work to show how one can make others work.[13] The queen's portrait, however, points not to her own force and power, but to that of the king. The markers of high status are clarified by the attributes of queenship—Marie's crown resting on a nearby table and her ermine-trimmed cape with fleur-de-lys lining. The defining quality of queenship—her relation to the king—is signified twice, first because the image appeared as a companion piece to Van Loo's portrait of Louis XV, and second because Louis appears within the painting as a portrait bust on the table. The king seems to be gazing down at his queen as she looks out at the audience. Although viewers cannot share the king's gaze, they can imagine themselves exchanging glances with the queen. At the same time, they see him looking at her and can envision him as re-presenting, or authorizing, or even authoring her. From the king's gaze the whole top half of the composition—the queen's face and upper body—is framed in a space defined by his triangle of vision.

The problem in making a public portrait of the queen is how to eulogize the absolute monarch through a portrait of his wife, how to show the king's force in a portrait of the queen. Marin has argued that in representation to be elegant is to show and to be one's appearance, and also to present oneself to others and by that to represent oneself through one's image in the gaze of others.[14] The queen here is represented through her image as the regal and elegant consort not only in the gaze of her subjects (those who are the actual viewers of the painting), but also in the gaze of her husband, the king—who is the real subject in and of the painting. Although Marin argues that to be elegant is to show and be shown, to assume both the subject and the object position, here the queen is the object of the king's showing. Marie Leszczynska is represented to us as queen, but the authority that allows her representation is vested elsewhere; her image always refers to that authority.

The portrait of the queen, then, creates a subject, "queen of France," that refers to a position a woman holds because she is wife to the king of France. Not an accident of birth, but a legal contract changes the historical woman into a queen. The title (*état*) of queen, like that of wife, held no authority or right to govern. And the queen held no relation to the kingdom or to the state independent of her relation to the king. Her function was to produce sons. As Maria Theresa wrote to Marie-Antoinette: "to bear children, that is why you have been summoned; it is by bearing children that your happiness will be secured."[15] Although the queen's fertility was a major concern, royalty was conferred only by the father. She was the medium through which power was exchanged between father and son. After the line was ensured, the queen was superfluous. Kings who outlived queens satisfied themselves with unofficial wives (e.g., those married without public acknowledgment), as Louis XIV did with Mme de Maintenon, or with mistresses, as Louis XV did with Mme du Barry. Power passed through the queen's body but was not part of her. The king's majesty could not be shared with her, but it could not be passed on without her.

This point returns me to the third and final proposition of the aesthetics of queenship noted above: "The king is monarch and has no companion in his royal majesty. External honors can be communicated to the wives of kings, but that which is of his majesty, representing his power and dignity, resides inextricably in his person alone." In terms of the relation between king and queen, the third proposition is very significant. In some respects they did not have the same relation as other married couples, especially when marriage was conceptualized as a uniting of two individuals into one "body," with the husband as the head. This view of marriage could not obtain for the king and queen, because only in *his* person, thought by tradition to be united to the state, resided majesty, power, and dignity.

The queen, moreover, did not share community property with the king. Another of the fundamental laws of France conceptualized the king's domain as an attribute of sovereignty, and sovereignty could not be subdivided or alienated, that is, shared with the queen or anyone else. What was acquired by kings went to the profit of his kingdom, which came to be thought of as the king's "most privileged spouse."[16] Thus the king had two spouses—the privileged one, or the kingdom, which shared his sovereignty, and the alienated one, or the queen, who was separated from it.

From the notion of a marriage between the king and the kingdom came the tradition of calling the dauphins the "children of France."[17] When the king is married to the nation and his children are the children of France, the queen is—at least metaphorically—displaced as mother of the (future) king. There could be no coordination between the queen's body and that of the other wife—the kingdom, or France.[18] Queens are theoretically and symbolically foreign to the kingdom, so the portrait of the queen operates no exchange between the real historical woman and the political body/state.

Where, then, does all of this leave the queen of France? Although she had no right to rule, did not share the king's majesty, and was alienated from kingdom and state, the queen was not, in practice, powerless. Under absolute monarchy queens could take part in administration, primarily by sitting on the king's council, consisting of his court and other devoted servants. Although the importance of this council declined between 1723 and 1789, Marie-Antoinette did gain permission to join it during the reign of Louis XVI. The queen could rule if and only if the king named her regent, but this was an office entirely separate from the fact of queenship, even though the two sometimes coincided. As regent, the queen ruled by appointment of her husband the king, usually in the name of her son the king. This opening for female power, however, was closed during the Revolutionary period. In March 1791, the National Assembly decreed that if the crown passed to an underage son, the king's closest *male* relative, as defined by the laws of succession, would become regent. The timing of this decree again reminds us that fear of female rule was particularly heightened by the specter of the "monstrous" Marie-Antoinette.[19]

Although the queen had no relation of her own to the kingdom, she was fated to live in the gaze of court and populace. As the king's consort, she was the object of elaborate court rituals and spectacles of viewing, and she had little or no private life, in the sense of a life apart from her position as queen. At court, the queen did not own her own body. She was dressed and undressed in elaborate ceremony; her giving birth was a major public spectacle. Yet she was not as completely a public person, or as completely the public's person, as was the king, for her theoretical relation to court and nation was that of outsider alien to the *chose publique.*

As an outsider, the queen could raise fears of overstepping her boundaries, of having too much power over the king, her husband, or the king, her son. In the first case, her power could come from the place where women were perceived to exercise their authority—the bedroom. Historically, however, this sort of female power was divided because the king took various official and unofficial mistresses. Holding a position at court, the official mistress could be much more than the king's sexual partner; she was often a friend, confidant, and trusted advisor. A wife, an official mistress, and a proliferation of unofficial ones helped ensure that female power was fragmented. Yet wives and mistresses did exercise power, if only covertly or behind the scenes, as Lynn Hunt has recently reminded us.[20] Louis XVI was not a womanizer and he had no official mistresses. Thus his queen, Marie-Antoinette, seemed the most influential woman in his life, and her influence was undiluted, a situation complicated by the perception that Louis was a weak ruler and man. Marie-Antoinette was an archduchess and daughter of an empress; she presented the real and imagined threat of allegiance to her mother's house.

Marie-Antoinette Portrayed

In the French imaginary, royalty was incestuous. The dauphin, the child of France, fulfilled the Oedipal fantasy of marrying his mother, France, at his coronation when she became his privileged spouse. In practice the historical woman who became queen of France, at least in the seventeenth and eighteenth centuries, represented a principle of exogamy. Because the importation of a (foreign) woman was necessary to the proper running of the monarchy, the queen of France can be construed as a sign of political alliance between two families or houses.

In relation to queenship as diplomatic exchange, the making and viewing of Marie-Antoinette's portrait has an important history. Before Louis XV would close the deal with Maria Theresa, a deal negotiated over four years, he wanted to see a portrait of the young archduchess. There seems to be a peculiar belief in the truth of the portrait or in its power to capture beauty, taken as a signifier of future fertility. But we cannot really know why Louis insisted on having this portrait. Perhaps he understood it as his prerogative since it was traditional to be supplied with such an image. For her part, Maria Theresa seems never to have been satisfied with any portrait, and she repeatedly delayed sending a definitive one, as if no artist could really capture the beauty of her daughter—always implying that there was more, something that could not be represented.[21] Already impatient, Louis wanted to send France's most distinguished portrait painter, the academician Drouais. But Drouais overestimated the king's desire and asked too high a price. In the end, in late January of 1769, Louis sent the painter Ducreux—who was not even an academician—to do the job. A hairdresser went with him because Maria Theresa wanted to ensure that her daughter would look as French as possible.[22] The portrait that sealed the deal is now lost.

If the history of making Marie-Antoinette's portrait is bound on one side by the French king, it is determined on the other by the Hapsburg empress. The approval of Maria Theresa, the queen's mother, seems to have secured Vigée-Lebrun her position as favored portraitist. The correspondence of Maria Theresa, her agent the comte de Mercy–Argenteau, and Marie-Antoinette shows the empress anxious to have appropriate images of her daughter. As a mother, she wanted private portraits to remind her of the child sent away; as empress, she wanted public statements of queenship. It was in conjunction with the latter that Vigée-Lebrun was first successful. The artist began making the queen's image by copying for the *menuplaisir* portraits that other artists had painted of Marie-Antoinette (a steady supply of such copies was needed to meet diplomatic requests). Why and how Vigée-Lebrun was called to paint the queen from life is not clear, but it is evident that both queen and empress were exasperated by the official images made by other painters.

Maria Theresa spent nearly a decade trying to obtain an official portrait of her daughter that pleased her.[23] After commissioning a work from the painter Liotard, she wrote to Marie-Antoinette in December of 1770: "I await the painting of Liotard with great expectations, but in your finery [*parure*] not in casual dress. [*négligé*] nor in a man's outfit. I want to see you in your proper station."[24] The work has been lost, but we know from correspondence that Liotard, a portraitist frequently employed by Maria Theresa, did not satisfy the empress' expectations. Her comment, however, also points to another aspect of the story. Smaller, private images of Marie-Antoinette did satisfy the mother, who, making a distinction between them and official portraits, allowed them more leeway in terms of costume. She even tolerated in painting what she disapproved in real life. Her remark about not wanting to see her daughter in a man's outfit recalls Joseph Krantzinger's famous portrait of Marie-Antoinette *en amazone,* that is, in a costume resembling a man's riding coat. Maria Theresa expressed her pleasure even at this portrait since it represented her daughter as she was, enjoying her activities.[25] Thus even as she warned Marie-Antoinette against the dangers of riding a horse—especially of riding *en homme,* which she found hazardous for future fertility—she relished these images and used them in her private spaces.[26] In August of 1771, she wrote to her daughter, "I have received your portrait in pastel, it is a good resemblance and it pleases me and the whole family. It is in the cabinet where I work, and the [second] framed image is in my bedroom, where I work in the evenings, so I have you with me before my eyes and you are always profoundly in my heart."[27]

The search for a suitable official portrait, however, went on for years, much to both women's exasperation. In 1774 Marie-Antoinette wrote to Maria Theresa: "It quite saddens me not to have been able to find a painter who catches my resemblance; if I found one I would give him all the time he wanted, and although he would be able to make only a bad copy, I would take great pleasure in dedicating it to my dear mama."[28] The letter responds to the unrealized desire of the mother, and three years later the daughter wrote to her in a similar vein on 16 June: "I put myself at the discretion of the painter, for as long as he wanted and in the attitude that he wished. I would give everything for him to be able to succeed and to satisfy my dear mama."[29] Finally, two years later a portrait arrived that suited Maria Theresa, a portrait painted by Elisabeth Vigée-Lebrun 1778; see photo insert). Here is the response the empress sent Marie-Antoinette after receiving the work in April 1779: "Your large portrait pleases me! Ligne has found it resembling, but it is enough for me that it represents your face, with which I am quite happy."[30]

Given that Vigée-Lebrun's image succeeded where so many others had failed, is it any surprise that Marie-Antoinette became attached to the painter who finally pleased her mama?

The work sent by Vigée-Lebrun is well within the tradition of the queen's official portrait. The symbolic accessories duplicate many of those seen in Van Loo's portrait of Marie Lzczynska; in particular, the queen is standing near a table on which rests the crown placed on a pillow decorated with fleur-de-lys. The curving figure that usually signaled a woman's body is again presented in a more stable triangular form; on one side the queen's extended arm masks the round of her hip, and on the other a virtual diagonal runs from her plumed headress down the slope of her shoulders and through her panier and skirt. That diagonal is emphasized by the direction of her gaze. As in Van Loo's portrait, the vertical accents—the straight arm and the hanging tassels adorning her dress—reinforce the stabilizing effect of the massive columns. Thus, despite the display of costume and surface, the queen's figure seems quite architectonic. Moreover, the artist uses to positive effect the long Hapsburg face. The right side is rendered in a sharp, straight profile; on the left her hair is pulled well back, and the vertical shadow cast along temple and neck stands out against the rounded and lightly rouged cheeks and chin. The hair, underplayed and kept in shadow, acts as a frame for the face. Despite her plumed headdress and wavy hair, Marie-Antoinette's highlighted face rises from her neck with a verticality nearly as regular and definite as that of the column beside her. Moreover, she holds the center of the composition easily. Her face is isolated against a rectangular space articulated by the door frame in the background, and light reflected from her white neck and chest, which are bare of necklace, pendant, or other jewels, ensures her maximum visibility.

Marie-Antoinette's image in this work is simplified over that of Louis XV's queen, although it is still opulent enough to bespeak royal status. Similarly, the artist maintains certain traditional elements, such as the swag of drapery that both adds complexity to the composition and theatricalizes the sitter. However, even the drapery swag is made to seem less self-consciously dramatic by reducing the complexity of its folds and tracing a more or less vertical fall rather than a grand diagonal sweep. It is not enough to attribute this difference to a change in taste, since in other images Marie-Antoinette was even more decorated than Marie Lzczynska. Overly embellished images of her daughter drew criticism from Maria Theresa, who felt they made Marie-Antoinette look like an actress. I believe that Vigée-Lebrun's simplifications represent the artist's appeal to the recipient of the portrait, who had repeatedly complained about overly decorated images. Given the numbers of painters called to represent the queen, the quest for the proper image of Marie-Antoinette could hardly have been news to the artistic community.

In her portrait of the queen, Vigée-Lebrun reduces the ornamentation by restricting the number of different elements in the painting (elements are repeated rather than varied) and by making these less decorative. She uses one dominant color for the costume, which makes this frilly dress seem more austere, more classic, and she restricts the color range of the entire composition, relying primarily on an overall white with strong red accents and more muted ones of gold and blue. Even the headdress is simplified, and because the hat's plume harmonizes in overall shape with the flowers on the nearby table, it seems integrated with the overall composition and not singled out as an attention-grabbing flourish. Vigée-Lebrun, moreover, has made the queen look serious and august. Marie-Antoinette does not engage the viewer; rather than acknowledge anyone's gaze, she stares out of the painting. Her expression resembles that usually reserved for important male sitters—for example, the king. Focused as it is on some thing—or some history—we cannot see, her look recapitulates that which Vigée-Lebrun gives to a bust of Louis XVI positioned on a plinth represented in the painting's upper right corner.

"Malicious People Said the Queen Appeared in Her Underwear"

The portrait of Marie-Antoinette *en chemise* made by Elisabeth Vigée-Lebrun is obviously not a state portrait, although a successful state portrait was probably her license to make this one. There was certainly a tradition of depicting the queen more informally; I have already mentioned some of those portraits of Marie-Antoinette sent to Vienna for her mother's private enjoyment. Informal portraits of the queen, however, did not often appear at the Salon, in public, as did the image of Marie-Antoinette *en chemise*. In this portrait, Vigée-Lebrun shows the queen standing at a table but set against a blank background, so it is not clear if the sitter is positioned in an interior or exterior space. Marie-Antoinette poses as she wraps a blue satin ribbon around a small nosegay that includes her signature flower, the rose. A few flowers lie on the tabletop, and a larger bouquet has already been arranged in a blue Sèvres vase decorated with a gilt satyr's head. For whom, one wonders, does the queen wind the ribbon as she looks out of the composition (at the viewer?) with a sideways and lopsided glance? Her person, moreover, is pushed up to the picture plane so that the viewer can fancy him- or herself in intimate conversation with the monarch. The entire image is coded for informality and refers to the artful naturalness of the picturesque. Marie-Antoinette's face is skillfully framed in a C-curve subtly formed by arms, ribbon, and hat plume, and her straw hat breaks the contours of the long Hapsburg face in a pleasing way. Her soft, unpowdered hair, lack of jewelry, and seemingly simple costume also token a studied naturalness associated with the look *en chemise.*

Why make the portrait *en chemise*? The letters between Marie-Antoinette and her mother suggest that even early on Marie-Antoinette wanted to see herself painted in her favorite costumes, undertaking her favorite activities. What does Marie-Antoinette want to be in the portrait *en chemise*? What desire is Vigée-Lebrun representing to her? What trap for her desire, as Louis Marin would say, is she presenting the queen? In showing the queen as a fashionable lady, Vigée-Lebrun has imaged, perhaps without realizing it, Marie-Antoinette's desire not to be queen of France. I am not suggesting anything like a wish for abdication, but a desire to separate herself, if only temporarily, from the demands of the office. I would like to distinguish this desire—if it is possible to do so—from the vision of Marie-Antoinette's escapist tendencies well represented in all kinds of writing, from serious historical studies to Hollywood movie scripts, and reworked every day for the visitors tromping through her private apartments at Versailles.

What I have in mind is a bit more sympathetic toward this admittedly spoiled woman, for while Marie-Antoinette likely wanted sometimes to escape her position as queen, she certainly had no desire to be less than a queen, even for a day. She wanted to be what she—willful woman that she was—wanted to be, not what French etiquette would make her. It was a revolt of sorts, but hardly a profound political one. Jacques Revel has well articulated the dilemma of Marie-Antoinette in writing of her pretension to conduct her life as she wished, to create a private space for herself apart from the official world of public representation. Marie-Antoinette "forgot the maxim that royalty has no right to private life."[31] Revel goes on analyzing her wish to create a private space symbolized by the Trianon: "In this case, the staging of the private sphere is at the origin of a degradation of the representation that it renders trivial, even ridiculous."[32] It is a joke, maybe even an outrage—a queen playing milkmaid with her Sèvres buckets and golden implements. We see class outrage, and we anticipate the final dramatization of the distinction between the queen playing at being a peasant and the real state of the French people. It is easy to imagine the queen, dressed as a milkmaid, uttering that apocryphal line: "Let them eat cake!"

Yet we forget today what other messages other audiences might have constructed from this portrait and the remaking of the sacred space of Versailles. What if one looks at this portrait from a perspective other than that of the Revolution, which in 1783 was scarcely a gleam in its fathers' eyes? How might a "public" of 1783 still attached to the monarchy, patrimoine, and gloire have read the desire encoded in the queen's portrait and at the Trianon? How they might have read these could, for a segment of the public, have been directed by the queen's enemies at court, for libels issuing from the court forged the first caricatures that were to haunt the queen through the Revolution.[33]

A decade before Marie-Antoinette's trial constructed her as the quintessential bad mother, Vigée-Lebrun unwittingly showed her as an immodest woman, providing enemies with yet more evidence against the queen.[34] Showing the work was, at least for the queen, a tactical error on Vigée-Lebrun's part. Maybe the artist was so captivated by a certain image of the queen (or by her desire to please a patron captivated by a certain image of herself) that she "forgot" what everyone knew by 1783: the Salon was becoming a school for virtue and morality, increasingly intolerant of immodest depictions. In 1783, many critics judged paintings according to the moral effect of their subject matter. In a Salon where critics found the most up-to-date history paintings those dedicated to great men, to heroic action, to women sacrificed for their virtue, how would this portrait of the queen of France signify? How would it be judged in relation to Virginius Killing His Daughter, for example, a story in which a moral ferocity shows no pity? What future did the queen en chemise suggest? Not the future of the past—the gloire of the French monarchy—but a future symbolized by the world of the Trianon. The emblem of the Trianon was the *chemise,* as commentators, including the royalist Rose Campan, have noted: "A dress of white percale, a fichu of gauze, a straw hat, these were the only adornments of the princesses."[35] It was as the queen of Trianon that Marie-Antoinette was displayed, judged, and condemned at the Salon of 1783. Although her condemnation then was not as consequential as it would be in '93, there is an underlying similarity in the charges against her. At her trial Marie-Antoinette was accused of damaging her son's— the former potential king's—sexual potency.[36] As the queen *en chemise,* she was castigated for feminizing a sacred space of the virile French monarchy with her society of women at Trianon. This violation— like that of her son—was all the more egregious because engineered by a foreign woman, by the *Autrichienne.*

If the Trianon was an escape from anything, it was an escape from the court with all its formality, rules, and, one imagines, tedium. In the portrait, Marie-Antoinette represents herself not in terms of a position at court, but in terms of a position in a larger society—as a fashionable woman. Taking the authority not to occupy her position as queen, Marie-Antoinette defied the sacrosanct laws of French court etiquette.[37] What Marie-Antoinette failed to realize, as many have pointed out, was that a queen could not do as she pleased. She was the first subject of the king and of France, the model of all others subjected to his power.

The Trianon

The two Trianons were conceived as resting places for the king to shelter him during the summer's heat, but both also took on other functions, both practical and symbolic. The Grand Trianon was a stage setting for Louis XIV. There the Sun King entertained his court, which was the privileged recipient of the prince's gracious gift. During a fête the king offered himself to the court as spectacle. The Grand Trianon in particular and the gardens of Versailles in general raise several important points. They were used for the convenience and pleasure of the king, and they participated in the symbolics of royalty. The Petit Trianon has a different history, but it too participated in the French monarchy's symbolics. Its domain was carved out in 1750, when Louis XV had a botanical garden established there. The cultivation of different species of plants extended the symbolism of the seventeenth-century gardens through which

Versailles contained the entire cosmos, represented symbolically in garden sculpture—the four elements, the four continents, the four seasons, and so forth. The botanist Bernard de Jussieu worked at the Petit Trianon and there applied for the first time the principles of his new system of classification. Gabriel designed the garden pavilion, built in 1750, which became Louis XV's resting place, as he stopped there on his garden walks. The Château du Petit Trianon (1763–68), built by the same architect, allowed Louis more extended visits, and became the place where he met Madame de Pompadour and where they entertained. His next mistress, Madame du Barry, later occupied the Trianon palace. Thus, although the domain of the Petit Trianon was generally associated with the symbolics of Versailles, its palace was associated with the king's pleasure. Perhaps it was already degraded by the strong aura of female presence and sexual intrigue.

In 1774, Louis XVI gave the Petit Trianon to Marie-Antoinette, who transformed the grounds into an English garden, which we can take as a symbol of the freedom and liberty she hoped to obtain there. With its aesthetics mimicking the look of natural growth through planned disorder, the English garden has long symbolized these values in contrast to the obviously regulated and trimmed formal French garden.[38] More important, perhaps, is that the English garden (like the English dress *en chemise*) was a foreign import into the heart of the French symbolic space. Replanting these gardens coincided with a general replanting of the estate after the trees had been cut down and sold for timber. Susan Taylor-Leduc has argued that the practical reason for the replanting was hidden under royal propaganda designed to influence public opinion. D'Angiviller, the royal official in charge of the project, wanted the replantation to be perceived as "a restoration of a symbolic space that would signal a return to a golden age of Bourbon rule under the young monarchs, Louis XVI and the queen, Marie-Antoinette."[39] D'Angiviller's fantasy of the replanting was hardly supported by the queen's English garden, with its serpentine paths, surprising views, and architectural follies. The Trianon's private function gave the lie to the image of public good cultivated by the director; as Taylor-Leduc has argued, the Trianon negated d'Angiviller's hope for restoring the park as a sign of royal and national power.[40] Moreover, the English garden represented what was fashionable and modern, not the French tradition and Bourbon rule.[41] One can imagine the director's dismay as the reputation of the queen's project spread far and wide. The court's malice took aim at these gardens and accused Marie-Antoinette of changing the name of her domain to "little Vienna." Madame Campan recalls these rumors in her memoirs, and although the particulars of the story may be unreliable, the tale jibes well with the other charges emanating from the court:

> From the moment she was in possession of the petit Trianon, it was spread about in some societies that she had changed the name of the pleasure pavilion that the king had just given her and had substituted that of little Vienna or little Schönbrunn. A man of court, simple enough to believe the rumor and desiring to enter into her society at the petit Trianon wrote to M. Campan to ask permission of the queen. He had in his letter called Trianon little Vienna.[42]

The image of the Trianon as "little Schönbrunn" may have been highlighted by copies of paintings that Marie-Antoinette had sent from Vienna and whose subjects recalled her childhood there. In particular, a 1778 copy by Wuchart represented the opera and ballet performed by the young archdukes and archduchesses at the marriage of Joseph II. It pictured Marie-Antoinette as a young girl dancing a minuet with her brothers. The French accused her of still dancing to their tune.

In its association with the Trianon, the portrait *en chemise* could be, and indeed was, read as indicating the queen's desire to escape being French, to bring what was alien into the heart of the French realm. Two other comments about the dress make this point. One appeared in a court libel, the *Secret Unpublished Correspondence concerning Louis XVI, Marie-Antoinette and the Court and the Town from 1777 to 1792*, which reported that the queen's fashion angered the silk makers at Lyon, who charged her with ruining a national industry for the profit of her brother Joseph, the Hapsburg ruler. How they thought her brother would benefit from the change is not clear.[43] A second remark directed to the portrait retitled it: "France as Austria reduced to covering herself with straw."[44]

It is difficult to exaggerate how much clothing mattered in the symbolic economy; its importance for Marie-Antoinette was established with the elaborate etiquette designed to ensure that neither the Hapsburg empress nor the Bourbon king would be slighted when the guardianship of an adolescent girl—the future queen of France—was transferred from Vienna to Paris. The transfer took place in 1770 on neutral territory, on an island in the Rhine under the domain of neither empire, where the French erected tents and other portable shelters. In one of those shelters the young Marie-Antoinette performed the ceremony of the toilette (or rather had it performed on her). She was divested of all her Austrian garb, stripped of all of her clothing, and redressed in garments fabricated entirely in France. She emerged from the tent, as if reborn, or at least converted.[45]

The portrait *en chemise* flouted the conventions of French etiquette and French dress and exposed Marie-Antoinette to the charge that her conversion was not sincere. Even if she had fully assimilated French culture, however, Marie-Antoinette would always be alien, a point dramatized by the many engraved portraits that captioned her two titles in the following order: archduchess of Austria and queen of France.[46] The portrait *en chemise*—or the libels it provoked—brought to light what was fundamental about the queen of France: she was alien to the kingdom. Marie-Antoinette as *Autrichienne* was not invented by the revolutionaries or even by her enemies at court. She was conceived with the fundamental laws of France. Even in the moments of the queen's greatest popularity, the *Autrichienne* was always there lurking in the shadows.

But more was encoded in Marie-Antoinette's portrait than the *Autrichienne*, and indeed, the portrait came to stand for some of the most common themes of the libels emanating from the court: the queen's foreign character, her extravagant spending, and her uncontrolled sexuality. The association with her spending was evident in 1783, for the queen was reputed to have dispensed outrageous sums for the decoration of the Trianon. The portrait appeared again in this context in 1785, connected to the Diamond Necklace Affair. It came out at the trial of La Motte, the woman impersonating the queen, that she had devised her costume after the one worn by Marie-Antoinette in the 1783 portrait by Vigée-Lebrun.[47] As to the queen's sexuality, the dress signaled the costume worn by Marie-Antoinette's friends characterized by libels as the "tribades of Trianon." This last association was damning not so much because people necessarily believed that lovemaking between women was actually rampant in the queen's circle, but because a location associated with the king and the French domain not only had been made foreign, but also had been feminized by Marie-Antoinette and her female friends. Male sexuality was banished and replaced by an intimacy among women.

Although men were among the invited guests, Trianon was primarily peopled by women and children who made their own rules and lived together without the ceremony or etiquette normally associated with the court. The king regularly visited the queen at the Trianon, but he never slept there. By representing Marie-Antoinette as the queen of the Trianon, Vigée-Lebrun made a portrait of the queen for which one can imagine no companion portrait of the king, who was alien to that realm. Her companions at the Trianon were her women friends. In fact, a counterpart to this portrait of the queen *en gaule* could be found in Vigée-Lebrun's portrait of the marquise de la Guiche, a member of the queen's intimate circle, as a milkmaid.

The image of the Trianon, with its aura of female intimacy, lingered long after the Revolution, and as Terry Castle has shown, women in the nineteenth century called up this myth to manufacture a lesbian identity:

> One cannot help but feel in the end, perhaps, that there is also something bizarrely liberating, if not revolutionary, about the transmogrification of Marie-Antoinette into a lesbian heroine. It is true that there is a nostalgic element in her cult: women who thought they "saw" her, like Hélène Smith, the "Dream Romances" writer and Moberly and Jourdain, were in one sense flagrantly retreating into the past, into a kind of psychic old regime. But in the act of conjuring up her ghost, they were also, I think, conjuring something new into being—a poetics of possibility. It is perhaps not too much to say that in her role as idealized martyr, Marie-Antoinette functioned as a kind of lesbian Oscar Wilde: a rallying point for sentiment and collective emotional intransigence. She gave those who idolized her a way of thinking about themselves. And out of such reflection—peculiar as its manifestations may often look to us now—something of the modern lesbian identity was born.[48]

Other Possibilities

Castle's notion of the poetics of possibility leads me to wonder if other women saw other sorts of possibilities in the figure of Marie-Antoinette. I am thinking here of republican women such Olympe de Gouges, who dedicated her "Declaration of the Rights of Woman" to the queen, and Germaine de Staël, who defended Marie-Antoinette in print. This is not to argue that the queen in any way supported or sympathized with the political goals of the French Revolution or generally supported women's rights. Although it is clear that Marie-Antoinette enjoyed close friendships with women at court and supported women artists, the queen showed no solidarity with women of different classes. This, however, does not mean that French women did not have some stake—no matter how remote—in the queen's status. At least some commentators argued that the Salic Law had a negative impact on all women. In his *Histoire des amazones anciennes et modernes* (1740), the abbé Guyon wrote that the Salic Law, "which has excluded them [women] from the throne of France, in our minds has made them lose a part of the esteem that several among them rightfully merit."[49]

Feminist historians and critics writing today increasingly draw attention to the relation between Marie-Antoinette's fate and that of all French women. Lynn Hunt, for example, writes: "The question of Marie-Antoinette and the issue of the status of women more generally were closely connected, even though Marie-Antoinette herself probably had no interest in women's rights and early French feminists had little concern for the queen."[50] Through an analysis of Germaine de Staël's *Réflexions sur le procès de la reine* (1793), Madelyn Gutwirth demonstrates that Staël understood much of what was at stake for women in the queen's trial and execution: "Whereas the courtly code had maintained a semblance of social integration for the women of the privileged class, the new republican code promises women honor as mothers. Staël clearly perceived that in killing the queen, a people 'neither just nor generous' was expressing both the death of the old and the feebleness of the new dispensation."[51]

Indeed, Staël addressed her defense of Marie-Antoinette to women and stressed their common cause with her: "Oh! you, women of all countries, of all classes of society, listen to me with the emotion I experience. The fate of Marie-Antoinette contains everything that can touch your heart: if you are happy, so was she."[52] A few lines later, she continues: "Republicans, constitutional monarchists, aristocrats, if you have known unhappiness, if you have needed pity, if the future raises in your thoughts any sort of fear, come together, all of you, to save her!"[53] Throughout her *Réflexions,* Staël exonerates the queen of the many crimes—and especially that of bad mother—charged against her, and concludes by suggesting to women not their collectivity in difference (of class, nationality, politics), but their similarity in sharing a single fate: "I return to you, women whose lives are all sacrificed with [that of] so tender a mother, whose lives are all sacrificed in the outrage that would be perpetrated against weakness by the annihilation of pity. It is the end of your dominion if ferocity reigns, it is the end of your destiny if your tears flow in vain."[54] Staël here panders to some of the most conservative clichés about woman's nature, but at the same time warns women of their precarious and vulnerable position in the social order. Marie-Antoinette's impending fate symbolized that vulnerable position, and earlier in the pamphlet Staël had reminded her readers that the slander used to damn Marie-Antoinette—especially that aimed at her sexuality—was the sort that could be used to ruin any woman.[55]

During the Old Regime, Marie-Antoinette had already provided some women with the image of an exceptional woman, a powerful woman descended from an even more powerful woman, who proved herself a supporter of women's endeavors. In 1774, for example, the *Journal des dames* reappeared under Marie-Antoinette's protection after a five-year suspension. Madame de Montanclos dedicated the new publication to Marie-Antoinette, who had lent her support in late 1773, when she was still dauphine. Although Marie-Antoinette may not have advocated many of the political and moral stances taken by the *Journal des dames,* she maintained her patronage of the publication. Nina Gelbart speculates that the queen was grateful to Madame de Montanclos, who seemed eager to uphold her as "an intelligent and virtuous model for the whole female sex."[56] Gelbart finds signs of Marie-Antoinette's gratitude at the Bibliothèque Nationale de France in gilt-edged copies of the journalist's later works, which carry the queen's personal arms.[57]

In the visual arts, Marie-Antoinette not only advanced the career of Elisabeth Vigée-Lebrun but was also a strong supporter of the artist Anne Vallayer-Coster. In a letter written on 15 September 1779, Mercy reported to Maria Theresa that Marie-Antoinette had left Versailles only to go to Paris to see the Salon. That day, Vallayer-Coster's image of a vestal crowned with roses, which belonged to the queen, was on display.[58] The actress Rosalie Dugazon was apparently devoted to the queen. During a performance of *Les Événements imprévus* in February 1792, she expressed publicly her devotion to Marie-Antoinette when she turned to face the empty royal seats, clasped hands to heart, and passionately sang, "Oh, how I love my mistress![59] Finally, today the Bibliothèque Nationale de France also houses many novels from the eighteenth century written by women and bound with the arms of Marie-Antoinette. It is not so important for the queen actually to have read the books; it was enough that she owned them to enhance a writer's reputation. French women, at least some of them, had a very specific stake in the queen's fate. Although women have long been patrons of the arts, queens who promoted women artists are rather more exceptional.

In view of this admittedly far less revolutionary poetics of possibility, it seems particularly ironic that those who wrote the first histories of representing this queen installed as her true portrait David's sketch of her on the way to the guillotine (see photo insert). Georges Duplessis, for example, believed he found her "authentic likeness" in David's work, particularly in the bone structure.[60] Writing at about the same time, other historians also selected David's work, finding the real queen in neither the portrait she found most resembling nor the one her mother found most pleasing. These authors were perhaps led by the image of immediacy suggested by a rapid sketch; or maybe they were seduced by the reputation of the great male artist; or it could be that the tendency to view Marie-Antoinette primarily from the perspective of the Revolution motivated their judgment. But David's drawing may have seemed the most "resembling" because it so well fits the stereotype of a royal person as one who acts with great dignity even (or especially) in the face of imminent annihilation. Finally following the proper etiquette, in David's image Marie-Antoinette sits tall and erect, apparently resigned to her fate. Here is how Henri Bouchot characterized the work:

> David had the last sitting with the queen, he saw her for a few seconds before him more majestic and more sovereign than Madame Le Brun or the others had known her. No rouge on her cheeks, no powder in her hair. A linen bonnet has replaced the toque of velvet, a little white robe garbs her miserably; it is again a portrait "en gaulle," the last one this time.[61]

Finding David's portrait the most majestic seems to me a misogynistic and perversely royalist gesture. In this image the woman-queen can be safely majestic and sovereign precisely because she has no power. Her hands tied behind her back, Marie-Antoinette is not threatening to the French Republic as the daughter of the Hapsburg empress, nor to her viewers as an unruly woman. She is here resigned to the role that, perhaps even more than the part of mother, patriarchy has reserved for woman—that of victim. I am not suggesting that she was the Revolution's victim, as royalist sympathizers would portray her; rather, she occupies the position of victim, the "feminine" place of the one destined to be attacked.[62] For some early commentators, perhaps David's portrait was the most authentic not because of its "bone structure," but because it showed Marie-Antoinette as she should have been when she was queen—dignified and helpless.

From the standpoint of many French citizens in 1793, Marie-Antoinette certainly represented the indecent privileges of aristocracy and the bankrupted principles of (a more or less) absolute monarchy. It would be folly to deny that she is fully entitled to represent a share of that meaning. But such a reading of the queen's image can no longer be cited, at least not after the recent work of Hunt, Maza, Gutwirth, Colwill, and others, without also noting that she, more than other likely candidates—and much more than the king—came to embody "the possible profanation of everything the nation held sacred."[63] In this context, David's sketch can be viewed as one more example of the interest focused on the queen's body, and more specifically as part of the attention that accompanied her on the road to the scaffold.

This is how Madelyn Gutwirth reads the image, pointing out that the king, garbed in court dress, rode to the guillotine in a closed carriage with his confessor. The queen, on the other hand, rode in an open cart, vulnerable to the eyes of all. Gutwirth sees in David's sketch the humiliation and abasement reserved for the woman-queen:

> David's excessively well-known sketch of her seems to reprove her proud, upright carriage as she sits bolt upright in the cart of her final journey. She looks like an aged hag (she was thirty-eight) [sic]; her reduction could not have been represented as more abject. . . .The sketch declares that there were to be no more queens in France, and all should heed her fate.[64]

Vigée-Lebrun's portrait of Marie-Antoinette and David's sketch of her must be read according to the different political circumstances in which they were produced. Marie-Antoinette in 1783 posed a threat not to the new French republic, as she would in 1793, but to certain interests at court and within the governing elite. What ties the two images together, however, is that in different ways each presents Marie-Antoinette not simply as the king's wife, but as the most notorious, dangerous, and powerful public woman in France. And a woman who acted in public—both in 1783 and in 1793—not only raised fears of sexual dedifferentiation, but also bore the blame for society's moral decline. Lynn Hunt reminds us that republican men were no more misogynist than their predecessors; her work demonstrates that neither were they less so.[65]

David's portrait pictures not so much an absolute monarch—for the queen could never be that in France—but a public woman vanquished, paying equally for her real and imagined political sins and

[Handwritten marginal note: "The king is allowed some noble trappings on his walk to the guillotine, but Marie Antoinette is not"]

gender bendings. In contrast is the 1783 portrait by Vigée-Lebrun, which transgresses first by showing the queen in a private role that did not suit the proper image of a king's wife and second by showing her as a woman with the will to reconfigure associations within the elite, to ignore the rules of court life and etiquette, to reconsecrate part of the king's domain. Of the two images, I prefer the one made in 1783; it lends Marie-Antoinette not the political power of a monarch's wife anxious to quell a popular revolution, and not the authority of the austere queen-mother who sits with her children in the official portrait—a piece of royalist propaganda—Vigée-Lebrun made in 1787. I prefer the portrait that allows Maria Theresa's daughter the power to define herself against established norms of seemly, modest, womanly behavior. I prefer Vigée-Lebrun's unofficial portrait, the one the sitter chose as her image, the one that shows Marie-Antoinette as the tribade of Trianon.

Notes

1. David Russell, *Costume History and Style* (Englewood Cliffs, N.J.: Prentice-Hall, 1983), 302–5; Blanche Payne, *History of Costume* (New York: Harper and Row, 1965), 437–40; and R. Turner Wilcox, *The Mode in Costume* (New York: Charles Scribner's Sons, 1958), 206–14.

2. Friedrich-Melchior Grimm et al., *Correspondance littéraire, philosophique et critique,* ed. Maurice Tourneux (Paris: Garnier Frères, 1877–82): 13:441–42. The more politically conservative journal *L'Année littéraire* gave a different explanation for the change in portraits: "It has been noted that that of the Queen, which had initially been shown in the Salon, was weak in tone and color; Madame *le Brun* has substituted for it another which is more effective; the graces of & resemblance to this August Princess are very well preserved." Elie Catherine Fréron, *L'Année littéraire* (Paris: Chez Mériot, 1751–89), 16:262–63.

3. *La Morte de trois milles ans au salon de 1783* (Paris, 1783). Collection Deloynes, 286: 6.

4. Elisabeth Vigée-Lebrun, *Souvenirs,* ed. Claudine Herrmann (Paris: Des femmes, 1986), 1:65–66.

5. Maxime de la Rocheterie and the Marquise de Beaucourt, eds., *Lettres de Marie-Antoinette.* (Paris: Alphonse Picard et fils, 1895), 89. Vigée-Lebrun's *Souvenirs* also contains a lengthy account of this work's positive reception. See Mary Sheriff, *The Exceptional Woman: Elisabeth Vigée-Lebrun and the Cultural Politics of Art* (Chicago: University of Chicago Press, 1996), 146.

6. Quoted in Roland E. Mousnier, *The Institutions of France Under the Absolute Monarchy 1598–1789,* trans. Arthur Goldhammer (Chicago: University of Chicago Press, 1979), 2:87.

7. Mousnier, *Institutions*, 1:650.

8. Ibid., 2:88.

9. Marcel Marion, *Dictionnaire des institutions de la France aux XVIIe et XVIIIe siècles* (Paris, 1923; reprint, New York: Burt Franklin, 1968), 340; Joan Kelly, "Early Feminist Theory and the *Querelle des Femmes* 1400–1789," in *Women, History, and Theory* (Chicago: University of Chicago Press, 1984), 85–86.

10. Quoted in Marion, *Dictionnaire*, 340.

11. Jeffrey Merrick, "Fathers and Kings: Patriarchalism and Absolutism in Eighteenth-Century French Politics," *Studies on Voltaire and the Eighteenth-Century* 308 (1993): 281–303.

12. On changing the king's image to that of benevolent father, see ibid.; see also Jeffrey Merrick, "Politics on Pedestals: Royal Monuments in Eighteenth-Century France," *French History* 5 (1991): 234–64.

13. Louis Marin, *The Portrait of the King*, trans. Martha M. Houle (Minneapolis: University of Minnesota Press, 1988), 27–28.

14. Ibid., 26.

15. Letter from Maria Theresa to Marie-Antoinette in *Correspondance sècrete entre Marie-Thérèse et le Cte de Mercy-Argenteau*, ed. Alfred d'Arneth and M. A. Geffroy (Paris: Didot, 1874), 1:104.

16. Sarah Hanley, *The Lit de Justice of the Kings of France: Constitutional Ideology in Legend, Ritual, and Discourse* (Princeton: Princeton University Press, 1983), 91–95; see also Mousnier, *Institutions*, 2:87.

17. Hanley, *Lit de Justice*, 97–98, and Mousnier, *Institutions*, 2:89–90.

18. At the Salon of 1783, for example, Ménageot showed an *Allegory of the Birth of the Dauphin* in which the dauphin is held in the arms of France. Descriptions of the work emphasize the connection between the two and also note that news of the British defeat at Yorktown arrived on the same day as the dauphin's birth. *Correspondance littéraire*, 13:381.

19. *Chronicle of the French Revolution* (London: Chronicle Publications, 1989), 304. The queen was still allowed her rights as a mother, and she could maintain custody of her underage son.

20. Lynn Hunt, *The Family Romance of the French Revolution* (Berkeley: University of California Press, 1992), 12.

21. Even after the portrait by Ducreux was presented to Louis, the comte de Mercy-Argenteau, Maria Theresa's agent at Versailles, let it be understood that Marie-Antoinette's beauty was actually quite superior to that represented by the portrait. At Vienna dissatisfaction with Ducreux's portrait may have prompted the commissioning of yet another likeness of Marie-Antoinette in the same costume and holding the same pose. J. Flammermont, "Les portraits de Marie-Antoinette," *Gazette des Beaux-Arts* 18 (1897): 5–21.

22. Marguerite Jallut, *Marie-Antoinette et ses peintres* (Paris: Noyer, 1955), 10; Flammermont, "Portraits de Marie-Antoinette," 16.

23. Although sitters (and critics) often complained about the resemblance of a portrait, I know of no other history of portrait making that is comparable to the one told in these letters. I retell this history to suggest why Vigée-Lebrun may have been selected by Marie-Antoinette as her favorite portrait painter.

24. Maria Theresa to Marie-Antoinette, December 1770, in *Correspondance* 1:105.
25. *Correspondance,* 1:157. Maria Theresa paid for this portrait. She apparently liked the work so well that she gave Kratzinger a bonus in addition to his price. See *Marie Antoinette: archiduchesse, dauphine et reine* (Paris: Editions des Musées Nationaux, 1955), 29.
26. On Maria Theresa's warnings, see *Correspondance* 1:104.
27. Maria Theresa to Marie-Antoinette, 17 August 1771, in *Correspondance,* 1:196.
28. Marie-Antoinette to Maria Theresa, 18 October 1774, in ibid., 2:248.
29. Marie-Antoinette to Maria Theresa, 16 June 1777, in ibid., 3:85.
30. Maria Theresa to Marie-Antoinette, 1 April 1779, in ibid., 3:303.
31. Jacques Revel, "Marie Antoinette in her Fictions: The Staging of Hatred," in Bernadette Fort, ed., *Fictions of the French Revolution* (Evanston, Ill.: Northwestern University Press, 1991), 120.
32. Ibid., 123.
33. See Lynn Hunt, "The Many Bodies of Marie-Antoinette: Political Pornography and the Problem of the Feminine in the French Revolution," in this volume.
34. On the trial of Marie-Antoinette see ibid.; and Elizabeth Colwill, "Just Another *Citoyenne*? Marie Antoinette on Trial 1790–1793," *History Workshop* 28 (autumn 1989): 63–87.
35. [Jeanne Louise Henriette] Campan, *Memoirs of Marie Antoinette* (Philadelphia: George Barrie & Sons, 1900), 1:183.
36. Hunt, "Many Bodies," 122–23. The queen was charged with having incestuous relations with her son and with damaging one of his testicles.
37. In a tour of the queen's rooms at Versailles in 1992, the guide told us how badly Marie-Antoinette had been brought up at Schönbrun; in particular, she had not been schooled in the proper manners. By all reliable accounts, however, life at Schönbrun was organized much differently than that at Versailles, and commentators have often suggested that in Vienna the Hapsburgs were the first bourgeois royal family.
38. Susan Taylor-Leduc, "Louis XVI's Public Gardens: The Replantation of Versailles in the Eighteenth Century," *Journal of Garden History* (summer 1994), 82–86.
39. Ibid. Hubert Robert's painting, *View of the Gardens at Versailles at the Time of the Clearing of the Trees, Winter, 1774–75, Entrance to the Tapis-Vert,* executed in 1777, shows the garden awaiting reforestation. Among the characters in the painting are the queen bending down to attend to her children, and the king in discussion with his advisors. For another analysis of this work, see Paula Radisich, "The King Prunes His Garden: Hubert Robert's Pictures of the King's Garden in 1775," *Eighteenth-Century Studies* 21 (summer 1988): 454–71.
40. Taylor-Leduc, "Louis XVI's Public Gardens," 87.
41. I thank Nicholas Mirzoeff for this observation.
42. Campan, *Memoires,* 84.
43. *Correspondance secrète inédite sur Louis XVI, Marie Antoinette, le cour et la ville de 1777 à 1792,* ed. [Mathurin] de Lescure (Paris: Plon, 1866), 2:228.
44. Quoted in Henri Bouchot, "Marie Antoinette et ses peintres," *Les lettres et les arts* 1 (1887 January 1): 46.

45. Discussions of this ceremony are found in all biographies of Marie-Antoinette; see, e.g., Stefan Zweig, *Marie Antoinette: The Portrait of an Average Woman*, trans. Eden and Cedar Paul (Garden City, N.Y.: Garden City Publishing, 1933), 13ff.

46. This order and captioning, although certainly not the case for all engravings, can be seen in a large number of them.

47. Sarah Maza, "The Diamond Necklace Affair Revisited (1785–1786): The Case of the Missing Queen," in this volume, 87–88.

48. Terry Castle, "Marie-Antoinette Obsession," in this volume, 230.

49. Abbé Jean Baptiste Denis de Guyon, *Histoire des amazones anciennes et modernes* (Paris, 1740), 1:52–53. It may be that women were treated no better in countries where women could ascend to the throne, but it is perhaps worth noting that French women were given civil rights, including the right to vote, much later than women in England and Germany.

50. Hunt, *Family Romance*, 89–90.

51. Madelyn Gutwirth, *The Twilight of the Goddesses: Women and Representation in the French Revolutionary Era* (New Brunswick, N.J.: Rutgers University Press, 1992), 301.

52. Germaine de Staël, *Réflexions sur le procès de la reine par une femme* (Montpellier: Les Presses du Languedoc, 1994), v.

53. Ibid., vi.

54. Ibid., xxx.

55. Ibid., xvi, and Gutwirth, *Twilight of the Goddesses*, 301.

56. Nina Rattner Gelbart, *Feminine and Opposition Journalism in Old Regime France: "Le Journal des Dames"* (Berkeley: University of California Press, 1987), 179.

57. Ibid.

58. The letter appears in *Correspondance*, 3:250. On the painting, see Marianne Roland Michel, *Anne Vallayer-Coster 1744–1818* (Paris: CIL, 1970), 269.

59. The actress refused to recant when ordered to do so, and she never appeared on stage again. *Chronicle of the French Revolution*, 265.

60. Georges Duplessis, "Introduction," in Eugène de Vinck de Deux-Orp, *Iconographie de Marie Antoinette 1770–1793* (Bruxelles: Olivier, 1878), n.p. Where he saw bone structure in this sketch is a mystery to me.

61. Bouchot, "Marie Antoinette," 58.

62. For a discussion of political attacks on wives and mistresses of rulers, see Maza, "Diamond Necklace Affair," 73–80. For a comparison of Marie-Antoinette to the "scapegoat," see Hunt, "Many Bodies," 131.

63. Hunt, "Many Bodies," 120.

64. Gutwirth, *Twilight of the Goddesses*, 301.

65. Hunt, *Family Romance*, 123.

The Diamond Necklace Affair Revisited (1785–1786): The Case of the Missing Queen

Sarah Maza

The real or imaginary political influence of queens, female regents, royal mistresses, and other first ladies seems especially likely to come under attack in times of political crisis. In recent years, Jacqueline Duvalier and Imelda Marcos have come to embody the corruption of their husbands' regimes, just as in earlier times revolutionary anger found targets in the mystical excesses of Alexandra Romanov and the French and Catholic allegiances of Henrietta Stuart.[1] The most famously infamous queen consort in European history remains the ill-fated Marie-Antoinette, whose narrow-minded frivolity and clumsy political meddling earned her early on in her reign the unflattering nicknames "l'Autrichienne" and "Madame Déficit."

[handwritten margin note: Maza is unsympathetic to Antoinette]

The loathing that attached to the wife of Louis XVI both before and during the French Revolution has been largely dismissed by most historians of the era as a mere detail in the gossipy history of court politics.[2] But two important recent trends in historiography seem to call for a reassessment of this seemingly old-fashioned subject. The political cultures of the Old Regime and French Revolution have been explored in a number of important and innovative studies published in the past few years, which address such topics as the structure of court politics, the birth of public opinion, and the meaning of rhetoric, pageantry, and iconography in the public sphere.[3] At the same time, some of the best of recent feminist scholarship has drawn attention to the importance of metaphors of gender and sexuality in the discourse of public life. Gender, as Joan Scott has recently argued, must be viewed not only as "a constitutive element of social relationships based on perceived differences between the sexes," but also as "a primary way of signifying relationships of power."[4]

Metaphors of gender and sexuality should figure prominently in any interpretation of the ideological transition from Old Regime to revolutionary political culture. The 1780s and 1790s in France, and later periods throughout Europe, witnessed the gradual demise of royal and aristocratic courts modeled on households—in which female rulers, relatives, and mistresses played a recognized (if often limited) role—and the ascendancy of entirely masculine representative bodies. In other works, the male-female world of familial and sexual bonds represented by Versailles was overpowered by the all-male contractual universe of the revolutionary assemblies.[5] Viewed within this framework, at this particular historical moment, the attitudes of French subjects toward the most politically conspicuous woman in the realm take on a new and broader significance: the growing resentment of the queen, which culminated in a particularly vindictive trial and execution in 1793, dramatically illustrates the brutal exclusion of women from the public sphere of the French Revolution.

Although the Austrian princess who married Louis XVI—and was viewed from the start as a pawn in the unnatural alliance between the Hapsburg and Bourbon dynasties—never enjoyed great popularity among her subjects, open attacks on the queen were extremely rare before the mid-1780s.[6] It has long been a commonplace of traditional historiography to attribute the demise of her public reputation to the particularly sordid and complicated scandal later known as the Diamond Necklace Affair, which burst open in 1785–86. And yet to anyone acquainted with even the bare facts of the case, then as now, it was and remains patently obvious that Marie-Antoinette was entirely innocent of any connection with the gang of bold schemers who used her name to pursue their goals. The standard accounts of the affair, however, conclude with the glibly tautological statement that the queen was widely viewed as guilty because large numbers of people wanted to believe in her guilt.[7]

This conventional assessment is not so much erroneous as insufficiently documented and, on the face of it, paradoxical: the vast majority of reports and pamphlets circulating at the time of the affair loudly proclaimed the queen's innocence and professed outrage at the idea that her "august name" had been defamed. My purpose here is to argue, first, that the queen's vulnerability to even the most implicit attacks upon her reputation is comprehensible only if the events of 1785–86 are replaced within the context of the political culture of the late eighteenth century with reference to earlier pamphlet literature denouncing the activities of women in the public sphere; and, second, that the quasi-official literature that appeared in connection with the case in the form of legal briefs managed to indict the queen without naming her openly. Whether consciously or not, the lawyers who penned these documents delivered an implicit message to their readers, one that made the female sovereign central to a sordid intrigue in which she had actually played no role.

Before the details of the Diamond Necklace Affair are laid out, it is necessary to review some of the features of late-eighteenth-century political life in France, which may explain the unpopularity of the prerevolutionary monarchs and the impact of the case on public opinion. A broad array of causes, ranging from political ineptitude to the military fiascos of the Seven Years' War to the writings of the philosophes, contributed to the onset, as early as the 1750s, of what historians have termed the "desacralization" of the French monarchy. For the purposes of this discussion, two structural developments seem especially worthy of consideration. The best known of these is the rise to political prominence, over the course of the century, of France's courts of high justice, under the leadership of the parlement of Paris. Parlement and monarchy had been at loggerheads since the seventeenth century, and after the death of Louis XIV they collided regularly over taxation and the rights of Jansenists.[8] Caught between an increasingly conservative church hierarchy, led by the bellicose archbishop Christophe de Beaumont, and the radical Jansenist sympathies of some of the parlement's judges and lawyers, Louis XV lost much of his political stature by proving incapable of arbitrating coherently between the warring factions.[9] At the same time, and well into the 1770s and 1780s, magistrates and lawyers courted public opinion effectively by printing and circulating *remontrances* against the monarchy, couching their demands in a patriotic language (contemporaries called it "republican") inspired by natural-law theories and by radical Jansenist ecclesiology.[10]

Challenges to royal and ministerial authority came not only from competing centers of political activity such as the parlement but from within the rarefied milieu of the court itself. Historians have recently begun to stress the new role played by erstwhile factional rivalries within the governing elite in undermining traditional forms of political legitimacy. Whereas earlier in the century disgraced ministers had been exiled from the court and the capital, under Louis XVI they were allowed to remain in Paris, where some of them organized effective oppositional networks: such were the parties that coalesced around the powerful duc de Choiseul after his fall in 1770, and around Jacques Necker after 1781.[11] Taking their cue from the parlements and the underground pamphleteers, these factions flooded the court and the city with everything from scurrilous libels to high-minded appeals to "the public" or the "tribunal of the Nation."[12]

Political strife within France's governing circles probably spawned most of the literature against Louis XV and his mistresses that began to circulate widely after that monarch's death in 1774. The late king's notorious debauchery, the power wielded by his mistresses Madame de Pompadour and later Madame du Barry, and the existence of a house of pleasure called the Parc aux Cerfs, where the monarch was provided with an unending series of nubile young women, were widely known secrets long before his death. Many a subject of Louis "le Bien-Aimé" shared the feelings of Jean-François Le Clerc, a veteran soldier arrested in 1757 for calling the king a "bugger" and complaining that the kingdom was governed "by two whores."[13] As Jules Michelet wrote hyperbolically, but not inaccurately, of Louis XV: "The philosophers pull him to the right, the priests to the left. Who will carry him off? Women. This god is a god of flesh."[14]

The two titular mistresses of Louis XV, the marquise de Pompadour and the comtesse du Barry, had played pivotal roles in the court intrigues of the reign. Madame de Pompadour lent her support to the duc de Choiseul, the omnipotent minister who dominated French foreign policy for a dozen years after his appointment in 1758. Choiseul's most outstanding achievement in those years was a diplomatic revolution that allied the French monarchy with its former continental rival, the Austrian Empire. The marriage of the French dauphin to the Austrian princess Marie-Antoinette in 1770 marked the apex of the duke's Austrian policy; although seemingly triumphant, Choiseul fell from power that very same year, brought down by the maneuvering of his political rivals. Chief among these were the so-called triumvirate of ministers who rose to prominence after his fall: Chancellor Maupeou, keeper of the seals; Abbé Terray, the somber and bilious controller–general of the realm; and the man who succeeded Choiseul as secretary of state for foreign affairs, the duc d'Aiguillon.[15] All three men were known to be implacable foes of the parlement; all three courted and secured the alliance of Pompadour's successor, Madame du Barry, who was rumored to have extended favors other than political to Maupeou and d'Aiguillon; and all three were highly unpopular among the public at large.

Maupeou and his colleagues were the targets of a torrent of hostile pamphlet literature after Maupeou provoked the most serious crisis of the prerevolutionary decades by disbanding the Paris parlement in 1771.[16] The advent of a new ruler in 1774, the reinstatement of the high courts, and the rapid demise of the hated triumvirate did not stem the tide of ill feeling surrounding Louis XV's "despotic" ministers and their alleged connections to Madame du Barry. The Choiseulist party, hoping to engineer the return of their leader to power—in which they proved unsuccessful—kept up a rearguard action against the three ministers and the "royal whore" who had patronized them.[17] Choiseul's followers were probably responsible for much of the abundant underground literature circulating in the 1770s and 1780s that described in scabrous detail the political intrigues and sexual exploits of Louis XV, his ministers, and Madame du Barry. As Robert Darnton has shown, even in a provincial town such as Troyes the clandestine bookseller Mauvelain kept his shelves well stocked with volumes bearing such titles as *Secret Anecdotes About Madame du Barry, Correspondence of Madame du Barry,* and *The Private Life of Louis XV.*[18]

By far the most successful of these *libelles* was a fat volume entitled *Les Fastes de Louis XV* [*The Annals of Louis XV*] (1782), a collection of anecdotes cobbled together from accounts published across the border in Switzerland, which Mauvelain ordered for his provincial readers on eleven occasions in the 1780s.[19] The opening pages of the book identify it clearly as emanating from the Choiseulist camp. The duke, intones the anonymous author, was Louis XV's only good minister, a man of "genius and perspicacity," who attracted followers because he was "lovable, generous, imposing and sensitive," but who could not alone "stem the waters of the flood of profligacy washing over the court and the town."[20] A model of political integrity, the duke had been brought down by "the tyrant Maupeou, the brigand Terray, the despot d'Aiguillon, . . . ministers, slaves crawling at the feet of a prostitute who had ascended in one leap from the brothel to the throne."[21]

How the Annals of Louis XV depict his reign

The scandalous tales that make up *Les Fastes de Louis XV* add up to a description of what might variously be termed the feminization, eroticization, or privatization of the public sphere under Louis XV. The beginning of this trend is simply ascribed to the machinations of the king's tutor, Cardinal Fleury, who plotted to distract the young monarch from his political duties, and to ensure his own power, by pushing the young man into the arms of his first mistress, Madame de Mailly.[22] The advent of Madame de Pompadour coincided with the conclusion of the War of the Austrian Succession, and the author identifies the peace of 1748 as the shameful moment when the king "put down his armor" and handed over the reins of his kingdom to his titular mistress. Under the "reign" of Madame de Pompadour, the Parc aux Cerfs, over which she presided, became the dark center of the realm, "an abyss for innocence and simplicity which swallowed up throngs of victims and then spat them back into society, into which they carried corruption and the taste for debauchery and vices that necessarily infected them in such a place.[23] Female sexuality run amok had, it seemed, taken over the "sacred center" of the kingdom.

The empire of women in Louis' court dictated the feminization of all men close to or at the center of power. A surprising passage of *Les Fastes* depicts Chancellor Maupeou not only as a supple, scheming, protean courtier, but also as a species of she-man: his dwelling contained "elegant furnishings and delicious boudoirs in which the most fastidious courtesan would not be out of place."[24] Maupeou's power was based on his ability to seduce, a talent he enhanced by painting his face white and powdering it with rouge.[25] But the man most thoroughly feminized by the rise of female power was, of course, the monarch himself. The most public figure in the realm, in fact the *only* public man, gradually withdrew from his designated sphere and retreated into "the private, slothful and voluptuous life for which he had been yearning," his conversation running increasingly to trivia and gossip.[26] The later advent of Madame du Barry further emasculated the monarch. "The king's scepter," the author slyly concludes, "a plaything in turn for love, ambition, and avarice became in the hands of the countess the rattle wielded by folly."[27]

The privatization of the king of France had as its counterpart the growing public role of the women who ruled over him, and not surprisingly, for Pompadour and du Barry had begun their careers as public women: the marquise's mother had risen in the world by trading on her charms, a talent she passed on to her daughter, and du Barry had first plied her trade in the dark streets of Paris and under the arcades of the Palais-Royal.[28] The displacement of unbridled female sexuality from its normally interstitial position in society to the center of power both reflected and generated social disorder. Both Pompadour and du Barry had clawed their way up the social scale and into the king's bed, the first from "the very lowest class" (she was, in fact, the daughter of a prosperous wholesale merchant), the second from the slums of the capital.[29] As their sexuality propelled these women into the highest spheres, it sent the king tumbling down the social scale as he moved from high-born mistresses to the middle-class Jeanne Poisson (later de Pompadour) to the vulgar du Barry, while his subjects died of hunger. "It is indeed essential," the author acidly concluded, "for a prince to get to know each one of his estates."[30]

Les Fastes de Louis XV thus summarizes most of the themes of the illegal pamphlet literature that chronicled the decay of the French monarchy under Louis XV: the anomalous ascendancy of women, the privatization of the public sphere, the role of female sexuality in inverting social and political hierarchies. On the face of it, the shafts aimed at the likes of Madame du Barry might seem to have little to do with the ruling queen of France: Marie-Antoinette was no ambitious shopgirl, but the well-bred scion of one of Europe's oldest dynasties and the wife of a popular king. And yet the connection between the former king's mistresses and the current king's wife was one that revolutionary literature made with a vengeance. One of the most popular pamphlets of the late 1780s, entitled *Essais historiques sur la vie de Marie-Antoinette,* [*Historical Essays Concerning the Life of Marie-Antoinette*] began with a lengthy parallel between du Barry and the queen, alleging that they shared the same taste for power and debauchery, the same "effervescence of passions": du Barry even came out ahead of the queen, for "the first almost honored a dishonorable position, while the second prostituted an estate that seemed invulnerable to degradation.[31] No party or political group, of course, held a monopoly on antifemale literature. Since the queen remained blindly loyal to the Choiseulist party at court, it is highly unlikely that they were responsible for any of the later literature attacking her. But the anti–du Barry literature described above was sufficiently widespread and well known to give special resonance to the scandal that erupted in 1785. By accidentally linking the queen's name to

those of two adventuresses whose careers closely resembled that of
Madame du Barry, the Diamond Necklace Affair greatly facilitated
the transition from attacks on the former reign to slanders of the
reigning queen.

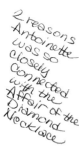
2 reasons Antoinette was so closely connected with the Affair of the Diamond Necklace

The fact that in the eyes of the public the queen became closely
implicated in the affair can be attributed to two causes: first, two of
the most interesting protagonists in the case were female; second,
Louis XVI committed the egregious blunder of turning the affair
over to the judges and lawyers of the parlement of Paris instead of
settling it privately.[32]

At the center of the scandal was a woman named Jeanne de
Saint-Rémi, whose talents for breathtakingly complex intrigue
matched those of the fictional characters of Laclos and Beaumarchais. Although her family was of provincial and utterly ruined nobility (her father had died in the poorhouse in Paris), she styled herself Jeanne de Valois, claiming descent from the French royal family
through a bastard line. By dint of charm and hubris, and by playing
on her alleged royal origins, the destitute young girl managed to
secure the help of wealthy protectors, notably the marquise de
Boulainvilliers, who provided her with a good education. In 1780
she married a penniless young officer of dubious nobility, Count
Nicolas de La Motte.

It was three years later, through Madame de Boulainvilliers, that
this talented con woman met the man whose gullibility was to ensure her of a seemingly endless source of revenue. The fifty-year-old
Louis de Rohan was a prominent member of the old and powerful
Rohan-Soubise clan, bishop of Strasbourg, grand almoner of France,
and former ambassador to Vienna. His prodigious wealth, and the
fact that he was already being hoodwinked by the notorious adven-
turer and magician Cagliostro, marked him out to the countess as an
ideal target. Better still, Rohan was driven by a powerful obsession
that could be put to good use: he yearned for high political office
and was convinced that only the queen, whom he had alienated
years before at the Austrian court, stood between him and his ambitions. La Motte had already tried her hand successfully at trading on
entirely fictitious connections with her "cousin" the queen for substantial sums of money. Soon the cardinal was composing missives
to the queen begging her to forget the past, and paying high prices
for evasive replies elegantly forged by Jeanne's associate Rétaux de
Villette.

Well aware that even the gullible Rohan might soon tire of this ineffective strategy, Jeanne and her husband decided to feed his fantasies with heartier fare. They searched the streets of Paris, eventually locating in the gardens of the Palais-Royal a young woman of easy virtue named Nicole Le Guay, whose features approximated those of the queen. It was on a summer's night of 1784, in the gardens of Versailles, that Rohan finally met his queen, the carefully dressed and coached Nicole, who stammered a few words at him before being whisked away by her mentors.

The time was ripe for Jeanne's finest hour, her most ambitious coup. The most famous jewel in France, a diamond necklace made up of 647 flawless gems, and worth over 1.5 million livres, was the masterpiece of the Parisian jewelers Boehmer and Bassange. Louis XV had commissioned it for Madame du Barry and then backed down before the jewel's price. In 1778 the necklace was offered to Louis XVI for his queen, but the latter had turned it down with the noble (though no doubt apocryphal) statement that the realm needed ships more than necklaces. By 1785, however, Madame de La Motte was able to persuade Rohan that the queen had her heart set on this expensive bauble, the purchase of which would ensure the cardinal's political fortune. A purchase order duly approved and signed by the queen was produced, and on the night of 1 February 1785 the object was delivered to Rohan and the countess, and handed over to a man purporting to be the queen's valet. The necklace, which Rohan was supposed to pay for in installments over the next several years, was promptly picked apart, and the gems were sold on the black markets of Paris and London.

The La Mottes' good luck was not to last for long, however. In July the jewelers sent Marie-Antoinette a cryptic note that mentioned "the finest diamonds known in Europe," and on 3 August the whole business came to light in a conversation between Boehmer and the queen's first chambermaid, Madame Campan.[33] On August 15 the nation was stunned by the arrest of Cardinal de Rohan at Versailles as he was preparing to conduct Assumption services clad in full pontifical regalia. A few days later the countess, Nicole Le Guay, and a few others were rounded up (Nicolas de La Motte had fled to London), and preparations began for the most sensational trial of the reign.

Nine months of feverish anticipation elapsed between the arrests and the trial. Despite attempts by the countess and her lawyers at shifting the blame for the swindle on to the shady Cagliostro, hardly anyone doubted her role in masterminding the swindle. The forgeries and theft of the necklace added up to a common criminal matter that could easily be disposed of; the real issue, as contemporaries quickly realized, lay elsewhere: should the cardinal be charged with "criminal presumption" and "lèse-majesté" for believing that the queen would stoop to dealing with the likes of La Motte and to assigning a nocturnal rendezvous? Or should he be acquitted on the implicit grounds that such behavior on the part of Marie-Antoinette was not at all implausible? Factions quickly aligned themselves for and against the cardinal. Those who most wanted to see him condemned, not surprisingly, were the queen and her supporters, most notably the baron de Breteuil, minister of the royal household, who had engineered the arrest; the family of the queen's close friend Madame de Polignac; and the king's prosecutor, Joly de Fleury.[34] Supporters of the cardinal included sizable portions of the upper clergy and high nobility, including a majority of the parlement; the influential Rohan-Soubise clan; and Breteuil's sworn enemy, controller–general Charles-Alexandre de Calonne.[35] The first verdicts handed down on 31 May 1786 proved neither surprising nor controversial: Jeanne de La Motte was condemned to whipping, branding, and life imprisonment; her husband, in absentia, to a life sentence on the galleys. Their accomplices suffered lesser penalties, such as exile, and Nicole Le Guay, who produced for the occasion a newborn child and a convincing tale of beleaguered innocence, was fully acquitted. But a furor erupted in court over the sentencing of Rohan, against whom the prosecutor requested a sentence of exile on the grounds of criminal temerity and disrespect for the monarchs. After hours of bitter dispute, the Grand'Chambre of the parlement returned a verdict of not guilty by a vote of thirty to twenty, and the cardinal left the Palais de Justice amidst the cheers of a jubilant crowd. At Versailles the queen wept tears of anger and humiliation.[36]

For the monarchs this outcome was bitterly ironic, in that it resulted from an act of great political integrity on Louis' part. As Rohan's secretary, the abbé Georgel, later observed, the king's decision to take the case before the magistrates was a "a solemn homage to the great influence of the laws which protect a citizen's honor," a testimony to "the sublime empire of reason in a well-ordered monarchy."[37] It is possible to read the case as yet another example of political legitimacy being undermined by fallout from the struggle between court factions: Georgel was convinced that Breteuil had known of the swindle very early on, and had allowed it to be played out in order to bring down his enemy Rohan.[38] But in bowing to the empire of laws, the monarch had also silenced his own voice and those of his courtiers, allowing the case to be presented to the public by the parties' lawyers. The latter were soon flooding the capital with printed trial briefs, or *mémoires judiciaires,* on behalf of their clients.

The lawyers involved in the case ranged widely in age, experience, and renown. The most prominent was Guy Jean Baptiste Target, who served as chief counsel to Rohan. The fifty-two-year-old Target had gained political notoriety in the early 1770s as one of the leaders of the opposition to Chancellor Maupeou's disbanding of the Paris parlement and had later served as a legal consultant to Louis XVI's brothers. The elegance and skill of his speeches and briefs in some of the most famous causes célèbres of the seventies and eighties had ensured his reputation as the nation's premier trial lawyer; in 1785 Target's career had recently been crowned by his appointment to the Académie Française.[39] The other defendants in the trial had to content themselves with the skills of much lesser luminaries. Jeanne de La Motte secured the services of one Maître Doillot, a competent jurist nearing retirement who had reputedly been smitten by her redoubtable charms. Nicole Le Guay's lawyer was Jean Blondel, a novice fresh out of law school, whose successful defense of his client launched his career. Pleading for the slippery Cagliostro was Jean-Charles Thilorier, a barrister from the provinces in his thirties, who went on to defend the marquis de Sade under the Revolution.[40]

For all of their differences, these men, as well as other lawyers involved in the case, had a good deal in common: they were men of law, members of the Paris bar, and *avocats au parlement,* barristers in the employ of the high court of justice whose political consciousness had been shaped by their order's support of the magistrates in opposition to the "tyranny" of Chancellor Maupeou. Target was the author of several important anti-Maupeou pamphlets, and although little is known of the other lawyers in the case, it is not unlikely that they shared with him the ideological leanings common in *parlementaire* circles: a suspicion of royal and ministerial authority forged by decades of clashes with the monarchy and a predilection for constitutional government that drew on sources as diverse as aristocratic liberalism, seventeenth-century natural-law theories, and radical

Jansenist ecclesiology.[41] It is at least certain that these men, like many of their colleagues in the order of barristers, opted for active political involvement in the upheaval of 1789: Blondel and Thilorier both became electors for the city of Paris prior to the convening of the Estates General, before holding public office under the Revolution, while Target went on to head the committee that drafted France's first constitution.[42] In short, the professional training and political allegiances of these lawyers made it unlikely that they would favor the sort of solipsistic and factional court politics of which Marie-Antoinette had become a central symbol.

These were the men from whose pens the public initially learned of the case known at the time as "l'affaire du cardinal." In Old Regime France, the procedure in criminal cases as codified by the great ordinance of 1670, was almost entirely secret, with magistrates examining defendants and witnesses privately behind closed doors.[43] On the basis mostly of indirect evidence from such proceedings, the parties' lawyers drew up written trial briefs, or *mémoires,* documents destined theoretically for the judges alone, but which in fact circulated widely beyond the courtroom. In the eighteenth century especially these *mémoires* became a category of pamphlet literature aimed at mobilizing public support for defendants, thereby putting pressure on the judges. The more sensational the case, the more trial briefs were churned out and hawked in the hopes of securing sympathy for the defendants, fame for their defenders, and healthy profits all around.[44]

Predictably, the Rohan affair provoked an outpouring of mémoires, an avalanche whose speed and volume increased as the trial approached. Four thousand copies of Doillot's first brief for Jeanne de La Motte were snatched up in November of 1785; by the following March, printings of briefs for even minor defendants in the case were reaching the tens of thousands, and by the time the trial got under way in May one or two were appearing each day.[45] The briefs for Jeanne de La Motte were distributed free in an attempt to rally support for her case; those for most of the other defendants sold for over one livre apiece, and manuscript versions of Target's first mémoire for Rohan were being peddled sub rosa months before its publication at the staggering price of thirty-six livres.[46] Whether these documents were sold or given out free, their appearance often provoked veritable stampedes around the houses of the lawyers and their clients: on the day Maître Thilorier produced his first brief for

[margin handwritten note: how the Criminal Courts operated]

Cagliostro, the police had to position eight guards at his door to stave off the crowd.[47]

Both the volume of mémoires produced—Target's brief for Rohan came out in three different simultaneous editions—and descriptions of the crowds of avid buyers suggest that these documents reached a fairly broad cross section of the Parisian population.[48] The author of an anonymous pamphlet published in 1786 describes himself strolling one morning in the vicinity of Maître Doillot's residence, only to be besieged by a frantic bustle. An onlooker informs him that the crowd is there waiting for an imminent mémoire distribution, whereupon a *clerc* collars him: "Monsieur, do you have any? Monsieur, do you have any?" Attempting a getaway, our man is nearly knocked over by the coach of a doctor who bellows: "Coachman, coachman, stop at that door!" Only after escaping the clutches of several other people, including a loud surgeon from Gascony, does the author escape, "sending to the devil both the lawyer and his brief."[49] Beyond the usual audience of upper-class readers and members of the legal profession, the trial briefs in the Diamond Necklace Affair seem to have appealed to broader segments of the reading public among the professional and even upper-artisanal groups of the capital.

No doubt the actual life stories of some of the protagonists in the case offered material likely to appeal to a semipopular audience: Thisorier's hugely successful brief for Cagliostro partly took the form of a picaresque novella following the enigmatic count's career from his obscure origins in the Middle East through his travels in Africa and Asia to his paramedical exploits at the greatest courts of Europe.[50] Meanwhile, the underground presses churned out sensational versions of the life story of Madame de La Motte, replete with the most unwieldy plots and subplots.[51] On the face of it, however, the appeal of the mémoires had little to do with politics: whatever the ideological leanings of the lawyers entrusted with the case, these were kept carefully under wraps for the occasion. The queen's personal conduct and reputation were issues far too sensitive to be broached explicitly in writings whose authors were known. Target's brief for Rohan was eagerly awaited on account both of the lawyer's reputation and of Rohan's well-known feud with the queen. The public's hopes were dashed, however, when instead of his usual flights of rhetoric, Target produced a tightly reasoned but dryly technical piece of writing.[52]

A close reading of some of these texts does, however, reveal the existence of a political subtext. The presence of the queen was implicit, I would argue, especially in the legal briefs written for or about Jeanne de La Motte and Nicole Le Guay. This argument is not meant to suggest conscious deviousness on the part of the lawyers; its likelihood derives rather from three of the points discussed earlier in this chapter. First, and most obviously, the queen's reputation and allegations about her social and sexual misconduct were recognized by contemporaries as the omnipresent, inescapable issues in the case; second, men such as Blondel and Doillot were more likely to be hostile to royal authority than overawed by it; and third, these texts were produced in an ideological climate in which the overlapping of female sexual and political activity had become a central metaphor for political decay.

Doillot's first mémoire for Madame de La Motte opened with a predictable description of the contrast between the high and mighty Rohan and his antagonist, a woman born in poverty and obscurity, but whose lineage, it was stressed, ranked higher than his.[53] A full three pages were then devoted to Jeanne's genealogy in order to establish her (apparently authentic) descent from a bastard line of the house of Valois. Doillot concluded, however, in the best of enlightened legal traditions, that "it is not on the basis of privilege deriving from her birth that she wishes to confront her adversary, but on the grounds of the equality of natural law that surpasses all human institutions."[54]

Doillot's odd rhetorical strategy, which consisted in heavily emphasizing his client's royal origins only to deny their explicit bearing upon the case, was duplicated time and again in his and other people's writings in defense of the countess.[55] An intriguing detail in one of Doillot's later writings for his client sheds more light on his purpose in arguing the case in these terms. What of the bill of sale for the necklace that she produced, signed with the words "Marie-Antoinette of France"? Doillot reminded his readers that newspapers all over Europe had initially reported that La Motte's real first name was Marie-Antoinette, and that since a Valois could claim to be part of the royal house "of France," the countess had innocently affixed her own signature to the document.[56] Although Doillot then went on to argue that La Motte had in fact not signed the document at all, his purpose in dragging this red herring across the path of his readers must have been related to his repeated stress on Jeanne's lineage: although explicitly arguing that Cagliostro and possibly Rohan were responsible for the swindle, he was implicitly making the point that Jeanne's identity was interchangeable with that of the queen, that her royal descent should partly exonerate her from blame, that the queen's misbehavior somehow legitimated other forms of female misconduct.

This theme of interchangeable female identities attains even greater complexity in the briefs that concern the lady of the Palais-Royal, Nicole Le Guay. Blondel's account, in his client's voice, of Jeanne de La Motte's first visit to the guileless Nicole is a consummate piece of melodramatic writing, in which the artful La Motte is shown entrapping her innocent accomplice by playing upon a combination of social authority and dangerous female intimacy:

> I offer a seat to Madame de La Motte: she herself draws it closer to mine. She sits down. Then she leans toward me with an air of both mystery and confidence, gives me a look that seems to suggest both the concern and the intimacy of friendship, tempered however by the dignified bearing of a lady of high rank about to confide an important secret to her protégé, and utters in low tones the strange words that follow.[57]

La Motte immediately brings up her close connection to the queen ("we are like two fingers on a hand"), while reassuring her young companion by means of seductive blandishments: "Trust me, *mon cher coeur*," she murmurs, "I am a lady of quality [*une femme comme il faut*] attached to the court."[58] The impressionable Nicole soon consents to assist the La Mottes in carrying out what she believes to be the queen's wishes. The alliance between La Motte and Le Guay is cemented by a refashioning of the latter's identity. Having introduced herself as the comtesse de Valois, the older woman announced that if her young friend wished to move in circles connected to the court, she too needed *une qualité*. And so in Blondel's account as well as many others, we learn of how Nicole Le Guay (no stranger in reality to dual identities, since she plied her trade as a courtesan under the nom de guerrre of Madame de Signy) became in the hands of her mentors the baroness d'Oliva. A mimetic impulse is evident in La Motte's choice of a name for her young protégé, for d'Oliva was an anagram of La Motte's own "royal" name, Valois.[59] What's in a name? A great deal in this case, since it was the Valois name that connected the trickster to the queen and its anagram that closed the circle linking prostitution to female sovereignty.

Another woman briefly entered the picture: the countess's chambermaid Rosalie assisted her mistress in dressing Nicole Le Guay for her appearance at night in the gardens of Versailles. The young girl was decked out for the occasion in an informal white linen dress and pink petticoat. Le Guay had no idea (or so her lawyer claimed) whom she was impersonating, no notion that this costume, known as a *robe en gaule,* was identical to the one sported by Marie-Antoinette in a recent portrait by Elisabeth Vigée-Lebrun.[60] While Rosalie arranged the young girl's hair, the countess dressed her with her own hands, stooping for the occasion, Blondel stressed, to playing second chambermaid to a young woman innocently masquerading as the queen.[61]

"Once the two women had finished serving as maids, Madame de La Motte resumed her rank as countess and the dignified mien of a protector," Blondel went on.[62] This insistence on the fluid character of Madame de La Motte's social identity served to underscore her vocation for intrigue: she was the exact female equivalent of the equally slippery and protean Cagliostro, though her femininity made her the more dangerous of the two. She and her husband had gathered around themselves a demimonde of fake counts, barons, and marquises, all of whom pursued social promotion by means of sexual and financial intrigue.[63] It was exactly this sort of marginal world, a degraded mirror image of high society, that had generated a Madame du Barry fully equipped with ersatz nobility and threatening sexual power. As Mary Douglas has argued, groups and individuals that exist at the margins of society are usually perceived as profoundly menacing, for they continually threaten to alter the shape of the social order by taking over its center.[64] Tricksters, whose skills enable them to impersonate a wide range of social types, and female prostitutes, whose sexual powers give them access to an equally broad cross section of society, appear as recurrent examples of such "liminal" types.[65] Du Barry had carried pollution and disorder to the center of political power by making her way directly to the king's bedroom. Under the reign of a more virtuous monarch, a La Motte had to operate indirectly, by merging her identity (and that of her double, d'Oliva) with that of the king's wife. In either case, however, female sexuality was perceived as the breach through which chaos could overtake the realm.

The pivotal scene in Blondel's two trial briefs, as in other accounts of the affair, was the nocturnal episode known as "la scène du bosquet," in which Nicole Le Guay impersonated the queen for Rohan's benefit. The lawyer argued, predictably enough, that Le Guay had been kept ignorant of the meaning of the intrigue, and of whom she was to represent in the scene for which she was coached—although she was told that the queen would be nearby watching over the proceedings.[66] Blondel then launched into a dizzying spiral of argumentation, the purpose of which was to demonstrate logically that since Nicole Le Guay was persuaded that the queen would be present at the scene, she could not have suspected that she was impersonating her:

> When one sets about representing a person, assuredly that person must not be present. Otherwise, the disguise becomes impracticable, and the man whom one wants to make the dupe of this fraud sees through it and is not taken in; and the person in charge of its execution [Nicole Le Guay] cannot believe that she is playing the role of a person who is present.[67]

The reader meanwhile is asked to identify with the young girl, to share her belief that Marie-Antoinette might very well be present at a midnight tryst set up by a woman of intrigue. Le Guay's triumphant acquittal testifies to her lawyer's skill in convincing the public that the queen was present at least in spirit that night in the groves of Versailles.

The argument that Marie-Antoinette could plausibly have been present at "la scène du bosquet" gains strength from the analogies between that scene as it was presented to readers and two contemporary texts it seems to echo, a famous play and a less famous pamphlet. Around the end of his first brief for Le Guay, Blondel himself gives the reader a hint as to one of his possible sources for recreating the scene: in describing the rewards heaped upon her for her part in the intrigue, Le Guay mentions that the countess had taken her to the theater to see the runaway success of 1784, Beaumarchais' *Marriage of Figaro*.[68] Madame de La Motte's taste for such fashionable theatrical entertainment is hardly surprising, given both her predilection for aping the high society that flocked to these events and her unquestionable talents as an actress and producer. As the abbé Georgel later remarked, the whole swindle amounted to a series of carefully staged scenes, complete with props and actors, played out for the benefit of a single spectator, Rohan.[69]

Blondel's briefs for Le Guay, of which twenty thousand copies at least were printed, enjoyed a success that can only be compared, in the 1780s, to that of Beaumarchais' play, with its unprecedented sixty-eight consecutive performances.[70] But the similarities between the mémoire and the play do not end there. *The Marriage of Figaro* does include a trial scene in act three, complete with references to lawyers and their briefs; beyond that, however, spectators of the play might well have recognized in Blondel's accounts of the affair some startling reminders of Beaumarchais' plot. The lawyer's depiction of the "high-born" La Motte and her maid Rosalie decking out the ambiguously innocent Nicole in lace and muslin was oddly reminiscent of the sexually charged scene in act two in which the pageboy Chérubin is dressed as a girl by the countess and Suzanne. The last act of the play (and of Mozart's opera, which follows it closely) takes place at night in an elegant park studded with kiosks and pavilions; in this setting, the countess and her maid, having exchanged clothes for the occasion, take advantage of the shadows and of their disguises to teach their respective husbands a lesson in trust and fidelity.

Both the play and the lawyer's brief, then, recount elaborately theatrical plots masterminded by women, of which high-born, powerful men (Rohan and Almaviva) are the dupes. One should not be misled by *Figaro*'s posthumous reputation as a politically subversive paean to the ambitions of talented commoners. As Robert Darnton and Thomas Crow have argued persuasively, Beaumarchais was perceived in the 1780s as an ally of the forces of political and stylistic conservatism: to radical critics such as Antoine-Joseph Gorsas, the relentless wittiness and erotic ambiguity of the play only served to confirm Beaumarchais' reputation as a spokesman for upper-class decadence.[71] Nor were contemporaries unaware of the forces that had made possible the play's opening in Paris in April of 1784 after years of protracted struggles with the censors. It had first been staged in private some months earlier on the estate of the comte de Vaudreuil, a member of the queen's inner circle and the lover of her most intimate friend, Madame de Polignac.[72] So enamored, in fact, was the queen of Beaumarchais' talent that she was rehearsing to play the female lead, Rosine, in a private production of his earlier *Le Barbier de Seville* around the time that the scandal erupted.[73] The striking similarities between certain episodes of the Diamond Necklace Affair and analogous scenes from Beaumarchais' play may amount to no more than an odd case of life imitating art; but if contemporaries noticed the resemblances, these must only have served as a reminder of the ubiquitousness of upper-class female intrigue, at the center of which stood the sovereign herself.

If the plots of Beaumarchais' plays make for an indirect link between Marie-Antoinette and the goings-on of "la scène du bosquet," a leitmotif of contemporary illicit pamphlet literature establishes the connection more directly. The earliest-known pamphlets attacking the queen's reputation, *Le Lever de l'aurore* [*The Break of Dawn*] and *Les Nuits de Marie Antoinette* [*The Nights of Marie-Antoinette*], began to circulate in the early 1770s. Although no copies of these works are known to exist (their authors were promptly jailed and the pamphlets destroyed), their titles allude to the young queen's well-known predilection for after-supper walks in the gardens of the Trianon and Marly in the company of friends and ladies-in-waiting.[74] Under the pens of hostile pamphleteers, these innocent pastimes became examples of the most unbridled licentiousness, with the young princess and her friends swapping lovers in the moonlit gardens of the palace. These episodes are taken up again in the much more prolific revolutionary literature against the queen, such as the popular *Essais historiques sur la vie de Marie-Antoinette,* of which eight different editions (along with two sequels) appeared in 1789. According to the author of that pamphlet, these scandalous nighttime outings were mainly female affairs: "Women from all walks of life had a role to play in this endless course in debauchery. Women of the court, chambermaids, the wives of high officials, of bourgeois, of the palace servants, and even grisettes, all of them intermingled for these promenades in the dark."[75] Here again social and sexual decay results from the dangerous confusion of female identities: the closer it came to the "sacred center" of royal power, the more female sexuality could act as a force potent enough to overpower conventional social and political distinctions. In the end, contemporaries could not entirely blame a Jeanne de La Motte or a Nicole Le Guay for their impersonations of the queen: these women were simply acting out a script dictated by the sovereign herself, and by the Pompadours and du Barrys who had preceded her.

The Diamond Necklace Affair provided a thematic source and repertory for the abundant and singularly venomous literature against Marie-Antoinette that began to appear in 1789. Whisked out of the Salpêtrière and over to London, thanks to the efforts of the queen's enemies, Madame de La Motte eventually produced (with the help, it was rumored, of the exiled Calonne) her own "candid" account of the events of 1784–85.[76] Her *Mémoire justificatif* of 1789 announces most of the themes that were played out ad nauseam in the pamphlets of the 1790s: Marie-Antoinette was a cold-blooded *politique* whose principal aim was to undermine the kingdom and

turn it over to her brother, the Austrian emperor; her political corruption was matched only by the personal debauchery made evident
by her indiscriminate passion for women as well as men, with Madame
de Polignac and La Motte herself figuring prominently among the
queen's many female lovers.[77] Well into the 1790s Jeanne de La Motte
was a recurrent figure in pamphlets that presented her as the archetypal plebeian victim of the evil political designs and sexual excesses
of the queen and Madame de Polignac.[78]

Meanwhile, the queen herself attained emblematic status in a
growing body of revolutionary literature denouncing the political
ambitions of female rulers and consorts. In 1791 there appeared a
grand synthesis on the subject, a five-hundred-page volume entitled
Les Crimes des reines de France [*The Crimes of the Queens of France*],
whose author, ironically enough, was a woman, Louise de Keralio.[79]
Reaching back into the dark ages, de Keralio's history began with the
mind-boggling crimes of early queens such as Frédégonde and
Brunehaut, moved on to dwell with relish on the "Italian vices" of
Catherine and Marie de Médicis, and culminated in a denunciation
of the worst of them all, the Austrian monster Antoinette. The introduction warns readers that if absolute power corrupts, absolute female power does so with a vengeance: "A woman for whom all is
possible is capable of anything; when a woman becomes queen, she
changes her sex," and it goes on to warn good monarchs against the
dangers of "a sex that must always be feared when it is displaced."[80]
The extraordinary frontispiece to the volume is an allegorical vision
of female rule (see photo insert). At the center of the image is a bed
occupied by a fishtailed siren wearing nothing but a diadem; with
her left hand, she drives a sword through the heart of a male ruler
whose body hangs lifeless across a throne; her right hand extends to
offer a cup of hemlock to aged male figures representing the virtues;
surmounting the bed is the bust of a satyr, which gloats lustfully
over the scene.

The publication of de Keralio's chronicle of the iniquities of female power coincided with the marked growth in early 1791 of anti-
monarchical agitation both in political clubs and in the Parisian
radical press.[81] Both before and during the Revolution, the most
venomous attacks on personal hereditary rule were first aimed
obliquely not at the king himself but at the mistresses and queens
who embodied the worst of monarchial power. Feminine nature,
characterized by deceit, seduction, and the selfish pursuit of private

interest, was construed as the extreme antithesis of the abstract principles of reason and law that were to govern the political sphere. Femininity, in short, became radically incompatible with the new definition of the public sphere.[82]

In the 1770s and 1780s this antithesis between female sexuality and the public sphere was first seized upon and exploited by political insiders pursuing factional interests within the world of the court. The Diamond Necklace Affair represents a broadening of these attacks, as outsiders to the political class, the parlement's lawyers, were forced to wrestle with a case whose implications concerned the personal reputation and sexual behavior of the queen. The lawyers who penned the trial briefs in the case had to deal obliquely, and gingerly, with these politically sensitive issues. But their writings also reached unprecedented numbers of readers, who were thus able openly to consume pamphlets in which a con woman and prostitute brazenly appropriated the queen's identity. The chameleonlike Jeanne de La Motte became implicitly, and then explicitly in 1789, the vehicle for an indictment of the corrupting effects of female power on all of society.

Whatever the social origins of this reaction against the presence of women in the public sphere, its ideological roots must no doubt be connected to the rise and dissemination of contractual theories of government. Eighteenth-century lawyers, well versed in the classic texts of seventeenth-century natural law, assumed that government and society originated in the free convenanting of rational beings; women, assumed to be by nature neither free nor rational, were not a party to this contract. Hence, as Carole Pateman has pointed out, the classic paradigm of the social contract nearly always implied a secondary contract that subjected women to their husbands: "What it means to be an 'individual,' a maker of contracts and civilly free, is revealed by the subjection of women within the private sphere."[83]

Under the Revolution the image of the public woman as a protean, erotic creature was struck down and replaced by the female allegory of the Republic, a warlike virgin wielding a pike or sword. As Marina Warner has perceptively observed, these abstract representations of Liberty or the Republic amounted to a complete denial of the sexual connotations of public womanhood: by virtue of their very conspicuousness, the bare feet and exposed breasts of Liberty or Marianne paradoxically denied eroticism, thereby forcing allegorical meaning onto the female form.[84] In this perspective, the Diamond Necklace Affair can be interpreted as the last political drama of female sexuality under the Old Regime, a prelude to, and harbinger of, the fall of public woman.

Notes

1. There exists no synthesis on the subject, but some suggestive remarks on the symbolic importance of personal rule in decaying autocracies can be found in the introduction to Michael Walzer, ed., *Regicide and Revolution: Speeches at the Trial of Louis XVI* (London: Cambridge University Press, 1974), esp. 27–31.
2. The question of the queen's reputation still figures prominently in anecdotal accounts of the period such as Claude Manceron, *Les Hommes de la liberté* (Paris: Robert Laffont, 1972–79), but is given only a few lines in the most recent authoritative survey of the scholarly literature, William Doyle, *Origins of the French Revolution* (Oxford: Oxford University Press, 1980), 90–91.
3. Most notably Lynn Hunt, *Politics, Culture, and Class in the French Revolution* (Berkeley and Los Angeles: University of California Press, 1984), and Keith Michael Baker, ed., *The Political Culture of the Old Regime* (Oxford: Pergamon Press, 1987).
4. Joan W. Scott, "Gender: A Useful Category of Historical Analysis," *American Historical Review* 91 (December 1986): 1067.
5. Joan B. Landes, *Women and the Public Sphere in the Age of the French Revolution* (Ithaca: Cornell University Press, 1988).
6. Henri d'Almeras, *Marie-Antoinette et les pamphlets royalistes et révolutionnaires* (Paris: Albin Michel, [1921]), chs. 7–8; Hector Fleischmann, *Les Pamphlets libertins contre Marie Antoinette* (Paris, 1908; reprint, Geneva: Slatkine, 1976). Both authors' evidence comes overwhelmingly from material published after 1789.
7. For instance, Alfred Cobban, *A History of Modern France* (London: Penguin Books, 1957), 1:117–20. Cobban's summary, in the most popular textbook covering this period, is probably drawn from the classic, exhaustively documented study by Frantz Funck-Brentano, *L'Affaire du collier* (Paris: Hachette, 1901). For a similar and equally popular account, see Stefan Zweig, *Marie Antoinette: Portrait of an Average Woman*, trans. Eden and Cedar Paul (New York: Garden City Publishing, 1933), chs. 14–17.
8. The abundant literature on this question is summarized and discussed by William Doyle, this generation's leading historian of the parlements, in *Origins of the French Revolution*, chs. 3–5, and in Baker, ed., *Political Culture*, ch. 9.
9. Dale Van Kley, *The Damiens Affair and the Unraveling of the Ancien Regime, 1750–1770* (Princeton: Princeton University Press, 1984), ch. 3.
10. Dale Van Kley, "The Jansenist Constitutional Legacy in the French Prerevolution," in Baker, ed., *Political Culture*, 169–202; Sarah Maza, "Le Tribunal de la nation," *Annales: Economies, Sociétés, Civilisations* 42 (1987): 80.
11. Doyle, *Origins*, 56–58.
12. Keith Michael Baker, "Politics and Public Opinion Under the Old Regime: Some Reflections," in Jack R. Censer and Jeremy D. Popkin, eds., *Press and Poli-*

tics in Pre-revolutionary France (Berkeley and Los Angeles: University of California Press, 1987), 208–13.

13. Van Kley, *Damiens*, 3, 239.

14. Jules Michelet, *History of the French Revolution*, trans. Charles Cocks (Chicago: University of Chicago Press, 1967), 54.

15. Cobban, *History of Modern France*, 1:90–99; Edgar Faure, *La Disgrâce de Turgot* (Paris: Gallimard, 1961), ch.1.

16. Durand Echeverria, *The Maupeou Revolution: A Study in the History of Libertarianism: France, 1770–1774* (Baton Rouge: Louisiana State University Press, 1985).

17. Doyle, *Origins*, 57.

18. Robert Darnton, *The Literary Underground of the Old Regime* (Cambridge, Mass.: Harvard University Press, 1982), 146.

19. Ibid., 139, 145–46.

20. *Les Fastes de Louis XV, de ses ministres, généraux, et autres notables personnages de son règne* ("À Villefranche, chez la Veuve Liberté," 1782), xl–xlix.

21. Ibid., lvi.

22. Ibid., 106–14.

23. Ibid., 351–52.

24. Ibid., 382.

25. Ibid., lvi.

26. Ibid., lvii–lviii.

27. Ibid., 381, 566.

28. Ibid., 705.

29. Ibid., xcviii, 263.

30. Ibid., 664, 698.

31. *Essais historiques sur la vie de Marie-Antoinette d'Autriche, reine de France* (London, 1789), 2, 70.

32. The following summary of the events leading up to the trial is based on the two most comprehensive and reliable accounts of the trial, Funck-Brentano, *Affaire du collier*, and Frances Mossiker, *The Queen's Necklace* (New York: Simon and Schuster, 1961); Mossiker provides a useful survey of the most significant accounts of the affair on pp. 594–98.

33. Madame Campan, *Memoirs of Marie Antoinette* (Philadelphia: George Barrie and Sons, 1900), 2:6–9.

34. Abbé Jean-François Georgel, *Mémoire pour servir à l'histoire des évènements de la fin du dix-huitième siècle* (Paris: A. Eymery, 1820), 2:70, 98–99, 131, 150.

35. Funck-Brentano, *Affaire du collier*, 244, 251, 323–24; Almeras, *Marie-Antoinette*, 281.

36. Funck-Brentano, *Affaire du collier*, 301–14; Mossiker, *Queen's Necklace*, ch. 22.

37. Georgel, *Mémoires*, 2:128.

38. Ibid., 2:70, 98–99.

39. Ibid., 2:123; Albert Poirot, "Le Milieu socio-professionel des avocats du parlement de Paris à la veille de la Révolution (1760–1790)" (thèse de l'École Nationale des Chartes, 1977), 2:183; Echeverria, *Maupeou Revolution*, 40–44.

40. Funck-Brentano, *Affaire du collier*, 278–83; Poirot, "Avocats," 2:29, 186.

41. Maza, "Tribunal de la nation," 79–80; Van Kley, "Jansenist Constitutional Legacy"; Elie Carcassonne, *Montesquieu et le problème de la constitution française au XVIII siècle* (Paris, 1927; reprint, Geneva: Slatkine, 1970), ch. 6.

42. Poirot, "Avocats," 2:29, 183, 186.
43. Maza, "Tribunal de la nation," 76; Mossiker, *Queen's Necklace*, 331–32.
44. Maza, "Tribunal de la nation," passim; Hans-Jürgen Lüsebrink, "L'Affaire Cléreaux (Rouen, 1786–1790): Affrontements idéologiques et tensions institutionnelles autour de la scène judiciaire au XVIII siècle," *Studies on Voltaire and the Eighteenth Century* 191 (1980): 892–900.
45. The publication of mémoires can be followed in the famous journal attributed to the bookseller Siméon-Prosper Hardy, in the volume covering the years 1785–86; Bibliothèque Nationale (hereafter BN) ms. Fr. 6685.
46. See, for instance, the entries in BN ms. Fr. 6685 for pp. 27–28, 29 May 1786: the mémoires for Bette d'Étienville, Rohan, and Nicole Le Guay sold for twenty-four or thirty-six sols; on La Motte's brief, see 6 November 1785; on the manuscript version of Target's brief, see 13 March 1786.
47. BN ms. Fr. 6685, 20 February 1786.
48. Funck-Brentano, *Affaire du collier*, 289.
49. *Observations de P. Tranquille sur le premier mémoire de madame la comtesse de La Motte* ("À La Mecque," 1786).
50. Jean-Charles Thilorier, *Mémoire pour le comte de Cagliostro* (Paris, 1786).
51. For instance, *Histoire véritable de Jeanne de Saint-Rémi, ou les aventures de la comtesse de La Motte* ("À Villefranche, Chez la Veuve Liberté," 1786).
52. Georgel, *Mémoires*, 2:158; BN ms. Fr. 6685, 19 May 1786.
53. Doillot, *Histoire du collier, ou mémoire justificatif de la dame comtesse de La Motte* (Paris, 1786), 3–5.
54. Ibid., 7–10.
55. See also Doillot, *Sommaire pour la dame comtesse de La Motte* (Paris, 1786), 14.
56. Ibid., 9–11.
57. Jean Blondel, *Mémoire pour la demoiselle Le Guay d'Oliva* (Paris, 1786), 14.
58. Ibid., 15.
59. Funck-Brentano, *Affaire du collier*, 150.
60. Blondel, *Mémoire*, 18–19: the scene is described again in his *Second mémoire pour la demoiselle Le Guay d'Oliva* (Paris, 1786), 16–17.
61. Blondel, *Second mémoire*, 16.
62. Ibid.
63. Funck-Brentano, *Affaire du collier*, ch. 13; *Histoire véritable de Jeanne de La Motte*, 48–49.
64. Mary Douglas, *Purity and Danger: An Analysis of Concepts of Pollution and Taboo* (New York: Praeger, 1966); see also Victor Turner, *The Ritual Process: Structure and Anti-Structure* (Ithaca: Cornell University Press, 1969).
65. For other applications of this concept, see, for instance, Sarah Maza, *Servants and Masters in Eighteenth-Century France: The Uses of Loyalty* (Princeton: Princeton University Press, 1983) ch. 3; Karen Halttunen, *Confidence Men and Painted Women: A Study of Middle-Class Culture in America, 1830–1870* (New Haven: Yale University Press, 1982), 27–30.
66. Blondel, *Mémoire*, 31; *Second mémoire*, 36.
67. Blondel, *Second mémoire*, 36.
68. Blondel, *Mémoire*, 41.
69. Other "scenes" produced by La Motte included various séances led by Cagliostro, and the delivery of the necklace for which La Motte "prepared the

theater" in her apartment at Versailles: "Ce furent véritablement une scène et une représentation" (Georgel, *Mémoires*, 2:59–62).

70. On the brief for Le Guay, BN ms. Fr 6685, 22 March 1786; Félix Gaiffe, *Le Mariage de Figaro* (Paris: Nizet, 1928).

71. Robert Darnton, "Trends in Radical Propaganda on the Eve of the French Revolution" (Ph.D. dissertation, Oxford University, 1964), 353–55; Thomas E. Crow, *Painters and Public Life in Eighteenth-Century Paris* (New Haven: Yale University Press, 1985), 225–26.

72. Frédéric Grendel, *Beaumarchais*, trans. Roger Greaves (New York: Thomas Crowell, 1977), ch. 14; Zweig, *Marie Antoinette*, 157–58.

73. Zweig, *Marie Antoinette*, 156; Almeras, *Marie-Antoinette*, 325.

74. See bibliography in Almeras, *Marie-Antoinette*, 399–403.

75. *Essais historiques*, 34.

76. Funck-Brentano, *Affaire du collier*, chs. 37–38.

77. *Mémoire justificatif de la comtesse de Valois-La Motte, écrit par elle-même* (London, 1789).

78. For instance, *Suplique à la nation et requête à l'Assemblée Nationale par Jeanne de Saint-Rémi de Valois* (n.p., 1790); *Adresse de la comtesse de La Motte-Valois à l'Assemblée Nationale pour être déclarée citoyenne active* (London, 1790).

79. [Louise de Keralio], *Les Crimes des reines de France depuis le commencement de la monarchie jusqu'à Marie-Antoinette* (Paris, 1791); the volume bears the name of Louis Prudhomme, editor of *Les Révolutions de Paris*. I am grateful to Lynn Hunt and to Carla Hesse for pointing out to me the likely author of the book. See also the article on Louise de Keralio in Louis Michaud, *Biographie universelle*, which also attributes *Les Crimes* to her.

80. [Keralio], *Crimes*, vii, ix.

81. Jack Censer, *Prelude to Power: The Parisian Radical Press, 1789–1791* (Baltimore: Johns Hopkins University Press, 1976), 96–98, 111–15.

82. See Landes, *Women and the Public Sphere*.

83. Carole Pateman, *The Sexual Contract* (Stanford: Stanford University Press, 1988), 11.

84. Marina Warner, *Monuments and Maidens: The Allegory of the Female Form* (New York: Atheneum, 1985), 277–92.

The Heroine of the Crime: Marie-Antoinette in Pamphlets

Chantal Thomas

Translated by Dena Goodman

A flock of little pamphlets, millions of stinging flies born in a stormy hour.

—Michelet

Short Works for Busy Times

The Old Regime did not believe in the event. The reigns succeeded one another according to the natural order of births and deaths. "The King is dead. Long live the King": this is not a new person who appears, it's a principle that continues (death grasps the living). The days have the rigidity of rituals. *The Political Journal* can report for any day, any month, of all the years past and future: "The King, the queen, the princes and princesses of the royal family have each in their turn received communion from the hands of their respective confessors." This immobility founded on religious observance is ridiculed by the revolutionary press. *The National Whip*, in February 1790, writes either as a made-up parody or following an event that actually happened: "Sunday, 31 January, the volunteers and grenadiers who attended the service at the King's chapel having not kneeled when the priest was preparing to give the benediction, the sergeant of grenadiers, *homme de tête*, went before the ranks and cried with all his might: 'Take care! On your knees.' The King, the Queen, and all those in attendance at the mass could not keep from laughing. One might have laughed less." The timeless—in the form of the repetition of the same gestures in the service of the rules of religion or those, worldly, but just as rigid, of etiquette—is disturbed. It no longer goes without saying. And while it continues stubbornly to perpetuate itself, it oscillates between the tragic and the ridiculous.

Pamphlet writing is a perfect expression of this acceleration of time, inseparable from the Revolution. Acceleration and diffraction. Not only do events unfold in a rhythm unknown before, but the scene of the event is multiplied, mobile, not always possible to capture. The rapid pace of printing and diffusion, the ubiquity, are the springs of the journalistic phenomenon, of which the pamphlet is an integral part; while at the same time it remains a book, in its material presentation. The pamphlet, as a material object, is a little book, "a work usually of minimal scope, satirical, injurious, defamatory," that attacks newsworthy questions.[1] The etymology of the word is unclear: I would choose the one that plays on the palm and a folded sheet of paper (*paume et feuillet*) and makes the pamphlet a folded sheet one holds in the palm of the hand. And it is true that the pamphlets had, for many of the characters who put them in play and denounced them, the meaning of a prediction. They could read in them, according to the words of a poem by Apollinaire, "their destiny written in the palm of the hand."

Small books of few pages, pamphlets were quickly written, even more quickly consumed. They corresponded to a complete change in modes of reading. In the popular milieus of the cities, and above all in the countryside, these were slow, repetitive, because to read was a poorly mastered operation, reduced in many cases, as long as the person was not completely illiterate, to an approximate deciphering. Moreover, outside of religious books, books were rare possessions. Thus the same ones were always taken up, learned by heart. As Roger Chartier has written, "the rapid advance of an ephemeral pamphlet literature, a mobile and nervous literature of value only as it related to current politics, rendered obsolete all of a traditional manner of reading connected to repetition of the same formulas from equally repetitious books (Books of Hours, almanacs, the fiction of the *Bibliothèque bleue*)."[2]

Pamphlets should be located in the context of both written and oral communication. They had a decisive role in the propagation of ideas by the spoken word (in the streets, in the marketplaces, in the workshops, the cabarets, etc.), without which it is impossible to understand the emergence of a revolutionary consciousness in a

France for the most part illiterate. "If it is unlikely that many *sans-culottes* could read the books of Rousseau or any other philosopher, it is certain that they knew them well enough for pamphleteers and political writers to refer to them and their fellows directly. This is suggested by numerous pamphlets that not only echo opinions spread about the neighborhoods and the markets, but were rewritten in a popular language. Consider *Père Duchesne;* and it is interesting to recall the remark attributed to a fishwife in a tract of 1789: 'Lady! I hope I know how to read.'"[3] This was not entirely certain, which is why orality held such a large place in the very simple style and vocabulary of the pamphlets.

Beginning with the titles, which alone were an entire program and which the peddlers would call out in the streets. Take, for example: *The Autrichienne on the Rampage, or the Royal Orgy; From the Fuckers of Good Taste to the National Assembly; The Delights of Coblentz or Libertine Anecdotes of French Émigrés; The Cloistered Whores, A Parody of the Visitandine Nuns; The Uterine Furors of Marie-Antoinette;* et cetera. Consider next the songs frequently included in the text. In *Historical Essays Concerning the Life of Marie-Antoinette* we find at the turn of a sentence, this song, to be sung to a tune from *The Marriage of Figaro*:

> What's the point of searching Castille
> For the stupidest of our Kings?
> The Bastille is demolished
> Goodbye to our Gothic laws
> How easily our heart jumps,
> In paying off the violins;
> Everything ends in songs
> Who needs cannons?

Titles bellowed at the top of one's voice, songs sung in chorus, words easily remembered because they were sung to well-known tunes— all of this puts the pamphlets in the register of vocal space, of the shout, of the refrain, situates them, too, in public space. From the spirit of the pamphlet arises also the inscription of graffiti. Almost no memory of all this fugitive writing on the walls of Paris remains. Aside from a few anecdotes, such as those which report that fire-proofed buildings were marked with the letters MACL, which everyone translated as "Marie-Antoinette cuckolds Louis."

The jubilation, the insight that motivates this writing passes above all in that which is external to it. Or, if one approaches the materiality of the text, in what Gérard Genette calls the "paratext" and, more precisely, the "editorial peritext." The pamphleteers tried hard to vary the fantastic designations:

> At Paris, at the home of the author and elsewhere with the permission of Liberty;
> At Paris, 100 leagues from the Bastille;
> At Paris, at the shops of the novelty sellers;
> At Paphos, in the printshop of Love;
> At Persepolis, at the sign of Astuce and of forsaken Virtue;
> At the riding school and in the bordellos of Paris;
> At Fuckopolis, *chez* Braquemart, Bookseller, Quick-draw Street, at the golden balls, with the permission of the superiors.

The reading of pamphlets contributed to the talk on the street, to the rumors of the crowds, to the movement of altercations, and to a certain kind of obscene, collective laughter as well. It is thus difficult to separate out the pamphlets, as soon as one is on the other side, at a distance from their actuality—put otherwise: in the silence of a library. This literature of anger, connected to moments of enthusiasm, of fanaticism, of immediate insights, lends itself as badly as possible to the seated position and to the internal and solitary reading of libraries. It is hard to imagine a greater distance between the declamation hurled out in the libels, tracts, and newspapers of the Revolution and the confined and highly supervised atmosphere of our way of approaching these texts. But it is important to keep this distance in mind and to know that the real difficulty of reading these works is surely not in deciphering them, but just in the very minimal part that they accord to writing. The difficulty, for the critic, lies also in the manipulation of a corpus necessarily full of lacunae. Destined for an immediate reading, grasped in the movement of action, numerous pamphlets have disappeared (we might even suppose that there is something unnatural in their conservation). On this foundation of incompleteness it is impossible to make a representative, exhaustive list of pamphlets.

The textuality of the pamphlets is ridiculous, often pathetic, almost always funny. However, it was indeed this discontinuous, brief, simplistic, profoundly poor literature (whether this poverty was authentic or mimicked by the pamphleteer), that aroused the public—a literature completely devoid of the breath of life, doubtless because the animation of breathing awaited the physical, living, improvisatory presence of readers.

Pamphlet writing followed the lineage of the exigencies of the present reclaimed by Diderot and the encyclopedists against the fixed traditions that, at the opera as well as the theater, aimed to abide by conventional figures, drawn from the mythology of the Olympian gods, and which represented more or less all the metaphors of the king. The pamphlets shattered the idea of the timeless. They put on the stage only contemporaries, radically deprived of any Olympian halo. No longer were grandeurs proclaimed. This was not the time for praise. Pamphlet writing focused, with a minimum of diversion, the hatred of the people on a small number of figures. The laying bare of innumerable vices of people in power was politically justified by a call for insurrection: "Must not an entire people now be struck mad to allow itself to be tossed about by the characters who are going to appear on the stage? Obedience is not imbecility; one wants to be guided along the path of truth, but not led over the precipice."[4]

The contemporary targets of the pamphlets tended to be the queen and her entourage. The use of pornography against the royal family and the aristocracy in power was not an innovation: "The genre was certainly traditional, going back to Louis XIV, whose amorous exploits were amply chronicled. But during the twenty years preceding the Revolution the attacks took on the aspect of political and social denunciation."[5] The noble characters who were the systematic target of the pamphlets were endowed with fixed character traits, with which they appeared in every pamphlet—psychological reminders that functioned like visual emblems in paintings. Louis XV was the "debauched *Fleur-de-Lycé*." His name was synonymous with egoism, lewdness, corruption. The following epigram expresses this clearly:

> The embalmer would be required,
> He has the smell of carrion;
> But to open him up, well, ugh!, why do it,
> Since there's sure to be no heart there.

During the reign of Louis XVI, the sexual debauches of Louis XV, his "harem" at the Parc aux Cerfs, and his attachment to du Barry were important not so much in themselves as to underscore the nullity of his successor. From this point of view, Louis XV had the same image as the comte d'Artois, Louis XVI's brother, presented as the sexual athlete par excellence. He was, among the princes of the blood, the most present in the pamphlets of the time. His frivolity, his licentiousness made him the privileged masculine hero of fictions that repeated ad infinitum the theme of the impotence of Louis XVI. Add to his impotence that he was also an alcoholic and "too good" (this excessive goodness being nothing but another manifestation of his inability to govern). All these negative elements contrasted with the erotic superpotency, the political devilry, of the "female monster" who was the queen, Marie-Antoinette. In fact, in this lewd saga that was constructed in pamphlet after pamphlet, Marie-Antoinette was the uncontested heroine. (We shall not analyze here the reasons for such a perfect fit for the function of target. They are multiple and can be laid out logically. But it is not at all certain that logic alone would exhaust this question.) Opposite Marie-Antoinette were only interchangeable, secondary masculine roles. The women were reduced to the roles of followers or slaves—with the exception of the duchesse de Polignac, who represented Marie-Antoinette's double, the two women being rewarded indifferently with the same title of "Messalina."

Pamphlet writing put on the stage a limited number of characters whom it was a matter of reducing to symbols of evil, without any possible nuance or ambivalence. These characters existed only in order to manifest the evil essence that constituted them. This willed simplicity did not imply, on one hand, any elaboration of plots (a difficulty of comprehension would attenuate the intended impact, the vehemence of the emotional reaction), or, on the other hand, any dispersion of the meaning of reported anecdotes. In a pamphlet, there are no gratuitous anecdotes. Everything has meaning—a meaning that can only develop the equation posed at the outset. The pamphlet exposes the misery or the blackness of a character placed by the aberration of a system of divine right in command of the realm. This is a literature that proposes a (negative) identity and poses against it all the episodes that illustrate it: the proof. This is why it can be continued indefinitely, like a litany. The brevity is not intrinsic to the construction of the pamphlets. They are short for reasons external to the time of reading, the appeal to violence, the sentences that are the equivalent of insults.

Laying Bare

Marie-Antoinette was not immediately, upon her arrival in France, subjected to the verve of pamphlets. During the first years of her reign, public opinion was indeed rather favorable to her. The hostility, when it came out, emanated from the court.[6] The first moment that provoked it was the court's sojourn at the château of Marly and the visit of Maximilien, the queen's brother: "Let us name the authors of this backbiting: it was the courtiers, a cruel and perfidious race. Each morning they brought from Marly to Paris a newspaper full of little anecdotes that circulated only as long as, by their nastiness, they poisoned the situation: thus appeared *The Break of Dawn*, a little libel, flat, obscure, and despicable."[7] The first pamphlets denounced the queen's acts of imprudence, her taste for gambling, her lack of respect for etiquette, and above all her coquetry. Around 1775 the rage for high hairstyles devastated the court. The queen set the example. She turned her back on the services of the official hairdresser of the royal family and gave her head up to the extravagances of a fashionable hairdresser. A serious mistake. The desacralization, through fashion, of the royal head was like a first, fatal step in the fall of the monarchy. The "Trinket Queen" suffered not only the reprimands of her mother, but also the irony of the public: "You must know that these feathers," wrote one pamphleteer, "are the most beautiful ornament with which a woman can embellish her hair. The flowerbeds that French industry varies in a thousand ways, and of which the sex adorns its head so agreeably, are again due to the taste and efforts of the Queen. Let us thank and not censure her."[8]

But the libels against Marie-Antoinette did not become serious, really animated by a will to destroy her, until the time of her first pregnancy (in 1778), and above all after 1781, the year the dauphin was born. The earlier theme of the impotence of the king was revived and aggravated by the claim that the dauphin was a bastard. This pamphlet war was conducted at the instigation of the comte de Provence. It was through contesting the lineage of the Bourbons that the offensive against the queen erupted. "[Sheets of paper] insinuated themselves everywhere. The Queen would find one at table when she unfolded her napkin; the King would come across one on his writing-desk among his official documents, in Marie-Antoinette's box at the theater, in front of her seat."[9] The small format of the pamphlets accorded with their irrepressible character.

The mounting hatred of the queen reached another peak in 1785, at the time of the Diamond Necklace Affair. From 1789 on, with the liberty of the press, the political and fantastic accusations against the *Autrichienne* maintained and animated revolutionary beliefs. They continued to satisfy the jealousies and quarrels that had nourished the royalist conflicts. At bottom, Marie-Antoinette *created unanimity*.

Whether they originated with the aristocracy—and that was where they started—or waved the flag of patriotism against royalty, the pamphlets against the queen made it possible to salvage an acceptable image of the king (until the irreversible date of the flight to Varennes). They are absolutely monotonous, regardless of their political coloration. Stylistically, they are all marked to a greater or lesser degree by popular formulas, inaccuracies, spelling mistakes. What difference did that make, since it did not at all change the manufactured quality of this mercantile writing, its anonymity? Because it was without an acknowledged statement of origins, and by the same token without textual originality, it established itself easily in the circulation of words—the whispered, insinuating, perfidious one of the court gossips, or that of the clamoring of the crowd. The pamphlets gave rumors a content, allowed them to be recast indefinitely. Concerning the "gross calumnies" uttered against the queen, *The Portfolio of a Red Heel* lays out their circuit: "A cowardly courtier hatched them in the shadows, another courtier put them in verse and in couplets, and through the ministry of valets got them passed along as far as Les Halles [the Parisian marketplace] and the Marché aux herbes. From Les Halles they were carried to the workshop, where, in turn, the craftsman returned them to the gentlemen who forged them, and who, without losing any time, hit the bull's-eye, asking each other, and in a tone of the most consummate hypocrisy: have you read them? Here they are."[10] This essentially Parisian rumor was indefatigable because it drew upon a source of unlimited fantasies: the body of the queen.

It was not the fact that the pamphlets exposed the nudity of Marie-Antoinette, it was the way in which they did it that was meant to shock. Because, traditionally, the body of the queen belonged to the public domain. It was an affair of state. This was evident in at least two episodes in the biography of Marie-Antoinette. The first was the ritual of her passage from Austria to France. A pavilion was built expressly for it on an island in the Rhine. The symbolic frontier was traced there. The young woman had to pass through a first room, surrounded by ladies-in-waiting. There she was stripped of everything she wore, clothes and jewelry. She crossed the fictional line naked and alone. On the other side her French identity awaited her in the form of a luxurious new outfit and new ladies-in-waiting, who did not speak the German language. The second episode, which belongs to a much more traditional ceremony, had to do with her lying-ins, which had to take place in public. Thus she barely escaped being suffocated to death by the crowd of courtiers who pressed in upon her bed in order to verify from as close as possible that there was no trafficking in babies.

This public exhibition of the body of the queen, of her nubile body or the body of a woman in the process of giving birth, did not penetrate her as an ideal (Georges Bataille: "A queen was a priori a more ideal, more ethereal being, than any other"). It was precisely because it did not stop incarnating royalty that it escaped the norms of modesty.

The pamphlets against Marie-Antoinette took up again this publicity of her body, but in the sense of a generalized prostitution. The pornographic fantasies that they staged played implicitly and unconsciously, according to Bataille, on a "back-and-forth movement from filth to ideal and from the ideal to filth," a movement that Bataille sees as being lived in "fury." In the human body, he identifies the foot with the lowest organ, in the concrete and moral sense of the term. The foot recalls getting stuck in the mud, shadows, dirtiness. Hence all the taboos of which it is the object. Thus, in Spain,

> the simple fact of letting the shod foot be seen beyond the hem of the skirt was considered indecent. Under no circumstances was it possible to touch the foot of a woman, this familiarity being, with only one exception, more serious than any other. Keep in mind, the foot of a queen was the object of the most terrifying prohibition. Thus, according to Madame d'Aulnoy, the comte de Villamediana being in love with Queen Elizabeth, dreamed of starting a fire in order to have the pleasure of holding her in his arms. The entire house, which cost a hundred thousand *écus*, was practically burnt to the ground, but he consoled himself by taking advantage of such a favorable occasion to take the queen in his arms and carry her up a small staircase. There he stole some favors from her and *as was much remarked upon in that country, he even touched her foot*. A young page saw it and reported it to the king, who avenged himself by having the count shot.[11]

In its own way, each pamphlet lit a fire. Except that the avowed aim was not to touch the foot of the queen, but to turn it to ashes.

The descriptions of the body of Marie-Antoinette tried to strip her bare in a way that would provoke a voyeuristic interest in the reader that would quickly give way to indignation. The spectacle of her nakedness had to be revolting. Of course, numerous pamphlets, more moderate, held to a banal libertine code. This was already a call to revolt, since to present a libertine queen was to denounce the scandal of her royal function. The libertine body was detailed according to stereotypical comparisons ("Below a finely turned neck, which puts alabaster to shame, / Sit two pretty tits, nicely molded, separate"),[12] or in a more lively style, one that mimics spontaneity ("Ah! what an ass! how tight and supple," exclaims d'Artois in *The Tipsy Autrichienne*).

Precious materials, rare stones or fabrics, allowed for metaphors that can hardly be classified due to their utter banality (all the libertine novels of the age used them). But in the case of the queen and the women of the court, they were understood with a connotation of wealth, of an entirely different way of life. In *The Sundial of Pleasures of the Court*, the sex of the duchesse de Polignac and of the queen are described in the following terms: "This one, shaded by a thick forest, whose blackness admirably sliced through her skin of white satin, offered up a striking contrast. The vase of the Divine surrounded by a blonde foam, and soft as silk, only contrasted with her alabaster body at its coral edges."[13] This language does not suggest any carnal vision (this is the least one could say!). But it confuses in the same envy the prohibited sex of Marie-Antoinette and the inconceivable luxury of the Petit Trianon . . . From her white marble dairy to her alabaster body, there is a single dream of possession, a single rage of impotence. Exacerbated by political tensions, the rage prevails over the impotence, her sex is no longer cast in the rococo style, but cast over to the side of defilement. In the pamphlets, in which the pornography is undergirded by misogyny, the licentiousness of Marie-Antoinette is presented as a defect, a pathology of the nymphomaniac. Her vagina is no longer a precious sculpture, but a "sponge" or, according to the contradictory logic of the unconscious, a "dried-out crust." It is repulsive. "My garden needs frequent watering. Otherwise it would soon become a dried-out crust. So get on with it . . . I'm burning."[14] No longer a question of Venus or the divine, the imagination that attributes to Marie-Antoinette the worst sexual excesses wishes to be relieved of all complicity. The farther she goes in the idea of her debauchery, the more, according to the voluntary and deadly mental division of puritanism, she exhibits the den of her vice under the repugnant form of a cesspool. Her depravity is revealed in the censure of it. The pamphlets, which strip off her clothes, reveal a sexuality that dishonors both the queen and the woman. The heights of the unbearable are attained—for understandable political reasons—when she is pregnant. Her pregnancy is everywhere declared to be illegitimate: "I'll hold on to it for my nine months, thanks to your thoughtlessness," she declares to the comte d'Artois in *The Life of Marie-Antoinette of Austria*. It is described in the most repellent way—the very antithesis of the virginal conception—as the very symptom of her uncontrollable and depraved sexuality. "The pregnancy of the queen advances; she is monstrous, she has enormous breasts which she has taken to displaying indecently."[15]

External and internal deformation. A pregnant Marie-Antoinette opens the possibility of casting a malicious look into the very depths of her womb and of discovering there the traces of a corruption so radical that one should be assured that if Marie-Antoinette followed the advice of [making] a "salutary divorce with men," it would be only to surrender herself more fully to her passion for women. "The indiscretion of one of the actresses of pleasure of our Antoinette has brought to light an inconvenience that causes considerable fear for the next lying-in, a descent or slackening of the womb occasioned no doubt either by the excess of debauchery or by the incompetence of the celebrated male midwife Varmont."[16]

Pamphlet writing, even as it regales its readers with pornographic subject matter, forbids them from getting aroused by its images. It plays hypocritically on the springs of righteous indignation. If this indignation is, or claims to be, so strong, it is because it is not made to deplore anything but immodesty. When the pamphlets present an orgiastic queen, a bacchante who set the tone for the entire court and the aristocracy of France, what makes these accusations of licentiousness so serious? Is it simply because they reveal the vice hidden under the appearance of virtue and make sex the sole operative motive for the decisions that emanate from Versailles? The violence demanded by these libertine pictures surpasses sexual behavior. It returns to it repeatedly only in order to recharge itself with a malicious energy and a politically useful resentment.

Aristocrat or libertine—these two words were synonyms in the language of the Revolution. They were equally insulting. The frivolity of the libertine, his art of leisure and pleasure, were regarded from the external point of view of suffering and privation. Licentiousness was decried in the revolutionary pamphlets as class arrogance. To the complicity of reading upon which libertine texts had been based until then, which postulated the same desire in the reader (that which produced in the work of Crébillon *fils* the art of

the unspoken, of the ellipsis), they substituted a militant cama-
raderie of agreement in order to condemn the debauchery of the
masters. But, under the pretext of better condemning it, they never
ceased to fix the eyes on it. It was the ambivalence of this literature
that spoke pleasure without pleasure, painted the most audacious
caresses without causing the slightest disturbance. The pamphlets
were not in the realm of pleasure. They were first and foremost the
acts of a revolution.

The pleasure of which they spoke was libertine, which is to say, at
the same time against nature and against the nation. The licentiousness of Marie-Antoinette was a serious and even a criminal matter
because, as a woman, she betrayed the duties of her sex in surren-
dering to it; and, as a queen, she exerted her hatred of the French
people. In *The Life of Marie-Antoinette of Austria,* we read:

> Because we must note that all these projects of revenge and of blood are
> cemented by the favors of love. If Antoinette had not joined to this lust-
> ful ardor the most heinous and horrible crimes, the narration of her life
> would be nothing but a voluptuous novel that would cause indifference
> itself to smile. But these heinous crimes are so strongly fused with those
> gallant intrigues that we have not been able to separate them.[17]

The obscene insight offered by these pamphlets did not come without a cost; it was imbricated in a continual interweaving of pornography and politics, that much more impressive for freely ignoring
the categories of reason.

Pornography and Politics

In the pamphlets, whenever the people intervened, they most often
played the role of the voyeur and of the person who recounted what
he saw. Voyeur, witness, reporter . . . According to the varying intensity of its pleasure and morality, it leaned more toward one character
or another. In *The Tipsy Autrichienne, or the Royal Orgy—Proverbial
Opera,* the spectator was a bodyguard who had "seen everything
through the door"—everything, that is to say, the queen and her "female Ganymede" (Jules de Polignac) fornicating in the company of
the comte d'Artois on the very body of a sleeping Louis XVI, an innovation, the "lustful Antoinette" is made to remark, that ought to be
added to the positions of Aretino. The guard, virtuously confused,
but moved in a literary way, is inspired with the following quatrain:

On the back of a human Monarch
I see the mother of all vices
Plunge into terrible delights
A depraved prince, a whoring Queen.

The same fiction of the accidental voyeur was utilized in the extremely virulent *Life of Marie-Antoinette of Austria, Queen of France, Wife of Louis XVI, King of the French* to recount the story of the rendezvous of Marie-Antoinette and Lafayette in a remote corner of the Tuileries palace, which looked out on the ditch surrounding the Place Louis XV and where she had just renewed "the libidinous scenes that had taken place in the woods of Versailles." And at the end of the same text, it was again a guard who, hidden, attended an orgy in the prison of the Temple. The actresses were Madame de Tourzel, the princesse de Lamballe, and the queen.

In certain pamphlets the exclusion was more insidious (and certainly more pleasurable). It was not that of the voyeur but that of the libertine object, seduced and abandoned at the capricious will not of the master but of the mistress, since under the reign of Louis XVI the arrogance of absolute power was entirely attributed to Marie-Antoinette, who thus came to amass in a single character the traditional vices of the king and his favorite. In *The Sundial of Pleasures of the Court,* the young page Chérubin tells the tale of his seduction and initiation by the queen (herself an adept of Cagliostro). Abandoned by her, he becomes the lover of Madame de Polignac, who, in turn, betrays him. He comes to understand, a little late, that "these treacherous people colluded to fool him." Having ceased to please, he receives an order of exile to America, to be carried out within twenty-four hours. In a foreign land, reflecting on his fate, he recalls this maxim practiced by Marie-Antoinette: "'Men . . . ,' she said, 'I treat them like an orange, when I've sucked out all the juice, I throw the peel far away from me.' Alas! I was really that orange."[18]

Reversing the classic scenes of seduction, the woman initiates the man into pleasure. She treats him as a sexual slave. When she has gotten her pleasure out of him, she disposes of him like squeezed fruit, kicks him out with her foot, like a dog. *The Amorous Evenings of General Mothier and the Beautiful Antoinette by the Little Spaniel of the Autrichienne* gives voice directly to the queen's dog, who complains of the cruelty of her inconstancy. "I was everything, now I am nothing," he moans (which was also her treatment of courtiers).

Marie-Antoinette could make use of men of the people in her debauches—the principle of the orgy is to use everyone, but only to humiliate them. Her sexual vampirism was part of a general system of expenses ruinous to France. Not only is the insatiable sexuality of Marie-Antoinette the scourge of the French (as a direct menace and as a motive for spending), but more basically, and according to a very Sadean movement, it was with this sexuality that Marie-Antoinette fed her taste for crime and, more precisely, her hatred of the French people. La Polignac declares to Marie-Antoinette: "We will only rest from the fatigues of love in working passionately for the destruction of a people who have the insolent pride to despise us."[19]

At the height of licentiousness, the queen dreams of drinking the blood of Frenchmen in a skull cup! The people, be they excluded or integrated by chance into the orgies of the Autrichienne, are always her victim. She only takes her pleasure against them. Her enjoyment really lies only in their end (and in their hunger). Vampire, castrator ("the two women with whom I had almost destroyed my virile potency," declares the poor Chérubin), Marie-Antoinette, by her hatred of the people, rejoins, according to a principle of universality proper to the spirit of the Revolution, the hatred of the human race. She is a monster, the product and instrument of a plot that outstrips her and whose origin is essentially feminine. The horror and the fascination that emanate from her take on mythic dimensions. They are fed by these links of terror and impotence, inextricably sexual and political, that men cannot face without being seized with delirium. In antiquity, this delirium gave voice to the sacred. Now, in the profane and prosaic form of the pamphlets, in their provocative simplicity, it is called the "voice of the people."

Let's listen to the terms in which it castigates Marie-Antoinette: "When in the past a plague desolated a country, the gods demanded an illustrious victim through the voice of oracles: the voice of the people is much more sure than that of oracles. The plague is much more terrible, more universal, longer, than the one that desolated Thebes; we do not seek blood, but an end to [our] troubles and a retreat that has become necessary."[20] This pamphlet was published in 1789. The punishment by enclosure, the subtraction from the world of the living (which, pushed to the extreme, evokes the torture of being buried alive), would for a long time be that which the pamphlets demanded. It was a measure meant to protect against a principle of impurity, more than it was a political sanction.

The Incorrigible

The pamphlets stage Marie-Antoinette as a main character. They also address themselves to her as an interlocutor, a reader. They thus propose as a goal to correct her. They admonish her to reform herself. "The *Essays* that we present today should bring repentance and remorse to the soul of a guilty woman." To correct herself, for the queen, would be to listen to the voice of the people that was supposed to be expressed in the pamphlets. Unfortunately, it goes without saying that nothing came of it. To the Rousseauist project of *saying everything* she opposed her will to *dissimulate everything*. She goes so far as to "display duplicity." Falsity, a specifically feminine trait, according to opinion, is presented as hereditary in the house of Austria. Marie-Antoinette thus could not but be a model of falsity. In the spirit of this duplicity, it is not surprising that she speaks a double language: the public one of dignity; the private one of filth.

In a footnote to *Royal Bordello*, it is spelled out to the reader, who might doubt it, that the queen converses in these terms with a marquis: "'Draw, Marquis, shoot; hurry up and f*** me. . . .' Such are the familiar expressions of this lascivious woman. We record her conversation word for word, as it actually took place since the arrival of Cardinal de Rohan. The reader will pardon our precision in reporting the facts. We are merely echoing this Messalina."[21] The pamphlets, at the same time that they revealed a base sexuality, denounced an obscene language, the only truthful one beneath the pretenses of refined speech.

Being thus obliged to mend her ways, how does Marie-Antoinette respond in the pamphlet literature? She soon acknowledges her active role in the pamphlet war and speaks of the enormous expenses that this defamatory production is costing her (see, for example, *The Life of Marie-Antoinette*, 3:32), she soon demands, in vain, censorship: "In Paris they're publishing my life story, the memoirs of the comtesse de Lamotte. Have all copies remanded: bring every one of them to me," she orders.[22]

The pamphlets agree on her hatred of the people. They maintain a vicious circle: "These pamphlets will only increase the hatred that I have conceived for the French people and from this time forth I swear to destroy them." (During her trial, Marie-Antoinette was accused of having these pamphlets written herself in order to sully the image of the French people.)

Far from reforming her, they harden her in her stubbornness to do evil. Marie-Antoinette proclaims the persistence of her identity as the criminal queen: "Do not doubt it, I am still the same."[23] As one pamphlet said:

> Antoinette as licentious as Messalina
> To pay for her crimes goes to the guillotine.

This is the playfulness of a rhyme; it's the Revolution in songs. But this is also how the passage to a deed is effected. The pamphlets are a moment in the action which they call forth. They correspond to this definition by Jean-Paul Sartre: "The word is a certain particular moment of action and has no meaning outside it."[24] An engaged word and one whose value lies only in its engagement, the pamphlet makes no claim to be inscribed indelibly in literary history. Even at the time, the pamphlets were not recognized as being part of literature. The *Mercure de France* did not take account of either pamphlets or newspapers in its chronicle. It maintained against these quickly produced works the long time of the work of art. By contrast, the marginal press, which lived according to the hurried rhythm of the Revolution, announced them and commented on them actively. The *Little Magazine of the Palais-Royal* printed the following: "I would like to inform the public of the printing of books that are new, clandestine, and prohibited by despotism and tyranny." Thus in its first issue (15 September 1789), it cited among works that were new or in press: "*Summary of the Life of Marie-Antoinette, Archduchess of Austria, Queen of France and of Navarre. A work published some years ago and newly reprinted based on a copy found in the Bastille. Truthful, verbose in style, a brilliant selection of little-known anecdotes; the historian might have supplemented the fidelity of his narrative with a little more energy. Be that as it may, the rank of the heroine of this work will always make it interesting."

In the course of her trial, the queen was accused of treason, but no convincing proof of it was then found. It was articulated by Jacques-René Hébert, another leading accuser, whose idea was a direct consequence of the pamphlet writings that, for years, made of her an erotic or criminal heroine, at least the equal of the marquis de Sade's Juliette. Marie-Antoinette was accused of incest. Summoned to explain herself, she said only: "If I have not responded, it is because nature refuses to respond to such a charge made against a mother. I call upon all those [mothers] who may be found here."[25]

Fair words in response to this peak of misogynist exultation that her trial represented. This is why, beyond the differences of political opinions, a feminine position is taken by personalities as different as Madame de Staël and Olympe de Gouges. In 1791, the latter, despite her revolutionary choices, wrote a declaration of the rights of woman dedicated to the queen.[26] In the same spirit in the month of August 1793, Madame de Staël published her *Reflections on the Queen's Trial.* She wrote: "They go awfully low to undermine the respect which the queen must inspire, by the use of the genre of calumny with which it is so easy to weaken all women." And later: "I return to you, *every* woman who is sacrificed in so tender a mother; all sacrificed by the attack which is committed on weakness by the annihilation of pity; this is what will become of your empire if ferocity reigns, what will be your destiny if your tears fall in vain."[27]

But "I call upon all mothers" is also ambiguous and politically contorted, since an attachment to the principle of hereditary monarchy can also be read in it—the motherhood vindicated here having nothing to do with the republican motherhood that, according to Jules Michelet, was the great discovery of the Revolution. In this sense, Marie-Antoinette would have been right up to the end what the pamphlet literature wanted to make of her: the irreducible, the enemy; as foreigner, as queen and favorite, as woman—as that in which all her privileges to a power that was justified only by her "good pleasure" was incarnated.

Notes

1. Marc Angenot, *La Parole pamphlétaire: Contribution à la typologie des discours modernes* (Paris: Payot, 1982), 5.

2. Roger Chartier, "Peasant Reading in the Age of Enlightenment," in *Cultural History: Between Practices and Representations,* trans. Lydia G. Cochrane (Ithaca: Cornell University Press, 1988), 166.

3. "Dame! j'savons lire, j'espère." George Rudé, *The Crowd in the French Revolution* (Oxford: Clarendon Press, 1959), 212.

4. *Essais historiques sur la vie de Marie-Antoinette, reine de France, pour servir à l'histoire de cette princesse* (1789), 7.

5. Henri-Jean Martin, "A la veille de la Révolution: crise et réorganisation de la librairie," *Histoire de l'édition française,* vol. 2 (Paris: Promodis, 1984), 525.

6. See Hector Fleischmann, *Les Pamphlets libertins contre Marie-Antoinette* (Geneva: Slatkine, 1976).

7. *Le Portefeuille d'un talon rouge* (178-), 11. It should be noted that the pamphlets are all anonymous, the editor's name an imaginative pretext, and the publication dates, when they exist, to be taken with caution.

8. Ibid., 27.

9. Stefan Zweig, *Marie Antoinette: The Portrait of an Average Woman* (Garden City, N.Y.: Garden City Publishing, 1933), 152.

10. *Portefeuille d'un talon rouge,* 12. The "bull's-eye" was a room at Versailles where courtiers gathered to exchange news.

11. Georges Bataille, *Oeuvres complètes* (Paris: Gallimard, 1970), 1:202.

12. *Les Amours de Charlot et Toinette* (1789), reprinted as *The Love Life of Charlie and Toinette* in Chantal Thomas, *The Wicked Queen: The Origins of the Myth of Marie-Antoinette,* trans. Julie Rose (New York: Zone Books, 1999), 187.

13. *Le Cadran des plaisirs de la Cour ou les Aventures du petit page Chérubin, pour servir de suite à la vie de Marie-Antoinette, ci-devant reine de France* (1789), 13.

14. *Le Bordel royal, suivi d'un entretien secret entre la reine et le cardinal de Rohan après son entrée aux Etats généraux* (1789), reprinted as *The Royal Bordello* in *Wicked Queen,* 222.

15. *Essais historiques,* 35. As a manifestation of the repellent vision of the queen's physique see, e.g., "The Austrian panther," in the photo insert. The caption reads: "Her hard eyes, treacherous and inflamed, breathe only fire and carnage in order to complete her unjust revenge; her nose and her cheeks are pimply and crimson from a corrupted blood that is distilled between her flesh and her leathery skin that is already livid; her fetid and infected mouth conceals a cruel tongue, which they say is forever altered with French blood."

16. *Essais historiques,* 6.

17. Ibid, 89.

18. *Cadran des plaisirs,* 38.

19. *Les Imitateurs de Charles IX ou les Conspirateurs foudroyés,* 19.

20. *Essais historiques,* 22.

21. *Royal Bordello,* 221.

22. Ibid., 226.

23. *Essais historiques,* 145.

24. Jean-Paul Sartre, *What Is Literature?* In *What Is Literature? and Other Essays,* ed. Steven Ungar (Cambridge, Mass.: Harvard University Press, 1988), 35.

25. *Actes du tribunal révolutionnaire* (Paris: Mercure de France, 1968), 97.

26. See Olympe de Gouges, *Oeuvres,* ed. Benoîte Groult (Paris: Mercure de France, 1986).

27. Germaine de Staël, *Réflexions sur le procès de la reine publiées dans le mois d'août 1793* in *Oeuvres complètes* (Paris: Trentt et Würtz, 1820), 2:32–33.

The Many Bodies of Marie-Antoinette: Political Pornography and the Problem of the Feminine in the French Revolution

Lynn Hunt

It has long been known that Marie-Antoinette was the subject of a substantial erotic and pornographic literature in the last decades of the Old Regime and during the Revolution itself. Royal figures at many times and in many places have been the subject of such writing, but not all royal figures at all times. When royal bodies become the focus of such interest, we can be sure that something is at issue in the larger body politic. As Robert Darnton has shown, for example, the sexual sensationalism of Old Regime *libelles* was a choice means of attacking the entire "establishment"—the court, the church, the aristocracy, the academies, the salons, and the monarchy itself.[1] Marie-Antoinette occupies a curious place in this literature; she was not only lampooned and demeaned in an increasingly ferocious pornographic outpouring, but she was also tried and executed.

A few other women, such as Louis XV's notorious mistress Madame du Barry, suffered a similar fate during the Revolution, but no other trial attracted the same attention or aired the same range of issues as that of the ill-fated queen. The king's trial, in contrast, remained entirely restricted to a consideration of his political crimes. As a consequence, the trial of the queen, especially in its strange refractions of the pornographic literature, offers a unique and fascinating perspective on the unselfconscious presumptions of the revolutionary political imagination. It makes manifest, more perhaps than any other single event of the Revolution, the underlying inter-connections between pornography and politics.

When Marie-Antoinette was finally brought to trial in October 1793, the notorious public prosecutor Antoine-Quentin Fouquier-Tinville delivered an accusation against her that began with extraordinary language, even for those inflamed times:

> In the manner of the Messalinas-Brunhildes, Frédégonde and Médecis, whom one called in previous times queens of France, and whose names forever odious will not be effaced from the annals of history, Marie-Antoinette, widow of Louis Capet, has been since her time in France, the scourge and bloodsucker of the French.

The bill of indictment then went on to detail the charges: before the Revolution she had squandered the public monies of France on her "disorderly pleasures" and on secret contributions to the Austrian emperor (her brother); after the Revolution, she was the animating spirit of counterrevolutionary conspiracies at the court. Since the former queen was a woman, it was presumed that she could achieve her perfidious aims only through the agency of men such as the king's brothers and Lafayette. Most threatening, of course, was her influence on the king; she was charged not only with the crime of having had perverse ministers named to office but more significantly and generally with having taught the king how to dissimulate—that is, how to promise one thing in public and plan another in the shadows of the court. Finally, and to my mind most strangely, the bill of indictment specifically claimed that

> the widow Capet, immoral in every way, new Agrippina, is so perverse and so familiar with all crimes that, forgetting her quality of mother and the demarcation prescribed by the laws of nature, she has not stopped short of indulging herself with Louis-Charles Capet, her son, and on the confession of this last, in indecencies whose idea and name make us shudder with horror.[2]

Incest was the final crime, whose very suggestion was cause for horror.

The trial of a queen, especially in a country whose fundamental laws specifically excluded women from ruling, must necessarily be unusual. There was not much in the way of precedent for it—the English, after all, had tried only their king, not his wife—and the relatively long gap between the trial of Louis (in December and January) and that of his queen ten months later seemed even to attenuate the necessary linkage between the two trials. Unlike her husband,

Marie-Antoinette was not tried by the Convention itself; she was brought before the Revolutionary Criminal Tribunal like all other suspects in Paris, and there her fate was decided by a male jury and nine male judges.[3]

Because queens could never rule in France, except indirectly as regents for underage sons, they were not imagined as having the two bodies associated with kings. According to the "mystic fiction of the 'King's Two Bodies'" as analyzed by Ernst Kantorowicz, kings in England and France had both a visible, corporeal, mortal body and an invisible, ideal "body politic," which never died. As the French churchman Bossuet explained in a sermon he gave with Louis XIV present in 1662: "You are of the gods, even if you die, your authority never dies. . . . The man dies, it is true but the king, we say, never dies."[4] It is questionable whether this doctrine still held for French kings by 1793, but it is certain that it never held for French queens. We might then ask why the destruction of the queen's mortal body could have had such interest for the French. What did her decidedly nonmystical body represent? In this chapter, I argue that it represented many things; Marie-Antoinette had, in a manner of speaking, many bodies. These many bodies, hydralike, to use one of the favorite revolutionary metaphors for counterrevolution, were each in turn attacked and destroyed because they represented the threats, conscious and unconscious, that could be posed to the Republic. These were not threats of just the ordinary sort, for the queen represented not only the ultimate in counterrevolutionary conspiracy, but also the menace of the feminine and the effeminizing to republican notions of manhood and virility.

Most striking is the way in which the obsessive focus on the queen's sexualized body was carried over from the pamphlets and caricatures to the trial itself. In the trial there were frequent references to the "orgies" held at Versailles, which were dated as beginning precisely in 1779 and continuing into 1789. In his closing statement Fouquier-Tinville collapsed sexual and political references in telling fashion when he denounced "the perverse conduct of the former court," Marie-Antoinette's "criminal and culpable liaisons" with unfriendly foreign powers, and her "intimacies with a villainous faction."[5] Herman, president of the court, then took up the baton in his summary of the charges against her: he too referred to "her intimate liaisons with infamous ministers, perfidious generals, disloyal representatives of the people." He denounced again the "orgy" at the château

of Versailles on 1 October 1789, when the queen had presumably encouraged the royal officers present to trample on the revolutionary
tricolor cockade. In short, Marie-Antoinette had used her sexual
body to corrupt the body politic either through "liaisons" or "intimacies" with criminal politicians or through her ability to act sexually upon the king, his ministers, or his soldiers.

In Herman's long denunciation the queen's body was also held
up for scrutiny for signs of interior intentions and motives. On her
return from the flight to Varennes, people could observe on her face
and her movements "the most marked desire for vengeance." Even
when she was incarcerated in the Temple her jailers could "always
detect in Antoinette a tone of revolt against the sovereignty of the
people."[6] Capture, imprisonment, and the prospect of execution, it
was hoped, were finally tearing the veil from the queen's threatening
ability to hide her true feelings from the public. Note here, too, the
way that Herman clearly juxtaposes the queen and the people as a
public force; revelation of the queen's true motives and feelings
came not from secrets uncovered in hidden correspondence but
from the ability of the people or their representatives to "read" her
body.

The attention to the queen's body continued right up to the moment of her execution. At the moment of the announcement of her
condemnation to death, she was reported to have kept "a calm and
assured countenance," just as she had during the interrogation. On
the road to the scaffold, she appeared indifferent to the large gathering of armed forces. "One perceived neither despondency nor pride
on her face."[7] More-radical newspapers read a different message in
her demeanor, but they showed the same attention to her every
move. The *Revolutions of Paris* claimed that at the feet of the statue
of Liberty (where the guillotine was erected), she demonstrated her
usual "character of dissimulation and pride up to the last moment"
(see engraving in photo insert). On the way there she had expressed
"surprise and indignation" when she realized that she would be
taken to the guillotine in a simple cart rather than in a carriage.[8]

The queen's body, then, was of interest, not because of its connection to the sacred and divine, but because it represented the opposite principle—namely, the possible profanation of everything
that the nation held sacred. But apparent too in all the concern with
the queen's body was the fact that the queen could embody so much.
The queen did not have a mystic body in the sense of the king's two

bodies, but her body was mystical in the sense of mysteriously symbolic. It could mean so much; it could signify a wide range of threats. Dissimulation was an especially important motif in this regard. The ability to conceal one's true emotions, to act one way in public and another in private, was repeatedly denounced as the chief characteristic of court life and aristocratic manners in general. These relied above all on appearances—that is, on the disciplined and self-conscious use of the body as a mask. The republicans, consequently, valued transparency—the unmediated expression of the heart—above all other personal qualities. Transparency was the perfect fit between public and private; transparency was a body that told no lies and kept no secrets. It was the definition of virtue, and as such it was imagined to be critical to the future of the Republic.[9] Dissimulation, in contrast, threatened to undermine the Republic: it was the chief ingredient in every conspiracy; it lay at the heart of the counterrevolution. Thus, for example, to charge Marie-Antoinette with teaching the king how to dissimulate was no minor accusation.

Dissimulation was also described in the eighteenth century as a characteristically feminine quality, not just an aristocratic one. According to both Montesquieu and Rousseau, it was women who taught men how to dissimulate, how to hide their true feelings in order to get what they wanted in the public arena.[10] The salon was the most important site of this teaching, and it was also the one place where society women could enter the public sphere. In a sense, then, women in public (like prostitutes) were synonymous with dissimulation, with the gap between public and private. Virtue could be restored only if women returned to the private sphere.[11] Rousseau had expressed this collection of attitudes best in his *Letter to M. d'Alembert on the Theatre* (1758): "Meanly devoted to the wills of the sex which we ought to protect and not serve, we have learned to despise it in obeying it, to insult it by our derisive attentions; and every woman at Paris gathers in her apartment a harem of men more womanish than she, who know how to render all sorts of homage to beauty except that of the heart, which is her due." And, as Rousseau warned ominously about women in the public sphere, "no longer wishing to tolerate separation, unable to make themselves into men, the women make us into women."[12] With her strategic position on the cusp between public and private, Marie-Antoinette was emblematic of the much larger problem of the relations between women and the public sphere in the eighteenth century. The sexuality of women, when operating in the public sphere through dissimulation, threatened to effeminize men—that is, literally to transform men's bodies.

Central to the queen's profane and profaning body was the image of her as the bad mother. This might take many, even surprising forms, as in Fouquier-Tinville's charge that she was the calumniator of Paris—described in his closing statement as "this city, mother and conservator of liberty." The queen was the antonym of the nation, depicted by one witness in the trial as the "generous nation that nurtured her as well as her husband and her family."[13] The nation, Paris, and the Revolution were all good mothers; Marie-Antoinette was the bad mother. It should be noted, however, that the nation, Paris, and the Revolution were motherly in a very abstract, even nonfeminine fashion (in comparison to Marie-Antoinette).

The abstractness and nonsexual nature of these political figures of the mother reinforces what Carole Pateman has tellingly described as the characteristic modern Western social contract:

> The story of the original contract is perhaps the greatest tale of men's creation of new political life. But this time women are already defeated and declared procreatively and politically irrelevant. Now the father comes under attack. The original contract shows how his monopoly of politically creative power is seized and shared equally among men. In civil society all men, not just fathers, can generate political life and political right. Political creativity belongs not to paternity but masculinity.[14]

Thus, La Nation had no real feminine qualities; she was not a threatening effeminizing force and hence not incompatible with republicanism. La Nation was, in effect, a masculine mother or a father capable of giving birth. Marie-Antoinette's body stood in the way, almost literally, of this version of the social contract, since under the Old Regime she had given birth to potential new sovereigns herself.[15]

Pateman is unusual among commentators on contract theory because she takes Freud seriously. As she notes, "Freud's stories make explicit that power over women and not only freedom is at issue before the original agreement is made, and he also makes clear that two realms [the civil and the private, the political and the sexual] are created through the original pact."[16] She is less successful, however, at explaining the preoccupation with incest in a case such as Marie-Antoinette's.

The charge of incest in the trial was brought by the radical journalist Jacques-René Hébert, editor of the scabrous Père Duchesne, the most determinedly "popular" newspaper of the time. Hébert appeared at the trial in his capacity as assistant city attorney for Paris, but his paper had been notorious for its continuing attacks on the queen. Hébert testified that he had been called to the Temple prison by Simon, the shoemaker who was assigned to look after Louis's son. Simon had surprised the eight-year-old masturbating ("indecent pollutions"), and when he questioned the boy about where he had learned such practices, Louis-Charles replied that his mother and his aunt (the king's sister) had taught him. The king's son was asked to repeat his accusations in the presence of the mayor and city attorney, which he did, claiming that the two women often made him sleep between them. Hébert concluded:

> There is reason to believe that this criminal enjoyment [*jouissance* in French, which has several meanings, including "pleasure," "possession," and "orgasm"] was not at all dictated by pleasure, but rather by the political hope of enervating the physical health of this child, who they continued to believe would occupy a throne, and on whom they wished, by this maneuver, to assure themselves of the right of ruling afterward over his morals.

The body of the child showed the effects of this incestuousness; one of his testicles had been injured and had to be bandaged. Since being separated from his mother, Hébert reported, the child's health had become much more robust and vigorous.[17] What better emblem could there be of effeminization than the actual deterioration of the boy's genitals?

As sensational as the charge was, the court did not pursue it much further. When directly confronted with the accusation, the former queen refused to lower herself by responding "to such a charge made against a mother."[18] But there it was in the newspapers, and even the Jacobin Club briefly noted the "shameful scenes between the mother, the aunt, and the son," and denounced "the virus that now runs through [the boy's] veins and which perhaps carries the germ of all sorts of accidents."[19] Since it seems surprising that republican men should be so worried about the degeneration of the royal family, it is not farfetched to conclude that the incest charge had a wider, if largely unconscious, resonance. On the most explicit level, incest was simply another sign of the criminal nature of royalty. As Hébert complained rhetorically to the royalists: "You immolate your brothers, and for what? For an old whore, who has neither faith nor respect for the law, who has made more than a million men die; you are the champions of murder, brigandage, adultery, and incest."[20] Although incest can hardly be termed a major theme in revo-lutionary discourse, it did appear frequently in the political pornog-raphy of both the last decades of the Old Regime and the revolu-tionary decade itself.[21] Perhaps the most striking example is the pornography of the marquis de Sade, which makes much of incest between fathers and daughters and between brothers and sisters.[22]

The official incest charge against the queen has to be set in the context provided by the longer history of pornographic and semi-pornographic pamphlets about the queen's private life discussed in several essays in this volume. Although the charge itself was based on presumed activities that took place only after the incarceration of the royal family in the Temple prison, it was made more plausible by the scores of pamphlets that had appeared since the earliest days of the Revolution and that had, in fact, had their origins in the political pornography of the Old Regime itself. When *Révolutions de Paris* ex-claimed, "Who could forget the scandalous morals of her private life," or repeated the charges about "her secret orgies with d'Artois [one of the king's brothers], Fersen, Coigny, etc.," the newspaper was simply recalling to readers' minds what they had long imbibed in un-derground publications about the queen's promiscuity.

Attacks on the queen's morality had begun as early as 1774 (just four years after her arrival in France) with a satirical lampoon about her early morning promenades. Louis XV paid considerable sums in the same year to buy up existing copies in London and Amsterdam of a pamphlet that detailed the sexual impotence of his grandson, the future Louis XVI.[23] Before long, the songs and "little papers" had become frankly obscene, and the first of many long, detailed pam-phlets had been published clandestinely. The foremost expert on the subject found 126 pamphlets he could classify in the genre of Marie-Antoinette, libertine.[24] Even before the notorious Diamond Neck-lace Affair of 1785, and continuing long after it, the queen was the focus of an always-proliferating literature of derision preoccupied with her sexual body.[25]

Although fewer than 10 percent of the anti-Marie-Antoinette pamphlets were published before 1789, they often provided the models for later publications.[26] It is difficult to find out much about the publication (the precise dates or location) or authorship of the prerevolutionary pamphlets, since they were necessarily produced clandestinely. As Robert Darnton has vividly demonstrated, those authors who can be traced were from the French version of Grub

Street.[27] Men such as Théveneau de Morande and the comte de Paradès worked sometimes for the French crown (as spies), sometimes for rival members of the court, sometimes for foreign printers, and always for themselves. The connection to members of the court is most significant, since it shows the intensity of the interlacing of social networks of communication under the Old Regime. The author of one of the best-known pamphlets, *Portfolio of a Red Heel,* made the connection explicit, tracing the circuit from courtiers to their valets, who passed the verses on in the market, where they were picked up by artisans and brought back to the courtiers, who then hypocritically professed surprise.[28] The "popular" images of the queen, then, had their origin in the court, not in the streets.

Politically pornographic pamphlets were often traced to London, Amsterdam, or Germany, where the most notorious of the French Grub Street types made their living, and the French crown evidently spent large sums having such pamphlets bought up by its agents abroad and destroyed before they could reach France. Indeed, this new industry seems to have become a very lucrative one for those hack writers willing to live abroad, since large sums were paid to secret agents and printers, who were most likely in collusion with the writers themselves.[29] In 1782 the *Mémoires secrets* described the government's reaction to the recently published *Historical Essays:*

> The dreadful *libelle* against the queen, of which I've spoken [in a previous entry], and others of the same genre, have determined the government to make an effort on this subject and to sacrifice money, which is very distasteful; with this help they have gotten to the source and asked for the assistance of foreign governments. They undertook searches in all of the suspect printing shops of Holland and Germany; they took away everything that deserved to be, and they have even had the printer-booksellers arrested who have taken the chance of coming to France to introduce their merchandise; they have had them condemned to large fines.[30]

Needless to say, copies still made their way into France; in 1783, 534 copies of *Historical Essays Concerning the Life of Marie-Antoinette* were officially destroyed at the Bastille prison along with many other offensive productions.[31]

Many of the major accusations against Marie-Antoinette were already present in the prerevolutionary pamphlets. The *Portfolio of a Red Heel* (also condemned in 1783) begins in classic eighteenth-century fashion with a preface from the presumed publisher announcing that someone had found a portfolio while crossing the

Palais-Royal (the notorious den of prostitution and gambling that was also the residence of the king's cousin, the duc d'Orléans, who was assumed to have paid for many of the pamphlets). In it was found a manuscript addressed to Monsieur de la H—— of the French Academy. It began, "You are then out of your mind, my dear H——! You want, they tell me, to write the history of tribades at Versailles." In the text appeared the soon-to-be-standard allegation that Marie-Antoinette was amorously involved with the duchesse de Polignac ("her Jules") and Madame Balbi. The comte d'Artois was supposedly the only man who interested her. These charges, as harshly delivered as they were, formed only part of the pamphlet's more general tirade against the court and ministers in general. Speaking of the courtiers, the author exclaimed, "You are an abominable race. You get everything at once from your character as monkeys and as vipers.[32]

The short and witty *Loves of Charlie and Toinette* took up much the same themes, though in verse, but this time focused exclusively on the queen, the comte d'Artois, and the princesse de Lamballe (who would become the most famous victim of the September Massacres in 1792). Marie-Antoinette was depicted as turning to lesbianism because of the impotence of the king. Then she discovers the delights of the king's brother.[33]

The long 1789 edition (146 pages in the augmented French edition) of the *Historical Essays Concerning the Life of Marie-Antoinette* (there had been many variations on the title since its first publication in 1781) already demonstrated the rising tone of personal hostility toward the queen that would characterize revolutionary pornographic pamphlets.[34] In the most detailed of all the anti-Marie-Antoinette exposés, it purported to give the queen's own view through the first person: "My death is the object of the desires of an entire people that I oppressed with greatest barbarism." Marie-Antoinette here describes herself as "barbarous queen, adulterous spouse, woman without morals, polluted with crimes and debaucheries," and she details all the charges that had accumulated against her in previous pamphlets. Now her lesbianism is traced back to the Austrian court, and all of the stories of amorous intrigues with princes and great nobles are given substance. Added to the charges is the new one that she herself had poisoned the young heir to the throne (who died in early 1789). Characteristic, too, of many of the later pamphlets will be the curious alternation between frankly pornographic staging—descriptions in the first person of her liaisons, complete with wildly beating hearts and barely stifled sighs of passion—and political moralizing and denunciation put into the mouth of the queen herself. The contrast with the king and his "pure, sincere love, which I so often and so cruelly abused" was striking.[35] The queen may have been representative of the degenerate tendencies of the aristocracy, but she was not yet emblematic of royalty altogether.

With the coming of the Revolution in 1789, the floodgates opened, and the number of pamphlets attacking the queen rapidly rose in number. These took various forms, ranging from songs and fables to presumed biographies (such as the *Historical Essay*), confessions, and plays. Sometimes the writings were pornographic with little explicit political content; the sixteen-page pamphlet in verse called *The Royal Dildo*, for example, told the story of Junon (the queen) and Hébée (presumably either the duchesse de Polignac or the princesse de Lamballe). Junon complained of her inability to obtain satisfaction at home, while pulling a dildo out of her bag ("happy invention that we owe to the monastery"). Her companion promises her penises of almost unimaginably delicious size.[36] In the much more elaborately pornographic *Uterine Furors of Marie-Antoinette, Wife of Louis XVI* of two years later, colored engravings showed the king impotent and d'Artois and Polignac replacing him.[37]

The Marie-Antoinette pamphlets reflect a general tendency in the production of political pornography: the number of titles in this genre rose steadily from 1774 to 1788 and then took off after 1789. The queen was not the only target of hostility; a long series of "private lives" attacked the conduct of courtiers before 1789 and revolutionary politicians from Lafayette to Robespierre afterward. Aristocrats were shown as impotent, riddled with venereal disease, and given over to debauchery. Homosexuality functioned in a manner similar to impotence in this literature; it showed the decadence of the Old Regime in the person of its priests and aristocrats. Sexual degeneration went hand in hand with political corruption.[38] This proliferation of pornographic pamphlets after 1789 shows that political pornography cannot be viewed simply as a supplement to a political culture that lacked "real" political participation. Once participation increased dramatically, particularly with the explosion of uncensored newspapers and pamphlets, politics did not simply take the high road.[39]

Marie-Antoinette was without question the favorite target of such attacks. There were not only more pamphlets about her than any other single figure, but they were also the most sustained in their viciousness. Henri d'Almeras claimed that the *Historical Essays* alone sold between twenty thousand and thirty thousand copies.[40] The year 1789 does appear to mark a turning point not only in the number of pamphlets produced but also in their tone. The pre-1789 pamphlets tell dirty stories in secret; after 1789 the rhetoric of the pamphlets begins self-consciously to solicit a wider audience. The public no longer "hears" courtier rumors through the print medium; it now "sees" degeneracy in action. The first-person rendition of the 1789 French edition of *Historical Essay* is a good example of this technique.

Obscene engravings with first-person captions worked to the same effect. The engravings that accompanied the long *Life of Marie-Antoinette of Austria, Wife of Louis XVI, King of the French; From the Loss of her Virginity to 1 May 1791,* which was followed by volumes two and three, entitled *Private, Libertine, and Scandalous Life of Marie-Antoinette of Austria, former Queen of the French,* are an interesting case in point. They showed Marie-Antoinette in amorous embrace with just about everyone imaginable: her first supposed lover, a German officer; the aged Louis XV; Louis XVI impotent; the comte d'Artois; various women (see photo insert); various ménages à trois with two women and a man (see photo insert); Cardinal de Rohan of the Diamond Necklace Affair; Lafayette; Barnave; and so on. The captions are sometimes in the first person (with the princesse de Guéménée: "Gods! What transports, ah! My soul takes off, words fail me"), sometimes in the second (with the comte d'Artois: "Groan, Louis, your *vigeur inactive,* outrages your too lascivious wife here"). The effect is the same: a theatricalization of the action so that the reader is made into voyeur and moral judge at the same time. The political effect of the pornography is apparent even in this most obscene of works. In volumes two and three, the pornographic engravings are interspersed with political engravings of aristocratic conspiracy, the assault on the Tuileries palace, and even a curious print showing Louis XVI putting on a red cap of liberty and drinking to the health of the nation in front of the queen and his remaining son and heir.[41]

That the pamphlets succeeded in attracting a public can be seen in the repetition of formulaic expressions in nonpornographic political pamphlets, "popular" newspapers, petitions from "popular societies," and the trial record itself. The *Historical Essay* of 1789 already included the soon-to-be-standard comparisons of Marie-Antoinette to Catherine de Médecis, Agrippina, and Messalina. These comparisons were expanded at great length in a curious political tract called *The Crimes of the Queens of France,* which was written by a woman, Louise de Keralio (though it was published under the name of the publisher, Louis Prudhomme).[42] The "corrected and augmented" edition dated "Year II" simply added material on the trial and execution to an already-long version of 1791.[43] The tract is not pornographic; it simply refers to the "turpitudes" committed by the queen as background for its more general political charges. Keralio reviews the history of the queens of France, emphasizing in particular the theme of dissimulation: "The dangerous art of seducing and betraying, perfidious and intoxicating caresses, feigned tears, affected despair, insinuating prayers" (p. 2). These were the weapons of the queens of France (which had been identified as the arms of all women by Rousseau). When the author comes to the wife of Louis Capet, she lists many of the queen's presumed lovers, male and female, but insists upon passing rapidly over the "private crimes" of the queen in favor of consideration of her public ones. Marie-Antoinette "was the soul of all the plots, the center of all the intrigues, the foyer of all these horrors" (p. 440). As a "political tarantula," the queen resembled that "impure insect, which, in the darkness, weaves on the right and left fine threads where gnats without experience are caught and whom she makes her prey" (pp. 445–46). On the next page, the queen is compared to a tigress who, once having tasted blood, can no longer be satisfied. All this to prove what the caption to the frontispiece asserts: "A people is without honor and merits its chains / When it lowers itself beneath the scepter of queens" (see photo insert).

The shorter, more occasional political pamphlets picked up the themes of the pornographic literature and used them for straightforward political purposes. A series of pamphlets appeared in 1792, for example, offering lists of political enemies who deserved immediate punishment. They had as their appendices lists of all the people with whom the queen had had "relationships of debauchery." In these pamphlets, the queen was routinely referred to as "bad daughter, bad wife, bad mother, bad queen, monster in everything."[44]

The movement from sexual misdemeanors to bestial metaphors was characteristic of much "popular" commentary on the queen, es-

pecially in her last months. In the *Père Duchesne* Hébert had incorporated the Frédégonde and Médecis comparisons by 1791, but still
in a relatively innocent context. One of his favorite devices was to
portray himself as meeting in person with the queen and trying to
talk sense to her.[45] By 1792 the queen had become "Madame Veto,"
and once the monarchy had been toppled, Hébert made frequent
reference to the "ménagerie royale." In prison the former queen was
depicted as a she-monkey ("la guenon d'Autriche"), the king as a
pig. In one particularly fanciful scene, *Père Duchesne* presents himself in the queen's cell as the duchesse de Polignac ("that tribade")
thanks to the effect of a magic ring, whereupon the former queen
throws herself into her friend's arms and reveals her fervent hopes
for the success of the counterrevolution.[46] After her husband had
been executed, the tone of hostility escalated, and Marie-Antoinette
became the she-wolf and the tigress of Austria. At the time of her
trial, Hébert suggested that she be chopped up like meat for pâté as
recompense for all the bloodshed she had caused.[47]

Local militants picked up the same rhetoric. In a letter to the
Convention congratulating it on the execution of the queen, the
popular society of Rozoy (Seine-et-Marne department) referred to
"this tigress thirsty for the blood of the French . . . this other Messalina whose corrupt heart held the fertile germ of all crimes; may
her loathsome memory perish forever." The popular society of Gar-
lin (Basses-Pyrénées department) denounced the "ferocious panther who devoured the French, the female monster whose pores
sweated the purest blood of the sans-culottes."[48] Throughout these
passages, it is possible to see the horrific transformations of the
queen's body; the body that had once been denounced for its debauchery and disorderliness becomes in turn the dangerous beast,
the cunning spider, the virtual vampire who sucks the blood of the
French.

Explicit in some of the more extreme statements and implicit in
many others was a pervasive anxiety about genealogy. For example,
the post-1789 pamphlets demonstrated an obsession with deter-
mining the true fathers of the king's children (they were often attributed to his brother, the comte d'Artois). In a fascinating twist on
this genealogical anxiety, *Père Duchesne* denounced a supposed plot
by the queen to raise a young boy who resembled the heir to the
throne to take the heir's place.[49] The culminating charge, of course,
was incest; in the trial, this was limited to the queen's son, but in the

pamphlet literature, the charges of incest included the king's brother, the king's grandfather Louis XV, and her own father, who had taught her "the passion of incest, the dirtiest of pleasures," from which followed "the hatred of the French, the aversion for the duties of spouse and mother, in short, all that reduces humanity to the level of ferocious beasts."[50] Disorderly sexuality was linked to bestialization in the most intimate way.

Promiscuity, incest, poisoning of the heir to the throne, plots to replace the heir with a pliable substitute—all of these charges reflect a fundamental anxiety about queenship as the most extreme form of women invading the public sphere. Where Rousseau had warned that the salon women would turn their "harem of men" into women "more womanish than she," the radical militant Louise de Keralio would warn her readers that "a woman who becomes queen changes sex."[51] The queen, then, was the emblem (and sacrificial victim) of the feared disintegration of gender boundaries that accompanied the Revolution. In his controversial study of ritual violence, René Girard argues that a sacrificial crisis (a crisis in the community that leads to the search for a scapegoat) entails the feared loss of sexual differentiation: "one of the effects of the sacrificial crisis is a certain feminization of the men, accompanied by a masculinization of the women."[52] A scapegoat is chosen in order to reinstitute the community's sense of boundaries. By invoking Girard, I do not mean to suggest that the French Revolution followed his script of sacrificial crisis, or that I subscribe to the nuances of his argument. In fact, the Revolution did not single out a particular scapegoat in the moment of crisis; it was marked instead by a constant search for new victims, as if the community did not have a distinct enough sense of itself to settle upon just one (the king or the queen, for example). Nevertheless, Girard's suggestion that an intense crisis within a community is marked by fears of de-differentiation is very fruitful, for it helps make sense of the peculiar gender charge of the events of the fall of 1793.

The evidence for a feared loss of sexual differentiation in the Revolution is in fact quite extensive. Just two weeks after the execution of the queen (which took place on 16 October 1793), the Convention discussed the participation of women in politics, in particular the women's club called the Society of Revolutionary Republican Women. The Jacobin deputy Fabre d'Églantine insisted that "these clubs are not composed of mothers of families, daughters of families, sisters occupied with their younger brothers or sisters, but rather of adventuresses, knights-errant, emancipated women, amazons."[53] The deputy Amar, speaking for the Committee on General Security of the Convention, laid out the official rationale for a separation of women from the public sphere:

> The private functions for which women are destined by their very nature are related to the general order of society; this social order results from the differences between man and woman. Each sex is called to the kind of occupation which is fitting for it. . . . Man is strong, robust, born with great energy, audacity and courage. . . . In general, women are ill suited for elevated thoughts and serious meditations, and if, among ancient peoples, their natural timidity and modesty did not allow them to appear outside their families, then in the French Republic do you want them to be seen coming into the gallery to political assemblies as men do?

To reestablish the "natural order" and prevent the "emancipation" of women from their familial identity, the deputies solemnly outlawed all women's clubs.

In response to a deputation of women wearing red caps that appeared before the Paris city council two weeks later, the well-known radical spokesman (and city official) Chaumette exclaimed:

> It is contrary to all the laws of nature for a woman to want to make herself a man. The Council must recall that some time ago these denatured women, these viragos, wandered through the markets with the red cap to sully that badge of liberty. . . . Since when is it permitted to give up one's sex? Since when is it decent to see women abandoning the pious cares of their households, the cribs of their children, to come to public places, to harangues in the galleries, at the bar of the senate?

Chaumette then reminded his audience of the recent fate of the "impudent" Olympe de Gouges and the "haughty" Madame Roland, "who thought herself fit to govern the republic and who rushed to her downfall."[54]

Marie-Antoinette was certainly not in alliance with the women of the Society of Revolutionary Republican Women, with Madame Roland or Olympe de Gouges; they were political enemies. But even political enemies, as Louise de Keralio discovered, shared similar political restrictions if they were women. Keralio herself was accused of being dominated by those same "uterine furies" that beset the queen; by publishing, Keralio too was making herself public. Her detractors put this desire for notoriety down to her ugliness and inability to attract men.[55] As Dorinda Outram has argued, women who wished to participate actively in the French Revolution were caught in a discursive double bind; virtue was a two-edged sword that bisected the sovereign into two different destinies, one male and one female. Male virtue meant participation in the public world of politics; female virtue meant withdrawal into the private world of the family. Even the most prominent female figures of the time had to acquiesce in this division. As Madame Roland recognized, "I knew what role was suitable to my sex and I never abandoned it."[56] Of course, she paid with her life because others did not think that she had so effectively restrained herself from participating in the public sphere.

Read from this perspective on the difference between male and female virtue, the writings and speeches about the queen reveal the fundamental anxieties of republicans about the foundation of their rule. They were not simply concerned to punish a leading counterrevolutionary. They wanted to separate mothers from any public activity, as Carole Pateman argues, and yet give birth by themselves to a new political organism. In order to accomplish this, they had to destroy the Old Regime link between the ruling family and the body politic, between the literal bodies of the rulers and the mystic fiction of royalty. In short, they had to kill the patriarchal father and also the mother.

Strikingly, however, the killing of the father was accompanied by little personal vilification. Hébert's references to the pig, the ogre, or the drunk were relatively isolated; calling the former king a cuckold ("tête de cocu") hardly compared to the insistent denigration of Marie-Antoinette.[57] Officials chose not to dwell on the king's execution itself. Newspaper accounts were formal and restrained. On the day of the event, one of the regicide deputies who spoke in the Jacobin Club captured the mood: "Louis Capet has paid his debt; let us speak of it no longer." Most of the visual representations of the execution (medals or engravings) came from outside of France and were meant to serve the cause of counterrevolution.[58] The relative silence about Louis among the revolutionaries reflects the conviction that he represented after all the masculinity of power and sovereignty. The aim was to kill the paternal source of power and yet retain its virility in the republican replacement.

The republican ideal of virtue was profoundly homosocial; it was based on a notion of fraternity between men in which women were relegated to the realm of domesticity. Public virtue required virility, which required in turn the violent rejection of aristocratic degeneracy and any intrusion of the feminine into the public. The many bodies of Marie-Antoinette served a kind of triangulating function in this vision of the new world. Through their rejection of her and what she stood for, republican men could reinforce their bonds to one another; she was the negative version of the female icon of republican liberty but nonetheless iconic for the rejection. She was perhaps also an object lesson for other women who might wish to exercise through popular sovereignty the kind of rule that the queen had exercised through royal prerogative. The republican brothers who had overthrown the king and taken upon themselves his mantle did not want their sisters to follow their lead. In this implicit and often unconscious gender drama, the body of Marie-Antoinette played a critical, if uncomfortable, role. The bodies of Marie-Antoinette could never be sacred by French tradition, but they could certainly be powerful in their own fashion.

Notes

1. Robert Darnton, "The High Enlightenment and the Low-Life of Literature," reprinted in *The Literary Underground of the Old Regime* (Cambridge: Harvard University Press, 1982), 1–40, esp. 29.
2. I have used the report on the session of 14 October 1793 in the *Moniteur Universel,* 16 October 1793.
3. At least that is how many judges signed the arrest warrant on 14 October 1793, according to the *Moniteur,* 16 October 1793. For the workings of the Revolutionary Tribunal, see Luc Willette, *Le Tribunal révolutionnaire* (Paris: Denoël, 1981). Since it was not established until March 1793, the tribunal was not in existence at the time of the king's trial.
4. As quoted in Ernst H. Kantorowicz, *The King's Two Bodies: A Study in Mediaeval Political Theology* (Princeton: Princeton University Press, 1957), 409 n. 319.
5. *Moniteur,* 27 October 1793, reporting on the trial session of 14 October.
6. Ibid.
7. Ibid.
8. *Révolutions de Paris,* no. 212 (3 August–28 October 1793).
9. I develop the notion of transparency in a somewhat different context in *Politics, Culture, and Class in the French Revolution* (Berkeley and Los Angeles: University of California Press, 1984), 44–46, 72–74.
10. On the philosophes' attitudes toward women, see Paul Hoffmann, *La Femme dans la pensée des lumières* (Paris: Éditions Ophrys, 1977), esp. 324–446.
11. I am indebted to the analysis of Joan B. Landes, *Women and the Public Sphere in the Age of the French Revolution* (Ithaca: Cornell University Press, 1988). Dorinda Outram concludes that the Revolution was committed to antifeminine rhetoric because it ascribed power in the Old Regime to women. I think that this exaggerates the identification of women with power in the Old

Regime, but it nonetheless leads to fruitful reflections about the way in which male revolutionary politicians tried to escape feelings of guilt. See Outram, *"Le Langage mâle de la vertu:* Women and the Discourse of the French Revolution," in Peter Burke and Roy Porter, eds., *The Social History of Language* (Cambridge: Cambridge University Press, 1987), 120–35, esp. 125.

12. Jean-Jacques Rousseau, *Politics and the Arts: Letter to M. d'Alembert on the Theatre,* trans. Allan Bloom (Ithaca: Cornell University Press, 1968), 100–1.

13. Quotes from *Moniteur,* 27 October 1793 and 18 October 1793 (the latter the testimony of Roussillon, a barber-surgeon and cannoneer).

14. Carole Pateman, *The Sexual Contract* (Stanford: Stanford University Press, 1988), 36.

15. Chantal Thomas argues that the anti-Marie-Antoinette pamphlets became especially virulent from the moment of her first pregnancy in 1777: *The Wicked Queen: The Origins of the Myth of Marie-Antoinette,* trans. Julie Rose (New York: Zone Books, 1999), 46–47. See also the article by Chantal Thomas in this volume.

16. Pateman, *Sexual Contract,* p. 12.

17. *Moniteur,* 18 October 1793.

18. *Moniteur,* 19 October 1793.

19. *Moniteur,* 20 October 1793.

20. *Père Duchesne,* no. 298 (October 1793).

21. On the last half of the eighteenth century, see Hector Fleischmann, *Les Pamphlets libertins contre Marie-Antoinette* (Paris, 1908; reprint, Geneva: Slatkine, 1976), esp. the chapter, "La France galante et libertine à la fin du XVIII siècle," 13–36.

22. See, for example, *La Philosophie dans le boudoir,* where Sade offers a defense of incest in the parodic tract "Français, encore un effort si vous voulez être républicains" (Paris: Gallimard, 1976), 229–30.

23. Fleischmann, *Pamphlets libertins,* 103–9.

24. Hector Fleischmann, *Marie-Antoinette libertine: Bibliographie critique et analytique des pamphlets politiques, galants, et obscènes contre la reine. Précédé de la réimpression intégrale des quatre libelles rarissimes et d'une histoire des pamphlétaires du règne de Louis XVI* (Paris: Bibliothèque des Curieux, 1911).

25. This essay was written before I had a chance to read the interesting and lively book by Thomas, *The Wicked Queen.* Her account differs from mine in several respects. It is especially strong on the analysis of the anti-Marie-Antoinette pamphlet literature, but has virtually nothing to say about the trial records.

26. Fleischmann gives likely publication dates for the 126 pamphlets that he found in *Marie-Antoinette libertine,* 277ff. These are not all separate pamphlets but include major revised editions. Fleischmann no doubt ignored some pamphlets in existence, but the basic balance of pamphlets is most likely correctly rendered in his bibliography.

27. Darnton, "High Enlightenment."

28. *Portefeuille d'un talon rouge, contenant des anecdotes galantes et secrètes de la cour de France* (reprint, Paris: Bibliothèque des Curieux, 1911), 22. Based on the edition dated "l'an 178-, De l'Imprimerie du Comte de Paradès." The passage is translated in Robert Darnton, "Reading, Writing, and Publishing," in *Literary Underground,* 201; see also 248, n. 63.

29. Fleischmann, *Pamphlets libertins,* 117–29. See also Henri d'Almeras, *Marie-Antoinette et les pamphlets royalistes et révolutionnaires: les amoureux de la Reine* (Paris: Librairie Mondiale, 1907), 299–328.

30. As quoted in d'Almeras, *Marie-Antoinette,* 309–10.

31. Fleischmann, *Marie-Antoinette libertine,* 64.

32. Quotes from the edition cited in n. 28 above.

33. Sections of the pamphlet are reproduced in d'Almeras, *Marie-Antoinette,* 56–60. According to Maurice Tourneux, this eight-page pamphlet was published in 1779, and it cost 17,400 livres for the crown to have it destroyed. It was reprinted several times after 1789 (*Marie-Antoinette devant l'histoire: Essai bibliographique* [Paris: Leclerc, 1895], 42).

34. See d'Almeras, *Marie-Antoinette,* 399–403, for title variations.

35. Quotations from *Essai historique sur la vie de Marie-Antoinette, reine de France et de Navarre, née archiduchesse d'Autriche, le deux novembre 1755: Orné de son portrait, et rédigé sur plusieurs manuscrits de sa main* ("À Versailles, Chez La Montensier [one of her supposed female lovers], Hôtel des Courtisannes," 1789), 4, 8, 19–20. Some have attributed this pamphlet to Brissot, but d'Almeras and Fleischmann both dispute this (d'Almeras, *Marie-Antoinette,* 339; Fleischmann, *Marie-Antoinette libertine,* 67–70). Fleischmann reports the view that the marquis de Sade wrote the second part of this 1789 edition (68). Earlier in 1789 a shorter, eighty-eight-page work titled *Essais historiques sur la vie de Marie-Antoinette d'Autriche, reine de France; pour servir à l'histoire de cette princesse* (London, 1789) struck a much less violent tone. It was not written in the first person, and though it discussed the queen's amorous intrigues in detail, it was not particularly pornographic in style. This version was written very much in the vein of attempts to convince the queen of her errors: "Fasse le ciel cependant que ces vérités, si elles sont présentées à cette princesse, puissent la corriger, et la faire briller d'autant de vertus qu'elle l'a fait par ses étourderies" (78).

36. *Le Godmiché royal* (Paris, 1789).

37. The publication page after the title read: "La mère en proscrira la lecture à sa fille. Au Manège. Et dans tous les bordels de Paris, 1791." It is interesting to note that one of the early editions of Sade's *La Philosophie dans le boudoir* included on its title page the obvious parody: "La mère en prescrira la lecture à sa fille." This was the 1795 London edition. See Pascal Pia, *Les Livres de l'Enfer, du XVIe siècle à nos jours* (Paris: C. Coulet and A. Favre, 1978), 2:1044.

38. See, for example, *Les Enfans de Sodome à l'Assemblée Nationale* (Paris, 1790), Enfer no. 638, Bibliothèque Nationale. For a general overview emphasizing the contrast between aristocratic degeneracy and republican health, see Antoine de Baecque, "Pamphlets: Libel and Political Mythology," in Robert Darnton and Daniel Roche, eds., *Revolution in Print: The Press in France, 1775–1800* (Berkeley and Los Angeles: University of California Press, 1989), 165–76.

39. See the remarks by Darnton in "High Enlightenment," esp. 33.

40. D'Almeras provides no evidence for this assertion, however (*Marie-Antoinette,* 403).

41. Enfer nos. 790–92, Bibliothèque Nationale.

42. The correct attribution was brought to my attention by Carla Hesse. While working on another project, I came across a denunciation that verified Keralio's authorship. The anonymous pamphlet *Les Crimes constitutionnels de France, ou la désolation française, décrétée par l'Assemblée dite Nationale Constituante, aux années 1789, 1790, et 1791. Accepté par l'esclave Louis XVI, le 14 septembre 1791* (Paris: Chez Le Petit et Guillemard, 1792) included the following:

> Dlle de Keralio. Ugly, and already over the hill; from [the days] before the revolution, she consoled herself for the disgrace of her *gray hair* and the indifference of men, by the peaceful cultivation of letters. Her principles were then pure, and her conduct was not at all inconsistent with the noble delicacy of her family. Giving way, since the revolution, to the demagogic disorders, doubtless dominated also by *uterine furors,* she married one Robert, a former lawyer, without talent, without a case, without bread, at Givet, and now a Jacobin-Cordelier. Abandoned by her family, despised by honest folk, she vegetates shamefully with this wretch, burdened with debts and opprobrium, working by the page, for the infamous *Prudhomme,* on the disgusting newspaper of the revolution of Paris. The *Crimes of the Queens of France* have pushed to the limit her shame, as well as her total wickedness.

43. The full title of the edition I used is *Les Crimes des reines de France depuis le commencement de la monarchie jusqu'à la mort de Marie-Antoinette; avec les pièces justificatives de son procès* ("Publié par L. Prudhomme, avec Cinq gravures. Nouvelle édition corrigée et augmentée. Paris: au Bureau des Révolutions de Paris, an II").

44. See, for example, *Têtes à prix, suivi de la liste de toutes les personnes avec lesquelles la reine a eu des liaisons de débauches,* 2d ed. (Paris, 1792), 28 pp., and the nearly identical *Liste civile suivie des noms et qualités de ceux qui la composent, et la punition due à leurs crimes . . . et la liste des affidés de la ci-devant reine* (Paris, n.d. [but Tourneux dates it 1792]).

45. *Père Duchesne,* no. 36 (1791).

46. *Père Duchesne,* no. 194 (1792).

47. *Père Duchesne,* nos. 296 and 298 (1793).

48. As quoted by Fleischmann, *Marie-Antoinette libertine,* 76.

49. *Père Duchesne,* no. 36 (1791).

50. *Vie privée, libertine et scandaleuse,* as reprinted in Fleischmann, *Marie-Antoinette libertine,* 173–74. This section concludes with the most extreme of all possible epitaphs: "Here lies the immodest Manon, Who, in the belly of her mother, Knew so well how to position her c———, that she f——— her father."

51. [Keralio], *Crimes,* vii.

52. René Girard, *Violence and the Sacred,* trans. Patrick Gregory (Baltimore: Johns Hopkins University Press, 1977), 141.

53. *Moniteur,* no. 39, 9 Brumaire year II, reporting on the session of 8 Brumaire, year II, 29 October 1793.

54. Quotes from Darline Gay Levy, Harriet Branson Applewhite, and Mary Durham Johnson, eds., *Women in Revolutionary Paris, 1789–1795* (Urbana: University of Illinois Press, 1979), 215–16, 219–20.

55. See quotation in n. 42 above.

56. Outram, *"Le Langage mâle de la vertu,"* 125, quotation, 126. See also the chapter on "Women and Revolution," in Landes, *Women and the Public Sphere,* 93–151.

57. *Père Duchesne,* no. 180 (1792), for example.

58. Lynn Hunt, "The Sacred and the French Revolution," in Jeffrey C. Alexander, ed., *Durkheimian Sociology: Cultural Studies* (Cambridge: Cambridge University Press, 1988), 25–43; quotation, 32.

Carle Van Loo, *Portrait of Marie Leczynska* (1741). Versailles: Musée du Château. Photo: Art Resource, New York.

· Queen doesn't exist w/o King
· she has no status
· family unit = father & children
· bust of ~~the~~ Louis XV in background

Elisabeth Vigée-Lebrun, *Portrait of Marie-Antoinette* (1778–79). Vienna: Kunsthistorisches Museum. Photo: Art Resource, New York.

Elisabeth Vigée-Lebrun, *Marie-Antoinette en chemise* (Salon of 1783).
Private collection, Germany. Photo: Art Resource, New York.

· no king
· underwear
· she's looking at you
· direct gaze is not modest
· no corset
· reflexion on country or king
  bad

The Wertmüller portrait
of Marie-Antoinette
(1785). Photo: National
Swedish Art Museum.

Jacques-Louis David, pencil
sketch of Marie-Antoinette
(1793). Paris: Musée du
Louvre. Photo: Art
Resource, New York.

Elisabeth Vigée-Lebrun, *Portrait of Yolande Gabrielle, comtesse* [later duchesse] *de Polignac* (1783). Photo: National Trust, Waddesdon Manor, and the Courtauld Institute of Art.

Vu peuple est sans honneur, et mérite ses chaines,
Quand il baisse le front sous le sceptre des Reines.

Frontispiece to [Louise de Keralio], *Les Crimes des reines de France* (1791).
Photo: University of Michigan Libraries.

La Panthère autrichienne. Photo: Bibliothèque Nationale de France.

Engraving of Marie-Antoinette with the princesse de Guémenée, one of her ladies-in-waiting, from *Vie privée, libertine, et scandaleuse de Marie Antoinette d'Autriche* (1793). Photo: Bibliothèque Nationale de France.

Engraving of Marie-Antoinette in embrace with a man and a woman from *Vie privée, libertine, et scandaleuse de Marie Antoinette d'Autriche* (1793). Photo: Bibliothèque Nationale de France.

Les Deux ne font qu'un (ca. 1791). Photo: Bibliothèque Nationale de France.

Marie Antoinette as a harpy (n.d.). Photo: Bibliothèque Nationale de France.

En montant à l'Echaffaud. Antoinette marcha par mégarde sur le pied de l'Exécuteur des Jugemens ; elle se retourna vers lui en lui disant, Monsieur, je vous demande Excuse, je ne l'ai pas fait exprès.

La Veuve Capet à la guillotine from *Les Révolutions de Paris*, no. 212 (1793).
Photo: Lynn Hunt.

94. Versailles — Trianon — Temple de l'Amour

The Temple d'Amour, near the Petit Trianon, Versailles, visited by Stephen Gordon in Radclyffe Hall's *The Well of Loneliness* (Garden City, N.Y.: Sun Dial Press, 1928). Photo: Stanford University Libraries.

W. Llewellyn, Portrait of Charlotte Anne Moberley, 1889. Reproduced with the kind permission of the Principal and Fellows of St. Hugh's College, Oxford.

1. CHARLOTTE ANNE ELIZABETH MOBERLY
from a painting by W. Llewellyn, 1889
St. Hugh's College, Oxford

Eleanor Frances Jourdain (c. 1912). Photo: Stanford University Libraries.

MᵐᵉDE LAMBALLE.

Marie Thérèse, princesse
de Lamballe. From
Adolphe Thiers, *Histoire
de la Révolution française*
(Paris: Furne, 1839).
Photo: University of
Michigan Libraries.

T. Johannot inv.   Pelée sc.

MORT DE MADAME DE LAMBALLE.

The death of the princesse de Lamballe, 1792. From Adolphe Thiers,
Histoire de la Révolution française (Paris: Furne, 1839). Photo: University
of Michigan Libraries.

Marie-Antoinette and Yolande de Polignac. From the lesbian periodical *The Ladder* (c. 1950s). Photo: Stanford University Libraries.

Eighteenth-century-themed cover of *The Well of Loneliness* by Radclyffe Hall (New York: Pocket Books/Simon and Schuster, 1974). Reprinted by permission of Pocket Books, an imprint of Simon and Schuster Adult Publishing Group.

SISTERS!

presents a

Benefit Lesbian Dance

for

The Lesbian Herstory Archives

Sunday, Jan. 20, 1991 • 5pm-10pm • Admission $10

Prizes for the most butch, femme, pc, pi, androgynous and heaviest leather

The Lesbian & Gay Community Services Center, 208 W. 13th St., NYC

"Marie-Antoinette" advertisement from *Outweek* (1991).

Italian postcard of Norma Shearer as Marie-Antoinette in *Marie-Antoinette*. Private collection.

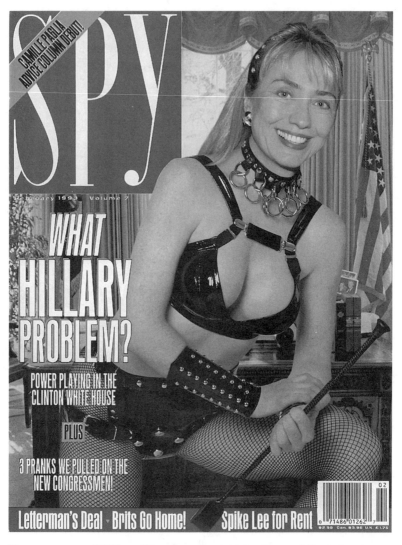

Photomontage of Hillary Clinton as dominatrix. Cover of *Spy* magazine (February 1993). Photo: Carolyn Jones. Paintbox composition: John Millo, FCL/Colorspace. Photo (Oval Office): UPI/Bettman.

Pass as a Woman, Act Like a Man: Marie-Antoinette as Tribade in the Pornography of the French Revolution

Elizabeth Colwill

The Court lost no time going à la mode;
Every woman turned both tribade and slut:
No children were born; it was easier that way:
A libertine finger took the place of the prick.[1]

The pamphlet in which these words appeared, suggestively entitled *The Uterine Furors of Marie-Antoinette,* was typical of an eighteenth-century pornographic genre that highlighted Marie-Antoinette's voracious sexual appetites, including her purported taste for women. The sexual proclivities of the Austrian princess, married to the French dauphin in 1770, had become the subject of rumor even prior to Louis' succession to the French throne in 1774. But the queen's allegedly polymorphous sexuality took on legendary proportions during the French Revolution. At that time, anonymous authors with a variety of political agendas turned their efforts to creating pamphlets with titles like *The Royal Dildo* or *National Bordello Under the Auspices of the Queen.*[2] The charge that the queen was a tribade—a common term in the early modern period for women who had sex with other women—was never the only sexual transgression cited in the pornographic pamphlets. One pamphleteer specified, for example, that "incest, adultery, the most sordid and shameful lubricity," as well as the "reversal of the sacred order of Nature were games for this lewd Messalina."[3] Pornographic pamphlets depicted the queen with an unusual range of sexual partners and in an imaginative array of sexual postures. Yet tribadism made a frequent appearance, and not just as the appetizer to a solid main course of heterosexual sex.[4]

The mythology surrounding Marie-Antoinette's sexuality has proven remarkably long-lived. Terry Castle has found in the queen a "code figure for female homoeroticism in the nineteenth century, even a kind of protolesbian heroine" for women who invoked her memory to affirm their own sexuality.[5] Heterosexual versions of this particular lesbian romance have persisted into the late twentieth century. The contemporary market for the French queen—whether packaged as a paper doll, staged in a comic strip, or used as a model for a white nightshirt ("What Marie-Antoinette wore to bed—she yearned for innocence")—suggests the current commodity value of our various Marie-Antoinette fantasies. Allen Kurzweil reports that in novelty stores, "Halloween masks bearing her high brow and blue eyes often outsell Catwoman and Nancy Reagan." Even Madonna has gotten into the act, dressing (or, more to the point, undressing) as the eighteenth-century queen.[6] Today, however, our students are more familiar with Marie-Antoinette's apocryphal pronouncement of aristocratic disdain, "Let them eat cake," than with her supposed lesbian loves. Yet none of us can separate this message about class from the queen's embodied—gendered and sexed—self. The Marie-Antoinette in our mind's eye, whether the object of nostalgia or of prurient scrutiny, simultaneously represents sexual, social, and political privilege, and sexuality continues to serve more broadly as a surreptitious way to constitute social difference.

Historians have not been immune to this public fascination with the queen. Important new scholarship has greatly increased our understanding of the political implications of the pornography that featured Marie-Antoinette, thereby fundamentally transforming our understanding of the sexual politics and the political culture of the Revolution.[7] But I will argue here that the figure of Marie-Antoinette-as-tribade belongs as much to a history of sexuality as it does to a history of revolutionary politics. Like the "lesbian" today, the "tribade" in the eighteenth century served as a flash point in debates about nature, rights, and sexual difference that remain as contested for us as they were for Edmund Burke or the marquis de Sade. What, then, if we were to turn our attention from the political significance of the queen's alleged taste for women, to the shifting meanings of the tribade in the eighteenth century? What if we were to read the pamphlets directed against Marie-Antoinette within a history of lesbianism?

Debating Sexual Difference

In some ways, reading Revolutionary pornography within this context necessarily complicates the historian's task. Given the instability of the language used to describe sexual relationships between women and the silences surrounding them in the available sources, the writing of lesbian history is fraught with challenges. Historians have located evidence of lesbian desire in every century, but the meanings of that desire vary according to historically determined conceptions of the desiring subject, gender difference, and sex itself.[8]

Uncovering the meanings of the Revolutionary pamphlets about Marie-Antoinette is particularly difficult. We know little about the social origins and political allegiances of authors and engravers, since most failed to sign their pornographic work. Just as troubling, it is virtually impossible to chart patterns of readership definitively. Like any other text, the pamphlets do not directly reflect the social landscape they purport to describe, and their content—exaggerated, parodic, ironic—further complicates their status as historical evidence. The accusations of tribadism tell us nothing about how women identified themselves or felt about one another, much less what they really did in bed. There is no way to know, after reading the pamphlets, whether Marie-Antoinette's alleged taste for women represented a response to an emergent lesbian subculture or whether the tribade in the pamphlets carried a primarily symbolic message in an era of intense political unrest. The pamphlets do, however, indicate concerns about the nature of the sexual order that mark a transitional moment in debates over sexuality in the eighteenth century.

The eighteenth century was the site of sexual as well as political upheaval. Indeed, the meanings of the tribade as a symbol actually derived from its status as an intervention in debates over political order and the parameters of sexual difference. The tribade of Revolutionary pornography was a key figure in a struggle that dated back to the ancients among medical, religious, and legal models of sexual commensurability versus sexual difference. Thomas Laqueur has argued that over the course of the eighteenth century, the sexes, once distributed along a natural continuum of man, hermaphrodite, and woman, came to be divided neatly into two complementary but fundamentally distinct beings: male and female.[9] Katharine Park and Robert Nye have challenged both the timing and the nature of this transition, throwing into question the very existence of the one-sex model. These debates are relevant to our analysis of the pornographic pamphlets at issue here, because the Revolutionary epoch was itself the site of competing models of sexual difference. Older models of difference, indebted in varying degrees to Galenic and Aristotelian traditions, were transformed as an older "metaphysical language" based on analogical thinking about sexual difference gradually gave way to a "biologistic and medicalizing terminology."[10]

The various models of sexual difference had important implications for gender identity and for the very meaning of the "nature" of man and woman. In early modern France, woman appeared in the writings of theologians and jurists in the image of Eve: sinful, unstable, and eager to escape her subordinate position. By the nineteenth century, however, educated elites had posited an identity between man's law and woman's nature, more frequently defined as constitutionally weak, sexually passive, and morally exemplary. Woman's weakness, once conceived as her susceptibility to pride and ambition—to wit, her propensity to make pacts with the Devil—appeared in subsequent centuries as neurasthenia or simple debility. Her strength, in contrast, came to reside in maternal love, for which doctors would construct ever more precise physiological bases.[11] This slow and uneven shift toward a sexual science compatible with Rousseauian ideals of complementarity also had important repercussions for sexual identity in the Revolutionary epoch.

A sex/gender system that polarized the bodies and natures of men and women on separate axes and assumed an exclusive attraction of each sex to its opposite would generate new barriers to the sexualities imaginable, though illegal, in the early modern period.[12] Randolph Trumbach has argued that by the end of the eighteenth century, a model based not only on two sexes (male and female) but also on four genders (man, woman, sodomite, and tribade) dominated much of the Western world. As physicians, philosophes, and moralists increasingly identified sexual practice with a gender identity rooted and naturalized in biological sex, sodomy came to represent a lifelong sexual nature rather than an occasional sexual act. By the early eighteenth century, Trumbach found, the British male libertine had to forego his boys and cleave only to women or else risk the stigma of belonging to a "third gender." The emergence of a "fourth gender" role for female "sodomites," he suggested, occurred between 1750 and 1840 as an earlier bisexual type was gradually supplanted by a more modern lesbian role for women who were attracted exclusively to other women and who adopted some elements of "masculine" behavior or dress.[13]

In France those whose sexual practice of gender identity failed to conform to their sex increasingly became the subject of gossip in the years prior to the Revolution.[14] Consider the case of the chevalier d'Eon, an aristocrat, soldier, and spy for the French government who passed as a woman passing as a man for half of his life. Forced by Louis XVI to dress in a manner that conformed to "her" (assumed) sex, d'Eon provides a dramatic example of increasing concern with gender boundaries in the final decades of the century. In 1777, the *Mémoires secrets* chided d'Eon for his "poor taste" in dressing alternately as a woman and as a man, when "all things conspired to confirm that his true sex is female."[15] As Jeffrey Merrick has discussed, scandal sheets and gossip columns exploited the symbolic uses of sex as they projected the image of French society ravaged by the "unnatural" sexual practices of degenerate aristocrats. Eighteenth-century physicians took new interest in female sexuality and its "aberrations," while prerevolutionary pamphlets confirmed the public rumors circulating about Marie-Antoinette's "favorite," and fashionable, "vice."[16]

As I will show, Marie-Antoinette occupies a liminal position in the debates over sexuality, for in the Revolutionary pamphlets, the nymphomaniacal queen appears both frighteningly feminine and threateningly virile. If her sexual polymorphism and feminine dress locate her within an earlier tradition of bisexual attraction, her masculinized behavior and sexual tastes sound more like the modern sapphist whom Trumbach identifies in late-eighteenth-century England.[17] Unlike the female soldiers and sailors of the early modern period who passed as men and sometimes married women, Marie-Antoinette passes as a woman in the pornographic pamphlets but acts like a man. My intention in this essay is not to fix Marie-Antoinette on one side or the other of the early-modern/modern divide, but rather to demonstrate that Marie-Antoinette-as-tribade, like representations of sodomitical clerics and courtiers, could have been read in many different ways, precisely because there was no eighteenth-century consensus on the "natural" boundaries of sex.

Eighteenth-century law and public opinion remained deeply intolerant of "unnatural" acts, whether insubordination within marriage, masturbation, or sodomy. Nonetheless, a range of evidence, from the emergence of a male subculture of "pederasts" identified by Michel Rey to the philosophes' subversion of clerical and absolutist culture analyzed by Bryant Ragan, suggests considerable controversy in the eighteenth century over the boundaries of the natural.[18] The coexistence of several interpretive paradigms for comprehending sexual difference authorized numerous, and in some cases contradictory, interpretations of Marie-Antoinette-as-tribade.

This essay places the "invention" of Marie-Antoinette's sex/uality in the context of late-eighteenth-century debates over the nature of sexual difference and explores the ways in which competing bodies of knowledge about gender and sex informed readings of Marie-Antoinette-as-tribade. I argue that Revolutionary pornographers did not merely reflect existing political, legal, and medical knowledge. They helped to reconfigure the terrain of sexual difference, and ultimately the possibilities of sexual identity, in the late eighteenth century. As pamphleteers evoked the image of Marie-Antoinette being sodomized with a dildo or flaunting a suspiciously male appendage, they intervened in debates about sex and status that would circumscribe the boundaries of what came to be defined as normalcy in the modern era.

Sexual Posturing

What was revolutionary about the pornography produced during the Revolution? At first glance, many of the charges directed against Marie-Antoinette and her "female favorites" appear tiresomely familiar. One can find denunciations of the "sultanate of women" in the sixteenth-century Ottoman Empire, disorderly wives in the rhetoric of John Knox, and women on top in carnival festivities.[19] In early modern Europe, critics of royal despotism excoriated wives and mistresses for exploiting their husbands' political influence. The tradition lives on, as political commentators pilloried First Lady Hillary Clinton for stepping beyond the confines of her appointed role.[20]

Nonetheless, Marie-Antoinette's rumored tribadism had historically specific political implications. Consider her final (fictive) testimony in *The Confession of Marie-Antoinette*: "People!" she protests, "because I ceded to the sweet impressions of nature, and in imitating the charming weaknesses of all the women of the court of France, I surrendered to the sweet impulsion of love . . . you hold me, as it were, captive within your walls?" As proof of the "excellence" of her character, she generously provides details of her amorous liaisons. Her husband's "incapacity in the venereal act" and the vital heat of her temperament forced her to turn for sexual satisfaction to the comte d'Artois, then Cardinal de Rohan, but even these efforts could not slake her sexual thirst. "Fucking was such a great need for me that I was forced to take into my service la Jule [sic] de Polignac, the most lascivious, libertine, intriguing, ostentatious woman who ever existed." Marie-Antoinette then specifies precisely what made sex with women so appealing: "Adroit in the art of stimulating the clitoris," La Polignac's attentions produced "one of those rare pleasures that cannot be used up, because it can be repeated as many times as one likes." Indeed, the queen exults, "I made such good use of this pleasure with her that it was well worth my time."[21] Although queens, regents, and royal mistresses had often been targets of vituperation, figuring prominently in sexual scandal literature, only Marie-Antoinette was tried and roundly convicted in the press as a tribade.

Equally significant was the historical juncture at which these charges appeared.[22] Rumors about Marie-Antoinette's sexuality took shape not merely at the site of a political revolution, but, more generally, within a nexus of eighteenth-century revolutions—commercial, cultural, and sexual. By the time the Revolution abolished the absolutist apparatus of royal censors, printers' guilds, and authorial privileges, journalists and publishers were already poised to profit from the opportunities offered by a newly liberated market.[23] The relatively low cost of pamphlets and the earlier proliferation of *cabinets de lecture* that provided reading materials for an annual fee, as well as booklenders' stalls that rented pamphlets by the hour, placed political pamphlets within the reach of Parisian artisanal classes as well as elites. What was revolutionary about the charges of the queen's sexual deviance was, in part, their growing audience and their potential for political mobilization.[24]

Furthermore, the charge that the queen was a tribade appeared in a literary genre—pornography—that was itself in transition. The Revolution, which constituted a turning point in the relationship of politics, pornography, and philosophy, stood at the threshold of the "ghettoization of pornography" in the modern era.[25] Early modern

French law recognized no firm distinction between "philosophic" and "licentious" books. Royal censors, concerned primarily with the maintenance of public order, confiscated politically subversive material, whether erotic or not.[26] As Lynn Hunt has argued, only after the Revolution did pornography emerge as a distinct genre. Shorn of its former connection to a subversive materialist philosophy, pornography was thereafter "devoted almost exclusively to the depiction of sexual pleasure as an end in itself."[27] Paradoxically, the increasing bifurcation of public and private in the nineteenth century helped to construct pornography as a private and therefore apolitical affair, an issue of sex rather than power, even as the state extended its regulation of the expanding industries of prostitution and pornography, and as the mass market for pornography generated fortunes for its producers. Pornography, feminist scholars have argued, is never innocent of relations of power, and is therefore always political in the broad sense of the term. But prior to an era that veiled pornography, like sexuality, under the mantle of privacy, pornography explicitly bespoke sexual politics.[28]

Both the structure and the content of the pornography at issue here differed from its predecessors. Although it drew on earlier forms of libertine literature that dated from the Renaissance, political pornography in late-eighteenth-century France was concerned less with arousal than with defining political through sexual order. The structure of many pamphlets—satires about the coupling of the "ferocious beast" that populated the court, songs that satirized Renaissance verse, confessions of sexual crimes interspersed with edifying political disquisitions—diluted the erotic potential of graphic sex. The following episode from the Diamond Necklace Affair, in which Cardinal de Rohan was implicated in a secret sale of jewels to the queen, transformed high political drama into sexual farce:

> When Rohan found himself shut up
> In this Bastille,
> With his eyes half shut,
> Did the bastard get it up?
> Like an idiot, the bloody fool would say:
> Fucking a cunt gets me locked away!
> But a fine, fine, fine,
> But a cunt, cunt, cunt,
> But a fine,
> But a cunt,
> But a queenly cunt,
> Is well worth the slammer.[29]

Even pamphlets with a cohesive narrative structure were most often presented in a parodic form more conducive to laughter than to lust. Some employed a vocabulary of excess to emphasize the degree to which Revolutionary France had succumbed to vice. In a parody of the Revolutionary faith in the laws of nature and science, the *Enfans de Sodome à l'Assemblée* [*Children of Sodom at the National Assembly*] applaud the triumphal announcement of the duc de Noailles that "*l'anti-physique,* derisively called 'buggery' by its detractors and 'bestiality' by the jurisconsults, will in the future be a science, known and taught in all the classes of society."[30]

If the body, as Nancy Armstrong has argued, functions as an "image or sign we use to understand social relationships," Revolutionary pornographers reconfigured the social order through a hierarchy of sexual partners and postures.[31] Unlike the materialists' models of pornography described by Margaret Jacob, in which bodies were interchangeable, the pornography of the Revolution specified precisely which bodies were doing what. Pornography worked by defining the distinct sexual tastes and practices of groups identified by title, political allegiance, or corporate loyalties. Male bisexuality, for instance, served in some pamphlets as visible proof of the illegitimate exercise of power by aristocrats, clerics, kings.[32] If, reasoned a fictitious marquis de Villette in *Les Petits bougres au manège* [*The Little Buggers at Riding School*], nature's "most precious gift" was the "ability to get it up, to fuck, and to come," and if, according to the rights of liberty and property "my balls belong to me," it followed that whether "I place them in a cunt or an ass, no one has the right to protest."[33] The particular crimes of prominent individuals often highlighted the depravity of the group as a whole. In *Le Bordel apostolique* [*The Apostolic Bordello*], Cardinals de Rohan and Bernis, heterosexual in their youth, turn to sodomitical pleasures in their "less vigorous" but ever libertine old age.[34] Some pamphleteers targeted both groups and prominent individuals. Consider the polymorphous perversity of the marquis, baron, and bishop who await Marie-Antoinette's favors in *The Royal Bordello,* and "bugger each other while awaiting their turn."[35]

Reading relations of power from physical postures is difficult precisely because ongoing debates over sexuality, not to mention different pamphlets, invested the same sexual act with different meanings. The strictures against sodomy in the early modern period applied to nonvaginal penetration of any kind, though in practice the juridical consequences of marital, bestial, and same-sex sodomy often differed dramatically. By the second half of the eighteenth century, I would argue, same-sex eroticism had begun to serve as the focal point of social anxieties formerly invested in a broader definition of sodomy. In 1762, Soulatges, a lawyer in Toulouse, defined the "sin against nature" as the "crime of someone who has immodest commerce with a person of his or her sex; it is committed," he specified, "by a man with another man or by a woman with another woman; of all the crimes against chastity, this is one of the most serious and most detestable according to divine and human law."[36] During the Revolution proper, as Lynn Hunt has shown, revolutionaries defined patriotic asceticism and homosocial bonds against the negative example of homoeroticism.[37] Pornographic pamphlets support this interpretation. Anal heterosexual intercourse (formally defined as sodomy) is conspicuously absent in most Revolutionary pamphlets that feature Marie-Antoinette, while same-sex coupling, both male and female, often takes center stage. The penal code adopted in 1791 by the Constituent Assembly remained silent on sodomy, thus freeing individuals, at least in theory, to dispose of their bodies as they chose.[38] The change, however, bespoke something less than simple liberation. Pamphleteers continued to denounce the "crime against nature," while the mechanism for policing same-sex desire shifted, if temporarily, from the courts to the province of public shame and self-control.

Despite fluctuations in the legal and moral status of various sexual practices, the hierarchy of sexual postures in the pornographic pamphlets followed a certain logic. Heterosexual sex held more status than same-sex coupling, and the "masculine" position ranked higher than the "feminine." Male/male sodomy was transgressive—either corrupt or despicable, depending on whether the man assumed a "masculine" or "feminine" position—while female same-sex sodomy signaled the double transgression of abandoning man and assuming his sexual prerogatives.

Pamphleteers from all points on the political spectrum used the charge of sodomy to discredit political opponents. In *Les Petits bougres au manège*, the fictitious marquis de Villette parodies the "Rights of Man" as the "Rights of Buggers" on the grounds that "female fuckers don't have the exclusive right to make [men] come."[39] As manhood came to connote freedom from all relations of dependence, representations of the rape of male counterrevolutionaries affirmed the natural rights of the Revolutionary men on top.[40] Heterosexual men mastered others in acts of homosexual rape, and even sodomites placed higher than the tribade on the sexual hierarchy if they assumed the "masculine" position. Men jockeyed for position by stigmatizing their enemies as powerless cuckolds and as "feminine" partners in same-sex liaisons. Those who played that feminine role were often accused of impotence. Indeed, the lowest rung was reserved for the impotent man, most notably the king himself. In the Revolutionary pamphlets, no lubricious strategy ever succeeded in reviving the "royal jewels" of Louis XVI.[41] Those of more plebeian stature were similarly subjected to withering scrutiny. In the "royal whorehouse," Marat, insufficiently endowed for any masculine role, is relegated to the lowliest position of servicing women as a "cunt-licker."[42] Conversely, astride a man, woman, or beast, a woman on top spelled disorder.

No woman spelled disorder more flamboyantly than Marie-Antoinette. Pamphleteers accused the queen of relations of debauchery with "all the tribades of Paris."[43] The comtesse de Polignac and the princesse de Lamballe, Marie-Antoinette's "female favorites," were the "tribades," other than the queen herself, who received the most public exposure. Suspicions about the nature of the queen's relationship with her female intimates first circulated in conjunction with rumors about the king's impotence when the royal couple took more than a decade to produce a male heir. As early as February 1770, the *Mémoires secrets* informed its readership of the appearance of "execrable couplets," read (avidly) although "detested by all good Frenchmen," which condemned Marie-Antoinette's illicit relationship with the princesse de Lamballe.[44] Jacques Revel has suggested that Marie-Antoinette's taste for privacy may have fueled the early rumors about sexual indiscretions. These rumors then assumed their own momentum through a process of cross-referencing by which the truth of the accusation was proven with references to other pamphlets. In the years before the Revolution, the queen's "dazzling" patronage of public women such as Mlle Arnould of the Opéra and Mlle de Raucourt of the Comédie Française reciprocally confirmed their (bad) reputations. Even the renowned artist Vigée-Lebrun came under sexual suspicion, Mary Sheriff has shown, after painting Marie-Antoinette scandalously *en chemise*.[45]

Given this prerevolutionary history of rumor and innuendo, it is not surprising that the Revolution provided a catalyst for an explosion of venom against aristocratic tribades. Some pamphleteers, particularly in the opening years of the Revolution, deflected the blame from the queen to her favorites. The charge that the queen's female consorts had betrayed her trust served to reconcile good patriots with the cause of constitutional monarchy. In the work of such pamphleteers, La Polignac, rather than the queen, conspired to drain the blood of the French people, dissolve the National Assembly, and drive the state into debt.[46] As late as 1792, one presumably royalist pamphleteer placed responsibility for the queen's sorry reputation at the feet of the "infamous *débauchée*" Polignac.[47] As Polignac "confessed" in verses entitled "The Grievances of the Fucking Bitch de Polignac, or Regrets on the Loss of the Cocks of France,"

> More than one pretty virgin
> Lying on my bed
> Gave up pricks altogether,
> Chose my lovely hand instead.[48]

Marie-Antoinette's predatory sexuality and immoderate lust for power had long served notice to the good king to put his household and his kingdom in order.[49] As a strategy to accuse their political enemies of treason and discredit the king, pamphleteers drafted long lists of the queen's partners in debauchery.[50] In earlier pamphlets Marie-Antoinette's friends were often guilty of the "base seduction of the queen," but the queen assumed ever more active and varied sexual postures as the Revolution radicalized.[51] "Ah buggeress!" she exclaims after a particularly satisfying interlude with Lamballe in a long *journée amoureuse*, "how expert you are in the art of amusing your sex."[52] By 1792, when the monarchy was overthrown, the queen's undifferentiated lusts amply demonstrated that majesty was utterly incompatible with Revolutionary virtue.

In some respects, then, representations of women's sexuality in the pamphlet literature of the Revolutionary period differed sharply from those in earlier pornographic narratives. Unlike the Renaissance pornography that celebrated sexual expression, the depiction of Marie-Antoinette as tribade during the Revolution warned *citoyens* and *citoyennes* to police the "natural" boundaries of desire. Unlike the self-confident and sexually polymorphous female libertines in eighteenth-century French pornography analyzed by Kathryn Norberg, Marie-Antoinette "confesses" to her perversion, thereby providing a rationale for her execution.[53] Like the pornographic fiction of the Enlightenment, the pornographic pamphlets of the Revolution were philosophically, politically, and sexually subversive. Unlike their antecedents, Revolutionary pamphlets explicitly replaced a social hierarchy of orders with a new "natural" order from which would develop both unprecedented experiments with democracy and legal/scientific systems of classification that would circumscribe public expressions of desire in the modern era.

The work of the marquis de Sade, particularly the novels written in the late 1780s and 1790s, exemplifies the complexity of the pornography of the Revolutionary epoch. On one hand, Sade wrote from within the prerevolutionary tradition of the lettered and philosophic libertine. The cohesive narrative structure of *Juliette* (1797) or *Justine* (1791), like that of *Thérèse philosophe,* made for the kind of eighteenth-century novel designed to be "read with only one hand."[54] On the other hand, Sade's sexual scripts, in Lynn Hunt's illuminating reading, stage the contradictions within Revolutionary ideology, carrying the republican family romance to the point of the absurd. As she demonstrates, the literary tropes and "parodic philosophizing" in *La Philosophie dans le boudoir* (1795) frequently mimic the Marie-Antoinette pamphlets.[55] The same is true of Sade's explicit evocations of mind- (and body-) bending sexual postures in *Juliette*, his obsession with the size and status of participants in the orgies in *Les Infortunes de la vertu* (1787), and the sheer violence of his sexual choreography in *Les Cent-vingt journées de Sodome* (1785), all of which echo central themes of the pamphlets at issue here.

But his work carried a different "revolutionary" punch. Whatever his professions of Revolutionary fervor, Sade remained an aristocrat invested in caste privilege and imprisoned by it, as cynical about liberty, equality, and fraternity as he was about the lettres de cachet that had sealed his fate.[56] His novels assimilated the egalitarian mechanism of Enlightenment pornography and the Revolutionary postures of the Marie-Antoinette pamphlets only to enlist them in the service of a modern disciplinary regime, elaborating what Pamela Cheek has aptly described as new "techniques for producing information" from the body. As he selected sexual subjects, measured genitals, produced sexual acts, and quantified their effects, this apostle of modernity extended an alliance between sexual arousal, scientific detachment, and political control that has provided a central paradigm for the pornographic imagination in the modern era.[57]

The tribade played a leading role in Sade's prose, as she did in the pamphlets directed against Marie-Antoinette. Her body—unnaturally virile yet terrifyingly feminine, changeable in both form and desire—stood for the illegitimacy of the ancien régime and the instability of the sex/gender system in the age of revolution. Yet the charge of tribadism was directed explicitly against a limited number of targets. The Jacobin press convicted Mme Roland of abandoning the proper feminine roles, but not the appropriate sexual postures. Olympe de Gouges was excoriated as a *femme-homme,* but not explicitly as a tribade. Even Marat's murderer, Charlotte Corday, denounced as a hermaphrodite, was not accused of sleeping with women.[58] La Polignac's public and insatiable lust for men and women, on the contrary, marked her as an archetypal *fille publique.*[59] The princesse de Lamballe's murder and rumored genital mutilation during the September Massacres served as retribution for the "unnatural" practices publicized in the pamphlets.[60] It appears, then, that given the absence of a modern lesbian subculture and the long association of aristocracy and sexual license, charges of tribadism during the Revolution proper were directed primarily at titled women.

Yet any woman whose public action brought her to the attention of her political opponents could find herself numbered among the accused. Théroigne de Méricourt, revolutionary proponent of rights for women, stars in *The National Bordello* in an unlikely nymphomaniacal partnership with Marie-Antoinette.[61] As Mary Sheriff has argued, the public easily conflated the activities of the *femme-homme* (a woman who encroaches on man's social roles) with those of the tribade (a woman who assumes a man's sexual desires). The actress, whose very profession signaled artifice, and the aristocrat, who practiced dissimulation, were subject to the same representational strategies that convicted the prostitute as an expert in deception. When political faultlines shifted, the artist, the activist, and the actress, like the aristocrat, could slip easily into the category of *femme publique,* linked in the public imagination with the tribade.[62]

> Fuckers from all ranks, source of your delights,
> Satisfied your tastes in offering you their nights.
> Limitless in your desires, your heart too libertine.
> Rendered you, in turn, a whore and tribade queen.[63]

As this quotation suggests, neither the Revolution nor pornography fits easily under the heading "liberating" or "oppressive." The charge of tribadism, issued under the banner of liberty, equality, and fraternity, leveled distinctions between orders as it severed elite women from former positions of influence.[64] It also fostered the very images of domestic womanhood that the Convention would soon turn against women's political clubs, and that would by the nineteenth century emerge in the purportedly universal guise of bourgeois domesticity. Pornography that explicitly targeted aristocratic women as tribades contributed tangibly to the Revolution, which legalized divorce, abolished primogeniture, and decriminalized sodomy, yet implicitly censured all women who encroached on the male political prerogative.[65] Marie-Antoinette's "passion for incest, filthy pleasures, and hatred for the French" in conjunction with her "aversion for the duties of wife and mother" marked her as an unnatural woman.[66] When pamphleteers juxtaposed the immoral conduct of "titled" (sapphic) women to the "modest virtue" of the (heterosexual) *bourgeoise,* they conflated the unfeminine, the immoral, and the unnatural in the figure of the tribade.[67] The disgust frequently expressed for the person of the queen—variously described as "ugly, wrinkled, worn-out, faded, hideous, frightful"—helped to redefine the parameters of royal power.[68] But to reshape the political in the vocabulary of sex was also to remake the sexual order.

The Tribade in Revolutionary Context

The figure of the tribade, ambivalently gendered and sexed and unnaturally privileged, collapsed political into sexual order in a manner that altered the boundaries of sexual difference. It did so in complicated ways. When it came to the sexual voraciousness of Marie-Antoinette and her female favorites, Revolutionary pornographers quite agreed. The multiplication of the sexual offenses imputed to the "Austrian bitch in heat, baring her ass to all comers," served to magnify political disorder and to highlight the virtues of heterosexual monogamy.[69] Yet the pamphleteers presented diverse, even contradictory, messages about the tribade. Some intimated that the tribade queen, like earlier "passing women," possessed a hermaphroditic body. Others maintained that her character, not her enlarged clitoris, was responsible for her deviant sexual tastes. While one author suggested that a woman's "pretty finger" could permanently supplant the penis, the next portrayed Marie-Antoinette swearing that "one prick alone is worth a scepter."[70] Individual pamphleteers wrote their own distinct visions of sexual and social relations into their pamphlets. The contradictory narratives in Revolutionary pornography suggest the extent to which sexual difference remained contested terrain in Revolutionary France.

Precisely because sexuality was the subject of such heated debate, Marie-Antoinette was susceptible to contradictory readings that reflected not only an allegiance to court or Convention, but also the reader's position in debates over the nature of tribadism itself. Readers who believed that nymphomania was the feminine norm and those who interpreted women's "excessive" desires as pathological, like readers who attributed Marie-Antoinette's tribadism to physical deformity and those who associated it with moral corruption, would have found images that reinforced their own positions in the pamphlets. For those familiar with the scandal sheets of the ancien régime, the pamphlets confirmed prerevolutionary rumors that the theatrical license assumed by aristocrats and actresses included a taste for women.[71] Followers of Rousseau could have used representations of incestuous and sodomitical, thus sterile, sexual practices as proof of the self-absorption of the female aristocracy, whose attraction to luxury, debauchery, and self-display stifled the maternal impulse natural to woman.

The boudoir of Madame de Polignac, for instance, is a "temple of libertinage" where a hall of mirrors magnifies obscenity to spectacular proportions. Although female anatomy is ill-equipped to satisfy the excessive transports of Polignac's sexual imagination, she claims that she can always take pleasure [*jouir*] in appearances. In an ongoing masquerade in which debauchery and dissimulation reign, nymphomania substitutes for maternity.[72] The charge of tribadism, then, ironically confirmed eighteenth-century pronatalists' concerns about a declining population and social disorder.[73] "If one day men abandon us," Marie-Antoinette confides to the princesse de Lamballe, "we know how to replace them."[74]

The wide range of possible resonances of the images in the pamphlets provides a key to their rapid proliferation during the Revolution. Marie-Antoinette-as-tribade was perversely appealing precisely because she violated the codes governing female sexuality in both the early modern and the modern periods. French law had long recognized female sodomy as a capital crime, as an aberrant practice that originated, it was once assumed, in an enlarged clitoris. But the few legal cases that historians have unearthed suggest that authorities defined the crime of female sodomy restrictively and punished transgressions infrequently.[75] The vital, if still fragmentary, work that has been done on the history of sexual relations between women in the early modern period demonstrates that European courts were far less concerned with women's transgressions than men's, a record consistent, as Judith Brown points out, with the phallocratic assumption that a woman's desire required satisfaction by a man. Terry Castle has rightly cautioned that a state's failure to prosecute female same-sex relationships aggressively should not be read as approval. Nonetheless, as other scholars have suggested, sexual relations between women appeared to pose a direct threat to patriarchal structures of church and state only when they were publicly flaunted and involved penetration.[76]

In the pornographic pamphlets of the Revolution, however, Marie-Antoinette poses exactly this threat. Her taste for women, while not exclusive, is publicly displayed and therefore, by definition, a public menace. Herein lies a key to the obsession with publicity in the sexual scripts. By rendering the queen's sex public, both in the sense of staging her sexuality for an audience and in casting her as an aggressive tribade, the pamphleteers placed her in a role that directly contravened older legal, ethical, and religious injunctions governing female sexuality.

The public nature of the queen's tribadism also provides a key to pamphleteers' preoccupation with both male and female specularity. The aristocratic women locked in amorous embrace on the frontispiece of *Les Bordels de Paris* are exposed to the reader, their transgressions magnified by a female voyeur who exposes her own sex in turn.[77] *La Boudoir de madame la Duchesse de P . . .* gives such techniques of sexual surveillance an autoerotic dimension. Since nature cursed women with nymphomaniacal desires without the appendage necessary to satisfy them, La Polignac here finds satisfaction only when gazing into mirrors that magnify the "lasciviousness of her mouth," and her own sexual "agitations," in the arms of her Adonis or her incubi.[78]

The sodomitical penetration narrated by the pornographers also breached the "natural" boundaries of female sexuality associated with the early modern period. When readers discovered that the queen had assumed a man's sexual prerogatives, they captured her in a criminal act that in former times could have earned the scaffold or the stake.[79] At a summit of pleasure in *La Journée amoureuse,* the queen is simultaneously masturbated and sodomized with an ivory dildo wielded by the princesse de Lamballe.[80] The implications of this doubly sodomitical act within early modern legal and religious paradigms would have been difficult to miss.

La Chasse aux bêtes puantes et féroces spelled out the mortal consequences of female sodomy. Although the *masters of the hunt* offer bounties for "ferocious beasts" who have "ravaged" kingdom, court, and capital, the she-wolf of Barbaria (La Polignac) achieves a special distinction. Having coupled "by a monstrous caprice of nature" with the Tiger (the comte d'Artois) and the Panther (Marie-Antoinette), as well as with a prodigious quantity of animals of different species, La Polignac is convicted on two counts of sodomy (bestiality and tribadism). The death penalty follows as a "logical" consequence: "twenty thousand livres for the one who kills her." Similarly, while many prominent members of the court figure on the *Liste des proscrits de la Nation*, La Polignac is most severely punished, for she has dared to act as a man. While the archbishop of Paris is banished to the kitchen, Polignac is "brought back to Paris to be hung and strangled until dead, and her body carried to the forked gibbet of Montfaucon."[81]

Like Marie-Antoinette, La Polignac violates modern, as well as early modern, norms that regulated women's sexuality. However unsavory the separate sins of Polignac, convicted by the pamphleteers for feminine dissimulation and sapphic practices, it is the polymorphous nature of her sexuality—or of her sex—that condemns her to "perpetual banishment." "Tribade, to satiate the fury of her temperament," she nonetheless takes her pleasure in the arms of any man who will "fill her coffers."[82] Sandwiched between a man and woman, this "modern Sappho" simulates, through the use of two orifices, the "delicious sensations that each spouse feels in the conjugal union." Tormented by nymphomania, she chastises nature: "Oh! that nature behaved shabbily in our regard by giving us such weak instruments of pleasure." Cheated of both a superior male anatomy and male lovers as "furious" as herself, she falls back upon the considerable resources of her imagination. In *La Boudoir de madame la duchesse de P . . .* her unnatural ambition extends to the antisocial desire to possess both male and female sexual organs, with which she could satisfy her own lust. In this exceptional pamphlet, La Polignac takes the fantasy of sexual polymorphism to its outrageous outer limits. Her fantasized body, independently capable of multiple sodomitical acts, represents a nightmarish perversion of Revolutionary fraternity.[83]

Although La Polignac took center stage in this particular porno-graphic drama, Marie-Antoinette more frequently assumed the starring role. Pamphleteers typically converted Marie-Antoinette's royal privilege into an anomalous sexual status. Both excessively feminine—sexual, dangerous, and dissimulating—and threateningly virile, Marie-Antoinette combined the transgressions of both, or all sexes within a single body. On one hand, in *Les Derniers soupirs de la garce en pleurs*, [*The Last Sighs of the Bitch in Tears*] the "frightful whore" is reduced to a repulsive feminine essence complete with sagging breasts, disease-ridden womb, and—"what a horrible sight! what a big hole!—a filthy cunt."[84] The violently misogynistic language of this pamphlet would have resonated on a number of levels by the end of the eighteenth century. The "repulsive" structure of the yawning vagina could have recalled the toothed vagina of ancient derivation. The "hideous clitoris" signified the enlarged organ of either the tribade or the hermaphrodite.[85] For some readers the description of the queen's genitals may have called to mind the African "Hottentot apron," or genital elongation, which had long excited the prurient commentaries of European travelers.[86]

However diverse the associations, such readings, on the one hand, highlighted the queen's noxious femininity. On the other hand, in an age when naturalists still debated the efficacy of "female semen" in procreation, such texts also offered the possibility of more sexually ambiguous readings. As a pupil of the abbé Maury in *Le Nouveau Dom Bougre à l'Assemblée nationale*, Marie-Antoinette learns the "way to fuck in the ass, the cunt, the armpits, the tits, the mouth, the hair, and the supple loins."[87] However, the queen is not content to act as the feminine recipient of masculine attentions. Instead of the "colder" metabolism considered natural to woman, Marie-Antoinette exhibits a suspiciously male heat.[88] Pamphleteers use verbs such as *décharger* (to ejaculate) to describe the ebb and flow of the queen's pleasures.[89] Even *Les Derniers soupirs de la garce en pleurs* marks Marie-Antoinette as male when she affirms that the sexual ministries of her "dear Désulland" produces "in my cunt the lively erection / That fills my senses with satisfaction."[90] Insatiably feminine in her taste for *vits roturieurs*, Marie-Antoinette here appears possessed of the hermaphrodite's indeterminate sexual anatomy.

Hermaphrodites in early modern Europe were occasionally able to gain social recognition and even civil rights if they chose a single gender identity on the basis of "which sex prevailed."[91] Unlike the hermaphrodite or the cross-dressing woman, who assumed male prerogatives only with men's clothes, Marie-Antoinette was taken for a woman who took the privileges of man.[92] "Flitting from one pleasure to the next, from one intrigue to the next," she reigned, claimed the pamphleteers, in her husband's name.[93] In refusing a single gender and usurping men's exclusive claim to politics and penetration, she violated the spirit of religious and Salic Law and ancient patriarchal injunctions to wifely submission, as well as more "enlightened" injunctions to domestic virtue and the sanctity of gender boundaries.[94] In no instance was the crime recuperable. The sexuality ascribed to Marie-Antoinette in the pornographic pamphlets stigmatized her as monstrous in her "uterine furors" in an age in which nymphomania could be invoked either as the feminine norm or to explain deviations from women's "natural" passivity.[95] Monstrous, too, was the range of her "odious pleasures," which violated the laws of God, on one hand, and "revolt[ed] love and outrage[d] nature," on the other.[96] Particularly monstrous was her lust for both women and men, a choice comprehensible, though sinful, to the degree that readers assumed that a desire for women did not compromise women's desire for men, but unnatural to the degree that they assumed a world divided into two sexes that should be attracted solely to their opposites. By some accounts, Marie-Antoinette was monstrous even in her biological sex, for, as one of her male partners alleged after a vigorous coupling reported in *La Journée amoureuse*, all was "not as it should be" in the royal *corps*.[97]

To readers familiar with stories such as that of Marie Garnier—who one fine sixteenth-century afternoon jumped a ditch and sprang a penis—the suspicions concerning the royal body could have suggested that the queen was a hermaphrodite, a "monstrous" condition to be sure, but one that had long been the subject of both scientific inquiry and popular interest.[98] After all, according to Galenic tradition, persons were male or female in varying degrees. But such an accusation would have had a different resonance for those skeptical readers who sought the source of sexual "deviance" in the corruption of the mind.[99] Ian Maclean has shown that in medical circles a discontinuous notion of sex difference had displaced Galenic concepts of a "middle spectrum" of sex by the beginning of the seventeenth century. Yet in *La Journée amoureuse*, Marie-Antoinette—

in her gender identity, her sexual practices, and even her sex—occupied precisely this unthinkable middle ground.[100]

While some pamphlets suggested the virile contours of the queen's physique, most emphasized her masculine character and behavior. Sexed female, Marie-Antoinette bore sole responsibility for her deviations from nature. Readers could have found in such pamphlets evidence that Marie-Antoinette was a "false" rather than "natural" hermaphrodite, who lacked a man's sexual organs but nonetheless mimicked his sexual performance.[101] But the label of "false hermaphrodite" would have placed the queen both within a familiar tradition of aristocratic libertinism and within a more modern and masculinized "sapphic" category. By the late eighteenth century, in the wake of Pierre Roussel's *Système moral et physique de la femme* (1775), widely disseminated among educated elites, and the "resexualization of the body" by European anatomists, this "false hermaphrodite," or tribade, would bear the stigma, to return to Randolph Trumbach's schema, of a fourth gender.[102] The Revolution thus marked a crossroads in the social construction of sexual relations between women, between the older assumption that woman's desire for woman, though wicked, could not substitute for woman's "natural" desire for man, and a modern vision that assumed the tribade's desire for her own kind negated heterosexual desire, not to mention public order and femininity itself.[103]

True, the years of revolution also saw the publication of Sade's *Juliette,* the most explicit and, in some sense, celebratory rendering of sex between women in that epoch. The novel opens in a convent where we first encounter our young heroine, a natural tribade, instructed in the virtue of vice by the philosophical abbess and a veritable phalanx of tribades. Among them appear the full spectrum of sapphic identities: the nymphomaniacal nun with undiscerning sexual tastes, the masculinized tribade whose enlarged clitoris permits her to sodomize other women, the libertine lady equipped with a dildo. Juliette's desires, unlike Marie-Antoinette's, are "naturalized," rather than criminalized, through extended philosophical monologues that juxtapose the perversion of marital monogamy to the natural pleasures of sodomy and tribadism. For Sade, pain provides the swiftest path to pleasure, and all women, like all men, are sodomites at heart. Yet Sade naturalized tribadism only to weave it into a sexual script of such murderous excess that desire logically culminates in death. Juliette's will to knowledge leads naturally to a scene in which, strapped into a dildo eight inches in circumference, she deflowers, sodomizes, and mutilates a ten-year-old schoolgirl. Although Sade's staging seems to authorize lesbianism by generalizing "deviance" in a way that Marie-Antoinette pornography does not, in the final analysis, both Sade's Juliette and the pornographers' Marie-Antoinette primarily signify lesbian desire as transgressive.

Like Juliette, Marie-Antoinette-as-tribade was a liminal figure who violated, as she assumed, the rights of man. She consequently earned the enmity of the French on the grounds of both sexuality and status. "Frenchmen, Republican People, may the world offer you the fraternal salute," exulted one pamphleteer in the aftermath of Marie-Antoinette's execution. "You have purged the earth of a monster" and plunged a "loathesome woman," an "infernal Fury," a "Messalina without shame" into the "night of death."[104] These were fighting words in 1793, words enlisted not only in the battle against monarchy and counterrevolution, but in a struggle to redraw the boundaries of deviance and normalcy. According to Kristina Straub and Julia Epstein, "ambiguous forms of sexuality and gender" constitute sites in which "power relations can be read."[105] The assault on Marie-Antoinette's allegedly polymorphous sexuality in the Revolutionary pamphlets is a case in point, for it was precisely in the instability of the sex/gender system of the Revolutionary epoch that new parameters of the natural and the unnatural were forged.

Marie-Antoinette, as a "true monster," occupies an anomalous position on both sides of the gender and sexual divide in the pornography of the Revolution. Janus-faced, she marks a profound disjuncture between the old and new regimes.[106] When Madame de La Motte, the queen's archenemy from the Diamond Necklace Affair, appears in the pamphlets as an innocent victim of the queen's flattery and "impure caresses," one can discern the trace of the seduced and abandoned maidens and aristocratic libertines dear to eighteenth-century novelists.[107] One can also find nonfictional early modern precedents in the coupling of "ordinary" women with sexually ambiguous, and legally culpable, partners, prosecuted for assuming the prerogatives of man.[108] On a more distant register, the stark disjuncture between the "masculine" libido of the tribadic pursuer and the faintingly "feminine" woman pursued in the *Lettre de la Comtesse Valois de La Mothe à la Reine de France* prefigures a much later distinction between the invert and her passive and guilt-ridden lover that achieved its consummate expression in Radclyffe Hall's *The Well of Loneliness*. The diverse symbolic resonances of Marie-Antoinette-as-tribade, then, are due to her position at the threshold of the modern era.

Marie-Antoinette was executed, in the final analysis, not as a hermaphrodite or an invert, but as a dethroned queen. Yet she was pilloried in the press for crossing back and forth between the codes that regulated female sexuality in the modern era, as well as for her status. She displays her sex and enjoys sodomy with a dildo; she not only desires women but also has sex with them publicly, sometimes in the company of men. What is more, she and La Polignac broadcast their taste for the solitary pleasures that so horrified the medical authorities of the era.[109] Randolph Trumbach has suggested that masturbation, on one hand, and same-gender sexuality, on the other, are the boundaries by which modern heterosexuality is established. The pornography directed against Marie-Antoinette is suggestive precisely because her libidinal excesses marked the emergent boundaries of female desire in the modern period. If Marie-Antoinette-as-tribade does not incarnate the "modern lesbian identity"—and she does not—the pamphlets contribute to a history of lesbianism nonetheless. Against Marie-Antoinette's lust for bodies, booty, and blood, the pamphlets defined the appropriate objects and limits of woman's desire. In stigmatizing Marie-Antoinette with a threatening virility and a deviant femininity, they circumscribed the boundaries of female sexuality in the modern era.

Marie-Antoinette-as-tribade survived in diverse modern incarnations ranging from "invert" to "bulldagger" to haunt the heterosexual imagination as a central marker of difference. But the insistence on difference, in its very urgency, betrayed a doubt. Were the boundaries of female desire more flexible, perhaps, than social order allowed? Let us return for clues to the *Confession de Marie-Antoinette,* which constructed Marie-Antoinette as the very embodiment of difference—an aristocratic threat to the social order—only to go one step further by bringing the crime home. "Young, and in the fortunate age of ardent passions," she confided, "surrounded by beings lit with the same flame, the same desires, devoured by the need to satisfy them, how could I resist their solicitations, their counsels?" "Put your wives in a similar position," demanded the former queen, raising the specter of the gendered order subverted from within. "Would they be more *sages*? You be the judge."[110]

Notes

1. *Les Fureurs utérines de Marie Antoinette* (n.p., n.d. [1791]), 6.
2. *Le Godmiché royal* (n.p., 1789), reprinted as "The Royal Dildo" in Chantal Thomas, *The Wicked Queen: The Origins of the Myth of Marie-Antoinette,* trans. Julie Rose (New York: Zone Books, 1999), 191–201; *Bordel national sous les auspices de la Reine* (n.p., 1790).
3. *Le Petit Charles IX* (n.p., 1789), 7.
4. In "The Many Bodies of Marie-Antoinette: Political Pornography and the Problem of the Feminine in the French Revolution," in this volume, 125–126, Lynn Hunt notes that the charge of Marie-Antoinette's involvement with Polignac and Mme de Balbi is already present in *Portefeuille d'un talon rouge* (1783).
5. Terry Castle, *The Apparitional Lesbian: Female Homosexuality and Modern Culture* (New York: Columbia University Press, 1993), 10, 107–49.
6. For the nightshirt, see the J. Peterman Company catalog, fall 1994, 70. For a student newspaper's pornographic comic, see "Springtime avec Marie," *The Pipe Dream,* State University of New York at Binghamton, 25 March 1988. For the "Cult of the Queen," see Allen Kurzweil, *Art and Antiques,* October 1993, 69–72. For Madonna, see postcard by Damaged Goods, London, 1991.
7. In addition to articles included in this volume, the voluminous literature on the libels directed against Marie-Antoinette includes: Antoine de Baecque, *La Caricature révolutionnaire* (Paris: Presses du CNRS, 1988); Claude Langlois, *La Caricature contre-révolutionnaire* (Paris: Presses du CNRS, 1988); de Baecque, "Pamphlets: Libel and Political Mythology," in Robert Darnton and Daniel Roche, eds., *Revolution in Print: The Press in France, 1775–1800* (Berkeley: University of California Press, 1989), 165–76; de Baecque, "Le Récit fantastique de la Révolution: Les Monstres aristocratiques des pamphlets de 1789," in Pierre Rétat, ed., *La Révolution du journal, 1788–1794* (Paris: Editions du CNRS, 1989), 235–46; Marie-Jo Bonnet, *Un Choix sans équivoque: Recherches historiques sur les relations amoureuses entre les femmes, XVIe–XXe siècle* (Paris: Denoël, 1981), 158–65; Vivian Cameron, "Gender and Power: Images of Women in Late Eighteenth-Century France," *History of European Ideas* 10 (1989): 309–32; Cameron, "Political Exposures," in Lynn Hunt, ed., *Eroticism and the Body Politic* (Baltimore: Johns Hopkins University Press, 1991), 90–107; *French Caricature and the French Revolution, 1789–1799* (Los Angeles: Grunwald Center for the Graphic Arts, Wight Art Gallery, University of California at Los Angeles, 1988); Nancy Davenport, "Maenad, Martyr, Mother: Marie-Antoinette Transformed," *Proceedings of the Consortium on Revolutionary Europe* (1986), 66–84; Annie Duprat, "La Dégradation de l'image royale dans la caricature révolutionnaire," in Michel Vovelle, ed., *Les Images de la Révolution française* (Paris: Publications de la Sorbonne, 1988), 167–76; Madelyn Gutwirth, *The Twilight of the Goddesses: Women and Representation in the French Revolutionary Era* (New Brunswick, N.J.: Rutgers Uni-

versity Press, 1992); Lynn Hunt, "Pornography and the French Revolution," in Hunt, ed., *The Invention of Pornography: Obscenity and the Origins of Modernity, 1500–1800* (New York: Zone Books, 1993), 301–39; Jeffrey Merrick, "Impotence in Court and at Court," *Studies in Eighteenth-Century Culture* 25 (1996): 187–202; Merrick, "Sexual Politics and Public Order in Late Eighteenth-Century France: The *Mémoires secrets* and the *Correspondance secrète*," *Journal of the History of Sexuality* 1 (1990): 68–84; Leah Price, "Vies privées et scandaleuses: Marie Antoinette and the Public Eye," *The Eighteenth Century: Theory and Interpretation* 33 (1992): 176–92; Jacques Revel, "Marie-Antoinette in Her Fictions: The Staging of Hatred," in Bernadette Fort, ed., *Fictions of the French Revolution* (Evanston: Northwestern University Press, 1991), 111–29; Chantal Thomas, "L'Architigresse d'Autriche: La Métaphore animale dans les pamphlets contre Marie-Antoinette," in Rétat, ed., *Révolution du journal,* 229–34; Thomas, *Wicked Queen.* I have benefitted greatly from this work. See Elizabeth Colwill, "Les Crimes de Marie-Antoinette: Images d'une femme mutine dans le discours révolutionnaire," trans. Ghislaine Mahler, in Marie-France Brive, ed., *Les Femmes et la Révolution française,* vol. 2: *L'Individuel et le social: Apparitions et représentations* (Toulouse: Le Mirail, 1990), 207–20; Colwill, "Just Another *Citoyenne*? Marie-Antoinette on Trial, 1790–1793," *History Workshop* 28 (1989): 63–87.

8. See especially Martha Vicinus, "'They Wonder to Which Sex I Belong': The Historical Roots of the Modern Lesbian Identity," *Feminist Studies* 18 (1992): 467–97. Randolph Trumbach, "London's Sapphists: From Three Sexes to Four Genders in the Making of Modern Culture," in Gilbert Herdt, ed., *Third Sex, Third Gender: Beyond Sexual Dimorphism in Culture and History* (New York: Zone Books, 1994), 527, suggests a connection between rumors surrounding Marie-Antoinette's "sapphic tastes" and "the development in France of a late-eighteenth-century sapphist role."

9. Thomas Laqueur, *Making Sex: Body and Gender from the Greeks to Freud* (Cambridge, Mass.: Harvard University Press, 1990); Londa Schiebinger, *The Mind Has No Sex? Women in the Origins of Modern Science* (Cambridge, Mass.: Harvard University Press, 1989); Randolph Trumbach, "Sex, Gender, and Sexual Identity in Modern Culture: Male Sodomy and Female Prostitution in Enlightenment London," *Journal of the History of Sexuality* 2 (1991): 186–203.

10. Katharine Park and Robert Nye, "Destiny Is Anatomy," *The New Republic,* 18 February 1991, 53–57.

11. Elizabeth Colwill, "'Women's Empire' and the Sovereignty of Man in *La Décade philosophique,* 1794–1807," *Eighteenth-Century Studies* 29 (spring 1996): 265–89.

12. See Ann Jones and Peter Stallybrass, "Fetishizing Gender: Constructing the Hermaphrodite in Renaissance Europe," in Julia Epstein and Kristina Straub, eds., *Body Guards: The Cultural Politics of Gender Ambiguity* (New York: Routledge, 1991), 80–111; Judith Brown, "Lesbian Sexuality in Medieval and Early Modern Europe," in Martin Duberman et al., eds., *Hidden from History: Reclaiming the Gay and Lesbian Past* (New York: NAL Books, 1989), 67–75; and, most dramatically, John Boswell, *Same-Sex Unions in Premodern Europe* (New

York: Villard Books, 1994). Gayle Rubin coined the phrase "sex/gender system" in "The Traffic in Women: Notes on the 'Political Economy' of Sex," in Rayna Reiter, ed., *Toward an Anthropology of Women* (New York: Monthly Review Press, 1975), 157–210.

13. See Trumbach's review essays, "The Origin and Development of the Modern Lesbian Role in the Western Gender System: Northwestern Europe and the United States, 1750–1990," *Historical Reflections* 20 (1994): 287–320, and "Sodomitical Subcultures, Sodomitical Roles, and the Gender Revolution of the Eighteenth Century: The Recent Historiography," in Robert Maccubbin, ed., *'Tis Nature's Fault: Unauthorized Sexuality during the Enlightenment* (Cambridge: Cambridge University Press, 1987), 109–21; Michel Delon, "The Priest, the Philosopher, and Homosexuality in Enlightenment France," in Maccubbin, ed., *'Tis Nature's Fault,* 122–31; G. S. Rousseau, "The Pursuit of Homosexuality in the Eighteenth Century: 'Utterly Confused Category' and/or Rich Repository?" in Maccubbin, ed., *'Tis Nature's Fault,* 132–68.

14. Merrick, "Sexual Politics."

15. *Mémoires secrets pour servir à l'histoire de la République des Lettres en France* (London, 1780), 7 September 1777; 10:216–17. See Gary Kates, *Monsieur D'Eon Is a Woman: A Tale of Political Intrigue and Sexual Masquerade* (New York: Basic Books, 1995).

16. *Sémonce à la Reine,* reprinted in Hector Fleischmann, *L'Histoire licencieuse: Les Maîtresses de Marie-Antoinette* (Paris: Les Éditions des Bibliophiles, [1910]), 245–49; Merrick, "Sexual Politics."

17. Trumbach, "London's Sapphists."

18. See Bryant T. Ragan, "The Enlightenment Confronts Homosexuality," in Jeffrey Merrick and Bryant T. Ragan, eds., *Homosexuality in Modern France* (New York: Oxford University Press, 1996), 8–29; Michel Rey, "Parisian Homosexuals Create a Lifestyle, 1700–1750: The Police Archives," in Maccubbin, ed., *'Tis Nature's Fault,* 179–91; Rey, "Police and Sodomy in Eighteenth-Century Paris: From Sin to Disorder," in Kent Gerard and Gert Hekma, eds., *The Pursuit of Sodomy: Male Homosexuality in Renaissance and Enlightenment Europe* (New York: Haworth Press, 1989), 129–46.

19. Leslie Pierce, "Shifting Boundaries: Images of Ottoman Royal Women in the Sixteenth and Seventeenth Centuries," *Critical Matrix* 4 (1988): 43–82; Rachel Weil, "'The Crown Has Fallen to the Distaff': Gender and Politics in the Age of Catherine de Medici, 1560–1589," *Critical Matrix* 1 (1985): 1–38; Natalie Zemon Davis, *Society and Culture in Early Modern France* (Stanford: Stanford University Press, 1975).

20. Jean-Pierre Guicciardi, "Between the Licit and the Illicit: The Sexuality of the King," in Maccubbin, ed., *'Tis Nature's Fault,* 88–97; Klaus Theweleit, *Male Fantasies,* vol. 1: *Women, Floods, Bodies, History,* trans. Stephen Conway (Minneapolis: University of Minnesota Press, 1987); Saint-Amand, "Terrorizing Marie-Antoinette."

21. *La Confession de Marie-Antoinette ci-devant Reine de France, au peuple franc* (n.p., n.d.).

22. The histories of licentious literature, satire, and censorship; of symbolic inversion and carnival; of the desacralization of the monarchy and secularization

of society; of the professionalization of medicine; and of the rise of nationalism all affected the meanings attributed to Marie-Antoinette's "tribadism." On eighteenth-century pornography, see Jean-Marie Goulemot, *Forbidden Texts: Erotic Literature and Its Readers in Eighteenth-Century France*, trans. James Simpson (Philadelphia: University of Pennsylvania Press, 1994).

23. Carla Hesse, *Publishing and Cultural Politics in Revolutionary Paris, 1789–1810* (Berkeley: University of California Press, 1991).

24. On authorship and censorship, see Hunt, "Pornography and the French Revolution," 311–21. On book lenders and reading practices, see Roger Chartier, *The Cultural Origins of the French Revolution*, trans. Lydia Cochrane (Durham, N.C.: Duke University Press, 1991), 69–70, 90–91. De Baecque estimates the prices of political pamphlets and caricatures at two to ten sous and ten to fifteen sous, respectively. *Caricature révolutionnaire*, 27.

25. Susan Gubar, "Representing Pornography: Feminism, Criticism, and Depictions of Female Violation," *Critical Inquiry* 13 (1987): 712–41.

26. Robert Darnton, *The Literary Underground of the Old Regime* (Cambridge, Mass.: Harvard University Press, 1982).

27. Hunt, "Pornography and the French Revolution," 302–5.

28. On the privatization of sexuality, see Robert Padgug, "Sexual Matters: On Conceptualizing Sexuality in History," in Kathy Peiss and Christina Simmons, eds., *Passion and Power: Sexuality in History* (Philadelphia: Temple University Press, 1989), 14–31.

29. *Les Fouteries chantantes* (n.p., 1791), 12. See Maza, "Diamond Necklace Affair."

30. *Les Enfans de Sodome à l'Assemblée nationale* (Paris, 1790), 2, 8–9, 15–17.

31. Nancy Armstrong, "The Gender Bind: Women and the Disciplines," *Genders* 3 (1988): 3.

32. On the association of homosexuality with the aristocracy, see Hunt, "The Many Bodies of Marie-Antoinette," 127; Robert Oresko, "Homosexuality and the Court Elites of Early Modern France: Some Problems, Some Suggestions, and an Example," in Gerard and Hekma, eds., *Pursuit of Sodomy*, 105–28.

33. *Les Petits bougres au manège* (n.p., n.d. [1790]), 8–13.

34. *Bordel apostolique, institué par Pie VI, pape* (Paris, 1790), 1–2.

35. *Bordel royal, suivi d'un entretien secret entre la Reine et le Cardinal de Rohan* (n.p., n.d.), reprinted as *The Royal Bordello* in Thomas, *Wicked Queen*, 219.

36. Quoted in Claude Courouve, *Les Assemblées de la manchette: Documents sur l'amour masculin au XVIII siècle* (Paris: C. Courouve, 1987), 7.

37. Hunt, "Pornography and the French Revolution," 308. On the Revolutionary refashioning of the body, see Dorinda Outram, *The Body and the French Revolution: Sex, Class and Political Culture* (New Haven: Yale University Press, 1989).

38. On the laws regulating sodomy, see Courouve, *Assemblées de la manchette*, 7–11. On the "quasi-toleration" of prostitution during the Revolution, see Susan Conner, "Prostitution in Revolutionary Paris," *Eighteenth-Century Studies* 28 (winter 1994–95): 221–40; Colin Jones, "Prostitution and the Ruling Class in Eighteenth-Century Montpellier," *History Workshop* 6 (1978): 7–28. Jill Harsin, *Policing Prostitution in Nineteenth-Century Paris* (Princeton: Princeton University Press, 1985), 85, notes, however, that the law of 19–22 July 1791 authorized police to enter places "notorious for debauchery."

39. While *Petits bougres* framed its critique of the National Assembly as a sarcastic defense of buggery, *Ode aux bougres* (n.p. 1789), 3, framed its assault on the "execrable, unworthy race" of *bardaches* as a "Hymne au Con."

40. For a convincing demonstration of the link between "homophobia and misogyny in the maintenance of masculinist sexual hegemonies," see Kristina Straub, *Sexual Suspects: Eighteenth-Century Players and Sexual Ideology* (Princeton: Princeton University Press, 1992).

41. For one example among many, see *Fureurs utérines. The Royal Dildo* suggests that the king's preference for the "cul" to the "con" had driven the queen not only to tribaderie, but also to adultery and "self-pollution" (193).

42. *Bordel national sous les auspices de la Reine* (n.p., 1790).

43. *Liste civile, suivie des noms et qualités de ceux qui la composent* (n.p., n.d.), 22.

44. *Mémoires secrets,* 21 February 1770, 9:48–49.

45. Ibid., 9 November 1777, 10:274–75, and 7 March 1777, 10:60; Mary Sheriff, "Woman? Hermaphrodite? History Painter? On the Self-Imaging of Elisabeth Vigée-Lebrun," *The Eighteenth Century* 35 (1994): 3–27, esp. 13–14.

46. In *Testament de Mme la duchesse de Polignac,* the queen appears as "good, honest, and compassionate," a "tender mother," and wife. Reprinted in Hector Fleischmann, *Madame de Polignac et la cour galante de Marie-Antoinette* (Paris: Bibliothèque des Curieux, 1910), 143–60. See, however, excerpts from *La Cause de la Révolution françoise* (n.p., 1790), in Hector Fleischmann, *Marie-Antoinette libertine* (Paris: Bibliothèque des Curieux, 1911), 117–22.

47. *Le Vrai caractère de Marie-Antoinette* (n.p., n.d. [1792]).

48. "Les Doléances de la foutue gueuse de Polignac," in *Fouteries chantantes,* 29–30.

49. *La Ligue aristocratique* (n.p., 1789), reprinted as *The Aristocratic League or The French Catalinas,* in Thomas, *Wicked Queen,* 229–37.

50. *Liste civile; Aristocratic League.*

51. See *Royal Bordello; La Chasse aux bêtes puantes et féroces* (Paris, 1789), 14; *Lettre de la Comtesse Valois de la Mothe* (Oxford, n.d.).

52. *La Journée amoureuse* (n.p., n.d.), 18.

53. Kathryn Norberg, "The Libertine Whore: Prostitution in French Pornography from Margot to Juliette," in Hunt, ed., *Invention of Pornography,* 225–52.

54. Goulemot, *Forbidden Texts;* Norberg, "Libertine Whore."

55. Lynn Hunt, *The Family Romance of the French Revolution* (Berkeley: University of California Press, 1992), 124–50, esp. 133–35.

56. On Sade's political loyalties, see Maurice Lever, *Sade: A Biography,* trans. Arthur Goldhammer (New York: Farrar, 1993), esp. 402–51.

57. I am greatly indebted here to Pamela Cheek's analysis of the affiliation between police writing and "sexualized writing" about prostitutes, in "Prostitutes of 'Political Institution,'" *Eighteenth-Century Studies* 28 (winter 1994–95): 193–219, esp. 198, and to Hunt's argument, in "Pornography and the French Revolution," that Sade simultaneously explored the subversive possibilities of pornography and forged key elements of the modern genre (330–31).

58. Sheriff, "Woman? Hermaphrodite? History Painter?" 7. For more typical charges directed against Corday, see Elizabeth Kindleberger, "Charlotte Corday in Text and Image: A Case Study in the French Revolution and Women's History," *French Historical Studies* 18 (fall 1994): 969–99.

59. *La Messaline française* (n.p., 1789).
60. Castle, *Apparitional Lesbian*, 131.
61. *Bordel national.*
62. Cheek, "Prostitutes of 'Political Institution'"; Sheriff, "Woman? Hermaphrodite? History Painter?"; Jeffrey Merrick, "The Marquis de Villette and Mademoiselle de Raucourt: Representations of Male and Female Sexual Deviance in Late Eighteenth-Century France," in Merrick and Ragan, eds., *Homosexuality in Modern France*, 30–53. In *Confession et repentir de Madame de P . . .* (n.p.,1789), Polignac slips easily from *l'antiphysique* to prostitution. In *Le Nouveau tableau de Paris* (Paris, 1790), Louis-Sébastien Mercier claimed that "healthy" arts and commerce had been supplanted by dissimulation, prostitution, and commerce in sodomy (3–4, 14).
63. *Cause de la Révolution françoise*, 122.
64. On representational strategies and gender politics in the age of revolution, see Gutwirth, *Twilight of the Goddesses;* Joan B. Landes, *Women and the Public Sphere in the Age of the French Revolution* (Ithaca: Cornell University Press, 1988).
65. See Hunt, "Many Bodies of Marie-Antoinette." On women's activism, see Dominique Godineau, *The Women of Paris and their French Revolution*, trans. Katherine Streip (Berkeley: University of California Press, 1998).
66. *Vie privée, libertine, et scandaleuse de Marie-Antoinette* (Paris, 1793), 5–6. For the charge that the queen abandoned her son on his deathbed, see F. Dantelle, *Description de la ménagerie royale d'animaux vivants* (n.p., n.d.), reprinted as *Description of the Royal Menagerie of Living Animals* in Thomas, *Wicked Queen*, 239–46, esp. 245.
67. *Messaline française; Les Imitateurs de Charles Neuf ou les conspirateurs foudroyés* (Paris, 1790); *Sémonce à la Reine*, 248.
68. Dantelle, *Description of the Royal Menagerie*, 241.
69. *Étrennes aux Fouteurs* (n.p., 1793), 3.
70. Cf. *Fureurs utérines*, 6; *Royal Dildo*, 196.
71. *Liste civile;* Merrick, "Sexual Politics," 72–74; *Mémoires secrets*, 9 November 1777, 10:274–75.
72. *Boudoir de Madame la Duchesse de P . . .* (n.p., n.d.), 2–4. See also *Royal Dildo;* Daniel Roche, *The Culture of Clothing: Dress and Fashion in the Ancien Regime*, trans. Jean Birrell (Cambridge: Cambridge University Press, 1994).
73. *Mémoires secrets*, 13:263, noted a troubling increase in the number of abandoned children [*enfants trouvés*].
74. *Journée amoureuse*, 67.
75. Brown, "Lesbian Sexuality"; Trumbach, "Sex, Gender, and Sexual Identity," 177; Rudolf Dekker and Lotte van de Pol, *The Tradition of Female Transvestism in Early Modern Europe* (New York: St. Martin's, 1989), 55–77.
76. Brown suggests that the "neglect of the subject [of lesbianism] in law, theology, and literature suggests an almost active willingness to *dis*-believe" ("Lesbian Sexuality," 69). In "The 'Nefarious Sin' in Early Modern Seville," Mary Elizabeth Perry argues that "the real crime of sodomy was not in ejaculating nonprocreatively, nor in the use of the anus, but in defiling or invading the male recipient's body" (in Gerard and Hekma, eds., *Pursuit of Sodomy*, 79).

James Saslow maintains that sexual relations between women were punished more severely to the extent that they might "counterfeit the office of a husband." "Homosexuality in the Renaissance: Behavior, Identity, and Artistic Expression," in Duberman et al., eds., *Hidden from History,* 95–96.

77. *Les Bordels de Paris* (n.p., 1790).

78. *Boudoir de Madame la Duchesse de P . . . ,* 2–4, 6.

79. Brown, "Lesbian Sexuality," 74.

80. *Journée amoureuse,* 50–51. Cf. *Royal Dildo,* in which Juno (Marie-Antoinette), disappointed by her impotent husband, masturbates with a dildo, then enjoys it with her female companion.

81. *Chasse aux bêtes puantes et féroces,* 6,14.

82. *Lettre d'un Savoyard au Roi* (n.p., 1789), 5.

83. *Boudoir de Madame la Duchesse de P . . . ,* 1, 5–6.

84. *Les Derniers soupirs de la garce en pleurs* (n.p., 1790), 12–13.

85. Jones and Stallybrass, "Fetishizing Gender," 90.

86. On the Hottentot apron, see Londa Schiebinger, *Nature's Body: Gender in the Making of Modern Science* (Boston: Beacon Press, 1993), 160–72. On the persistent association between the enlarged clitoris and tribadism, see Bonnet, *Choix sans équivoque,* 76–79.

87. *Le Nouveau Dom Bougre à l'Assemblée nationale* (n.p., [1790]).

88. Ian Maclean, *The Renaissance Notion of Woman: A Study in the Fortunes of Scholasticism and Medical Science in European Intellectual Life* (Cambridge: Cambridge University Press, 1980), 34–35.

89. *Journée amoureuse,* 14–15. On seminal fluids, see Schiebinger, *The Mind Has No Sex?* 180.

90. *Derniers soupirs,* 5.

91. Jones and Stallybrass have argued that the "supplementary figure of the hermaphrodite comes to stand for the lability of the whole gendering process," ("Fetishizing Gender," 83). On early modern distinctions among hermaphrodism, cross-dressing, and homoeroticism, see Trumbach, "London's Sapphists," esp. 116, 119.

92. In " 'Passing Women': A Study of Gender Boundaries in the Eighteenth Century," Lynn Friedli notes that most women who "passed" were prosecuted for fraud rather than sexual offences. In G. S. Rousseau and Roy Porter, eds., *Sexual Underworlds of the Enlightenment,* (Manchester: Manchester University Press, 1987), 237.

93. Dantelle, *Description of the Royal Menagerie,* 245.

94. Jeffrey Merrick, "Fathers and Kings: Patriarchalism and Absolutism in Eighteenth-Century France," *Studies on Voltaire and the Eighteenth Century* 308 (1993): 281–303; Merrick, "Sexual Politics."

95. One has only to compare the titles of pamphlets such as *Les Fureurs utérines* with D.-T. de Bienville's *La Nymphomanie, ou Traité de la fureur utérine* (Amsterdam, 1771) to recognize the extent to which they drew upon contemporary medical discourses.

96. *Sémonce à la Reine,* 245.

97. *Journée amoureuse,* 63.

98. On Marie, see Jones and Stallybrass, "Fetishizing Gender," 84–85; Laqueur, *Making Sex,* 126–27.

99. In the words of Herdt, "although a significant discourse on monsters and hermaphrodites had abounded for centuries, this approach was replaced with the modern period's conception of the homosexual as a hermaphrodite of the soul." "Introduction," in Herdt, ed., *Third Sex, Third Gender,* 23.

100. Maclean, *Renaissance Notion of Woman,* 32–33.

101. Sheriff, "Woman? Hermaphrodite? History Painter?" 4–5.

102. Schiebinger, *The Mind Has No Sex?* 190; Trumbach, "London's Sapphists."

103. Trumbach, "Sex, Gender, and Sexual Identity," 128–30. Michel Rey argues that by the eighteenth century, police understood sodomy not as sin but as "an offense against the social order." "Police and Sodomy in Eighteenth-Century Paris," 145.

104. *Testament de Marie Antoinette, veuve Capet,* reprinted as *The Testament of Marie-Antoinette, the Widow Capet* in Thomas, *Wicked Queen,* 249–55, esp. 249.

105. Epstein and Straub, eds., *Body Guards,* 7.

106. *Sémonce à la Reine.*

107. *Lettre de la Comtesse.*

108. Jones and Stallybrass, "Fetishizing Gender," 88–89; Valerie Traub, "The (In)Significance of 'Lesbian' Desire in Early Modern England," in Jonathan Goldberg, ed., *Queering the Renaissance* (Durham, N.C.: Duke University Press, 1994), 62–83.

109. Polignac is labeled "la Ganimède femelle" in *L'Autrichienne en Goguettes ou l'Orgie Royale* (n.p., 1789).

110. *Confession de Marie-Antoinette.*

Ambiguous Identities:
Marie-Antoinette and the
House of Lorraine from the Affair
of the Minuet to Lambesc's Charge

Thomas E. Kaiser

On the evening of 19 May 1770—four days into Marie-Antoinette's fairytale wedding at Versailles—Louis XV, grandfather to the awkward groom, was nervous—even more so, perhaps, than the teenage newlyweds. Despite an inconvenient rainstorm that had delayed the fireworks display, the elaborate festivities of previous days had gone smoothly enough. But at this point in the nuptials something far worse than a rainstorm—indeed, something almost unthinkable—seemed about to happen. Hoping to eclipse the elaborate festivities his Hapsburg in-laws had staged earlier in Vienna to celebrate the marriage, the king of France—at a time of growing financial exigency—had built a costly new theater at Versailles, where an extravagant dress ball was to take place.[1] Yet it now appeared that no one, or at least no one who mattered outside the royal family, would attend. Less than two weeks earlier, the cream of the court nobility had organized a boycott of the ball, going so far as to issue a protest petition signed by nearly two hundred courtiers explaining the reason.[2] What was the cause of their discontent? Through the intervention of the Austrian ambassador, Mercy-Argenteau, and with the support of the French foreign minister, Choiseul, a certain Madame de Brionne had asked Louis to bestow some special sign of recognition at the wedding upon the house of Lorraine, to which she belonged by marriage. Complying with this request, Louis had authorized Madame

[handwritten margin note: The nobles of Versailles have refused to attend the ball at the new theatre in honor of Marie Antoinette's marriage to the Dauphin]

171

de Brionne's second daughter—the fifteen-year-old Anne-Charlotte, princesse de Lorraine—to dance just after the princes of the blood and before the dukes and peers at the dress ball, a court festivity during which guests traditionally danced in declining order of rank and no one danced twice before all the designated dancers had danced once.[3] This exceptional grace, claimed the indignant petitioners, entailed a major assault upon the order of privilege, because it acknowledged the unjust claims of the house of Lorraine to status above the peers and interrupted the historic continuity between the ranks of the peers and that of the princes. The interruption was so grievous, they claimed, that it would cause immense damage to "the dignity of the nation and of the crown no less than to the prerogatives of the French nobility."[4] As one contemporary verse parody of the nobles' complaint put it, "Sire, the grandees of your Kingdom / Will regard with much pain / A princess of Lorraine / Precede them at the ball."[5]

The king had replied with his own communiqué. In it, Louis had minimized the constitutional significance of his act, reassured the nobles he had no intention of altering standard court practice, and requested their compliance on an occasion "when I want to indicate to the empress [Marie-Antoinette's mother, Maria Theresa] my recognition of the gift she has given me, [her daughter] who . . . will be my happiness for the rest of my days."[6] But Louis' plea also insensitively reasserted the notion of a hiatus between the princes and the peers, which prompted the boycott. Upon hearing of the courtiers' intentions, Louis was reportedly so upset that, tears welling up in his eyes, he angrily threw his hat on the ground. "This is a poor way to receive the lovable dauphine," muttered the groom.[7] But displeasing the bride was hardly the king's most important concern. More serious was the risk of offending the Austrian emperor, Joseph II, known for his anti-French attitudes, and Maria Theresa, who, in the words of one observer, might just possibly "risk the lives of millions of men for a minuet."[8] As Madame de Brionne argued to Mercy, the affair engaged high matters of diplomacy; despite the courtiers' threat to boycott the dress ball, she refused to retract her request on the grounds that "we cannot submit without failing the emperor."[9]

On the morning of the ball, the nobles' tempers were still hot. The duchesses, despite the personal invitations they had been sent by the king, were among the fiercest protesters and advocates of a hard line.[10] Some of the duchesses conspicuously delayed dressing for the occasion to show their pique, while others openly threatened to leave the court forever.[11] As evening approached, the situation did cool down. The protesters reconsidered their decision to boycott the ball, especially the duchesses, who ruminated on the expense they had gone to in purchasing their wardrobe, and ultimately there were enough court nobles in attendance for the ball to be considered a success.[12] Yet many invited guests did not show up, while of those courtiers who did appear, some refused to dance, some retired to the grilled loges, and some left early. Even this modest level of participation was achieved only at the cost of confusing matters of *préséance*. In an unusual procedure, the court had scheduled the comte d'Artois, the dauphin's younger brother, to dance twice—preceding and just after Mademoiselle de Brionne—that is, before all the other designated dancers had danced once.[13] In addition, the king, who was understandably relieved that the full boycott had not materialized, further sought to calm the ruffled feathers of the nobility by promising the duchesses they would have priority over the house of Lorraine at the next royal wedding ball.[14] In the end, one observer reckoned, the battle had yielded a draw: the house of Lorraine gained little additional prestige, but no one was entirely content, and some of the nobles were still fuming.[15] Still, the affair of the minuet was over.

Or was it? Tempting as it would be to relegate this apparently ridiculous comedy to a footnote in the history of *moeurs* at Versailles, contemporaries took it seriously enough, and I think it has far more significance when viewed in the larger perspective of French Austrophobia that coalesced around Marie-Antoinette.[16] The extravagant vilification of Marie-Antoinette, which so tainted the monarchy, as I have argued elsewhere, was a product not only of her crossing gender boundaries,[17] but also of the specific ends for which her supposed usurpation of power was allegedly used, in particular the subversion of France by the Hapsburgs.[18] Marie-Antoinette's chief problem was that, like other queens born abroad to rival dynasties, she was suspected of not having sufficiently exchanged national identities, as required by the marital "traffic in women" that sealed alliances and treaties under the Old Regime.[19] For this reason she was viewed as the crucial link between foreign and domestic "despotism."

The purpose of this article is to demonstrate that the affair of the minuet was important in the defamation of Marie-Antoinette, first because it gave reason for influential nobles in particular to resent her marriage to the future king from the very outset of her new life in France, and second because it focused attention on her association with the house of Lorraine—a house that had long been regarded as subversive of French national interests. Whereas these incriminating associations were hardly the result of her own initiatives, Marie-Antoinette in later years compounded the political damage they caused her by conspicuously supporting the escalating demands for court favors by the unpopular house of Lorraine throughout her reign. In the end, the affair of the minuet served as a connecting link between two imagined conspiracies against France: one that surrounded the historic role of the house of Lorraine as a threat to French security and one that surrounded Marie-Antoinette as the perpetrator of crimes against the French nation.

I

Although it was a duchy of the Empire, Lorraine was subject to progressive French encroachment beginning in the High Middle Ages.[20] Until the 1730s, its reigning house maintained a precarious semiautonomy by intermarrying with and paying homage to ruling dynasties in both France and Germany. The result of this double-dealing was to raise suspicions among Germans that Lorraine natives were really Francophiles, and among the French that they were Germans who harbored deep antagonism toward France. Thus, one French ministerial report of 1732 described the people of Lorraine as "hating the French and loving the Germans whom they resemble closely enough."[21] Within the royalist historiographical perspective, the ruling house of Lorraine was viewed as a persistent engine of disloyalty and subversion, despite the multiple honors and privileges extended to it in and by the French court on the basis of its claim to descend from Charlemagne.[22] As the duc de Saint-Simon put it in a typical formulation, the house of Lorraine had committed "crimes without limit and number" in an effort to "devour this kingdom and to assassinate its royal race, in order to usurp its provinces and more often its crown."[23] Indelibly associated with the Guises—one of its family branches, which had played a major destabilizing role during the late-sixteenth-century Wars of Religion—the house of Lorraine had allegedly continued its dubious career into the seventeenth century, most notably in the 1630s, when the duc de Lorraine had allegedly committed "every imaginable crime . . . against the person of the king, his state, and his ministers."[24] What made this unregulated ambition particularly threatening, in the view of the historian Pierre Dupuy, was its manipulation from abroad by the Austrian Hapsburgs, who sought to use the house of Lorraine as a tool for dominating the French kingdom from within. "The duc de Lorraine," he charged, "has taken up arms against France only because of the inducement and persuasion of the emperor . . . so that one can say that he has been like the instrument of their passion and of their hatred against France."[25] Thus long before Marie-Antoinette ever set foot in France, the house of Lorraine, whose kinship with the disloyal Guises remained "only too well known" in the eighteenth century, was closely linked in French political memory with a fifth-column movement subversive of the national interest.[26]

What gave this threat even more weight in court circles was the disruption the house of Lorraine had caused in the traditional order of precedence. As the only true *princes étrangers,* Saint-Simon contended, the house of Lorraine had aspired to usurp the king's role as regulator of ranks and orders, all the better to assign itself a rank it did not merit, just after the princes of the blood and before the peers.[27] And when did this usurpation allegedly transpire? During the Wars of Religion, that is to say, when the Guises were sufficiently strong and the crown sufficiently weak for a house with interests and pretensions "altogether opposed to the laws, maxims, and interests of [the country]" to usurp a dignity they never legitimately enjoyed.[28] Thus in Saint-Simon's view, the house of Lorraine had long combined illegitimate presumption with disloyalty, making it a threat not only to the nobility, but also to the nation insofar as its efforts at self-advancement had corrupted the French constitution.

The long-standing dubious reputation of the house of Lorraine was only enhanced by the complex process through which Lorraine was incorporated into France beginning in 1736.[29] According to the settlement of the War of the Polish Succession, Lorraine was to pass to Stanislaus, father of the queen, Marie Leszczynska, and when he died, to the French crown. The process was to begin immediately when its hereditary heir renounced his and his family's right to rule the duchy in exchange for his becoming duke of Tuscany upon the death of the current, moribund duke. Who was this heir? None other than Francis Stephen, intended husband to Maria Theresa and future father to Marie-Antoinette. Now, the entire rationale for Francis Stephen's renunciation of Lorraine was that, as the spouse of Maria Theresa and as a possible future emperor, he could not remain duc de Lorraine without endangering French security from inside the kingdom, since Lorraine lay geographically at the "heart of France" and its possession by an Austrian emperor would provide him with a launching pad for endless mischief.[30] Indeed, if ever an emperor of Germany became duc de Lorraine and Bar, French negotiators told the Austrians flatly, "we would no longer exist as a national body."[31] The main problem in all these delicate arrangements was that there were many legal grounds for doubting the legitimacy of the renunciation, it being altogether possible that Francis Stephen would one day reassert his rights to Lorraine using the vast resources of the empire.[32]

What made this possibility all the more disturbing was the reputation Francis Stephen had established as a notorious Francophobe—in Saint-Simon's words, "a born enemy of France."[33] Although a Lorraine native, he was educated at the Viennese court, had served the emperor as vice-regent of Hungary, and was so out of touch with French culture that he was obliged to spell the French language phonetically.[34] In France, he was thought to have been Germanized to the point where he had adopted Austrian prejudices toward foreigners, especially the French. According to one report, Francis Stephen once remarked that he had no more regard for French people than for a whore.[35] Indeed, his own mother, distraught over her family's loss of Lorraine, claimed that her son's pro-Austrian sensibilities, as evidenced by his willingness to renounce his family's ancient domain, showed that he had been "bewitched" by the Hapsburgs.[36]

Hapsburg "sorcery" aside, subsequent developments gave the French every reason to fear that Francis Stephen would use the resources of the empire to undermine French security by reasserting his claims to Lorraine.[37] Austria nearly recaptured the duchy during the War of the Austrian Succession, when in 1744 Prince Charles, brother of Francis Stephen, led an Austrian army into neighboring Alsace. There, despite his reportedly cruel campaign of burning crops, raping nuns, and massacring civilians, he raised concerns that the people of Lorraine might support his efforts to put the duchy back under the rule of its ancient house.[38] Henceforth, the terms *autrichien* and *lorrain* connoted "traitor to the *patrie*" and were frequently applied to those writers of hand-copied newsletters who demonstrated a pro-Austrian bias.[39]

Despite the failure of Prince Charles's incursion and the alliance France struck with Austria in 1756, which was largely attributed to the diabolical machinations of Madame de Pompadour, French Austrophobia generally and fears of internal subversion in connection with the recapture of Lorraine in particular did not subside. To the contrary, they were fanned by the *parti dévot*—that court circle, including the king's family and associated ministers, who were opposed to the king's mistresses and later Marie-Antoinette. Austrophobia gained strength when Marie-Antoinette's brother, Joseph II, who seemed to have inherited his father's intense Francophobia,[40] became emperor in 1765 and thereafter conducted an erratic foreign policy opposed to French interests.[41] In 1772, the French ambassador to Austria, the future Cardinal de Rohan, informed Versailles of fresh reports circulating in Vienna that Joseph intended to abscond with Alsace and Lorraine. Although these reports were brushed off by Joseph as implausible Prussian lies when Rohan brought them to his attention, they did wind up exciting the "most serious attention on the part of the king."[42]

Returning now to the affair of the minuet, it first should be recalled that the original request for some special sign of recognition for the house of Lorraine was made by a Madame de Brionne, who was a major player in the cutthroat politics of court privilege and a tireless advocate of her family's interests. Born Louise-Julie-Constance de Rohan in 1734, she had married Charles Louis de Lorraine, comte de Brionne, in 1748, a match that united two prominent families with claims as *princes étrangers*. Madame de Brionne bore two sons and two daughters and was widowed in 1761.[43] Known for her beauty, she became the mistress of her cousin, the future Cardinal de Rohan, and then of the powerful manager of French foreign policy, the duc de Choiseul, who was himself from Lorraine and the son of a prominent diplomat working for its reigning house. Madame de Brionne's correspondence shows that she and her Lorraine in-laws remained extremely close to their Hapsburg relations.[44] They frequently exchanged greetings on holidays and family occasions, such as the birth and death of family members, and Maria Theresa, Francis Stephen, and later Joseph II agreed to serve as godparents to some of Madame de Brionne's children. For years she milked this tie for all it was worth, risking offense through violations of Viennese court etiquette to gain privileges and special consideration for her offspring in the Hapsburg entourage.[45] She lobbied especially hard on behalf of her elder son, the prince de Lambesc, who became a favorite of Joseph as a military attaché shortly before Marie-

Antoinette's wedding. Although the house of Lorraine enjoyed no permanent special status at the Viennese court, the French ambassador to Austria informed Choiseul that Lambesc was being shown the same honors that a prince of the blood would receive at Versailles.[46] "The comtesse de Brionne," observed Choiseul, "can only be extremely grateful for the reception that the prince de Lambesc has received in Vienna, and we truly share her sensibilities."[47]

Not content with working the east side of the Rhine, Madame de Brionne also lobbied hard for her children in France, where her family by marriage had held the prestigious office of *grand écuyer* since 1658. What needs stressing here is that far from undercutting her influence at Versailles, her Hapsburg ties only enhanced her credit with the king, since the rapprochement between France and Austria, cemented by the alliance of 1756 and Marie-Antoinette's marriage to the dauphin, inclined Louis XV to show considerable solicitude toward the house of Lorraine-Hapsburg. Hardly blind to the potential for personal benefit created by these developments, the house of Lorraine, especially Madame de Brionne, sought to harvest its rewards almost immediately.[48]

Although Madame de Brionne's lobbying of the king was not always successful, she did win a notable concession in 1761, when on the death of her husband she arranged for the passage of the office of *grand écuyer* to her elder son, the prince de Lambesc. What made this grace especially valuable were not only the emoluments of the office itself, but also the extra prestige that the house of Lorraine acquired as a result of Lambesc's being, at age ten, fifteen years younger than was normally necessary to hold it.[49] In 1767, she successfully recovered for her family the coveted *tabouret* (privileged seat) formerly held by the prince de Rochefort, and she placed the prince de Lambesc in the regiment of the marquis de Castries, notwithstanding Lambesc's still tender age of sixteen.[50] In seeking these and other favors from the court, Madame de Brionne put to good use her close relationship with the comte de Mercy-Argenteau, the Austrian ambassador posted to France in 1766, who had once considered marrying one of her daughters.[51] But still more useful for her efforts at self-promotion was her association with Choiseul and with his wife, who apparently did not resent her husband's affair and received Madame de Brionne graciously at the Choiseul residence of Chanteloup.[52] Among other favors, including the permission to dance before the dukes and peers at Marie-Antoinette's wedding, Choiseul helped negotiate an advantageous marriage for her elder daughter with the prince de Carignan of the house of Sardinia in 1768.[53] In short, indelibly associated with her former lover Choiseul and the unpopular Austrian alliance, Madame de Brionne was arguably the most conspicuous female emblem of the Lorraine-Hapsburg dynasty at Versailles until the marriage of Marie-Antoinette to the dauphin.

The union of Maria Theresa's daughter with the grandson of Louis XV bore all the marks of Choiseul's diplomacy.[54] Indeed, only considerations of protocol prevented Choiseul himself from greeting the Austrian archduchess as she entered French territory.[55] Saturated by allusions to and symbols of the dynastic union between the Bourbons and Hapsburgs, the nuptials also made many allusions to Marie-Antoinette's roots in Lorraine, through which she passed on the way to her wedding.[56] While there she visited her family's ancestral tombs in the Church of the Cordeliers in Nancy and accepted a formal compliment in Commercy recalling her descent "from a family that for nearly a thousand years has reigned in our hearts."[57] Further driving home the connection was the publication of a new genealogical treatise showing the common origins of the houses of Lorraine and Hapsburg, and the circulation of a family tree indicating the blood ties among the houses of Bourbon, Hapsburg, and Lorraine.[58]

The reaction of the French people to these historical reminders is hard to determine, but it was in all probability ambivalent at best. To the baron Grimm, the genealogical treatise could only recall the family that "had contemplated wresting away the scepter of one of the most beautiful kingdoms of Europe from the house of Bourbon."[59] What was crucial to Madame de Brionne was the fact that the marriage threw open the doors to even greater prospects for the house of Lorraine. As the duc de Croÿ acutely noted, she "wanted to profit from the moment that the house of Lorraine, having obtained, permanently it seemed, the title of emperor, and having dignified the house of Austria, gave a princess as wife to the dauphin, with whom the king appeared very content to assure the peace of Europe."[60]

In this light, it becomes clear that Louis' accommodation of Madame de Brionne's request for special recognition represented one further reminder of what the marriage meant in political terms. For years, the *parti dévot* had been at war with Choiseul and the Austrian alliance. They had worked hard to vilify Choiseul as a traitor to

France's best interests and to portray the alliance as "unnatural" and a deception whereby Austria would undermine France's rightful place as Europe's dominant power.[61] Keenly aware, as one contemporary put it, that they would never control "the mind of an archduchess [Marie-Antoinette] whose actions will always be directed either by the affection she feels for the princes of Lorraine or by the counsels of the ambassador of the imperial court,"[62] the *dévots* had tried to delay the dauphin's marriage to Marie-Antoinette, while they searched for an alternative spouse among the house of Saxony, that is, the house of the dauphin's recently expired mother, Marie Josèphe.[63] Outmaneuvered by Choiseul, they were forced to resign themselves to the Hapsburg match. But this meant the loss of a battle, not the war. Rough times were ahead for Choiseul, who was fired in late 1770, and for the new dauphine, whose alleged influence over the future king made her appear a dangerous lobby for the Austrian alliance. Recalling two centuries of efforts by the house of Lorraine to subvert the rights of the French nobility, the affair of the minuet could only remind the court and nation of the disruption a suspect ally, Austria, might cause to France. In short, it served to highlight and connect three simultaneous violations of the "natural" order: the domination of France by Austria, the usurpation of rank by the house of Lorraine, and the manipulation of the dauphin and soon-to-be king by Marie-Antoinette.

Developments following the affair only deepened and widened the breaches caused by it. For one thing, the nobles' protest elicited snickers outside the court and a much-publicized parody that held the nobles up to ridicule for challenging the pretensions of Madame de Brionne while disregarding traditional rankings among themselves in their deliberations.[64] For another, the affair fed an already raging controversy over the relative status of the *princes étrangers* and the dukes and peers, which led to the publication of learned treatises challenging and defending the rights of the powerful Rohans, in particular.[65] These squabbles provided an irresistible target for the acid pen of the publicist Pidansat de Mairobert, who profited from the occasion by ridiculing the claims of the dukes and peers to ancient lineage and indicting the entire French nobility for marrying daughters of financiers, actresses, and other "public women, originating from the most infamous places of debauchery," out of cupidity and lust.[66] Moreover, if the affair of the minuet most directly affronted the dukes and peers, in early 1775, a second spat in-

volving Marie-Antoinette and *préséance* erupted that offended the
princes of the blood. This storm occurred when her brother Maximilien insisted, with the open support of the queen, that on his stay
in Versailles the princes pay a visit to him before he visited them,
thereby provoking another boycott of a royal function. The upshot
was that the queen's relationships with the princes were poisoned,
while, as private Austrian accounts confirm, Marie-Antoinette suffered a great drop in popularity among the public, who clearly sided
with the princes.[67]

In addition, there were the never-ending bouts of self-promotion
by Madame de Brionne and her children. Far from distancing herself from Madame de Brionne and the house of Lorraine, the queen
showered them with favors, often at some considerable political cost
to herself. Her motives in doing so are not altogether clear. Her
mother's lobbying on their behalf and the queen's genuine feeling
for her kinsmen probably played a role; so, too, in all likelihood did
her continued loyalty to the dismissed minister Choiseul and his circle and the belief that she had to consolidate and maintain her political base at court.[68] In any case, she replaced Choiseul as the chief
conduit for favors requested by associates of the house of Lorraine.[69]
"I had the pleasure of giving the *lorrains* special attention," she
wrote her mother when choosing members of her household.[70]

In 1775, Madame de Brionne's elder son, the prince de Lambesc,
was granted the honor of carrying Louis' cape during the coronation. A year later he was made *chevalier* de l'Ordre du Saint Esprit in
a ceremony that allowed the house of Lorraine once again to assert
its precedence over the dukes and peers—despite the fact that at
twenty-five he was five years younger than normally required.[71]
Similarly in 1780, his brother, the prince de Vaudémont, was made a
commander in Lambesc's regiment before he was of age, with the result that another major blowup occurred among the high nobility.
According to Mercy, this grace was a direct product of the queen's
patronage and would not have aroused nearly the same effervescent
reaction had it not been for the preexisting "excessive jealousy of the
high nobility for princes of the house of Lorraine."[72] Under pressure
from that quarter, the king delayed granting the honor. But this
move only raised the hackles of Madame de Brionne, who loudly
protested that the delay devalued the grace and violated the traditional French policy of conferring exceptional favors on the princes
of Lorraine. To advance her argument, Madame de Brionne sent her

daughter Anne-Charlotte—the controversial interloper in the affair of the minuet—to remonstrate with the queen through letters and a personal interview. At this point, Marie-Antoinette declined to press the case of her troublesome clients any further and the matter was henceforth dropped, but the queen nonetheless reassured Madame de Brionne that the house of Lorraine would continue to receive "effective signs of her goodness and protection."[73]

In reviewing the whole affair, the politically acute Mercy, who had already sensed the danger Madame de Brionne posed to his charge, reported that her actions did "inspire in the queen some suspicions of abuse of her favor."[74] But the lesson she might have learned certainly did not last long. As Mercy put it, "the impression [of abuse of her favor] was only momentary and left behind no detectable mark."[75] And, indeed, the flow of favors continued. The biggest prize went to the prince de Lambesc in 1785, when he was given command of the Royal-Allemand, a regiment dating back to the sixteenth century that included some foreigners and natives of Alsace and Lorraine—a fact that, as we will see, would have important consequences.[76]

As if her persistent demands for favors on the part of the house of Lorraine did not put the queen in enough jeopardy, Madame de Brionne further compromised the queen by meddling in political affairs and frequently battling with royal ministers, particularly, although not exclusively, with those in the *dévot* camp. A year into Louis XVI's reign, she sent Marie-Antoinette a memorandum in which she criticized the ministry headed by the comte de Maurepas and advocated the reinstatement of the disgraced duc de Choiseul. When the queen presented the memorandum to Louis XVI, he reacted with the same undisguised horror and disgust he normally showed when Choiseul's name was mentioned, demanding that henceforth "no one speak to me of that man!"[77] Madame de Brionne also offended Turgot, the controller-general, with her persistent demands for special treatment, prompting him to snap back on one occasion that under Louis XVI, "the reign of women is over."[78] Similarly, when in 1780 she complained to Maurepas that it was "indecent" for French relatives of the German imperial family to have to solicit favors from persons beneath them, he told her off by saying that members of the imperial family who were discontented with the king's treatment could go back where they had come from.[79] Another of her offensive initiatives was her protest to the king against the reforms of the finance minister Jacques Necker, which entailed cuts in court patronage generally and risked reducing patronage to her family in particular. Despite the display of all her charms before the king, she was, according to one source, "very badly received," a reception that Madame de Brionne's heavy drinking—which was later held up to public scorn in a widely circulated song—was unlikely to make any the warmer.[80] Nor were the offenses of the Brionne family limited to court circles. In 1780, a carriage carrying the prince de Lambesc and his brother ran over a number of pedestrians as it forced its way through the crowded rue Saint-Antoine without stopping, causing witnesses to run after the carriage shouting curses and provoking a public outcry. Madame de Brionne tried to make amends in this incident, reminiscent of Dickens' *Tale of Two Cities,* by providing an injured priest with two hundred livres in *rentes* and by asking her children to make a formal apology to the priest, but they refused. The upshot, according to the *Mémoires secrets,* was "a scandal to which the whole populace was witness" and "for which philosophers who shiver at the barbarity of the deed would have demanded an example of vigorous prosecution of justice to contain grandees, [who were] insufficiently punished in such cases."[81]

What did Marie-Antoinette get in return for protecting these compromising cousins? Certainly not loyalty. When the chips were down during the Diamond Necklace Affair, Madame de Brionne not only deserted the queen, but vociferously supported the cause of her own kinsman and former lover, Cardinal de Rohan.[82] "Madame de Brionne," the queen reported to Joseph, "who for twenty years appeared to have had no relations with him [Rohan], has involved herself in this affair with an enthusiasm that has led her to do a thousand foolish things."[83] This desertion must have been an especially bitter pill for Marie-Antoinette to swallow. She did finally turn on Madame de Brionne, blocking her international campaign to make Talleyrand—the lover of Anne-Charlotte, of Madame de Brionne's daughter-in-law (the beautiful princesse de Vaudémont), and probably of Madame de Brionne herself—a cardinal, by enlisting Mercy to put counterpressure on the Pope through Austria's ambassador in Rome.[84] Yet Marie-Antoinette did not turn on the house of Lorraine as a whole, but to the contrary, conspicuously continued to protect Madame de Brionne's two sons. At no point did Lambesc become persona non grata at the court, as evidenced by the king's willingness to grant Lambesc's vehement petition for privileged seating during the upcoming Assembly of Notables in early 1787.[85] As the queen wrote to Mercy in 1789 after recommending the prince de Lambesc to Joseph, "the more his mother was on bad terms with me in the past, the more I have personally praised the two brothers."[86] Thus by the eve of the Revolution, Marie-Antoinette had put no significant political distance between herself and the house of Lorraine, the bill for which would soon fall due.

II

Although a number of recent historians have demonstrated the intensification of the sexual defamation to which Marie-Antoinette was subject after 1789, it is equally significant that she provided the nucleus around which growing fear of Austria and its suspected agents cohered. Even before 1789, her very real but largely ineffective lobbying efforts on behalf of Austria had conjured up images of murder, sexual license, and the export of French treasure to her brother, the Austrian emperor Joseph II. In the spring of 1790, the term "Austrian Committee" began to infiltrate French political rhetoric, a term connoting a secret conclave headed by the Marie-Antoinette who sought to subvert the Revolutionary government and turn control of France over to the duplicitous Austrians. These charges were echoed in rumors circulating in the provinces—particularly those areas on the borders of Austrian-held territories—regarding the export of French food and gold and the suspicious activities of self-described "deserters" from the Austrian army who had crossed into France. By the spring of 1792, such concerns had grown to the point where the faction around Jacques-Pierre Brissot could successfully invoke the "Austrian Committee" as a bogeyman time and again in their campaign to push France into a war against Austria, for which the Legislative Assembly voted almost unanimously on 20 April.[87]

Fears about the fate of Lorraine and its surrounding territories, which echoed similar alarms sounded over the course of the Old Regime, featured prominently in the larger "case" against Austria and the queen during the Revolution. In early 1790, *Le Moniteur* "revealed" a plot of the royal council to sell Lorraine to Austria, a sale that the French government, despite its impending bankruptcy, would itself allegedly finance by extending a loan of six million livres to the emperor.[88] Also in 1790, an end to French sovereignty over Alsace and Lorraine was proposed by German publicists seeking territorial compensation for German princes who had lost seignorial rights in eastern France because of recent Revolutionary antifeudal legislation. Openly supported by the king of Sweden, this proposal was followed a year later by a similar one when, in the course of negotiating an alliance with Austria, Prussia raised the possibility of an Austrian recovery of Alsace and Lorraine in case of war with France.[89] The ventilation of plans for Austrian territorial reacquisitions in Alsace and Lorraine could only have aggravated an already inflamed French Austrophobia.

Rumors of an Austrian military effort to conquer eastern France circulated throughout the country during the summer of 1790, amidst other disturbing reports. One alleged that the king might leave Paris to set up a countergovernment in Lorraine, another that Lorraine had been selected to serve as one portal through which Austrian and Prussian troops would pour into the nation and, assisted by internal enemies, stir up anarchy and impose despotism: "There is no doubt that blood would flow in great waves, and that they [the troops] would seek to pitilessly slit our throats with the help of all the betrayals that their perfidious hearts could invent."[90] Little wonder, then, that when in 1790 Austria invoked its right to send troops across French territory on the basis of a 1769 agreement, armed peasants were reported rushing toward the border in the nearby Ardennes and shouting, "To arms! Here is the enemy!"[91] What these developments indicate is that the centuries-old fear of a Lorraine-based subversion of the nation by the Hapsburgs—a fixture of French political culture underlying the affair of the minuet—had now escalated into near public panic over an apparently clear and present danger.

As the most conspicuous emblem of Lorraine in France and the imputed chief of the "Austrian Committee," Marie-Antoinette could hardly escape implication in these and similar developments, an outcome that her own actions reinforced. In the early years of the Revolution, the queen stubbornly made good on her promise of support for Madame de Brionne's sons. Thus when the émigré princes de Lambesc and de Vaudémont petitioned for permission to enlist in the emperor's armies and demanded compensation for offices they had lost as a result of the Revolution, the queen lobbied a reluctant Louis to grant the "just demands advanced by M. de Lambesc on behalf of himself and his family."[92] Such protection, it should be noted, followed even in the wake of the most notorious incident involving the house of Lorraine—Lambesc's cavalry charge of 12 July 1789.

The basic facts regarding this charge are well established, although there is considerable dispute over the details.[93] With tensions rising in Paris over escalating food prices, the dismissal of Necker on 11 July, and fears of a coup d'état by the crown against the National Assembly, crowds closed down the theaters and took to the streets to protest the actions of the government on 12 July. When in the evening they entered the Place Louis XV from the Place Vendôme carrying busts of Necker and the duc d'Orléans taken from Curtius' waxworks exhibits, there followed a number of skirmishes with the forces of order. The prince de Lambesc, commander of the Royal-Allemand, was ordered to clear the square with his armed cavalry, who pursued the crowds into the neighboring Tuileries gardens. Assaulted by stones and verbal insults, the Royal-Allemand charged the crowd. One detachment did brief battle with members of another regiment, the Gardes Françaises, although this conflict does not seem to have occurred as a direct result of Lambesc's charge.

What is significant about Lambesc's charge in this context is not the event itself but its aftermath. As regards Lambesc, the incident prompted the sudden suspension of his career in France, since his actions immediately marked him as an assassin of the people. Indeed, Lambesc, who had already earned a reputation as a callous aristocrat in the hit-and-run incident of the rue Saint-Antoine in 1780, was forced to flee for his life.[94] On 13 July he made a brief visit to Versailles, where he reported to the king, who ordered Lambesc and his regiment to decamp for the Rhine.[95] Moving eastward along a route that the king and his family would closely follow two years later, Lambesc and the Royal-Allemand were badly received wherever they went. In Châlons they were denied provisions and, as in Paris, pelted with stones.[96] In Dun, despite efforts to hide their identity, they were recognized, attacked by yet another mob of outraged citizens, and shot at along the way. Abandoning the Royal-Allemand to its own fate, Lambesc crossed the border alone into Luxembourg on 1 August. He returned to France only in 1817 after pursuing a distinguished career as a field marshal in the counterrevolutionary armies of the Austrian emperor. Lambesc thus became one of the most prominent émigrés, deserting France a mere two weeks after the first and probably most notorious émigré of them all, the comte d'Artois, whom the Revolutionary literary imagination would depict as sharing the same circle of hell as the "traitor" Lambesc.[97] Lambesc was soon followed into exile by the virulent counterrevolutionary Madame de Brionne and his brother. Having enhanced their counterrevolutionary reputation by helping to repress a bitter mutiny at Nancy in August 1790 and assisting in the king's failed escape plans during the Varennes fiasco in June 1791, all but about forty members of the Royal-Allemand emigrated in May 1792. Like Lambesc and his brother, they eventually served in the forces of France's enemies.[98]

A second important result of Lambesc's charge was the elaboration of a popular myth surrounding it. Rumors of an immense slaughter immediately stalked Paris, with some observers claiming that Lambesc had been "massacring everyone in the Place Louis XV."[99] The periodical press retailed stories of a peaceful old man with a cane ruthlessly struck down by Lambesc's sword.[100] In his version of the story, the journalist Nicolas Ruault reported that Lambesc had severed the head of a venerable physician after crushing the hapless old man under the hooves of his horse, an act that had "terrified the whole city."[101] These accounts distorted a battle that was in fact far less bloody, but they nonetheless contributed to what officers of the Royal-Allemand later referred to as "the furor of a people whom writers had fooled and led into error" and prompted the prosecution of Lambesc in absentia by the Châtelet of Paris in the fall of 1789.[102]

Particularly interesting from the standpoint of this article was the common representation of the Royal-Allemand as a regiment of suspicious "foreigners" at a time when other detachments were liberating themselves from royal command and swearing that as "national," not "royal," troops, they would never spill the blood of the French, "their brothers and their friends."[103] The assertion that the Royal-Allemand was staffed by foreigners—Germans, in particular—was repeated so often in press accounts that the officers of the regiment felt obliged to refute it in a published self-justification. The regiment did contain some Germans, they pointed out, but, notwithstanding its name, the Royal-Allemand also comprised "good French citizens." Even the German members, they argued, had been raised according the same "principles" as the native French.[104] Yet it is doubtful that the protests of the Royal-Allemand officers did much to convince the public of their credentials as patriots. For the regiment did, in fact, comprise officers from Germany and the sensitive border areas of Lorraine and Alsace; and their willingness to commit violence on behalf of the king gave them a political coloration sharply different from that of the Gardes Françaises—their antagonists of 12 July—who enjoyed much closer social ties to the people of Paris and became conspicuous allies of the popular movement against royal "despotism" during the summer of 1789.[105] Lambesc's charge, in short, reinforced the impression that the king was relying on "foreign" troops, in particular "Germans" from Lorraine and Alsace, to maintain control of the popular movement, and that these troops had assaulted his own people.

As might be expected, Lambesc's demonization contributed to the demonization of Marie-Antoinette, just as Lambesc, according to the officers of the Royal-Allemand, "was doubly accused at this time because he is a relative of the queen."[106] The clearest evidence of this mutually reinforcing defamation lies in the role of Marie-Antoinette in the pamphlet literature directed against Lambesc and the role of Lambesc in the pamphlet literature targeted at Marie-Antoinette. In both genres, Lambesc was represented as an all-too-willing henchman of the evil queen. Thus in the notorious *Private and Scandalous Life of Marie-Antoinette,* the anonymous author described Lambesc as a devoted enforcer of the "committee of Antoinette," who pledged to use his blindly obedient "Germans" to inspire hatred and spill French blood.[107]

In another anonymous *libelle* purporting to be his "testament," Lambesc, an "abominable traitor and vile assassin" in his own right, was depicted as the queen's sexual hostage. "Without principles, without *moeurs,* without delicacy," declared the prince, "the royal prostitute has captivated my heart, my feelings, conjointly with those of thousands of others, and . . . because of the singular and shameful consideration she has for me, my will has always been dependent on hers." The imputation of a sexual relationship between the queen and Lambesc led to further charges of polymorphous promiscuity: on Lambesc's part to an alleged liaison with the queen's alleged lesbian lover, Madame de Polignac, and on the queen's part to an alleged affair with the comte d'Artois, reputedly the father of her children.[108] Such accusations echoed similar ones found in other pamphlets, one of which asserted that Lambesc had traveled through Europe in the company of a "beautiful castrato," and many others that collectively depicted Marie-Antoinette as engaging in virtually every imaginable sexual practice and cavorting with virtually every conceivable sexual partner.[109]

Yet sexual delinquence was hardly the principal transgression that representationally joined the queen with Lambesc. Lurking just beneath the charge of sexual trespass was the allegation of treason, made all the more plausible by their common association with the house of Lorraine—a dynasty of *princes étrangers* that had never been considered fully French, indeed had long been suspected of national subversion. In the eyes of some observers, accusing the queen and Lambesc of committing treason against a country to which neither really belonged by origin or imputed sentiment might have appeared to be stretching the meaning of "treason" beyond fair use. Yet just as Marie-Antoinette and Lambesc seemed to straddle the divide between male and female in their ambiguous sexual identities, so too did their Lorraine origins, coupled with the high offices they occupied in France and their notorious deeds, both invite charges they were covertly working on behalf of the Hapsburgs and make them seem sufficiently French to justify claims they had betrayed the nation. Thus, even if Lambesc, the commander of a "German" regiment in France with broad experience in the armies of Joseph II, could be described by one pamphleteer as possessed of "German" frankness, he was also portrayed as sufficiently Gallicized to have "adopted the agreeable vices of the court of France."[110]

Historical memory, particularly the collective recollection of the conniving Guises during the sixteenth-century French religious wars, clearly played a large role in the definition of these ambiguous identities. Lambesc, according to one report—inaccurate, as it turned out—had been hanged from a hook and his body mutilated by an angry crowd of people once they had recognized him as a descendant of the Guises.[111] In another text, also notable for its allusion to cross-gendering, Marie-Antoinette was represented as "a courageous man, worthy of honoring the noble blood of Guise," the branch of the house of Lorraine that the author held responsible for the butchering of thousands of Protestant leaders during the Saint Bartholomew's Day Massacre in 1572 and all the other major atrocities of the Wars of Religion over four successive reigns.[112] If such civil strife was what the house of Lorraine had achieved in the distant past, no less terrifying was what it had accomplished over the *longue durée*, most especially since the striking of the 1756 alliance, which had brought the most prominent contemporary representative of the house of Lorraine, Marie-Antoinette, to Versailles. In the view of Jean-Louis Carra, one of the chief "exposers" of the "Austrian Committee" conspiracy against the Revolutionary government, it was upon the latest incursion of the house of Lorraine into France

> that [French] inhabitants and their properties have been the toys of their despots, princes or sovereigns; that these despots, all enemies of the nation, have granted the most important positions only to perfidious foreigners or to well-compensated French rogues; that the people have been governed for thirty years strictly according to the counsels of the court of Vienna, uniquely concerned with putting them under the yoke of slavery [and] draining our treasury to gratify the voracity of a horde of insatiable foreigners; . . . [that the] court has become an arsenal for manufacturing chains, which have weighed more and more heavily upon an oppressed nation, and for sharpening daggers and stilettos that Italians introduced into France at the time of the Medici.[113]

Although surely bearing the inflections of Revolutionary discourse, such language had a more remote provenance, extending back to the days of the Guise and running through the affair of the minuet all the way to Lambesc's infamous charge.

III

During her trial in October 1793, Marie-Antoinette was asked whether "at the time of your marriage to Louis Capet, you had not conceived the project to reunite Lorraine with Austria?"[114] This accusation—expressed as a question—has gone largely unnoticed by scholars. But it is significant especially in the context of this article, for it forcefully demonstrates that contemporaries during the Terror had not lost sight of the former queen's supposed dynastically linked treason among all the other fantastic crimes attributed to her. By the time of the Revolution, recollections of the faintly comical affair of the minuet had faded sufficiently to suffer distortion, but memories of the house of Lorraine's deadly threat to French national security surely remained fresh in the minds of a good many French citizens.[115]

As regards Marie-Antoinette's personal fate, the suspicions arising from this indelible fixation are important for historians to consider, because they help explain how a young princess who had enjoyed such exceptional popularity upon her arrival in France could so quickly lose public favor and become so exceptionally vilified.[116] They also demonstrate how necessary it is to enter into the rich details of her political associations in order to account for her fate. Already targeted by the *parti dévot* as the emblem of an alliance they detested, Marie-Antoinette, through no fault of her own, was implicated in a highly resented attack on the hierarchy of noble privilege in the affair of the minuet as a result of her association with Madame de Brionne. But she compounded this injury on her own initiative by visibly supporting her brother Maximilien in his spat with the princes of the blood and by casually disregarding court etiquette. Her identification with and embrace of a well-placed Lorraine lobby anchored by the ex-minister Choiseul is understandable given the continued importance of clientage in the snake-pit politics of Versailles, the rise of an "administrative" monarchy notwithstanding.[117] Yet she was able to reap little advantage from her association with the house of Lorraine. Choiseul was dismissed at the end of 1770, never to return, leaving Marie-Antoinette to lobby for the unpopular Franco-Austrian alliance without him. Her patronage of Madame de Brionne and her children won her few friends and many enemies, who had long resented their pretensions; when she badly needed the fidelity of her cousins, during the Diamond Necklace Affair, they deserted her and supported Cardinal de Rohan. Even after the Revolution had eliminated the court as the chief nexus of political power, a rich residue of resentment and fear remained. Lambesc's notorious charge—in which a commander from the house of Lorraine deployed his force of "Germans" to assault a "peaceful" crowd of protesting patriots—evoked memories of the atrocities of the Guises; and it appeared that similar horrors might recur at a time when the Hapsburgs were believed to be once again casting a lean and hungry look on Lorraine and Alsace. All this, in the end, was put on the account of Marie-Antoinette, chief embodiment of the dreaded "Austrian Committee." Little wonder that she was feared, hated, and eventually beheaded, even if Madame de Brionne and her sons were able to escape across the border before the Terror got them.

Notes

1. Emmanuel, maréchal duc de Croÿ, *Journal inédit du duc de Croÿ, 1718–1784* (Paris: Flammarion, 1906–7), 2:392. Croÿ's is the most thorough account of the affair and I draw much of my description from it, but see also notes 3 and 16 below. On the preparations at Versailles for the wedding, see Denis-Pierre-Jean Papillon de la Ferté, *Journal de Papillon de la Ferté, intendant et contrôleur de l'argenterie, menus-plaisirs et affaires de la chambre du roi (1756–1780)*, ed. Ernest Boysse (Paris: P. Ollendorff, 1887), 250ff. The cost of the wedding was protested in an anonymous pamphlet, *Idée singulière d'un bon citoyen, concer-*

nant les fêtes publiques qu'on se propose de donner à Paris & à la cour, à l'occasion du mariage de Monseigneur le Dauphin, mentioned in Mouffle d'Angerville, *La Vie privée de Louis XV* (London, 1781), 4:180.

2. Croÿ, *Journal,* 2:432–33.

3. Friedrich Melchior, baron Grimm, *Correspondance littéraire, philosophique et critique,* ed. Maurice Tourneux (Paris: Garnier frères, 1877–82), 9:40.

4. Ibid., 9:35. Under the Old Regime, the peers consisted of the princes of the blood (blood relatives of the king) and the highest of three orders of dukes, the dukes and peers, of which there were slightly fewer than fifty in the eighteenth century. By this time, the functions of the peers had become largely ceremonial in nature, but they did have the right to sit in the *parlement* of Paris, the kingdom's foremost sovereign court, which led to protracted disputes over precedence. It was critical to the pretensions of the dukes and peers that there was as little distance as possible between them and the princes of the blood, which is one reason why during the regency of the duc d'Orléans they challenged the right of Louis XIV's legitimated bastards to follow the princes of the blood in line to the throne. For two excellent treatments, see Jean-Pierre Labatut, *Les Ducs et pairs de France au XVIIᵉ siècle: Étude sociale* (Paris: Presses Universitaires de France, 1972), and Harold A. Ellis, *Boulainvilliers and the French Monarchy: Aristocratic Politics in Early Eighteenth-Century France* (Ithaca: Cornell University Press, 1988). The *princes étrangers* were members of houses deemed sovereign unto themselves, including those of Lorraine, Savoy, Rohan, Bouillon, and Monaco. At court they were accorded honorific privileges not enjoyed by the dukes and peers, such as the right to attend receptions for ambassadors without removing their headgear. For a brief analysis, see Marcel Marion, *Dictionnaire des institutions de la France au XVIIᵉ et au XVIIIᵉ siècles* (Paris: A. Picard, 1923), 455.

5. "Mémoire au Roi, 15 June 1770," Bibliothèque de la Mazarine, Ms. 2385.

6. Croÿ, *Journal,* 2:433. In fact, there were precedents for interrupting the order of precedence at state balls to accommodate special requests. A particularly relevant one occurred on the occasion of Louis XIII's baptism in 1606, when during the grand ball the duc de Lorraine took precedence "by order of the king, in consideration solely that he was the godfather." Théodore and Denys Godefroy, *Le Cérémonial français* (Paris, 1649), 2:181. The order of dance on that occasion is listed on page 183.

7. Croÿ, *Journal,* 2:434.

8. Ibid.

9. Quoted in Claude de Pimodan, *Le Comte F.-C. de Mercy-Argenteau, ambassadeur impériale à Paris sous Louis XV et sous Louis XVI* (Paris: Plon-Nourrit, 1911), 89.

10. Croÿ, *Journal,* 2:433.

11. Grimm, *Correspondance littéraire,* 9:40.

12. Croÿ, *Journal,* 2:436, 409.

13. For the order of the dance, see ibid., 2:410–11.

14. Ibid., 436.

15. Ibid., 412. Grimm reached a different conclusion, namely, that the house of Lorraine had lost more than it gained. Grimm, *Correspondance littéraire,* 9:40.

16. The affair was mentioned frequently in contemporary literature. Aside from the accounts in Croÿ and Grimm, see Mathieu-François Pidansat de Mairobert,

L'Observateur anglois, ou correspondance secrète entre Milord All'Eye et Milord All'Ear (London, 1777–78), vol. 1, letter 4; Mouffle d'Angerville, *Vie privée de Louis XV*, 4:186–87.

17. Versions of this argument have been put forward by Elizabeth Colwill, "Just Another *Citoyenne?* Marie-Antoinette on Trial, 1790–1793," *History Workshop* 28 (1989), 63–87; and by Sarah Maza and Lynn Hunt in this volume.

18. Thomas E. Kaiser, "Who's Afraid of Marie-Antoinette? Diplomacy, Austrophobia, and the Queen," *French History* 14 (2000): 241–71. For other treatments of Austrophobia, see Michael Hochedlinger, "'La cause de tous les maux de la France': Die 'Austrophobie' im revolutionären Frankreich und der Sturz des Königstums 1789–1792," *Francia: Forschungen zur westeuropäischen Geschichte* 24.2 (1997): 73–120; Gary Savage, "Favier's Heirs: The French Revolution and the *Secret du Roi*," *The Historical Journal* 41 (1998), 225–58.

19. Gayle Rubin, "The Traffic in Women: Notes on the 'Political Economy' of Sex," in Rayna R. Reiter, ed., *Toward an Anthropology of Women* (New York: Monthly Review Press, 1975), 157–210. The changing national identities of foreign-born queens has not, to the best of my knowledge, been treated comparatively. For another instance in which suspicions regarding loyalties were aroused, see A. Lloyd Moote, *Louis XIII, the Just* (Berkeley: University of California Press, 1989), 278–81. During the Fronde, rumors circulated that Queen Anne d'Autriche was selling out France for the benefit of her family, the Spanish Hapsburgs. See *Discours sur le gouuernement de la Reyne depuis sa régence* (1649) in C[élestin] Moreau, ed., *Choix de Mazarinades* (Paris: J. Renouard, 1853), 2:4, in which the author, who disbelieved the charges, nonetheless asserted that there were "malicious-minded people . . . [who] have already said that being Spanish, the Queen would not fail to make a disadvantageous peace with the King [of Spain] her brother, . . . that she was going to abandon the interest of the French to advance the good of her country, . . . that although she is in France, her heart is in Spain."

20. For a general overview, see Michel Parisse, ed., *Histoire de la Lorraine* (Toulouse: Privat, 1977).

21. "Mémoire sur le duché de Lorraine (1732)" by M. d'Audiffret, *envoyé extraordinaire* to the courts of Mantua, Parma, Modena, and Lorraine, in Archives du Ministère des Affaires Étrangères (henceforth AAE) Correspondance Politique (henceforth CP) Lorraine 124, fol. 154. See also Rohan Butler, *Choiseul*, vol. 1: *Father and Son, 1719–1754* (Oxford: Clarendon Press, 1980), 171.

22. See, for example, Louis Chantereau Le Febvre, *Considérations historiques sur la généalogie de la maison de Lorraine. Première partie des mémoires* (Paris, 1642), preface. For background, see Gaston Zeller, "Le Traité de Montmartre (6 février 1662) d'après des documents inédits," *Mémoires de la Société d'archéologie lorraine et du Musée historique lorrain* 62 (1912): 5–74.

23. Louis de Rouvroy, duc de Saint-Simon, *Écrits inédits de Saint-Simon*, ed. M. P. Faugère (Paris: Hachette, 1880–93), 3:277.

24. Pierre Dupuy, *Traitez touchant les droits du roy très-chrestien sur plusieurs estats et seigneuries par divers princes voisins: et pour prouver qu'il tient à iuste titre plusieurs prouinces contestées par les Princes Estrangers* (Paris, 1655), 551.

25. Ibid., 561.

26. Croÿ, *Journal*, 2:427.

27. Saint-Simon, *Écrits inédits*, 3:302–8. For an analysis, see Labatut, *Ducs et pairs*, pt. 3, chap. 2.

28. Saint-Simon, *Écrits inédits*, 3:452.

29. Joseph-Othenin-Bernard de Cléron, comte de Haussonville, *Histoire de la réunion de la Lorraine à la France* (Paris: Michel Lévy frères, 1854–59).

30. AAE Mémoires et Documents (henceforth MD) France 418, fol. 215.

31. AAE CP Autriche 191, fol. 98. In 1732, before the renunciation was negotiated, Barbier reported that France opposed the election of Francis-Stephen as emperor, "because it is not in its interest to have as so close a neighbor a duc de Lorraine, emperor, and that it could not happen without leading to a war in nearly all Europe." Edmond-Jean-François Barbier, *Journal historique et anecdotique du règne de Louis XV* (Paris: J. Renouard, 1847–56), 1:476–77.

32. AAE CP Lorraine 127, "Observations sur les préliminaires de paix qui cèdent le duché de Bar avec l'expectative de la Lorraine," fol. 163ff.

33. Louis de Rouvroy, duc de Saint-Simon, *Mémoires*, ed. A. de Boislisle (Paris: Hachette, 1879–1919), 15:203. On Francis-Stephen, see Hubert Collin, "François-Étienne, dernier duc de Lorraine (1729–1737) et premier empereur de la maison de Lorraine-Habsbourg (1745–1765)," in Jean-Paul Bled et al., eds., *Les Habsbourg et la Lorraine: Actes du colloque international* (Nancy: Presses Universitaires de Nancy, 1988), 151–59.

34. Derek Beales, *Joseph II*, vol. 1: *In the Shadow of Maria Theresa, 1741–1780* (Cambridge: Cambridge University Press, 1987), 39–40.

35. Henri Baumont, *Études sur le règne de Léopold duc de Lorraine et de Bar (1697–1729)* (Paris: Berger-Levrault, 1894), 379 n. 2.

36. Ibid., 384.

37. AAE CP Lorraine 127, "Observations," fol. 163.

38. For a recent treatment of the events, see Reed Browning, *The War of the Austrian Succession* (New York: St. Martin's Press, 1993), chap. 10. On reports of Prince Charles' cruelty, see Barbier, *Journal*, 2:400–401.

39. Frantz Funck-Brentano, *Figaro et ses devanciers* (Paris: Hachette, 1909), 98–99.

40. Beales, *Joseph II*, 1:123–25.

41. On the impact of these developments, see Kaiser, "Who's Afraid of Marie-Antoinette?"

42. AAE CP Autriche 320, fols. 192, 204, 238. Frederick the Great noted that "the French accuse [Joseph] of having an aversion against their nation and of planning to reconquer Lorraine, Alsace, and Flanders." Letter to Prince Henry, 2 February 1777, in Frederick II, *Politische Correspondenz Friedrichs des Grossen*, ed. G. B. Volz et al. (Berlin: A. Duncker, 1879–1939), 39:46.

43. On Madame de Brionne and her family, see vicomte Jacques de Fleury, *Le Prince de Lambesc, grand Écuyer de France* (Paris: Plon, 1928).

44. Bibliothèque Nationale (henceforth BN) Ms. Fr. 6677.

45. See, for example, Princess Charlotte to Madame de Brionne, 9 June 1768, BN Ms. Fr. 6677, in which the writer reproves Madame de Brionne for her unorthodox method of making requests.

46. Croÿ, *Journal*, 2:427; AAE CP Autriche 312, fol. 88.

47. AAE CP Autriche 312, fol. 108.

48. BN Ms. Fr. 6677, fol. 38ff.

49. Fleury, *Prince de Lambesc*, 26ff.
50. Ibid., 108–9, 115.
51. Pimodan, *Comte F.-C. de Mercy-Argenteau*, 58–60.
52. Alfred Arneth and M. Auguste Geffroy, eds., *Correspondance secrète entre Marie-Thérèse et le comte de Mercy-Argenteau* (Paris: Firmin-Didot frères, 1874), 1:140n.
53. Fleury, *Prince de Lambesc*, 103.
54. Among Choiseul's chief concerns when proceedings for the marriage began to gain momentum in 1768 was Russian expansion into Poland, which Vienna showed few signs of opposing. See AAE CP Autriche 309. For negotiations on the marriage, see AAE MD France 426. See also Maurice Boutry, *Le Mariage de Marie-Antoinette* (Paris: Émile Paul, 1904) and *Autour de Marie-Antoinette* (Paris: Émile-Paul, 1906).
55. Boutry, *Autour de Marie-Antoinette*, 125–26.
56. Baron Max de Zedlitz, *Marie-Antoinette à Nancy (10 Mai 1770)* (Paris: J. Mersch, 1906).
57. *Mercure de France* 98 (June 1770): 163–64. The familial association with Lorraine would be renewed seven years later, when on his celebrated tour of France Joseph II frequented the same tombs in Nancy and received a loud ovation at an artillery school in Metz. See Boutry, *Autour de Marie-Antoinette*, 333.
58. [Beatus Fidelis Anton Johan Dominik, baron de Latour-Chatillon de Zurlauben], *Tables généalogiques des augustes maisons d'Autriche et de Lorraine, et leurs alliances avec l'auguste maison de France* (Paris, 1770); *Mercure de France* 99 (August 1770): 185.
59. Grimm, *Correspondance littéraire*, 9:33.
60. Croÿ, *Journal*, 2:427.
61. See Kaiser, "Who's Afraid of Marie-Antoinette?"
62. Général-Major de Martange to Prince Xavier de Saxe, 24 October 1767, in Charles Bréard, ed., *Correspondance inédite du Général-Major de Martange* (Paris: Picard, 1898), 418.
63. Martange to Prince de Saxe, 15 September 1767, in ibid., 404.
64. Grimm, *Correspondance littéraire*, 9:38.
65. Henri Griffet, *Traité des différentes sortes de preuves qui servent à établir la vérité de l'histoire* (Liége, 1769); [Joseph-Balthasar Gibert], *Mémoires sur les rangs et les honneurs de la cour; Pour servir de réponse aux trois derniers chapitres du Traité des preuves qui servent à établir la vérité de l'Histoire, par le P. Henri Griffet* (n.p., n. d.); abbé Jean-François Georgel, *Réponse à un écrit anonyme, intitulé "Mémoires sur les rangs et les honneurs de la cour"* (Paris, 1771). Gibert was secretary of the peers and helped draft the protest. The connection between the affair of the minuet and the controversy over the rights of the *princes étrangers* in general and the Rohans in particular is made by Pidansat de Mairobert, *L'Observateur anglois*, 1:166.
66. Pidansat de Mairobert, *L'Observateur anglois*, 1:169–70, 174.
67. Jacob-Nicolas Moreau, *Mes souvenirs* (Paris: Plon, 1898–1901), 2:149. See the anonymous letters on the impact of the affair published in Pimodan, *Comte F.-C. de Mercy-Argenteau*, 152 n. 1.

68. Thus upon the terminal illness of her uncle Charles de Lorraine, Marie-Antoinette lamented to her mother on 16 June 1780 about "how sad it was to see the last representative of the house of Lorraine expire." Arneth and Geffroy, *Correspondance secrète*, 3:436.

69. See the *placet* submitted to her that year on behalf of the chevalier de Tristay de Châteaufort. A Lorraine nobleman whose family had long served in the houses of Lorraine and Hapsburg, he had fallen on hard times, and now, upon the strongest endorsement of Maria Theresa, sought the protection of the new queen. AAE MD Fr. 1377, fols. 347–51.

70. See the exchange on the subject in Arneth and Geffroy, *Correspondance secrète*, 2:140, 156.

71. Grimm, *Correspondance littéraire*, 9:41; Fleury, *Prince de Lambesc*, 26ff., 141–42, 149–50.

72. Arneth and Geffroy, *Correspondance secrète*, 3:419.

73. Ibid., 420.

74. Ibid., 2:357, 3:420.

75. Ibid.

76. Fleury, *Prince de Lambesc*, 212–13; *Relevé d'erreurs et d'impostures consignées dans les journaux, comme faits réels*, no. 3 (10 May 1790), 102.

77. François Métra, *Correspondance secrète, politique & littéraire* (London, 1787–90), 1:339–40.

78. Siméon-Prosper Hardy, *Journal*, BN Ms. Fr. 6681, fol. 480.

79. Louis Petit de Bachaumont, *Mémoires secrets pour servir à l'histoire de la république des lettres en France depuis MDCCLXII jusqu'à nos jours* (London, 1777–89), 15:71.

80. Ibid.; Marc-Marie, marquis de Bombelles, *Journal* (Geneva: Droz, 1977–93), 2:276.

81. Bachaumont, *Mémoires secrets*, 15:115–16.

82. See Maza, "Diamond Necklace Affair Revisited," in this volume.

83. Marie-Antoinette, *Lettres de Marie-Antoinette: Recueil des lettres authentiques de la reine*, ed. Maxime de la Rocheterie and Le Marquis de Beaucourt (Paris: A. Picard et fils, 1895–96), 2:86.

84. Jack F. Bernard, *Talleyrand: A Biography* (New York: Scribner, 1973), 56–57.

85. "Mémoire donné au Roy par S.A. Mgr. Le Pce. de Lambesc au sujet de la place à occuper par le grand écuyer de France à l'ouverture de l'Assemblée de Notables du 22 fev. 1787," in Archives Nationales (henceforth AN) K677 no. 122.

86. Marie-Antoinette, *Lettres*, 2:142–43.

87. For a more detailed discussion of these developments, see Kaiser, "Who's Afraid of Marie-Antoinette?" See also Hochedlinger, "La Cause"; Savage, "Favier's Heirs."

88. *Moniteur universel*, 11 July 1789, 1:145.

89. Albert Sorel, *L'Europe et la Révolution française* (Paris: E. Plon, Nourrit et cie, 1887), 2:149, 241; T.C.W. Blanning, *The Origins of the French Revolutionary Wars* (London: Longman, 1986), 114.

90. AN D29 bis 32, no. 334.

91. *Moniteur universel*, 29 July 1790, 5:246.

92. *Pièces imprimées d'après le décret de la Convention Nationale, du 5 décembre 1792, l'an premier de la République* (Paris, 1793), 3:254.

93. For a close analysis of the primary sources and the conflicting interpretations of them, see Paul G. Spagnoli, "The Revolution Begins: Lambesc's Charge, 12 July 1789," *French Historical Studies* 17 (1991): 466–97; for Lambesc's own account, see Charles-Eugène de Lorraine, prince de Lambesc, *Précis historique et justificatif de Charles-Eugène de Lorraine, prince de Lambesc* (Trier, 1790).

94. For these events, on which the following account is partly based, see Edmond Cleray, "Un Précédent de 'Varennes:' L'Émigration du prince de Lambesc (juillet 1789)," *Annales des sciences politiques* 24 (1909): 531–37.

95. This directive was part of a general policy the Assembly imposed on Louis to demilitarize the area around Paris. See Jacques Godechot, *The Taking of the Bastille, July 14, 1789*, trans. Jean Stewart (New York: Scribner, 1970), 258.

96. *Le Sabreur des Tuileries dans l'embarras. Nouvelle authentique et intéressante* (Paris, 1789), 12.

97. *Testament préalable à la juste exécution projettée du traître et assassin le prince Lambesc . . . Suivi du Crédo des Traîtres, ou la profession de foi de ce Prince criminel & des autres Aristocrates, & leur Méa-Culpa* (Paris, 1789), 20; see also *Descente du prince Lambesc aux enfers* ([Paris], n.d.), 6, where Lambesc is likewise depicted as a "traitor" consigned to hell.

98. Samuel F. Scott, *The Response of the Royal Army to the French Revolution: The Role and Development of the Line Army, 1787–93* (Oxford: Clarendon Press, 1978), 114–15.

99. Quoted in Spagnoli, "The Revolution Begins," 485.

100. *Révolutions de Paris,* no. 1 (12–17 July 1789), 2–6.

101. Nicolas Ruault, *Gazette d'un Parisien sous la Révolution: Lettres à son frère, 1783–1796,* ed. Anne Vassal (Paris: Perrin, 1976), 156.

102. *Relevé d'erreurs,* 105; *Procès du prince de Lambesc: Résumé général de ce procès, ou Résultat des réflexions qu'il fait naître d'après le rapprochement de chaque déposition* (Paris, 1790), 3. Someone really was killed as a result of Lambesc's charge, but this casualty was largely forgotten for reasons Spagnoli tries to explain. See "Revolution Begins."

103. See, for example, Ruault, *Gazette,* 152, 156; and *Révolutions de Paris* 1 (12–17 July 1789), 4. This notion lives on in the current literature. Thus William Doyle refers to them as "German cavalry" in *The Oxford History of the French Revolution* (Oxford: Clarendon Press, 1989), 109.

104. *Relevé d'erreurs,* 102.

105. Ibid.; Scott, *Response of the Royal Army,* 61; Godechot, *Taking of the Bastille,* 84.

106. *Relevé d'erreurs,* 101.

107. *La Vie privée et scandaleuse de Marie-Antoinette, ci-devant reine des Français* (Paris, year I), 2:88–93.

108. *Testament préalable,* 3, 4, 6, 15.

109. *Les Nouveaux projets de la cabale dévoilés, ou Lettre du prince de Lambesc au marquis de Belsunce* (Caen, n.d.), 3ff.

110. Ibid., 11.

111. *La Mort du ci-devant prince Lambesc pendu par le peuple à Chambéri, en Savoye* ([Paris], n.d.), 5–6.

112. *Révolutions de Paris,* 43 ([1–8] May 1790), 265–66, n. 1.

113. *Annales patriotiques et littéraires de la France, et affaires politiques de l'Europe* 298 (27 July 1790), 194.

114. Gérard Walter, ed., *Actes du tribunal révolutionnaire* (Paris: Mercure de France, 1968), 128.

115. *Portefeuille d'un talon rouge* (Paris, 178-), for example, erroneously asserted that it was Madame de Brionne herself who danced ahead of the dukes and peers. Reprinted in Hector Fleischmann, *Les Maîtresses de Marie-Antoinette* (Paris: Éditions des Bibliophiles, 1910), 221.

116. On Marie-Antoinette's early popularity, see Kaiser, "Who's Afraid of Marie-Antoinette?"

117. On the lingering importance of clientage in court politics until the end of the Old Regime, see Peter Campbell, *Power and Politics in Old Regime France, 1720–1745* (London: Routledge, 1996).

Marie-Antoinette Obsession

Terry Castle

I

What might it mean to suffer from Marie-Antoinette obsession? In the approved manner of the late-nineteenth-century sexologists, Krafft-Ebing, say, or Havelock Ellis, let us begin anecdotally, with several case histories. In 1900 the Swiss psychologist Theodore Flournoy, professor of psychology at the University of Geneva, published *From India to the Planet Mars,* an investigation of the case of "Hélène Smith," a celebrated spirit medium active in Genevan spiritualist circles in the 1890s. While in a state of hypnotic trance Smith claimed to have had three previous incarnations—as a fourteenth-century Indian princess named Simandini, as an inhabitant of the planet Mars, and as Marie-Antoinette, the doomed queen of France. During her seances, which she conducted with the help of a mysterious "control" from the spirit world named Leopold, who communicated by rapping on a table, Smith was able to "relive" these past lives in precise, often bizarre detail. Flournoy, an experimental psychologist with an interest in spiritualism and the occult, began observing Smith's trances in 1894, and in his book offered an account of these visionary "cycles" while also speculating along Freudian lines about their psychological origins.[1]

The "Hindoo" and "Martian" cycles were outlandish enough: in fourteenth-century India, Smith revealed, she had lived at the court of a ruler named Sivrouka; on Mars, she had been an individual named Pouzé Ramié. While entranced, she was able to produce long passages of automatic writing—sometimes in a language resembling Sanskrit (of which she claimed no conscious knowledge) and sometimes in a so-called Martian dialect. Flournoy devotes several chapters of meticulous philological analysis to these fascinatingly cryptic compositions.[2] Yet the Marie-Antoinette cycle was, if any-thing, even more colorful. Were one to give it attention proportion-ate to its importance in Smith's "somnambulic life," Flournoy ob-served, a hundred pages would not suffice.[3]

Smith's royal "romance" typically began with a communication from Leopold, her spirit control. Leopold, it was revealed, was an otherworldly manifestation of the eighteenth-century Italian magi-cian Joseph Balsamo, otherwise known as Cagliostro, who had once—at least according to Smith—been passionately in love with Marie-Antoinette. While under Leopold's spiritual control, which she experienced as a kind of possession, Smith spoke in "the deep bass voice of a man," used masculine gestures, and frequently pro-fessed her love for the ill-fated French queen in an Italian accent. Soon, however, she progressed to reincarnating the spirit of An-toinette herself. At such moments she would pantomime with a handkerchief or an imaginary fan, pretend to take snuff, mimic the action of throwing back a train, and address those present as though speaking to members of a court. On one occasion she identified two male sitters as "Philippe d'Orléans" and "Mirabeau" and engaged them in conversation on eighteenth-century political matters. At another séance in 1896, Flournoy reports, Smith addressed "touch-ing exhortations to a lady present whom she took for the Princesse de Lamballe." This poignant encounter, "Leopold" later informed witnesses, was a "reproduction of the last evening which the un-happy queen, sustained by her companion in captivity, passed in this world."[4]

Admittedly, Smith's royal incarnation had its ludicrous aspects. Spectators sometimes caught out "Her Majesty" in peculiar anach-ronisms. At one séance attended by Flournoy in 1896 Smith ac-cepted a cigarette from the man she called "Philippe," despite the fact that she did not smoke in ordinary life. "But the remarks of the persons present upon the historical untruthfulness of this feature," Flournoy notes, "must have registered, and bore fruit, since at the following seances she did not seem to understand the use of tobacco in that form; she accepted, on the other hand, with eagerness, a pinch of imaginary snuff, which almost immediately brought about by autosuggestion a series of sneezes admirably successful."[5] When participants spoke of such things as telephones or bicycles, Smith-as-Marie-Antoinette would at first seem to comprehend their mean-ing, then (observing "the smile of the sitters") would somewhat sus-

piciously feign "sudden ignorance and astonishment in regard to
it."[6] Even the skeptical Flournoy, however, was forced to admit that
Smith's embodiment of the queen was often convincing, if not moving. "When the royal trance is complete," he wrote, "no one can fail
to note the grace, elegance, distinction, majesty sometimes, which
shine forth in Hélène's every attitude and gesture."

> She has verily the bearing of a queen. The more delicate shades of expres-
> sion, a charming amiability, condescending hauteur, pity, indifference,
> overpowering scorn flit successively over her countenance and are mani-
> fested in her bearing, to the filing by of the courtiers who people her
> dream. . . . Every thing of this kind, which cannot be described, is perfect
> in its ease and naturalness.[7]

However deeply rooted in hysteria, he concluded, it was all a most
"sparkling romance."

Seven years after the publication of *From India to the Planet
Mars,* in June 1907, a writer in the British *Journal of the Society for
Psychical Research* described a similar fantasy having to do with Marie-
Antoinette. Under the heading "Dream Romances" the anonymous
author—who allowed herself to be identified only as someone of
"strongly developed artistic sensibilities"—confessed how she had
been haunted since youth by an apparition that she believed to be
the ghost of the French queen. The haunting had begun in early
childhood, when a "strange woman" in a long old-fashioned dress,
with "masses of grey hair, done up in a fashion quite unlike to the
people I was accustomed to see," appeared in her bedroom and tenderly caressed her face as she lay in bed.[8] Her mother's attempts to
convince her that there was no such woman failed: in fact the apparition returned even when her mother kept watch in the room.
Soon the writer came to look upon her nightly visitor as a "secret
friend" and especially admired her beautiful kindly face and deep
blue eyes. These last, she says, were "brilliant like stars, though at
times the lids looked very heavy, as though she had been crying."
The apparition never spoke to her, she recollected, but this seemed
natural to her at the time: "I felt that we understood one another."[9]

Gradually the conviction came over her that her spectral visitor
was none other than Marie-Antoinette. Espying her mother dressing
one evening for a masquerade ball, she recognized her mother's costume—"of the Louis XVI period"—as identical to that of her silent
friend. She became obsessed with reading about the French Revolution and developed a private cult around the queen's memory. In her

teens, she says, she "spent hours at the South Kensington Museum, gazing at Marie-Antoinette's bust, examining her toilet-table with its little rouge pots, etc." "I can honestly say my happiest hours were spent in contemplating these treasures, though it was always with an emotion bordering on tears that I faced the bust of the queen."[10]

Later on, though the nighttime visits gradually ceased, she continued to have fantastic dreams and waking visions in which she saw the woman she believed to be Marie-Antoinette performing characteristic actions—playing cards, for example, "with Louis XVI and Madame Elizabeth," or listening to music, seemingly "in a palace or else a park." Once, while in a hotel room at Margate, she had a vision of the queen imprisoned in the Conciergerie in the final days of her life—her expression "haggard and agonized," her hair entirely white, and her eyes fixed in "a strange, glassy look." When the writer rushed forward to embrace her, the apparition abruptly vanished. A few years later, upon visiting Versailles for the first time, the writer experienced an eerie sense of déjà vu and a dreadful "choking sensation" upon entering the queen's former apartments.

During these hallucinatory episodes, the writer says, she sometimes saw herself as well, though oddly enough as a boy, "never as a girl." Her most terrifying vision of this kind came one night at a hotel in Paris on the rue St. Honoré. There she dreamed that she saw a huge crowd assembled outside the window and Marie-Antoinette passing by in a tumbril. Then she saw herself in male guise, "struggling frantically to push my way through and shouting incessantly: 'The queen! Let me get to the queen! I must get to the queen!'" Then again: "I was under the scaffold, stabbing furiously at the legs of the executioner to prevent him from doing his gruesome work, while the crowd jostled me back. Then I gave a horrible shriek . . . and that was the end of my dream." To this day, she added, she was unable to walk down the rue St. Honoré or across the Place de la Concorde (former site of the guillotine) without a horrible sensation of fear and revulsion.[11]

The writer of "Dream Romances" confessed that she had learned to be reticent about her strange experiences: since childhood, she admitted, friends and relations had laughed at her royal fancies, and she feared further humiliation once her case became widely publicized. Nonetheless, she concluded her brief memoir with a tremulous appeal for understanding. At times, she opined, she felt herself "on the point of reconstructing a consecutive remembrance of some former existence while in France, but no sooner do I seem to hold the thread I lose it, which is a very painful sensation." Lacking such remembrances, she could think of no other "plausible explanation" for her visions. Yet she remained hopeful that on returning to France she would solve her haunting mystery once and for all.[12]

Four years after the publication of "Dream Romances" yet another case of Marie-Antoinette obsession came to public attention—perhaps the most *outré* of all. In a book entitled *An Adventure*, published by Macmillan in 1911, two English spinsters identified only as "Miss Morison" and "Miss Lamont" described how during a sightseeing tour of the gardens at Versailles near the Petit Trianon in 1901 they had encountered the apparition of the queen and several members of her court. The story was not a hoax: the Misses Morison and Lamont, it was subsequently revealed, were in fact two eminently respectable female academics, Charlotte Anne Moberly and Eleanor Jourdain, the principal and vice principal, respectively, of St. Hugh's College, Oxford (see photo insert). Not only were they in earnest; for the next fifteen years they continued to enlarge upon their tale, often in the face of exquisite public ridicule.

Their "adventure" had been as follows. On the afternoon of 10 August 1901, after touring the main palace of Versailles (which neither had visited before), the two ladies had gotten lost somewhere in the surrounding grounds while looking for the Petit Trianon, the famous rustic retreat of Marie-Antoinette. After trying unsuccessfully to get their bearings—or so they maintained—they had encountered a succession of unusual-looking personages: a peasant woman and girl in picturesque rural costumes, two men in green liveries and three-cornered hats, an ugly and strangely "repulsive" pockmarked man sitting by a kiosk, a running man with buckled shoes, a man dressed like a footman, and finally a beautiful fair-haired lady in an "old-fashioned" dress and pale green fichu. The latter sat sketching on the lawn near a small building they assumed to be the Trianon. As they walked toward it, both were overwhelmed by a powerful feeling of melancholia and oppression. Once inside the building, however, where a jolly French wedding party was in progress, they recovered their spirits and the rest of their visit passed uneventfully.[13]

Returning to Versailles a few months later, Moberly and Jourdain were unable to retrace their steps, finding much of the scenery around the Trianon mysteriously altered. At the same time—or so

they claimed—they learned that 10 August, the date of their first
visit, had been the anniversary of the 1792 sacking of the Tuileries,
when Marie-Antoinette and Louis XVI had been forced to flee for
their lives and take refuge in the hall of the National Assembly.
Shocked and excited by the coincidence, the two of them gradually
evolved the theory that they had somehow traveled back in time—
perhaps by entering "telepathically" into the reveries of Marie-
Antoinette as she huddled with Louis XVI and their children in the
National Assembly right after the sacking of the royal palace. Under
those anxious circumstances—the two surmised—the queen must
have relieved her spirits by thinking back, nostalgically, to the final
happy summer she had spent at the Petit Trianon in 1789. By some
uncanny process, they concluded, what they had seen in 1901 were
those very images of the Trianon—and of the people associated
with it in 1789—that had flitted, phantomlike, through the queen's
thoughts in 1792.

Convinced that their theory was correct, Moberly and Jourdain
now began an exhaustive—indeed, obsessional—search for proof.
Between 1901 and 1911 they combed archives and libraries, reading
everything they could lay their hands on about Marie-Antoinette
and the Trianon. They presented their findings in *An Adventure,*
complete with footnotes, maps, appendices, and other scholarly-
looking paraphernalia. As far as they were concerned, the mystery
had been solved: every person seen in 1901 was precisely identified
with someone present at the Trianon in 1789. The two men in green,
for example, were identified as members of Marie-Antoinette's private *gardes suisses;* such royal guards, Moberly and Jourdain informed their readers, invariably wore liveries of exactly this color
while on duty at the Trianon. The sinister pockmarked man was
identified with the queen's would-be enemy, the comte de Vaudreuil:
the count's face, according to several old memoirs they had consulted, had been scarred by smallpox. The running man was identified as one of the queen's pages: he wore buckled shoes of exactly the
kind fashionable "after 1786"—and so on. The sketching lady, the
two maintained, was none other than Marie-Antoinette herself. Her
"pale green fichu," they wrote, was identical to one they had found
described in the notebooks of Mme Éloffe, the queen's dressmaker,
from July 1789. After completing these demonstrations, Moberly
and Jourdain concluded *An Adventure* with a lyrical epilogue entitled "A Reverie: A Possible Historical Clue"—a blatantly fictional

stream-of-consciousness account (mostly composed by Moberly) of the supposed thoughts and reflections of Marie-Antoinette on 10 August 1792.[14]

Hardly surprisingly, given its bizarre subject matter and the prominence of its authors, *An Adventure* produced a storm of controversy. Among the more scathing attacks on the book was Mrs. Henry Sidgwick's review in the *Journal of the Society for Psychical Research* in which she accused Moberly and Jourdain of outright folly and self-deception. What they had encountered at Versailles in 1901, she contended, were merely "real persons and things" that they had subsequently "decked out by tricks of memory (and after the idea of haunting had occurred to them) with some additional details of costume suitable to the times of Marie-Antoinette."[15] In *Psychical Research* (1911) the scientist W. F. Barrett took a similar line: the two ladies' claims, he thought, were the result of "lively imagination stimulated by expectancy" and lacked any "real evidentiary value."[16] Such skepticism, however, only prompted Moberly and Jourdain to further asseverations. In 1913 they published a revised edition of *An Adventure* with a section entitled "Answers to Questions We Have Been Asked," in which they reiterated their belief that they had indeed seen the queen and members of her court, not unusually dressed gardeners, tourists, film actors, or people in masquerade costume, as Sidgwick and others had suggested.[17] The controversy ultimately outlived them. Though Jourdain died in 1924 and Moberly in 1937—each staunchly maintaining the truth of their story to the end—books and articles disputing the claims of *An Adventure* continued to appear well into the 1950s. As late as 1976 the two ladies' literary executor published her own debunking explanation of the "Trianon ghosts" in a lengthy essay in *Encounter*.[18]

Why so many apparitions of Marie-Antoinette? The simplest answer, of course, may be that some hidden chain of influence links the three cases. Flournoy's book on Hélène Smith, translated into English in 1901, was well known enough in England in 1907 for the author of "Dream Romances" to have been aware of it; in their introduction to "Dream Romances," the editors of the *Journal of the Society for Psychical Research* themselves called attention to it.[19] In turn, Moberly and Jourdain, writing in 1911, could easily have read either Flournoy's book or "Dream Romances" and used one or both as inspiration for *An Adventure*. Several contemporaries in fact suspected them of appropriating the Marie-Antoinette theme. W. F.

Barrett, in his attack on *An Adventure* in 1911, mentioned both *From India to the Planet Mars* and "Dream Romances" in his remarks and hinted that some act of conscious or unconscious borrowing had taken place.[20] In *The Ghosts of Versailles: Miss Moberly and Miss Jourdain and Their Adventure*, a three-hundred-page "critical study" published in 1957, Lucille Iremonger, who had been a student at St. Hugh's, argued that since Eleanor Jourdain read French, she could easily have read Flournoy's book when it appeared in 1900 in its original language. The book had been successful and had gone through three editions within a few months.[21]

Yet to posit that some sort of copycat syndrome must have been at work in a sense merely restates the original problem. The communication, as if by infection, of delusional ideas from one person to another is of course not unknown to psychologists. One need only think of the witch-hunting manias of the Middle Ages, outbreaks of St. Vitus' dance in the sixteenth and seventeenth centuries, the collective hallucinations seen on World War I battlefields, or the UFO and Elvis Presley sightings of our own day to appreciate the contagious power of certain delusional ideas. And yet, even allowing for an element of hysterical contagion in the cases under consideration, the basic psychological issue is still left unresolved. To plagiarize someone else's fantasy of seeing Marie-Antoinette is, after all, just as peculiar as coming up with such a fantasy on one's own. What was it about Marie-Antoinette—and Marie-Antoinette alone—that she should become so extraordinarily present, more than one hundred years after her death, to four presumably intelligent, well-educated, and otherwise conventional women?

Flournoy's remarks on Hélène Smith in *From India to the Planet Mars* suggest a way into the problem. Flournoy, who was one of the earliest disciples of Freud, explained Smith's "royal romance" in classic psychoanalytic terms as the hysterical manifestation of an unconscious hostility toward her parents. Like Anna O. (to whom he compares her), Smith had been born into comfortably bourgeois circumstances, yet grew up feeling misunderstood and unappreciated by her parents—"like a stranger in her family and as one away from home."[22] This emotional isolation led by turns, he hypothesized, to "a sort of instinctive inward revolt against the modest environment in which it was her lot to be born, a profound feeling of dread and opposition, of inexplicable malaise, of bitter antagonism against the whole of her material and intellectual environment."[23]

As a teenager, Smith expressed this yearning "for a life more brilliant than her own" decoratively, by turning her parents' sitting room into a kind of Beardsleyesque salon, complete with Japanese vases, engravings, and miniature hanging lamps. Later, however, in her twenties, she began to manifest her dissatisfaction more eccentrically—by falling into states of "obnubilation" (i.e., hypnotic trance), joining in seances, and indulging in "megalomaniac" reveries.[24]

That Smith should have fixed upon Marie-Antoinette as her primary alternative personality made sense, according to Flournoy, on two counts. "The choice of this role," he maintained,

> is naturally explained by the innate tastes of Mlle. Smith for everything that is noble, distinguished, elevated above the level of the common herd, and by the fact that some exterior circumstance fixed her hypnoid attention upon the illustrious queen of France in preference to the many other historic figures equally qualified to serve as a point of attachment for her subconscious megalomaniac reveries.[25]

The latter circumstance, he speculated, had been an engraving—first seen by Smith in 1892 or 1893—depicting a scene from Alexandre Dumas' *The Memoirs of a Physician* (1846–48), one of a series of historical romances written by Dumas about life under the ancien régime. In the scene in question, the sixteen-year-old Marie-Antoinette, shortly to ascend the throne of France (Dumas' novel is set in 1773), meets the mysterious magician-doctor Joseph Balsamo (Cagliostro), who invites her to look into the future by gazing into the water in a magic decanter. Seeing the terrible fate in store for her, the dauphine faints dead away. Soon after being shown the engraving, the entranced Smith announced "through the table" that she was Marie-Antoinette and "Leopold," her control, whose spiritual identity had previously been unclear, was Cagliostro. One could only surmise, wrote Flournoy, that the sight of the engraving had somehow "given birth to this identification of Hélène with Marie-Antoinette, as well as to that of her secondary personality of Leopold with Cagliostro."[26] As for the melodramatic touches Smith brought to her role as the queen—her parting embrace of the supposed "princesse de Lamballe," for example—these could be explained, he thought, by the intellectual context in which Smith had grown up: sentimental stories having to do with the queen and the French Revolution were, after all, among "the classes of facts" best known "in France today," he concluded.[27]

The central argument here—that Hélène Smith's Marie-Antoinette impersonation was a way of getting back at unresponsive parents—

strikingly anticipates Freud's argument, of course, in the well-known essay "Family Romances" from 1909. The fantasy of being descended from royalty, Freud thought, had its origins in the unconscious resentment that children felt toward their mothers and fathers. There were "only too many occasions," he contended, "on which a child is slighted, or at least feels he has been slighted, on which he feels he is not receiving the whole of his parents' love, and most of all, on which he feels regret at having to share it with brothers and sisters."[28] In retaliation for such slights, the child was wont to imagine himself a stepchild or adopted child, and to replace his parents in fantasy with others, "occupying, as a rule, a higher social station." For Hélène Smith—whom Flournoy describes as "disgusted" by her "insipid and unpleasant surroundings" and "wearied" by "ordinary, commonplace people"—the act of becoming Marie-Antoinette was conceivably simply a convenient means of avenging herself upon "vulgar," uncomprehending parents and of intimating to the world that she had indeed been "born for higher things."[29]

A similar argument, one suspects, could be made about the authors of "Dream Romances" and *An Adventure*. In the case of the "Dream Romances" writer especially, it is difficult not to invoke the obvious psychoanalytic allegory. The writer hints that her childhood was unhappy; her mother in particular seems to have neglected her. She speaks of lacking any sense of "those intimate blood-ties that generally exist between members of the same family," and of being reproached by her relations for a want of "esprit de corps." In the fantasy of the secret friend, the beautiful spectral woman who comes at night to give comfort, it is almost impossible not to see an element of symbolic wish fulfillment. "Many an evening, when my parents were entertaining guests, or had artistes to sing and play, which kept me awake," the writer somewhat broodingly relates, "the presence of my unknown friend comforted me. She remained with me for hours, and sometimes put a cool, slender hand on my head while she bent down to look at my face."[30] Here at last was someone, she insinuates—a queen, no less—to give her the attention she deserved. That her real mother inevitably objected to these "nervous fancies" seems only to have increased their intoxicating power over her: as with Hélène Smith, revenge seems to have played an important role in the larger wish-fulfillment structure.

In the case of Moberly and Jourdain the biographical picture is more complicated, yet similar psychological factors may have been at work. Both women were members of large families, even by Victorian standards: Moberly was the seventh of fifteen children, Jourdain the first of ten, and each felt overshadowed by siblings. Both had cold and forbidding mothers: Moberly's always wore a "severe matron's cap" and refused to call her husband by his first name; Jourdain's was known for her sarcastic tongue.[31] Both women's fathers, in turn, blatantly preferred sons to daughters. Moberly's father—for many years the headmaster of Winchester and later bishop of Salisbury—did not believe in educating women; Moberly acceded to the principalship of St. Hugh's only after his death, and largely by accident. Jourdain's father, also a clergyman and scholar, seems to have taken little interest in his eldest daughter's academic career, even when she became the first woman to undergo a viva voce examination in modern history at Oxford in 1886.[32]

Hostility toward these unsatisfactory parents may have motivated certain aspects of *An Adventure*. Like the "Dream Romances" writer, Moberly and Jourdain both seem to have envisioned Marie-Antoinette, at least in part, as a kind of idealized maternal substitute: the obsession with finding her at the Trianon (and later, symbolically, in their researches) could, at a pinch, be read as a search for that "mother love" their real mothers seem not to have supplied. One of the crucial pieces of evidence they put forth in support of their claim that the sketching lady of 1901 was in fact the French queen, interestingly, was the so-called Wertmüller Antoinette, a portrait from the 1780s depicting the young Marie-Antoinette with her two children, which they said "brought back" the lady's features exactly (see photo insert). Conveniently enough, the early-nineteenth-century memoirist Madame Campan had declared the Wertmüller portrait the truest likeness of the queen.[33] But the image may have interested them for another reason: with its insistent visual focus on the queen's maternal body (reinforced by the crudely triangular composition). It also satisfied, perhaps, subliminal longings in both women for a compensatory image of maternal tenderness.

Finding a new mother in Marie-Antoinette was in turn a way of retaliating against powerful yet impervious fathers. Of course, from one perspective Moberly and Jourdain's *Adventure* might be read as a coded plea for paternal approval: the elaborate mimicry of scholarly conventions, the ponderous footnotes, and the obsessional adumbration of "evidence" all suggest a desire to placate (if only superficially) emotionally distant scholar-fathers. By becoming Oxford dons, and part of the first trailblazing generation of English women academics, Moberly and Jourdain had from the start not-so-secretly modeled themselves on imposing male parents. And yet one also senses a subterranean animosity in *An Adventure*—an urge to show up, as it were, these same authority figures. By using the sober devices of masculine scholarship to tell a decidedly fabulous and "gynocentric" story, Moberly and Jourdain found a way, perhaps, of subtly arraigning those patriarchs—real and symbolic—who seemed to discount them and their achievements.[34]

Suggestive as it may be, however, the standard Freudian model of the family romance still leaves the most puzzling feature in the cases before us unexplained. Psychoanalysis describes the royal fantasy only in negative and generalized terms—as a mode of psychic protest or revenge. And yet in the peculiar passion with which Hélène Smith, the "Dream Romancer," and Moberly and Jourdain made the Marie-Antoinette connection we sense something more than mere atavistic complaint. There is an idiomatic, loverlike intensity about each woman's fixation, a lyrical-romantic ardor powerfully suffused with what can only be described as homosexual pathos. These, above all, are homoerotic fantasies, in which the queen plays the part of both seductive object of desire and visionary emblem of female-female bonding.

We sense this pathos most strikingly, perhaps, in the case of the "Dream Romances" writer, whose Marie-Antoinette fantasies are startling for both their erotic intensity and openly transsexual aspects. The writer's vision of Antoinette leaning over her bed at night—leaning into her, as it were—to caress and be caressed is as much a lover's as a child's vision, replete with heterodox possibility. In these hours of voluptuous communion, she notes, "I had full leisure to note every detail of her face, which seemed to me very beautiful." Later she speaks of the queen as "dearer to me than anyone in the world."[35] The fantasy of being a boy seems to have licensed these curiously sapphic devotions: the writer betrays no embarrassment at declaring—or embracing—a female love object. At times, it is true, she veils her passion in transvestite melodrama: the dream she describes in which she sees herself, in heroic male guise, attempting to save Marie-Antoinette from the guillotine has an air about it of sentimental kitsch, though it is perhaps no less compelling for that. The fantasy of gallantry allowed her love to flourish; in erotic self-obfuscation she found release.

Similar themes can be discerned in the visions of Hélène Smith. Smith, as Flournoy notes, was unmarried: indeed, she used her psychic gift to resist men and matrimony from an early age. Despite her "profound isolation of heart," she told the psychologist, "I could not make up my mind to marry, although I had several opportunities. A voice was always saying, 'Do not hurry: the time has not arrived; this is not the destiny for which you are reserved.'"[36] Later she personified this "voice" in the figure of "Leopold," her spirit control. Leopold played the role of invisible watchdog in Smith's life, addressing her harshly whenever she allowed herself to be approached by men. Once during her adolescence, she said, Leopold had had "an explosion of wrath" when her middle-aged family doctor (like Herr K. in Freud's case history of Dora) attempted to kiss her.[37] On another occasion he violently berated her for accepting a rose from a man on a streetcar.[38]

With the evolution of Smith's career as a medium and the development of the "royal romance" in the early 1890s, Leopold came to assume an even more prominent role in her psychic life. Smith at times described feeling herself mysteriously "becoming or being" Leopold:

> This happens most frequently at night, or upon awakening in the morning. She has first the fugitive vision of her protector; then it seems that little by little he is submerged in her; she feels him overcoming and penetrating her entire organism, as if he really became her or she him.[39]

As in the case of the "Dream Romances" writer, this alternative male self—bizarrely realized—gave Smith access to a sphere of explicitly homoerotic emotion. Leopold's dramatic assertion "through the table" that he was actually Cagliostro and in love with Marie-Antoinette became for Smith, one suspects, a phantasmagorical way of signifying her own sexual attraction to the French queen, whom at other moments, of course, she also impersonated. Taken over by the spirit of "the powerful and manly Count of Cagliostro," wrote Flournoy, "[Smith's] eyelids droop; her expression changes; her throat swells into a sort of double chin, which gives her a likeness of some sort to the well-known figure of Cagliostro."[40] Her words, paradoxically addressed to herself (as Marie-Antoinette), came forth "slowly but strong" in "the deep bass voice of a man." While one hesitates to label Smith's fantasies as lesbian in any simplistic sense—the "Hindoo" and "Martian" cycles reveal a sexual personality of quite staggeringly polymorphous perversity—there is a strong suggestion here that her "royal romance," so weirdly enacted, was powerfully informed nonetheless by latent homosexual interests.

Compared with these colorful goings-on, Moberly and Jourdain's rather more straightforward hallucination of Marie-Antoinette at the Trianon may seem a bit tame. And yet theirs is in some ways the most homosexual vision of all, as the biographical background to *An Adventure* makes clear. At the time of the fateful excursion to Versailles in August 1901, Moberly and Jourdain were virtual strangers to each other, having met in Paris only a few weeks before. A mutual friend had recommended Jourdain to Moberly for the vacant post of vice principal at St. Hugh's, where Moberly had served as principal since 1886. The sightseeing trip was in part an experiment to see if the two women could work together compatibly. It was a success in more ways than one. Following the experience at the Trianon, Moberly and Jourdain not only became colleagues at St. Hugh's and collaborators on *An Adventure* but lived together (in a relationship described by one observer as that of "husband and wife") for the next twenty-three years, until Jourdain's death in 1924.[41]

What this sequence of events suggests, of course, is that the vision of Marie-Antoinette in some way triangulated—or made possible—Moberly and Jourdain's own lifelong homoerotic attachment. In the months immediately following the Trianon experience, as Lucille Iremonger records in *The Ghosts of Versailles,* the two women became inseparable friends: "The shy woman [Moberly] liked the sociable one [Jourdain]; the plain unfeminine creature warmed to the little charmer, flowery hats, silken ankles and all." The joint obsession with Marie-Antoinette seemed to underwrite their courtship: "Soon, too soon, many thought, the vacations which Annie Moberly had once spent with relations . . . were all spent searching for 'proof' for the Versailles 'adventure' in company with Miss Jourdain."[42] It was as if, indeed, Marie-Antoinette had brought them together.

At a deeper level Moberly and Jourdain seem to have been using the figure of the queen to legitimate, if only unconsciously, their own unorthodox emotional needs. Certainly the story in *An Adventure* can be read as a kind of lesbian legitimation fantasy. In both its details and overall structure it seems to dramatize a movement away from masculine sexuality toward a world of female-female love and ritual. The pseudonymous Miss Morison and Miss Lamont, lost in a mysterious garden, are questing after the palace of a beautiful queen. After numerous adventures, including a frightening en- counter with a "repulsive-looking man" (the kiosk man), they en- counter, as if in a vision, the beautiful queen herself. In the guise of the sketching lady, she seems to bring about a kind of mystical mar- riage between them. Ever after, the two resolve, they will testify to- gether to what they have seen. Their symbolic odyssey ends, fittingly enough, with a real marriage, when they come upon the French wedding party, inside the "female" space of the Trianon itself.[43]

Later, when *An Adventure* met with attack, Moberly and Jourdain defended their claims so fiercely, one suspects, because they were trying in part to maintain this subliminal fiction of legitimation. It was as if they needed the queen in order to justify themselves as "husband and wife"—women living together in a potentially in- criminating homosexual dyad—before a hostile and rejecting world.[44]

Why this recurrent association between Marie-Antoinette and female homoeroticism? To get at the meaning of such obsession, it seems to me, we need to look beyond the somewhat specialized fic- tions of the family romance to something much broader: to what we might call "cultural romance" or the dynamics of collective fantasy. Hélène Smith, the "Dream Romances" writer, and Moberly and Jourdain were not the only women of the later nineteenth century, it turns out, haunted by ghostly dreams of Marie-Antoinette. Particu- larly among women in England, where sympathy for the ancien régime had long been a staple of popular romantic sensibility, Marie-Antoinette was in fact a kind of cult figure—the object of a widespread and often curiously eroticized group fixation. A host of hagiographical biographies from the period, such as Sarah Tytler's *Marie-Antoinette* (1883), dedicated to one whose tribulations "will never cease to melt all hearts, so long as manly pity and womanly tenderness endure," bear witness to the phenomenon.[45]

This fixation needs to be differentiated at once, I think, from what might loosely be called the heterosexual fascination with the queen traceable in the works of eighteenth- and nineteenth-century male writers. Edmund Burke's famous description of Marie- Antoinette in her prime "glittering like the morning-star, full of life, and splendor, and joy," or Thomas Carlyle's romantic paean to the hapless queen, fated to end her life among the most "vicious" of men, or even Charles Dickens' chivalrous asides on "the Widow Capet" in *A Tale of Two Cities*, while laden with historical pathos, nonetheless seldom display the same peculiar intimacy, the clandestine, excitable joy, and the uncanny urge to bring back to life so palpable in the fantasies of her female admirers.[46]

For subtly inspiring the feminine fixation (in all of its strange embodied tenderness), I would like to argue, were shadowy rumors having to do with Marie-Antoinette's own purported homoeroticism. That Marie-Antoinette was herself a lover of women had been rumored at least since the 1770s, when stories about her scandalous friendships with women had circulated freely in court circles. In the years before the Revolution antiroyalist propagandists had in turn taken up the rumor, giving it sensational play in a series of widely distributed obscene pamphlets and broadsheets. In an effort to undo the damage done to her reputation by such assaults, the queen's nineteenth-century apologists tried to defend her by emphasizing the "romantic" (and hence platonic) nature of her female friendships. And yet precisely by dwelling on the issue they also succeeded, paradoxically, in keeping the problem of her sexuality before the public eye. By the end of the century, not only were the rumors about Marie-Antoinette's homosexuality still alive, but she had become for certain of her female admirers a kind of secret heroine— an underground symbol of passionate love between women. It made sense that Hélène Smith, the "Dream Romances" writer, and Moberly and Jourdain should have used her to underwrite their own homoerotic romances, for she had already been thoroughly coded, as it were, into late-nineteenth-century culture as the "sapphic" queen par excellence.

II

How had rumors of Marie-Antoinette's homosexuality come to haunt the nineteenth century? Without question the queen herself had something to do with it—though exactly how much is still a matter of debate. Whether Marie-Antoinette was "really" a lesbian, if indeed the term can be said to apply under the circumstances, remains in dispute. Stefan Zweig, author of *Marie Antoinette: The Portrait of an Average Woman* (1933) and the first modern biographer to discuss the question with anything resembling frankness, thought that she had indeed had homosexual affairs—if only, as it were, by default. She was at heart, he argued, "a thoroughly natural, an essentially feminine woman, gentle, tender, ready to surrender herself to the embraces of the male." Owing to Louis XVI's mysterious impotence, however, during the first seven years of their marriage—from 1770 to 1777—she had been forced to turn elsewhere in order "to gratify her physiological requirements." "She had need," he affirms, "of someone who would relieve her spiritual and bodily tensions, and since, for propriety's sake, she would not (or would not yet) seek it from a man, Marie-Antoinette at this juncture involuntarily turned towards a woman friend."[47] The doting princesse de Lamballe (see photo insert) was the first of these intimate friends, only to be supplanted later by the dashing comtesse de Polignac (see photo insert), who inspired in the queen "a sort of super-heated falling in love."[48] Only the curing of Louis XVI's impotence in 1777, and Marie-Antoinette's subsequent motherhood, Zweig concludes, turned her sexual interests back in a more conventional direction.[49]

Other biographers are more equivocal. Both Dorothy Moulton Mayer in *Marie Antoinette: The Tragic Queen* (1968) and Joan Haslip in *Marie Antoinette* (1987) deny the lesbian allegation; Mayer, in fact, dismisses it as "rubbish." Yet both also linger, somewhat ambiguously, on the subject of Marie-Antoinette's unusual interest in other women. During the first years of her reign especially, Mayer writes, when the young queen lived "without hope of any normal sexual life with her husband," she turned for "love and understanding" to various attractive women at court, such as the raven-haired Polignac.[50] Haslip dwells at length on the queen's emotional susceptibility to pretty women. In the delicate princesse de Lamballe, with her "huge blue eyes and long blonde curls," she writes, Marie-Antoinette thought she had found the "ideal companion"; later infatuations included the "exquisite" Lucie Dillon (who became one of the queen's ladies-in-waiting), an unnamed actress, and the "insinuating" Polignac, who used her position to enrich her large and ambitious family.[51]

Whatever the truth of the matter, it is clear that rumors about Marie-Antoinette's homosexuality had begun to spread across France—and even to England—well before the French Revolution. "They have been liberal enough to accuse me of having a taste for both women and lovers," she wrote to her mother, Empress Maria Theresa of Austria, in 1775.[52] In the years leading up to the Revolution, antiroyalist propagandists elaborated on the charge in a host of secretly published pornographic *libelles* designed to inflame public sentiment against her. In the anonymous *Portfolio of a Red Heel* (1779) and the *Historical Essay Concerning the Life of Marie Antoinette* (1781), for example, the queen was accused of bringing the vice of "tribadism" with her from Austria into France and of having affairs with the comtesse de Polignac and Madame Balbi. In the scurrilous *Love Life of Charlie and Toinette* (1779) she was depicted in "criminal" embraces with the princesse de Lamballe. And in the grossly obscene *The Royal Dildo* (1789), in the guise of the goddess "Junon," she was shown deploying a dildo on her female lover "Hébée" (Polignac or Lamballe) after complaining about her husband's impotence—a motif revived in the equally scandalous *Uterine Furors of Marie-Antoinette, Wife of Louis XVI* of 1791 (see photo insert for similar images).[53]

Lesbianism was not the only form of sexual transgression attributed to Marie-Antoinette in the *libelles:* it was often alleged that she had also had adulterous affairs with the king's brother, the comte d'Artois, and numerous other male figures at court. But the charge of homosexuality was unquestionably the one that clung most damagingly. At the start of the Revolution, especially abroad, it turned otherwise sympathetic observers against her. "The queen of France," wrote Hester Thrale Piozzi in disgust in her diary in 1789, "is at the Head of a Set of Monsters call'd by each other *Sapphists,* who boast her example; and deserve to be thrown with the She Demons that haunt each other likewise, into Mount Vesuvius."[54] Later, when the Revolution turned violent, the "tribadism" accusation seems to explain some of the unusually sadistic actions of the Parisian crowd. After the princesse de Lamballe was brutally murdered and mutilated during the September Massacres in 1792, for example, a screaming and drunken mob carried her head on a bloody pike to the Temple (where Marie-Antoinette and her family were imprisoned) with the grotesque demand that the queen be forced to "kiss the lips of her intimate." Only the intervention of a prison governor, who convinced the mob to parade the head through the streets of Paris so that all might enjoy the "trophy" of victory, kept them from imposing this ghastly (yet telling) humiliation upon her.[55] In turn, at Marie-Antoinette's trial just before her execution in October 1793, the "crime" of her homosexuality was invoked again, mingled with others (including a charge of incest with her own son) and made part of the Revolutionary Tribunal's death-dealing case against her.[56]

Which isn't to say that the rumor went unchallenged. True, during the queen's lifetime, amid the turmoil of insurrection, little could be done to stop the flow of scurrilous *libelles,* thousands of copies of which circulated freely in France up until the time of her execution.[57] But in the years immediately following the defeat of Napoleon and the restoration of the monarchy in 1814, a host of royalist apologists and defenders of the ancien régime stepped forth, determined to rehabilitate her reputation. Laying the lesbian rumor to rest as swiftly as possible, obviously, was a crucial part of this revisionist project.

The first of Marie-Antoinette's nineteenth-century apologists, the staid Madame Campan, tried to defuse the lesbian charge by underplaying it as much as possible. In the course of her 450-page *Private Life of Marie Antoinette* (1823), the former lady-in-waiting at Versailles referred to the rumor only once, and then only euphemistically. Two "infamous accusations," she allowed, had been made against the queen in her lifetime: "I mean the unworthy suspicions of too strong an attachment for the Comte d'Artois, and of the motives for the tender friendship which subsisted between the Queen, the Princesse of Lamballe, and the Duchess of Polignac."[58] After rebutting the first charge in detail, she responded to the second more vaguely, as if to keep her readers from thinking too long about it: "As to the intimate connection between Marie-Antoinette and the ladies I have named, it never had, nor could have, any other motive than the very innocent wish to secure herself two friends in the midst of a numerous Court; and notwithstanding this intimacy, that tone of respect observed by persons of the most exalted rank towards majesty never ceased to be observed."[59] Something indeed so "infamous," it seemed, was best passed over as rapidly and obscurely as possible. Beginning with the Goncourt brothers, however, subsequent defenders of the queen's reputation settled on a far more flamboyant and paradoxical strategy. Instead of obscuring Marie-Antoinette's relations with other women, they sought to romanticize them. In their *History of Marie Antoinette,* the relentlessly hagiographical biography they published together in 1858, the Goncourts presented Marie-Antoinette as a tragic heroine brought low by the malignity of fate and of "le peuple," who persistently misrepresented her character and actions. Her friendships with women, they maintained, had arisen simply out of an innocent yet heartfelt desire for intimacy and companionship. In the early part of her reign, oppressed by the alien formality of the French court, she had instinctively gravitated toward companions in whom she could confide freely and tenderly. In the serene princesse de Lamballe, she discovered "tolerance, simplicity, amiability, calm playfulness"; in the enchanting Polignac, "an intriguing sweetness" and a charming wit that came as refreshment to her often-weary spirit.[60] Those who later calumniated her, wrote the Goncourts, simply did not understand the purity of feeling that inspired such delicate "tenderness."

Over time and through adversity the heroic nature of these attachments had been revealed. Between Marie-Antoinette and the comtesse de Polignac, the Goncourts contended, there had subsisted a devotion so powerful that only the queen's heart-rending command after the storming of the Bastille that Polignac flee the country for her own safety convinced her beloved "friend" to leave her side. The grief-filled letters that subsequently passed between them, the brothers enthused, were a veritable "masterpiece" of female-female love:

> What an incomparable baring of the soul! What delicate matters delicately expressed! And what words, such as women only possess—one alone can evoke a world of feeling! The kindly sob, the sweet sadness resembles the lamentation of a great soul, and sorrow is exalted to the heroism of tears.[61]

As for the tragic bond between Marie-Antoinette and the unfortunate princesse de Lamballe, this was from the start one of those "rare and great loves that Providence unites in death"—an almost supernatural-seeming devotion.[62] As with Polignac, the queen had begged her "dear Lamballe" to escape in 1789, but to no avail: the princess had ultimately proved her love by giving up her life for the woman she adored. Following the news of Lamballe's terrible death, wrote the Goncourts, Marie-Antoinette sat immobilized in her prison room in the Temple, seeing nothing, like a statue. It was as if, they suggested, she were still in communication with her friend— "as if that bloody blonde head behind the curtains were to gaze at her forever!" No more poignant moment, perhaps, was to be found in all the annals of the Revolution.[63]

Between 1860 and 1900 a host of Marie-Antoinette biographers followed in the Goncourts' footsteps, elaborating on the heroic friendship theme. In works such as Amélie Lenormant's *Quatre femmes au temps de la Révolution* (1866), Charles Duke Yonge's *Marie Antoinette* (1876), Julie Lavergne's *Légendes de Trianon, Versailles et Saint-Germain* (1879), Sarah Tytler's *Marie Antoinette* (1883), Lord Ronald Cower's *The Last Days of Marie Antoinette*

(1885), Pierre de Nolhac's *La Reine Marie-Antoinette* (1890), M. C. Bishop's *Prison Life of Marie Antoinette* (1894), Anna L. Bicknell's *Story of Marie Antoinette* (1897), and Clara Tschudi's *Marie Antoinette* (1898) one finds the same sentimental motifs cropping up again and again: the queen's "sisterly" tenderness for Lamballe and Polignac, their bravery on her behalf, her terrible grief at separating from them in the darkest days of the Revolution. The gruesome martyrdom of Lamballe made her a special object of fascination, and in numerous works of the period, such as W. R. Alger's *The Friendships of Women* (1872), Sir Francis Montefiore's *The Princesse de Lamballe* (1896), and the pseudonymously authored *Secret Memoirs of Princess Lamballe* (1901), she appears as a full-blown romantic heroine in her own right (see "The Death of the Princesse de Lamballe," later reproduced by Montefiore, in the photo insert).[64]

There can be no doubt what message these later nineteenth-century defenders of the queen were trying to get across: many of them openly affirmed Marie-Antoinette's sexual purity and blasted the "vile falsehoods" perpetrated in her name. "A reciprocity of friendship between a queen and a subject," declaimed one of them, excoriating the "blackest calumny" made against the queen and the comtesse de Polignac in the 1770s,

> by those who never felt the existence of such a feeling as friendship, could only be considered in a criminal point of view. But by what perversion could suspicion frown upon the ties between two married women, both living in the greatest harmony with their respective husbands, especially when both became mothers and so devoted to their offspring? This boundless friendship DID glow between this calumniated pair—calumniated because the sacredness and peculiarity of the sentiment which united them was too pure to be understood by the groveling minds who made themselves their sentencers.[65]

At the same time, however, by the breathless, titillating, even obsessional manner in which they dwelt upon these "sacred and peculiar" attachments, they also managed, paradoxically, to reinfuse them with a curious erotic charge.

The queen's intimacy with the ill-fated princesse de Lamballe (that "ever-regretted angel") seemed especially to invite embellishment of this sort. Consider, for example, the apologists' oddly voluptuous handling of what one might call the "sledge party episode" from Madame Campan. In her memoir of 1823 Campan had mentioned in passing that during the unusually cold winter of

1775–76, Marie-Antoinette, nostalgic for the customs of her Austrian youth, had taken to riding out with friends in sleighs around the snowy countryside outside Paris. It was during these "celebrated sledge parties" (condemned by her enemies at court), wrote Campan, that the queen became "intimately acquainted with the princesse de Lamballe, who made her appearance in them wrapped in fur, with all the brilliancy and freshness of the age of twenty; the emblem of spring, peeping from under sable and ermine."[66]

In her 1883 biography of Marie-Antoinette, Sarah Tytler transformed this brief description into a homoerotic set piece—at once magical and fetishistic. After marveling first over how "the Queen's white horses, blue velvet harness, and gold and silver tinkling bells startled the Boulevards with a vision from fairyland," she lingered, like a sentimental novelist, on the imagined face of the princess, sensuously pinked by the cold: "Almost rivaling the Queen's face in beauty was another young face rising above the wraps of martin and ermine, with the delicate complexion heightened by the snow-wind."[67] Later on, describing Marie-Antoinette's supposed reveries after Lamballe's death, Tytler lovingly evoked the image again: "She [Marie-Antoinette] was once more gliding over the snow plain, unspotted by a single drop of blood, and a fair young face, gathering gladness from her own, was close to hers."[68] Nor was Tytler the only nineteenth-century female biographer to reimagine these romantic excursions: "Marie-Antoinette," rhapsodized Anna L. Bicknell in her own biography of the queen from 1897, "delighted to recall the pastimes of her childish days at Vienna, had sledges prepared, in which she flew over the frosted ground with the Princesse, who, fair and fresh as a rose under her rich furs, looked like spring itself in midwinter."[69]

Other writers lingered voyeuristically over episodes from later, more tragic times. During her first separation from the princesse de Lamballe, wrote Sir Francis Montefiore in his lachrymose 1896 life of the princess, Marie-Antoinette was so anguished by her companion's absence from court she had her portrait painted "on the looking glass of the room she most frequented."[70] On another occasion, in 1791, after the queen and Louis XVI had made their unsuccessful flight from Paris and had been recaptured at Varennes, she sent the princess a ring, set with a lock of her now-whitened hair and with the pathetic words "bleached by sorrow" engraved upon it. The melancholy Lamballe in turn sent the queen a repeater watch ("to remind her of the hours we have passed together") and expressed the gallant wish to "live or die" near her.[71] Among the last possessions taken from Marie-Antoinette on the day of her final removal to the Conciergerie, it was poignantly noted, had been a tearstained miniature of the princesse de Lamballe.[72]

Perhaps the most suggestive of all the post-Goncourtian defenses was the mawkish *Secret Memoirs of Princess Lamballe*—dedicated once again to Lamballe and the "saint-like martyred" queen she served. This blatantly fictionalized work, the real authorship of which remains uncertain, purported to be a selection of extracts from the princesse de Lamballe's journal up until 1792, edited and annotated by an Englishwoman, "Catherine Hyde," who claimed to have been the princess's confidential secretary and secret messenger during the first years of the Revolution. The relationship between Lamballe and the queen, Hyde complained, had often been unjustly maligned. By presenting Lamballe's diary (with which she had supposedly been entrusted just before the princess's death), Hyde wished to demonstrate, she said, how "heavenly" the love between "this august, lamented, injured pair"—her mistress and the queen—in fact had been.[73]

What the *Memoirs* is really, however (besides an obvious hoax), is a maudlin, almost prurient paean to the joys of female bonding. Thus the "princess's" description of how she and Marie-Antoinette first met, when the queen paid a visit to her and her father-in-law, the duc de Penthièvres, soon after the death of the princess's young husband in 1775:

> It was amid this gloom of human agony, these heart-rending scenes of real mourning, that the brilliant star shone to disperse the clouds, which hovered over our drooping heads,—to dry the hot briny tears which were parching up our miserable vegetating existence—it was in this crisis that Marie-Antoinette came, like a messenger sent down from Heaven, graciously to offer the balm of comfort in the sweetest language of human compassion. The pure emotions of her generous soul made her unceasing, unremitting, in her visits. . . . But for the consolation of her warm friendship we must have sunk into utter despair![74]

Not long after, writes the princess, she began dining "tête à tête with Her Majesty," who continued to shower her with tokens of affection. During one especially intimate conversation, she recalls, "my tears flowing down my cheeks rapidly while I was speaking, the Queen, with that kindness for which she was so eminently distinguished, took me by the hand, and with her handkerchief dried my face."[75] Then the queen announced her intention to appoint her superintendent of her household at Versailles. With the arrival of the princess Elizabeth, the queen's sister-in-law, the scene escalated into a rhapsodical three-way communion: "The Queen took me by the hand. The Princess Elizabeth, joining hers, exclaimed to the Queen, 'Oh, my dear sister! let me make the trio in this happy union of friends!'"[76] And soon after, writes the princess, Marie-Antoinette embraced her again, exclaiming, "Death alone can separate us!"[77]

In her own numerous commentaries on the princess's narrative, the mysterious "Catherine Hyde" lingers on similar themes. Her own love for the princess, she claims, was as fervent as that of the princess for Marie-Antoinette. Nicknamed by her Italian-speaking mistress her "cara Inglesina," Hyde often risked her life, she says, by going in boy's clothes to deliver secret messages between the princess and the queen during the first years of the Revolution.[78] So devoted was she to the royalist cause she refused to leave her patroness even in 1792, when Lamballe was confined with the queen in the Tuileries: "I begged [the princess's] forgiveness, and on my knees implored that she would not send me away in the hour of danger."[79] Their eventual parting, which supposedly took place only when Marie-Antoinette ordered the unwilling Hyde on a last secret mission to Italy, was almost unbearably poignant: "I took her hand; I bathed it with my tears, as she, at the same moment, was bathing my face with hers. . . . The Princess Lamballe clasped me in her arms. 'Not only letters,' exclaimed she, 'but my life I would trust to the fidelity of my *vera, verissima, cara Inglesina!*'" Witnessing this orgiastic display of emotion, says Hyde, Marie-Antoinette was herself wracked by uncontrollable sobs.[80]

At the moment of farewell, Hyde says, the princess seemed to become a radiant, unearthly, almost spectral apparition—"animated by some saintlike spirit, with scarcely a consciousness of its own existence, and with no thought but that of consoling those around, and no desire but that of smoothing their path to those mansions of eternal peace to which she had already, by anticipation, consigned herself." Indeed, her servant recalls, "her countenance beamed with a serenity perfectly supernatural," while "the graces that played about her bespoke her already the crowned martyr of Elysium."[81]

Hyde falls into the language of the apparitional again in the concluding pages of the *Memoirs,* when she describes her grief upon hearing of the terrible death of the princess during the September massacres—supposedly at the hands of a mulatto whom Lamballe had supported since childhood:

> Words cannot express what a void I felt on returning some years after these horrible calamities to Paris, to find that no trace of the angelic form of my beloved benefactress had been suffered to remain; that no clue had ever been discovered to the sod which enwraps her mutilated body; that there was not even a tombstone to point out the resting place of her mangled frame. There would have been happiness in communing with her spirit over her burial place. What a school for royalty and earthly grandeur! . . . How often have I left the sons of mirth and gayety paying libations to Bacchus to pass an hour at the grave of Marie-Antoinette, lamenting I could not enjoy the same consolation, and unburden the anguish of my soul in solemn prayer, over her martyred friend.[82]

In lieu of such intimacy, Hyde is forced to make do with memories—above all, of the "divine" friendship subsisting between her beloved mistress and the same Marie-Antoinette, over whose grave she now weeps. That friendship remains, she ends grandiloquently, "an everlasting monument that honors their sex."[83]

What would imaginative contemporaries such as Hélène Smith, the "Dream Romances" writer, or Moberly and Jourdain have made of such spectral romancing? The answer, I think, is not far to seek. Though ostensibly concerned with laying the rumor of her homosexuality to rest, Marie-Antoinette's late-nineteenth-century biographers found themselves, like the ghost-obsessed author of the *Secret Memoirs,* ineluctably haunted by it, unable to let it go—unable to keep themselves from embellishing obsessively and ambiguously upon it. By idealizing Marie-Antoinette's friendships with women, they sought, obviously, to exorcize the specter of her putative lesbianism once and for all. Yet precisely by dilating so ardently on the exalted nature of her same-sex friendships, they succeeded in transforming her into a symbol of homoerotic romance. In the very act of supposedly "delesbianizing" Marie-Antoinette they made her over—paradoxically—into a subject for crypto-lesbian reverie.

For women such as Hélène Smith, caught up in dreams of homage and desire; the melancholic "Dream Romances" writer, haunted by her ghostly lady; or the jointly besotted Moberly and Jourdain, unable or afraid to act out their homosexual impulses in any other way, the fantasy of occult connection with Marie-Antoinette must have seemed a safe yet also powerfully gratifying way of articulating otherwise inadmissible erotic desires. Marie-Antoinette was safe, theoretically, because she was "innocent." "If the unfortunate Queen," as Catherine Hyde assured her readers, "had ever been guilty of the slightest of those glaring vices of which she was so generally accused, the Princess [de Lamballe] must have been aware of them; and it was not in her nature to have remained the friend and advocate, even unto death, of one capable of depravity."[84] Yet the very fiction of Marie-Antoinette's innocence, so feverishly adumbrated in the biographies, facilitated the subversive workings of lesbian romance. It opened up a space for erotic fantasy, made possible a host of spectral encounters. "The Queen of France," wrote one of her fantasists, "had love in her eyes and Heaven in her soul."[85] Imagining such love—indeed, basking in its reflected light—the clandestine lover of women might find consolation and secret communion, a ghostly authorization for half-conscious but nonetheless potent desires.

III

In pronouncing Marie-Antoinette a code figure for female homoeroticism, even a kind of protolesbian heroine, I run the risk, I realize, of being accused of indulging in a little imaginative projection myself. After all, it might be argued, Marie-Antoinette is remembered today mainly for the egregious (and apocryphal) "Let them eat cake" and the sensational manner of her death, not for any presumed sexual irregularity.[86] Even if it is true that her biographical image in the nineteenth century was oddly colored by homoerotic elements, and that women such as Hélène Smith, the "Dream Romances" writer, and Moberly and Jourdain covertly fantasized about her as a lover of women, is that enough to declare her, as I have done here, the object of a collective lesbian fixation? To some, the fact that Marie-Antoinette's putative lesbianism is not, for the most part, common knowledge today may suggest that her nineteenth-century biographers were in fact more successful at suppressing the rumor of her homosexuality than I have allowed.

The most compelling evidence for Marie-Antoinette's cult figure status, I would like to suggest by way of coda, is to be found in the lesbian literary-cultural tradition itself—especially in works of fiction written by and about lesbians in the first decades of the twentieth century. The homosexuality of Marie-Antoinette is in fact a kind of communal topos in lesbian writing of the early twentieth century: a shared underground motif or commonplace. If Hélène Smith, the "Dream Romances" writer, and Moberly and Jourdain used Marie-Antoinette unconsciously, so to speak, to symbolize erotic impulses of which they were themselves only half aware, twentieth-century lesbian writers and artists have exploited the queen's image far more artfully and self-consciously to symbolize, if not glamorize, the possibility of love between women. Indeed, to the extent that they have continued to romanticize Marie-Antoinette, modern lesbian writers have taken up where her nineteenth-century biographers left off, but with one crucial difference: they affirm rather than obfuscate the sexual nature of her intimacies with women.

The first English writer to invoke Marie-Antoinette specifically as a lesbian icon, as far as I have been able to discover, is the little-known Rose Laure Allatini, whose *Despised and Rejected,* published under the pseudonym A. T. Fitzroy, appeared in 1918. This remarkable novel (which was immediately banned on account of its powerful antiwar sentiments and homoerotic plot line) is the story of a young woman and a young man who become engaged on the eve of the First World War. Both are pacifists; each is also unconsciously drawn to members of his or her own sex. When the man falls in love with a fellow conscientious objector, he recognizes his homosexuality and breaks off the engagement. The woman is then forced to confront her own homosexual desires. Over the course of the novel, which ends with the man's imprisonment, the two find a new (and surprisingly hopeful) emotional bond in the recognition of their shared nature.

It is not simply that Allatini's heroine's name is Antoinette. (Though brought up in England, she is supposedly the child of French émigrés.) In the opening scene of the novel, a number of guests in a hotel, including Antoinette, are diverting themselves by performing a little costume drama about the French Revolution. The play's author, a somewhat silly young woman named Rosabel, has written it in honor of Antoinette, whom she idolizes. When Antoinette perversely chooses the part of Charlotte Corday instead of that of her namesake, the infatuated Rosabel is sorely tried: "Antoinette, darling, I do think it's such a pity—though of course you know best, and I'm sure you're simply wonderful as Charlotte Corday—but I did write Marie-Antoinette's part on purpose for you—so sweet that you've got the same name, isn't it? And I know I'm no good in the part." Rosabel, the narrator observes, "was ready to lavish great floods of adoration on her friends or on characters in history or fiction. At present the said adoration was equally divided between Antoinette de Courcy and the 'Unhappy Queen.' "[87]

The scene is meant to be satirical, of course, with the joke on Rosabel. (Later on, when war breaks out, she abruptly switches her affection from Marie-Antoinette to the queen of Belgium, whom she sees as "just as unfortunate and more up-to-date.") But it also suggests something about Allatini's heroine, Antoinette. Though opting here for the part of Charlotte Corday, Antoinette cannot escape, as it were, from her fateful name—or from the powerful homoerotic emotion with which it is so obviously associated. In the same hotel is Hester, a mysterious older woman with whom Antoinette herself will soon become wildly infatuated. Though Antoinette resists her feelings for Hester—turning instead to men and hopes of marriage—she is caught out by the end of the novel, when she realizes that she has loved the older woman all along. The elaborately homoerotic invocation of Marie-Antoinette at the outset might thus be said to function as a kind of proleptic hint to the reader—as the cipher, or symbolic intimation, of Antoinette's own emerging lesbian desires.

An even more striking invocation of the Marie-Antoinette topos occurs in *The Well of Loneliness,* Radclyffe Hall's openly polemical classic of lesbian fiction from 1928. Midway through that novel, Hall's lonely young heroine, Stephen Gordon, who has yet to confide in anyone her tormented knowledge of her own homosexuality, pays a visit to Versailles in the company of Jonathan Brockett, a sympathetic yet oddly effeminate artist friend who has taken her under his wing. Brockett guides her through the rooms of the palace—"repeopling the place for Stephen so that she seemed to see the glory of the dancers led by the youthful Roi Soleil; seemed to hear the rhythm of the throbbing violins, and the throb of the rhythmic dancing feet as they beat down the length of the Galerie des Glaces." But "most skillfully of all," the narrator observes, "did he recreate for her the image of the luckless queen who came after; as though for some reason this unhappy woman must appeal in a personal way to Stephen."[88]

As soon as Stephen and Brockett enter the dead queen's apartments (where Stephen is inexplicably moved) Brockett's comments become oddly insinuating:

Brockett pointed to the simple garniture on the mantelpiece of the little salon, then he looked at Stephen: "Madame de Lamballe gave those to the queen," he murmured softly.

She nodded, only vaguely apprehending his meaning.

Presently they followed him out into the gardens and stood looking across the Tapis Vert that stretches its quarter mile of greenness towards a straight, lovely line of water.

Brockett said, very low, so that Puddle [Stephen's servant] should not hear him: "Those two would often come here at sunset. Sometimes they were rowed along the canal in the sunset—can't you imagine it, Stephen? They must often have felt pretty miserable, poor souls; sick to death of the subterfuge and pretences. Don't you ever get tired of that sort of thing? My God, I do!" But she did not answer, for now there was no mistaking his meaning.[89]

The episode, which concludes with the two of them visiting Marie-Antoinette's "Temple d'Amour," close by to the Petit Trianon (see photo insert), is incomprehensible without some knowledge of the homoerotic biographical traditions surrounding the queen in the later nineteenth century. Clearly Hall expected her lesbian readers to understand the reference to "Madame de Lamballe" and to find in Brockett's cryptic history lesson a consoling, if melancholy, image of homosexual communion. (The subtle parody of Moberly and Jourdain's *An Adventure* also seems intentional.)[90] Evoking the love between queen and princess, Brockett manages, as if by a delicate semaphore, to communicate to Stephen both the fact of his own homosexuality and his unspoken awareness of her own. In turn, grasping his meaning, she is suddenly able to see her lesbianism in a larger emotional context. Marie-Antoinette functions here as a kind of potent ancestor spirit whose spectral presence at once liberates and affirms Stephen's own half-acknowledged erotic desires. Later on, when Stephen at last finds happiness with a woman lover, she will in fact return to Versailles with her, as if in tribute to her unseen benefactress.[91]

In several other well-known lesbian novels of the twenties and thirties, the ghost of Marie-Antoinette, though unnamed, hovers discreetly behind the scenes. In Virginia Woolf's *Orlando* (1928), memories of Marie-Antoinette (and the rosy-cheeked Lamballe) seem to haunt the courtship scenes of Orlando and Sasha, the Russian "princess," who begin their androgynous romance by riding out in sledges, then skating, over the ice of the frozen Thames. ("And then, wrapped in their sables, they would talk of everything under the sun; of sights and travels; of Moor and Pagan; of this man's beard and that woman's skin; of a rat that fed from her hand at table; of the arras that moved always in the hall at home; of a face; of a feather. Nothing was too small for such converse, nothing was too great.")[92]

In *Extraordinary Women* (1928), Compton Mackenzie's comic satire on lesbian expatriate society on Capri in the 1920s, the gallant Anastasia Sarbécoff, an impoverished member of the sapphic colony on the island of Sirène, "[steps] out as dauntlessly toward an old age of penury as the French nobility stepped forward to the guillotine"; another character presents herself as "deliciously *ancien régime*."[93] (Though not, obviously, a lesbian, the whimsical Mackenzie seems to have had a remarkable intuitive understanding of contemporary lesbian tropes.)

Rather more somberly, in a dreamlike passage in Djuna Barnes' *Nightwood* (1936) Robin Vote, the homosexual wife of the luckless would-be aristocrat Felix Volkbein, dresses herself in the magnificent, dilapidated costumes of a woman of the later eighteenth century:

> Her skirts were moulded to her hips and fell downward and out, wider and longer than those of other women, heavy silks that made her seem newly ancient. One day [Felix] learned the secret. Pricing a small tapestry in an antique shop facing the Seine, he saw Robin reflected in a door mirror of a back room, dressed in a heavy brocaded gown which time had stained in places, in others split, yet which was so voluminous that there were yards left to refashion.[94]

Captivated, yet unable to penetrate her uncanny alienation, Felix concedes defeat:

> Looking at her he knew that he was not sufficient to make her what he had hoped; it would require more than his own argument. It would require contact with persons exonerated of their earthly condition by some strong spiritual bias, someone of that old regime, some old lady of the past courts, who only remembered others when trying to think of herself.[95]

In Antonia White's *Frost in May* (1933), the adolescent heroine's boarding-school beloved "[moves] in her haze of charm like Marie-Antoinette."[96] And in Sylvia Townsend Warner's *Summer Will Show* (1936), set in Paris during the 1848 revolution, the heroine Sophia Willoughby's female lover is stabbed on a barricade by a mulatto boy whom Sophia has raised up, in a scene that weirdly recalls the melodramatic demise of the princesse de Lamballe as recounted by "Catherine Hyde" in the anonymous *Secret Memoirs of Princess Lamballe.*[97]

Marie-Antoinette's ghost lingers on, finally, even in more recent lesbian writing and iconography. In the 1950s Lennox Strong published an article in *The Ladder,* the first national lesbian magazine, detailing Marie-Antoinette's putative affairs with women; the article was reprinted in a collection of *Ladder* reprints in 1976 (see photo insert).[98] In 1985 Florence King invoked the memory of the princesse de Lamballe in her lesbian coming-of-age story, *Confessions of a Failed Southern Lady;* a character in Jeanette Winterson's homoerotic historical romance *The Passion* (1987) "still [prays] for the soul of Marie-Antoinette."[99] Images of Marie-Antoinette likewise continue to crop up in contemporary visual representations of female homosexuality. The cover of a 1974 paperback edition of *The Well of Loneliness* shows two women in quasi-eighteenth-century costume, one of whom wears a cameo of a woman resembling the queen at her neck (see photo insert). An advertisement for a women-only dance in the gay and lesbian magazine *Outweek* (1991) shows another pair of women, one dressed in the rustic-rococo style adopted by Marie-Antoinette in the 1780s (see photo insert). And most amusingly, perhaps, in the rock video "Vogue" (1990), the pop icon Madonna, also dressed as Marie-Antoinette, offers her own ambiguous paean to late-twentieth-century lesbian chic.[100]

From one angle the lesbian rehabilitation of Marie-Antoinette—a process that I have argued can be traced back to the Goncourt brothers—might be derided, of course, as hopelessly politically incorrect. From the late nineteenth century onward, from Hélène Smith and Radclyffe Hall to *Outweek* and Madonna, what I have defined as Marie-Antoinette "obsession"—her overt or covert celebration as homoerotic icon—might easily be condemned as an apolitical, aestheticized, even reactionary subcultural phenomenon. Since the turn of the century, the queen's numerous acolytes have shown little interest in her actual political beliefs (except, embarrassingly, to defend them) or her scabrous role in some of the events leading up to the French Revolution. Of the feckless, manipulative, often ruthless figure who comes across in more objective histories, those who romanticize her love of women have had virtually nothing to say.[101]

And yet one cannot help but feel in the end, perhaps, that there is also something bizarrely liberating, if not revolutionary, about the transmogrification of Marie-Antoinette into a lesbian heroine. It is true that there is a nostalgic element in her cult: women who thought they "saw" her, like Hélène Smith, the "Dream Romances" writer, and Moberly and Jourdain, were in one sense flagrantly retreating into the past, into a kind of psychic Old Regime. But in the act of conjuring up her ghost, they were also, I think, conjuring something new into being—a poetics of possibility. It is perhaps not too much to say that in her role as idealized martyr (as in *The Secret Memoirs of Princess Lamballe* or *The Well of Loneliness*) Marie-Antoinette functioned as a kind of lesbian Oscar Wilde: a rallying point for sentiment and collective emotional intransigence. She gave those who idolized her a way of thinking about themselves. And out of such reflection—peculiar as its manifestations may often look to us now—something of the modern lesbian identity was born.

Notes

1. Theodore Flournoy, *From India to the Planet Mars: A Study of a Case of Somnambulism with Glossolalia,* trans. Daniel B. Vermilye (New York: Harper, 1900).
2. See, for instance, Flournoy's speculations on the relationship between Smith's "Hindoo" language and Sanskrit; ibid., 314–36. Among the experts Flournoy consulted regarding Smith's linguistic productions was his colleague at the University of Geneva, the renowned philologist and founder of semiology, Ferdinand de Saussure.
3. Ibid., 342.
4. Ibid., 349. "Leopold," as Flournoy notes, seems here to have gotten his chronology wrong: Marie-Antoinette actually outlived the princesse de Lamballe by over a year.
5. Ibid., 352.
6. Ibid., 354.
7. Ibid., 346.
8. "Dream Romances," *Journal of the Society for Psychical Research* 13 (June 1907): 91. The author of the narrative has not been identified. According to the editors of the journal, the account was forwarded to them by an associate of the society, a Mrs. Stapleton, of 46 Montagu Square, London, W. Mrs. Stapleton, they said, claimed she had known the writer intimately for many years, and believed her report of her experiences to be a "literally accurate one."
9. Ibid., 92.
10. Ibid., 93.
11. Ibid., 96.

12. Ibid.

13. See Elizabeth Morison and Frances Lamont [Charlotte Anne Moberly and Eleanor Jourdain], *An Adventure*, 2d ed. (London: Macmillan, 1913), 1–25. In synopsizing here and elsewhere the complicated background to *An Adventure*, I have drawn on Lucille Iremonger's *The Ghosts of Versailles: Miss Moberly and Miss Jourdain and Their Adventure: A Critical Study* (London: Faber and Faber, 1957); and Joan Evans, "An End to *An Adventure:* Solving the Mystery of the Trianon," *Encounter* 47 (October 1976): 33–47. For a closer look at some of the psychobiographical issues involved in the Trianon case, see Terry Castle, "Contagious Folly: *An Adventure* and Its Skeptics," *Critical Inquiry* 17 (summer 1991): 741–72.

14. During her fictional reverie, the musing Marie-Antoinette "sees" the very objects and persons seen by Moberly and Jourdain in 1901—with one amusing addition. Thinking back to her last day at the Trianon and how she sat sketching on the lawn, she suddenly remembers "two strangers" who walked past her onto the terrace. Thus, presumably, did Moberly and Jourdain, imagining the doomed queen imagining them, seek to lend "telepathic" credibility to their own richly phantasmagorical vision.

15. Mrs. Sidgwick's anonymous review appeared in the June 1911 supplement to *The Proceedings of the Society for Psychical Research.* It is also reprinted in full in chap. 12 of Iremonger's *Ghosts of Versailles.*

16. W. F. Barrett, *Psychical Research* (London, 1911), 201.

17. Moberly and Jourdain, *An Adventure*, 100–20. *An Adventure* went through four editions in all—in 1911, 1913, 1924, and 1955. Each edition was also reprinted. The different editions vary considerably; some, for instance, include the appendices and "A Rêverie," while others do not.

18. The first book devoted to debunking *An Adventure* was J. R. Sturge-Whiting, *The Mystery of Versailles: A Complete Solution* (London: Rider and Co., 1938). It was followed not long after by David Landale Johnston, *The Trianon Case: A Review of the Evidence* (Ilfracombe, N. Devon: A. H. Stockwell, 1945). A spate of critical essays on *An Adventure* appeared in the 1950s: W. H. Salter, " 'An Adventure': A Note on the Evidence," *Journal of the Society for Psychical Research* 35 (January 1950): 178–87; W. H. W. Sabine, "Is There a Case for Retrocognition?" *Journal of the American Society for Psychical Research* 44 (April 1950): 43–64; and Léon Rey, "Une Promenade hors du temps," *Revue de Paris* (December 1952), the first French essay on the subject. (An annotated French translation of *An Adventure*, complete with preface by Jean Cocteau and critical introduction by Robert Amadou, appeared under the title *Les Fantômes de Trianon* in 1959.) The most exhaustive critique of *An Adventure*, however, was undoubtedly Iremonger's 1957 *Ghosts of Versailles.* Iremonger devoted much of her book to an ad feminem attack on Moberly and Jourdain themselves, whom she suspected of outright double-dealing. Joan Evans' *Encounter* piece of 1976, while also skeptical in essence, was in part an attempt to defend Moberly and Jourdain against Iremonger's no-holds-barred personal attack.

19. "Dream Romances," 90.

20. Barrett, *Psychical Research,* 201.

21. Iremonger, *Ghosts of Versailles*, 180.

22. Flournoy, *From India to the Planet Mars*, 27.

23. Ibid., 26.

24. See ibid., 48–75, for a detailed clinical assessment of Smith's "spontaneous automatisms" and trance states. Throughout his study Flournoy emphasizes the hysterical nature of Smith's symptoms, referring to them at one point as "eruptions from the subliminal volcano."

25. Ibid., 342.

26. Ibid., 342–43.

27. Ibid., 406.

28. Sigmund Freud, "Family Romances" (1909), trans. James Strachey, in *The Standard Edition of the Complete Psychological Works of Sigmund Freud* (London: Hogarth Press, 1959), 9:237–38.

29. "The emotional disposition which I have depicted," writes Flournoy in one particularly florid passage, "which is one of the forms under which the maladaptation of the organism, physical and mental, to the hard conditions of the environment, betrays itself, seems therefore to me to have been the source and starting-point for all the dreamings of Hélène in her childhood. Thence came these visions, always warm, luminous, highly colored, exotic, bizarre; and these brilliant apparitions, superbly dressed, in which her antipathy for her insipid and unpleasant surroundings betrays itself, her weariness of ordinary, commonplace people, her disgust for prosaic occupations, for vulgar and disagreeable things, for the narrow house, the dirty streets, the cold winters, and the gray sky." *From India to the Planet Mars*, 30–31.

30. "Dream Romances," 92.

31. Iremonger, *Ghosts of Versailles*, 30 and 65.

32. Ibid., 73.

33. Moberly and Jourdain, *An Adventure*, 33.

34. In an uncomplimentary aside on Eleanor Jourdain in *The Ghosts of Versailles*, Iremonger argues that the first women to go up to Oxford and Cambridge became "unsatisfactory imitations of the men they at once envied and resented," subject to unconscious "feelings of defiance" as well as "affectations and intellectual conceit" (68–69). For a more sympathetic account of later-nineteenth-century women in English universities—and of the unique social and psychological pressures they faced—see Martha Vicinus, " 'One Life to Stand by Me': Emotional Conflicts of First-Generation College Women in England," *Feminist Studies* 8 (fall 1982): 602–28, as well as her *Independent Women: Work and Community for Single Women, 1850–1920* (Chicago: University of Chicago Press, 1985).

35. "Dream Romances," 92–93.

36. Flournoy, *From India to the Planet Mars*, 27.

37. Ibid., 89.

38. Ibid., 129–31.

39. Ibid., 119.

40. Ibid., 104.

41. See Evans, "An End to *An Adventure*," 34–35.

42. Though she never once uses the word *lesbian* to describe them, Iremonger's interest in her subjects' emotional predilections often verges on the prurient. Quoting an unnamed St. Hugh's source, she animadverts on Jourdain's "unhealthy" relationships with various students in the college, who reciprocated by falling in love with their principal: "An illuminating punning phrase which had currency at that time was, 'Have you crossed Jordan yet?' In other words, have you fallen under the sway of this woman who is acknowledged to be consciously exercising her charm to bind students to her?" According to the mistress of Girton, Iremonger concludes, "a lot of kissing went on"; see *Ghosts of Versailles,* 87–88.

43. Such a symbolic reading seems particularly appropriate given the fact that the Petit Trianon served as Marie-Antoinette's private retreat and "maison de plaisir." Inside its elegant alcoves, which she had had charmingly decorated in the rococo style, she often entertained female favorites such as the comtesse de Polignac. According to Stefan Zweig, within this "inviolable kingdom"— her "island of Cythera"—not even the king himself was allowed to enter without the queen's permission. See Zweig, *Marie Antoinette: The Portrait of an Average Woman,* trans. Eden and Cedar Paul (Garden City, N.Y.: Garden City Publishing, 1933), 106–8.

44. Moberly and Jourdain's wishful use of a supernatural third party to triangulate, and thereby legitimate, their lesbian relationship will not appear so bizarre, perhaps, when one considers other such triangles existing between homosexual women in the period. Radclyffe Hall and Lady Una Troubridge, for example, formed a similar spiritual triangle with Hall's deceased ex-lover "Ladye," Mabel Batten, with whom they communicated regularly through a spirit medium for over twenty years. See Michael Baker, *Our Three Selves: The Life of Radclyffe Hall* (New York: Morrow, 1985), 84–97.

45. Sarah Tytler [Henrietta Keddie], *Marie Antoinette* (New York: G. P. Putnam's Sons, 1883), 216.

46. See, for example, Edmund Burke, *Reflections on the Revolution in France* (1790; reprint, Harmondsworth, Eng.: Penguin Books, 1969), 169–70; Thomas Carlyle, *The French Revolution: A History* (1837; reprint, London: Folio Society, 1989), 1:487, 2:322–25; and Charles Dickens, *A Tale of Two Cities* (1859; reprint, Oxford: Oxford University Press, 1988), 313, 335. Marie-Antoinette's male admirers, interestingly enough, frequently discounted the importance of her early life, including her achievements as queen, in order to concentrate instead solely on her final days and execution. As Lord Ronald Gower somewhat sententiously put it in his *Last Days of Marie Antoinette: An Historical Sketch* (London: Kegan Paul, Trench, 1885), "the Queen's life becomes chiefly interesting as it approaches its end, and is chiefly remarkable by showing how a woman, whose early years were trifled thoughtlessly away, and who in later life, most unfortunately for her family, herself, and her adopted country, mixed herself in politics, where women are ever mischievous, was raised through suffering to an heroic level" (v–vi). This teleocentric focus was often linked with an almost prurient interest in the physical details of her so-called martyrdom and dissolution. One detects a displaced hint of this interest in *A*

Tale of Two Cities, when one of Madame Defarge's accomplices contemplates condemning Lucie Darnet to the guillotine: "'She has a fine head for it,' croaked Jacques Three. 'I have seen blue eyes and golden hair there, and they looked charming when Samson held them up.' Ogre that he was, he spoke like an epicure" (444). The blue eyes and blonde hair mentioned here seem to me an unmistakable iconographic allusion to Marie-Antoinette, who was noted for both. By contrast, for whatever reasons, the queen's female acolytes tended on the whole to downplay the actual horror of her demise. Their focus, almost always, was on her charmed life before the Revolution, or (as in the case of the "Dream Romances" writer) on somehow bringing her "back to life," magically, as a kind of loving and poetic apparition, in the mind's eye of the reader.

47. Zweig, *Marie Antoinette,* 119–20.

48. Ibid., 121.

49. Zweig attributes Louis XVI's seven-year impotence to phimosis, a contraction of the orifice of the prepuce, which made it impossible for him to ejaculate; ibid., 21. It has often been reported—though recent biographers are more skeptical—that Louis underwent a successful operation to cure the problem in 1777 at the behest of Marie-Antoinette's brother, Emperor Joseph II of Austria. See Joan Haslip, *Marie Antoinette* (London: Weidenfeld and Nicolson, 1987), 100.

50. Dorothy Moulton Mayer, *Marie Antoinette: The Tragic Queen* (New York: Coward-McCann, 1968), 79–80.

51. Haslip, *Marie Antoinette,* 64–65 and 83–84.

52. Ibid., 84.

53. On the publishing history of the *libelles,* see Henri d'Almeras, *Marie-Antoinette et les pamphlets royalistes et révolutionnaires: les amoureux de la reine* (Paris: Librairie Mondiale, 1907); Hector Fleischmann, *Les Pamphlets libertins contre Marie-Antoinette* (Paris: Les Publications Modernes, 1908); and *Marie-Antoinette libertine: Bibliographie critique et analytique des pamphlets politiques, galants, et obscènes contre la reine* (Paris: Bibliothèque des Curieux, 1911). The pornographic pamphlets against Marie-Antoinette have recently attracted considerable attention from literary critics and historians of the Old Regime. See, in particular, Chantal Thomas, *The Wicked Queen: The Origins of the Myth of Marie-Antoinette,* trans. Julie Rose (New York: Zone Books, 1999); and the brilliant essay by Lynn Hunt (to which I am here much indebted), "The Many Bodies of Marie-Antoinette: Political Pornography and the Problem of the Feminine in the French Revolution," in this volume.

54. Hester Thrale Piozzi, *Thraliana: The Diary of Mrs. Hester Lynch Thrale, 1776–1809,* ed. Katharine C. Balderston (Oxford: Clarendon Press, 1951), 2:740. Hearing of "Anarchy" in France and Marie-Antoinette's travails at the hands of the revolutionists in December of 1790, Thrale remarked, only slightly more charitably, "God will I hope touch her noble Heart *now* with *natural* Passions, and shewing her the Vicissitudes of this Life, turn her Thoughts to Eternity" (2:788–89).

55. Zweig, *Marie Antoinette,* 375

56. Haslip, *Marie Antoinette,* 287.

57. According to Henri d'Almeras, the *Essai historique* alone, reprinted in various forms in the 1780s, sold between twenty thousand and thirty thousand copies; *Marie-Antoinette*, 403. As Lynn Hunt notes in her essay on the *libelles*, however, he provides no evidence for this statistic.

58. Jeanne Louise Henriette Campan, *The Private Life of Marie Antoinette, Queen of France and Navarre, with Sketches and Anecdotes of the Court of Louis XVI* (New York: Scribner and Welford, 1887), 115.

59. Ibid.

60. Edmond and Jules de Goncourt, *Histoire de Marie-Antoinette* (Paris: Charpentier, 1878), 104–5 and 116–17.

61. Ibid, 266.

62. Ibid., 105.

63. Ibid., 373.

64. Somewhat later works in the same hagiographical vein include Hilaire Belloc's *Marie Antoinette* (London: Methuen, 1909) and Nesta H. Webster's *Louis XVI and Marie Antoinette Before the Revolution* (New York: G.P. Putnam's Sons, 1937) and *Louis XVI and Marie Antoinette During the Revolution* (New York: G.P. Putnam's Sons, 1938). See also Joseph Adelman, *Famous Women: An Outline of Feminine Achievement Through the Ages with Life Stories of Five Hundred Noted Women* (New York: E. M. Lonow, 1926). Not content merely with romanticizing her, Marie-Antoinette's early-twentieth-century biographers frequently used her story as an excuse for riding various hobbyhorses of their own. Belloc's rather crabbed and neurotic account is full of gratuitous anti-Semitic asides. And in the bizarre concluding paragraphs of *Louis XVI and Marie Antoinette During the Revolution*, Webster took Marie-Antoinette's fate as an occasion for warning against the international "conspiracy" of Freemasonry.

65. Catherine Hyde, ed., *Secret Memoirs of Princess Lamballe: Being Her Journals, Letters, and Conversations During Her Confidential Relations with Marie Antoinette* (Washington, D.C. and London: M. W. Dunne, 1901), 83.

66. Campan, *Private Life of Marie Antoinette*, 92.

67. Tytler, *Marie Antoinette*, 84.

68. Ibid., 188.

69. Anna L. Bicknell, *The Story of Marie-Antoinette* (New York: Century, 1897), 94. Admittedly, some of the revisionist biographers recognized the compromising element in the sledge-party episode and tried to defuse it. In a comically bathetic passage in the fictionalized *Secret Memoirs of Princess Lamballe*, for example, the sledge parties of queen and princess are rewritten as missions of charity.

70. Francis Montefiore, *The Princesse de Lamballe: A Sketch* (London: Bentley and Son, 1896), 29.

71. Ibid., 146–47.

72. Tytler, *Marie Antoinette*, 189.

73. Hyde, *Secret Memoirs*, 2.

74. Ibid., 69–70.

75. Ibid., 72.

76. Ibid., 74.

77. Catherine Hyde here appends an ominous footnote in which, like Moberly and Jourdain later, she imagines the fateful date of 10 August 1792: "Good Heaven! What must have been the feelings of these true, these sacred friends, the shadow of each other, on that fatal Tenth of August, which separated them only to meet in a better world!" Ibid., 86.

78. Among the errands Hyde claims to have made in boy's clothes on the queen's behalf was one to the National Assembly, where she observed a debate between Mirabeau and the abbé Maury; ibid., 300. On another occasion, she says, she disguised herself as a milliner and went to spy on Danton, who tried to seduce her (303–5).

79. Ibid., 280.

80. Ibid., 312–13.

81. Ibid., 310.

82. Ibid., 334.

83. Marie-Antoinette's nineteenth- and early-twentieth-century biographers frequently used ghostly metaphors to describe her, especially—as one might expect—in melodramatic passages dealing with her last days and death. In *Marie Antoinette,* trans. E. M. Cope (London: S. Sonnenschein, 1907), Clara Tschudi spoke of her "blanched face" and "almost spectral appearance" at her trial (282); in *The Last Days of Marie Antoinette,* Lord Gower described her as "pale as death" on the way to the scaffold (158). Certainly her appearance deteriorated dramatically while she was imprisoned in the Temple and the Conciergerie; most famously, by the last year of her life, her once-luxuriant blonde hair had gone completely white. She also suffered at this time from constant uterine hemorrhages, which undoubtedly contributed as well to her wraithlike appearance. But one also senses in the persistence with which her biographers describe her appearance as "ghostly" or "unearthly" an impulse to invest her story with uncanny elements. Sometimes a supernatural theme surfaces directly. At the end of her 1897 biography of the queen, Bicknell asserted that when Marie-Antoinette's executioner displayed her head to the crowd after guillotining her, her face "expressed perfect consciousness, and the eyes looked on the crowd" with an expression of "intense astonishment, as of some wonderful vision revealed" (*Story of Marie-Antoinette,* 324–25). In his 1909 biography of the queen, Belloc claimed that in Germany on the night of 16 October 1793, just after her execution, her distant cousin, George of Hesse, "saw the White Lady pass, the Ghost without a face that is the warning of the Hapsburgs, and the hair of his head stood up" (*Marie Antoinette,* 394). In the context of such weird ruminations, the apparition-seeing of the "Dream Romances" writer and Moberly and Jourdain is perhaps not as wholly eccentric as it might at first appear.

84. Hyde, *Secret Memoirs,* 344–45.

85. Ibid., 83.

86. According to the editors of the *Oxford Dictionary of Quotations,* 3d ed. (1979), the infamous words, "Qu'ils mangent de la brioche," were probably never uttered by Marie-Antoinette. The expression antedates her: Rousseau in his *Confessions* referred to a similar remark as a well-known saying. In his *Relation d'un voyage à Bruxelles et à Coblentz en 1791* (Paris: Canel, 1823), Louis

XVIII attributed the phrase "Que ne mangent-ils de la croûte de pâte?" ("Why don't they eat pastry?") to Marie-Thérèse (1638–83), the wife of Louis XIV.

87. A. T. Fitzroy [Rose Laure Allatini], *Despised and Rejected* (1918; reprint, London: GMP, 1988), 20–21.

88. Radclyffe Hall, *The Well of Loneliness* (New York: Pocket Books, 1974), 239.

89. Ibid.

90. That Hall was familiar with *An Adventure* and its authors seems to me likely indeed, given her lifelong interest in occultism and psychical research. Hall and Una Troubridge's twenty-year homosexual relationship paralleled Moberly and Jourdain's in interesting ways; both couples felt themselves deeply susceptible to supernatural influences. In Brighton in 1920, in the company of Troubridge, Hall saw the apparition of a mutual friend inspecting an automobile in a garage. Like Moberly and Jourdain before them, the two sent an account of their experience to the editors of the *Journal of the Society for Psychical Research,* who published it in the April 1921 issue under the title "A Veridical Apparition."

91. See Hall, *Well of Loneliness*: "The Hameau [Marie-Antoinette's model village at the Trianon] no longer seemed sad to Stephen, for Mary and she brought love back to the Hameau" (329). There is evidence to suggest that the Trianon was a site of romantic pilgrimage for Hall and Una Troubridge as well: in her doting life of Hall published after Hall's death, Troubridge mentions their sightseeing trips in the 1920s to "Versailles and the Trianon," as well as to the Conciergerie, the final prison of Marie-Antoinette. See *The Life of Radclyffe Hall* (New York: Citadel Press, 1963), 88.

92. Virginia Woolf, *Orlando: A Biography* (New York: Harcourt Brace Jovanovich, 1956), 45.

93. Compton Mackenzie, *Extraordinary Women: Theme and Variations* (London: Hogarth Press, 1986), 15, 39.

94. Djuna Barnes, *Nightwood* (New York: New Directions Books, 1961), 42.

95. Ibid., 44.

96. Antonia White, *Frost in May* (New York: Dial Press, 1980), 121.

97. In the *Secret Memoirs,* Hyde describes the death blow of the princesse de Lamballe thus:

> Nearest to her in the mob stood a mulatto, whom she had caused to be baptized, educated, and maintained, but whom, from ill-conduct, she had latterly excluded from her presence. This miscreant struck at her with his halbert. The blow removed her cap. Her luxuriant hair (as if to hide her angelic beauty from the sight of the murderers, pressing tigerlike around to pollute that form, the virtues of which equaled its physical perfection), her luxuriant hair fell around and veiled her a moment from view. An individual, to whom I was nearly allied, seeing the miscreants somewhat staggered, sprang forward to the rescue; but the mulatto wounded him. The Princess was lost to all feeling from the moment the monster first struck at her. But the demons would not quit their prey. She expired, gashed with wounds. (328)

In Warner's novel, the mulatto Caspar leads a *gardes mobiles* assault on the barricade where Sophia and her lover, Minna Lemuel, are loading rifles for the insurgents and then turns—equally violently—against his former mentor:

> With the certainty of a bad dream, there, when [Sophia] looked up, was
> Caspar's profile outlined against the smoky dusk, tilted, just as it had been
> on those summer evenings at Blandamer House, when he played his guitar,
> leaning against the balustrade. . . .
>
> "Why, it's Caspar!"
>
> It was Minna's voice, warm, inveterately hospitable. He glanced round.
> With a howl of rage he sprang forward, thrust with his bayonet, drove it
> into Minna's breast.
>
> "Drab!" he cried out. "Jewess! This is the end of you."
>
> A hand was clapped on Sophia's shoulder, a voice told her she was a
> prisoner.
>
> "One moment," she replied, inattentively. With her free arm she pulled
> out the pistol and cocked it, and fired at Caspar's mouth as though she
> would have struck that mouth with her hand. Having looked to aim, she
> looked no further. But she saw the bayonet jerk in Minna's breast, and the
> blood rush out.

Warner alters certain details of the original scene (as in the immediate retribution that Sophia wreaks on Caspar), but the similarities are also, I think,
unmistakable. Sylvia Townsend Warner, *Summer Will Show* (New York: Penguin Books–Virago Press, 1987), 382–83.

98. Lennox Strong, "The Royal Triangle: Marie-Antoinette and the Duchesse de
Polignac," in Barbara Grier and Coletta Reid, eds. *Lesbian Lives: Biographies of
Women from "The Ladder"* (Baltimore: Diana Press, 1976), 180–85. Among
the bibliographic sources cited by Strong are two of the romanticizing biogra-
phies from the turn of the century: Bicknell's *Story of Marie Antoinette,* and
Hyde's *Secret Memoirs.*

99. Florence King, *Confessions of a Failed Southern Lady* (New York: St. Martin's
Press/Marek, 1985), 70; Jeanette Winterson, *The Passion* (New York: Grove Press,
1988), 16. King's reference, though seemingly flippant, is in fact an especially interesting one in the context of lesbian thematics. Describing several bossy grade-
school teachers whom she disliked intensely, King complains that "they were not
happy unless everybody was engaged in an activity big enough to require what
they called 'give and take,' like marching on the Tuileries with equal parts of the
Princess de Lamballe's dismembered corpse on our pikes." Against such enforced
jollity, the introverted King sought refuge, she says, in intimate friendships with
one or two other intellectually minded and sensitive girls.

100. On Madonna's paradoxical role as lesbian (as well as heterosexual) icon, see
Alice Echols, "Justifying Our Love? The Evolution of Lesbianism Through
Feminism and Gay Male Politics," *The Advocate,* 26 March 1991, 48–53.

101. In her *Ladder* piece, Lennox Strong, it is true, betrays some ambivalence about
Marie-Antoinette's self-indulgence and lack of concern for her suffering subjects. Given the amount of money Marie-Antoinette spent on "pretty frip-
peries" for her favorites, writes Strong, it was not surprising that the people of
France ended up hating "their beautiful but expensive queen." "The rest is history," she concludes philosophically, "bloody and even evil, but not wholly
unjustified"; "Royal Triangle," 184.

"We're Just Little People, Louis":
Marie-Antoinette on Film

Laura Mason

In 1938, with much fanfare and advance notice, MGM released the lavish costume drama *Marie-Antoinette* (see photo insert). Designed as a star vehicle for Norma Shearer, one of the most popular Hollywood actresses of the decade, the film's supporting cast included matinee idol Tyrone Power as Marie-Antoinette's supposed lover, Count Axel von Fersen, the aging Shakespearean actor John Barrymore as an aging Louis XV, and Robert Morley as a singularly befuddled and inept Louis XVI. Although MGM executives mismanaged the film's production, they promoted an energetic ad campaign for the finished product and arranged for Shearer to reprise her role on the *Maxwell House Coffee Radio Hour*. In the end, *Marie-Antoinette* achieved only moderate commercial success, but it met with a generally favorable critical reaction. Praised by the *New York Herald Tribune* as "the most sumptuous historical spectacle of the year," it was named one of the ten best movies of 1938 by *Film Daily* and was nominated for four Academy Awards.[1]

Today, the film seems to have little critical merit. Norma Shearer was not an especially talented actress under any circumstances, but even her limited abilities suffered in *Marie-Antoinette,* as her mugging and muttering went unchecked by the minimalist direction of W. S. Van Dyke (known as "One-Shot Woody" for his breakneck production style). Tyrone Power veered in the opposite direction, giving a flat, nearly affectless performance. Judged in cinematic terms, the film's greatest appeal is kitsch: it boasts remarkable costumes, theatrically overstated performances by Robert Morley and Joseph Schildkraut (as Philippe d'Orléans), and a weepy celebration of a kindhearted but misunderstood queen. And yet, while *Marie-Antoinette* may have few aesthetic merits, it is significant in representing a popularized American vision of the French Revolution and, in company with *Tale of Two Cities,* it is one of fewer than a half dozen such films that continue to find a contemporary audience through video.[2]

Scholars have traditionally shied away from films such as this, preferring to treat cinema that restricts itself to domestic history: French films about the French Revolution, for example, or American films about the Civil War.[3] Certainly there are clear disciplinary reasons for this approach, but it has imposed an unnecessarily narrow perspective on rich bodies of cinematic work. American filmmakers by no means restricted themselves to the domestic experience, and their breadth of inspiration was increasingly important as movies became the principal form of American mass culture in the thirties and forties. Aggressively marketed and filling an ever-greater portion of Americans' leisure time, movies provided audiences across the country with common texts that offered lessons about politics, culture, and sexual mores; they became, as Margaret Thorp argued in 1939, a "new form of collective symbolism."[4] And historical films constituted no small part of this collective symbolism. However, as filmmakers ranged widely, to embroider American and European pasts alike, and so seem to offer an important new source of filmgoers' historical knowledge, they remained profoundly rooted both temporally and geographically. And so they produced films whose representations of the past were profoundly shaped by current and American concerns, as well as by the classic narrative style that dominated Hollywood in those years.[5]

Marie-Antoinette is just such a film. Ostensibly based on Stefan Zweig's biography of the French queen, the film's narrative and characterizations were shaped by the genre requirements of the Hollywood standard and infused with concerns that plagued Americans at the end of a decade of economic depression. Generic conventions determined the film's representation of historical causality, for in order to achieve the Hollywood desideratum of temporal and narrative unity MGM scenarists cast the events and personalities of Marie-Antoinette's life as the principal causes of the French Revolution. Meanwhile, the turmoil over sex roles that rumbled through American society in the thirties governed the explanatory weight given particular events and personal characteristics. Faced with the economic disruption of older family structures and sex roles, Americans turned their attention away from women's struggle for personal and professional independence to focus instead on the blow that the Depression dealt to ideals of masculine strength and self-sufficiency. And this shift markedly shaped the way in which the French queen's life was represented cinematically, producing a very precisely gendered vision of Old Regime France. In *Marie-Antoinette*, the heroine's search for an ideal masculine authority serves the narrative by giving cause for the French Revolution at the same time that it reflects prevailing concerns in Depression-era America about the status of contemporary masculinity.

Stefan Zweig's biography of Marie-Antoinette, published in German in 1932 and translated into English in 1933, was subtitled *The Portrait of an Average Woman*. The author introduced his work by explaining that his purpose was to strip away both the hagiographic and the demonizing impulses that had characterized earlier descriptions of Marie-Antoinette, in order to reveal the "mediocre woman" whom history required to play a part in a "profoundly moving drama."

> Had it not been for the outbreak of the Revolution, this insignificant Habsburg princess . . . would have continued . . . to live her life after the fashion of hundreds of millions of women of all epochs. She would have danced, chattered, loved, laughed, made up her face, paid visits, bestowed alms; she would have borne children and would at long last have died in her bed, without ever having lived in any true sense of the term.

But, Zweig continued, the suffering and misfortunes of the Revolution reshaped the French queen, "until all the greatness derived from a long line of ancestors (though till now hidden) had been brought to light. . . . Just before the mortal, the transient fame perished, the immortal work of art was perfected. Marie-Antoinette, the mediocrity, achieved a greatness commensurate with her destiny."[6]

In writing this biography, Zweig faced the complex task of explaining the contours and development of Marie-Antoinette's individual character, as well as the relationship between her life and the period in which she lived; thus he had, to a certain extent, to explain the causes of the French Revolution. Zweig argued that the single most important detail in the life of Marie-Antoinette and in the development of the French nation was Louis XVI's impotence, which prevented him from consummating his marriage for almost seven years. The public and private consequences of this impotence were equally disastrous. The king's "secret shame" (Zweig's nomenclature) rendered him shy and retiring, incapable of exerting his will over wife or subjects. Meanwhile, Marie-Antoinette, frivolous and sexually frustrated, turned to an extravagant lifestyle that attracted the attention and hostility of enemies at and away from court. To make matters worse, she intervened in political affairs on impulse, responding to personal whims or the prompting of the ambitious duchesse de Polignac. Marie-Antoinette developed neither the knowledge about nor the sustained interest in politics that had been the source of the domestic and diplomatic successes of her mother, Maria Theresa.

Zweig went on to describe the scandal of the Diamond Necklace Affair, when extortionists used the queen's name to defraud a jeweler of an extremely expensive necklace, as the catalyst of long-simmering discontents. Regardless of the queen's innocence, even total ignorance of the original affair, her name had been dragged through the mud and she henceforth became a scapegoat for the troubles that plagued France. The long-hostile nobility accused her of isolating them from the king, just as the mistresses of Louis XV had done in earlier decades. Meanwhile, an increasingly cultured and self-confident bourgeoisie claimed that Marie-Antoinette was responsible for forfeiting France's international prestige even as she fed its debts. Finally, the overburdened peasantry came to believe that it was the queen's extravagance, rather than inefficient economic structures and an anachronistic system of taxation, that was the source of their ills.

Thus, while Stefan Zweig focused on Marie-Antoinette's life, he situated it within the broader context of eighteenth-century politics and culture. He sought to explain why the queen's contemporaries hated her, and how the seemingly personal details of a family life at court dovetailed with broader historical change to contribute to the causes of the Revolution. But context, like Zweig's avowed hostility toward hagiography, was stripped away by the scenarists, directors, and actors who turned the biography into a film.

Ironically, biography is a likely source for a classic Hollywood narrative because, as David Bordwell has explained, these narratives are character-centered and driven by the protagonist's desire to overcome obstacles in pursuit of a specific goal. "It is easy to see in the goal-oriented protagonist an ideology of American individualism and accomplishment, but it is the peculiar accomplishment of the classical cinema to translate this ideology into a rigorous chain of cause and effect."[7] The protagonist's efforts acquire even grander significance in historical films, for they do not simply drive the story forward; they become the principal cause of historical events. Thus, in *Marie-Antoinette*, the protagonist's private search for love and conjugal guidance set in motion the events that led to the collapse of the French monarchy and the opening of the French Revolution.

The central dilemma of Marie-Antoinette's life is foreshadowed in the first scene of the film. Having announced to her daughter that she will be wed to the dauphin of France, Maria Theresa offers advice for a union that sounds more like bourgeois marriage than political alliance. Marie-Antoinette must try, she urges, to accustom herself to the manners of the French and become a good queen and a good wife; to do so she must, above all, "trust to your husband." However, the futility of Maria Theresa's parting words are revealed upon the princess's arrival at Versailles. Tall but pudgy, clumsy, and thoroughly tongue-tied, the dauphin seems far from the kind of husband upon whom an adolescent girl might depend for guidance. Matters go from bad to worse on the wedding night itself. After the marriage bed has been blessed and the court withdraws to leave the royal couple in isolation, Marie-Antoinette attempts to win over the withdrawn dauphin and accomplish aspirations that are both domestic and dynastic. But the dauphin silences her chatter about how many children they might have by blurting out an explanation that was, doubtless, rendered enigmatic by the conditions of the Hays Code. "There will be no heirs to the throne . . . because of me." Having revealed to Marie-Antoinette that he can make her neither wife nor mother, he swears her to secrecy on the matter and leaves her alone to collapse in tears on the empty marriage bed.

The rest of the film's narrative, which resumes two years later, is set in motion by the dauphin's physical and psychological impotence. Frustrated by Louis' refusal to play the husband and defend her against attacks by the king's mistress Madame du Barry, Marie-Antoinette makes an alliance with the ambitious and reptilian duc d'Orléans. Under d'Orléans' patronage, the dauphine becomes the center of a dazzling and scandalous social life until she disgraces herself by publicly snubbing du Barry, thus provoking Louis XV to prepare her return to Vienna with the explanation that she has failed to bear an heir. Worse yet, d'Orléans abandons the dauphine upon hearing of her disgrace. During the night that follows, Marie-Antoinette encounters the handsome Swedish count Axel von Fersen and, falling in love, prepares to embrace the annulment of her marriage. But upon returning to the palace, she learns that the king is on his deathbed and the dauphin has undergone a mysterious transformation with the result that "now we can truly be one." Fersen tells the queen that she must live openly and honestly, doing what is best for her people, and he leaves for America. Marie-Antoinette becomes a good wife, a good mother, and a good queen, but her subjects cannot forget the past because the scorned and ever-ambitious d'Orléans, turning from palace intrigue to rabble-rousing, stirs them to revolt. The French Revolution ensues; Fersen returns to mastermind the royal family's escape; the attempt fails and eventually Louis, then Marie-Antoinette herself, goes to the scaffold.

Just as filmmakers shaped the events of Marie-Antoinette's life in France to achieve narrative unity, so they represented the unhappy queen and her cohorts according to Hollywood principles of character development: each figure embodies one or two principal traits that define him or her and, more importantly, motivate the plot.[8] At the film's center is, of course, Marie-Antoinette, whose character is defined by her search for love and her desire to fulfill her mother's aspirations by becoming a good queen. But Marie-Antoinette's ability to accomplish these goals is alternately thwarted and facilitated by the men she encounters in France, encounters that, logically, bring the male characters' essential traits into play. Each of these men—Louis, d'Orléans, and Fersen—may be said to be trying out for the role of husband in Marie-Antoinette's life: in other words, each is potentially the man who will offer her the love and guidance she needs to accomplish her goals. And as they represent different conjugal possibilities, so each character represents a different kind of maleness; but only the ideal, truly masculine type—Fersen—will succeed.

In making gender a central preoccupation of *Marie-Antoinette*, Hollywood filmmakers found a certain affinity with the period that they represented. Sex roles and sexual practices played an important part in political discourse developed during the final years of the Old Regime and throughout the first half of the Revolution itself. After the death of Louis XV in 1774, libelous pamphlets accused the late king's mistresses, Madame de Pompadour and her successor, Madame du Barry, of using their sexuality to control the king and involve themselves in the politics of the court. These accounts employed pornographic detail to depict key players and to drive home their central point: that the dominance of women at court corrupted politics and emasculated the men who should properly be running the country. For a variety of reasons, these same kinds of attacks came to focus on Marie-Antoinette in the mid-eighties, in the wake of the Diamond Necklace Affair. And as libelists made these accusations in pornographic pamphlets, more sober arguments about the corrupting influence of women's involvement in politics were developed by recognized members of the Enlightenment, most notably by Jean-Jacques Rousseau.[9] These two strands of thought came together during the Revolution, to reach their zenith in 1793 when Revolutionary prosecutors went beyond accusing Marie-Antoinette of treason to claim that she had committed incest with her son.[10]

Marie-Antoinette initially seems to follow the lead of eighteenth-century criticism, problematizing women's place in politics through visual criticism of the inappropriate and potentially emasculating influence of Madame du Barry. We first see her feeding a clothed poodle that stands uncomfortably on its hind legs as du Barry asks the king, "Have you ever had a gallant more decorous or obedient?" But this woman's nastiness proves to be motivated by simple feminine jealousy, as she complains of having been abandoned by her courtiers when the dauphine arrived at court, and her concerns seem properly familial in their emphasis on dynasty. For, astonishingly, it is Madame du Barry who proves to be most concerned about Marie-Antoinette's failure to bear an heir to the throne, and so her mocking of the dauphine—which twice serves as a crucial plot device—is founded on the desire to continue a lineage from which she herself is excluded. Meanwhile, the other harpy of eighteenth-century literature, Marie-Antoinette, is shielded from all hint of accusation by the very structure of the film's plot, which requires that she play the part of demure heroine.

Women's potential for harm is, however, peripheral to Marie-Antoinette for other than generic reasons, for the film's gender concerns were also shaped by the society in which and for which it was produced. Pornographers and political theorists in eighteenth-century France were, in part, able to blame their social and political anxieties on women because they could find a handful of remarkable and exemplary figures: women who, as *salonnières* or members of the court, decisively shaped the political and intellectual life of the realm. In twentieth-century America, on the other hand, a women's movement that was only nascent had been powerfully undermined by the economic crisis of the Depression. By the end of the 1930s, women had suffered both economically and culturally: while the Depression cost them a disproportionate share of the labor market, new Hollywood production codes encouraged representations of women that promoted sexual discretion and the sustenance of nuclear families headed by men.[11] *Marie-Antoinette*'s representation of women was consistent with this transformation, for the film celebrates a heroine whose love exceeded worldly ambition and transcended all obstacles, even death.

But women's status and representation were not the only gender issues of the thirties. Masculinity was in flux as well, and it was on this point that *Marie-Antoinette* delivered its most pointed commentary. Unemployed or underemployed, American working men felt a keen loss of status in the 1930s; as their earning power declined, many believed that their positions as heads of households were endangered as well. Couples reported that their sexual relations diminished in these years as women's increasingly important contributions to the family economy freed them from the compulsion to agree unfailingly to sex, or as men's impaired self-esteem impinged on their virility.[12] Against this background, *Marie-Antoinette*'s exploration of masculinity can be seen as both reflecting and paying attention to concerns that were common within the film's projected audience.

We have already given brief consideration to Louis XVI's impotence, both literal and figurative. And it is, in truth, his figurative impotence that is the greater source of trouble. Marie-Antoinette initially agrees to keep her (nominal) husband's secret and stand by his side, and we are given to understand that she does so faithfully for two years; we next see her whiling away a deadening afternoon with a female friend while Louis comes and goes from his workshop like a happy child. But when du Barry viciously attacks the dauphine's barrenness and Louis refuses to bring the matter to his father's attention, Marie-Antoinette loses all patience. "This woman only dares to insult me because you seem to despise me," she rages at Louis. "I want life to be rich and full and beautiful." She goes on to make clear that it is not the dauphin's actual failure at being a husband that is the source of her discontent; it is his refusal even to play the part. Determined to seek other means to have herself recognized as the dauphine of France, she turns to an alliance with the duc d'Orléans, the king's cousin and a scorned minion of Madame du Barry.

In the world of *Marie-Antoinette,* d'Orléans proves to be the most dangerous character at court, perhaps in all of France, and his untrustworthiness is made manifest to the viewer by his sexually ambiguous appearance. Even at a court in which all men wear silk and lace, d'Orléans is distinctively feminized: his eyebrows are penciled into a permanent arch, and he alone among all the characters, male or female, has a mouth obviously painted into a cupid's bow: his gestures are delicate, his expression sneering, and he speaks in an unnaturally high voice. The physical impression is reinforced by Marie-Antoinette's innuendo when she refuses him a kiss at an artist's ball by sneering, "Perhaps you don't have enough *allure,* Philippe." When d'Orléans replies that it may be his "*excess* of allure" that has caused her to refuse him the kisses she gives other men at court, Marie-Antoinette slaps him. And this gesture reveals the full dimensions of the character, for the duc d'Orléans visibly relaxes and allows a smile of pleasure to cross his face. "Thank you," he whispers as, finally, he and the dauphine kiss.

Vito Russo has argued that, in the films of the twenties and thirties, effeminate male characters served as measures of the masculinity of the "real" men who surrounded them, and this is the heavily laden role accorded to d'Orléans.[13] D'Orléans underscores masculine weakness because his ability to join Marie-Antoinette's inner circle makes clear the extent of Louis' impotence and renunciation of authority.[14] But the duke is not the benign or comic measure that Russo describes; rather, he is a malignant presence who undermines the dauphine's standing and, finally, strikes at the very root of the tiny bourgeois circle of the royal family. Under his tutelage, Marie-Antoinette gambles, attends "artists' balls," and spends outrageous sums of money on clothes and jewels—activities that damage her and the court's reputations and which will, in the end, serve d'Orléans' efforts to rouse the populace against the monarchy.

If d'Orléans first serves to measure the impotence of Louis XVI, he later throws into relief the sufficient and appropriate masculinity of the man who will act as Marie-Antoinette's savior: Count Axel von Fersen. Representationally, Fersen's appearance is as evocative as that of his antithesis. While the latter carries court fashion to outrageous excess, the former shuns it almost altogether. His clothes are dark and simple; he does not even wear a powdered wig. And as with d'Orléans, Fersen's behavior confirms the suggestion of his appearance from his first meeting with Marie-Antoinette. While still under the thrall of the evil duke, the dauphine invites Fersen into a gaming house to help her win a turn at forfeits. Rejecting the warning of his companion in the street, who tells him that it is Marie-Antoinette who has beckoned, Fersen joins her circle only to find that they are pretending to be an actor's troupe. Once among this company, where d'Orléans vies with the women in ogling the count, Fersen's self-possession and reserve stand in marked contrast to the laughter and innuendo being exchanged by the other men. Playing along with the ruse that Marie-Antoinette is an actress, Fersen claims that she is known throughout Paris for kindness and easy virtue alike. When he persists in this judgment even after the dauphine has claimed her true identity, Fersen makes clear his unswerving scrupulousness and the fact that he sees the woman rather than the royal symbol.

It is moral rigor and a determination to recall Marie-Antoinette to her duty that characterize Fersen throughout. The count declares his love for the dauphine only after she has fallen into disgrace, and he retreats as she prepares to ascend the throne, explaining that nothing must stand between Marie-Antoinette and her people. It is clearly this scrupulousness and authority that the young woman has sought all along, for she tells Fersen rapturously, "With you I'll be everything I'm meant to be: serious and helpful and . . . a *good* Queen." Even when he leaves, it is with the command that she continue to meet the standard he has set for her.

> *Fersen:* If you need me, I shall come to you.
> *Antoinette:* I shall always need you.
> *Fersen:* And if I should ask you, "Was it well done?" you would tell me, "It was well done."

Until this point, Marie-Antoinette has been the active one who sets goals, takes action, makes future plans, but now Fersen, in exerting the authority she seeks, has fixed her in place. Appropriately enough, then, it is he who walks away from this meeting, the camera racing backward before him, as Marie-Antoinette stands silently in the deepening shadows of the background.

Fersen's declaration of love and Louis XV's death occur in scenes that follow upon each other to constitute the central turning point of the film. Here, the context shifts from static Old Regime to revolutionary climate as both members of the royal couple achieve sexual maturity. But the transformation is not absolute: the old king's death may have rendered the dauphin sexually potent, but he remains the psychological innocent who relies upon Marie-Antoinette for guidance. Meanwhile, she has found a masculine power to back her throne and so can play her part by becoming, quite literally, a queen-mother. She bears children and includes the king among them, preparing his speeches, guiding his policy, and imposing economies on the royal household that become manifest in costumes with increasingly discreet necklines.

But history has determined that this will not be a film with a happy ending, and it is the unwelcome return of the unmanly man, the duc d'Orléans, that proves to be the royal family's undoing. Frustrated in his ambitions by his break with Marie-Antoinette, d'Orléans turns to rabble-rousing. He stirs class hatred by circulating stories among the people about royal expenditures. And the crowd that he rouses is as unmindful of proper authority as had been the youthful dauphine: they refuse the offers of assistance from a deputy to the Assembly and shout instead that they will head to the Bastille. Worse yet, they are as ignorant of proper gender roles as the duc d'Orléans, for when a crowd invades the royal household in the Tuileries Palace, a man steps forward to slap Marie-Antoinette. Here, finally, Louis takes action by restraining the man with the reminder "It's cowardly to strike a woman."

But Louis' action is brief and fails to be decisive. The rest of the film, like the rest of Zweig's biography, unwinds as a series of disappointments and humiliations that lead almost inexorably to the scaffold. The extent of d'Orléans' corroding influence on the royal family is made clear in scenes of pathos that follow upon one another as Louis joins his family for a last dinner in the prison of the Temple before heading to the guillotine and then, immediately after the king's execution, guards arrive to wrest the dauphin from the arms of his weeping mother, Marie-Antoinette. Deprived of her double role of queen-mother by the emasculate d'Orléans, Marie-Antoinette ages quickly and follows her husband to the guillotine. But death is cinematically subverted: the viewer is spared the sight of the queen's head falling beneath the blade as the film gives the last scene to Fersen, who stands alone above the city, preparing to cherish the memory of the woman who would do as he commanded and say, "It was well done."

My point here is not that Hollywood somehow got the history of the French Revolution wrong; Pierre Sorlin, Marc Ferro, and others have argued eloquently that, like more traditional forms of historical writing, cinematic representations of history involve interpretation.[15] Rather, I am concerned with the particular kinds of interpretations that *Marie-Antoinette* promoted. Above all, American filmmakers drew on their own national traditions and contemporary concerns in representing eighteenth-century France. Unable to conceive of a world in which women actively shaped politics and culture, they painted a picture of Old Regime society that suffered bitterly from the absence of bourgeois marriages and households headed by men. Had Marie-Antoinette's affairs been left to follow a more "natural" course, the film implies, we would not have known of her at all; not, as Zweig suggests, because she was a particularly mediocre woman but simply because she was a woman. Under other circumstances, she would have remained happily in the shadows where she belonged because she had found fulfillment in a patriarchal marriage. And ironically, this is where Hollywood hagiographers found an unexpected point of contact with some of their historical subjects, for in making masculinity the only potential savior of the French throne, they implied that they found the notion of womanly authority as monstrous as had pornographers and republicans in the eighteenth century.

Notes

1. Jack Jacobs and Myron Braum, *The Films of Norma Shearer* (South Brunswick: A. S. Barnes, 1976), 212–19; James Robert Parish, Gregory W. Mank, and Richard Picchiarini, *The Best of MGM: The Golden Years (1928–1959)* (Westport, Conn.: Arlington House Publishers, 1981), 131–33.

2. In *La Victoire en filmant, ou, la Révolution à l'écran* (Nancy: Presses Universitaires de Nancy, 1989), Roger Viry-Babel lists 281 films made internationally between 1897 and 1989 about the French Revolution; 41 are American. *Marie-Antoinette* has been available for sale and rental on video since 1990. It can be rented in 453 of the 2,323 American Blockbuster Stores (about one-fifth), the largest video rental chain in the United States. *Tale of Two Cities* (1936), starring Ronald Colman, is available in 1,308 stores (more than half). Figures on Blockbuster available from Blockbuster Video Public Relations Office.

3. See, for example, Pierre Sorlin, *The Film in History: Restaging the Past* (Oxford: Blackwell, 1980); Marc Ferro, *Cinema and History,* trans. Naomi Greene (Detroit: Wayne State University Press, 1988); K. R. M. Short, ed., *Feature Films as History* (Knoxville: University of Tennessee Press, 1981).

4. Quoted in Garth Jowett, *Film: The Democratic Art* (Boston and Toronto: Little, Brown, 1976), 266. Jowett includes the quote approvingly in his more general discussion of American filmgoing habits during the 1930s.

5. Pierre Sorlin has demonstrated how present concerns and national traditions shape films that treat domestic histories. I would argue that geographically and temporally local concerns exert a still more decisive influence in films that purport to describe other national histories. See Sorlin, *Film in History*.

6. Stefan Zweig, *Marie-Antoinette: The Portrait of an Average Woman*, trans. Eden and Cedar Paul (Garden City, N.Y.: Garden City Publishing, 1933), xiii, xiv–xv.

7. David Bordwell, "The Classical Hollywood Style, 1917–1960," in David Bordwell, Janet Staiger, and Kristin Thompson, *The Classical Hollywood Cinema: Film and Mode of Production to 1960* (New York: Columbia University Press, 1985), 16.

8. Ibid.

9. For a more detailed discussion of pornographic attacks on Louis XV's mistresses and their association with attacks against Marie-Antoinette, see Sarah Maza, "The Diamond-Necklace Affair Revisited (1785–1786): The Case of the Missing Queen," in this volume.

10. Lynn Hunt, "The Many Bodies of Marie-Antoinette: Political Pornography and the Problem of the Feminine in the French Revolution," in this volume; Joan Landes, *Women and the Public Sphere in the Age of the French Revolution* (Ithaca: Cornell University Press, 1988); Elizabeth Colwill, "Just Another *Citoyenne*? Marie-Antoinette on Trial, 1790–1793," *History Workshop* 28 (autumn 1989): 63–87.

11. On production codes, see Marjorie Rosen, *Popcorn Venus: Women, Movies, the American Dream* (New York: Coward, McCann, and Geoghegan, 1973); Molly Haskell, *From Reverence to Rape: The Treatment of Women in the Movies*, 2d ed. (Chicago: University of Chicago Press, 1987); Jowett, *Film*. On the economic impact of the Depression on women, see Nancy Woloch, *Women and the American Experience* (New York: Alfred A. Knopf, 1984); Peter G. Filene, *Him/Her/Self: Sex Roles in Modern America*, 2d ed. (Baltimore: Johns Hopkins University Press, 1986).

12. Woloch, *Women and the American Experience*, 439–46; Filene, *Him/Her/Self*, 149–60.

13. Vito Russo, *The Celluloid Closet: Homosexuality in the Movies*, rev. ed. (New York: Harper and Row, 1985), chap. 1, "Who's a Sissy?"

14. Louis' immaturity is underscored by a ball scene in which the camera pans up from the dance floor to find the dauphin watching from the balcony—like a small child—as he eats an apple.

15. Sorlin, *Film as History*; Ferro, *Cinema and History*.

Terrorizing Marie-Antoinette

Pierre Saint-Amand

Translated by Jennifer Curtiss Gage

In order to understand Marie-Antoinette's peculiar situation during the French Revolution and the negative political representations of her, we might consider the more recent case of Hillary Clinton. Amazingly, despite the two hundred years that separate these two figures, they illustrate that political conceptions of women are still subject to the same collective fears and anxieties. The hatred trained upon Hillary Clinton during the 1992 presidential election was reproduced in the very same language as the discourse of infamy that sent Queen Marie-Antoinette to the guillotine on 16 October 1793. In fact, the fear of women in power, of woman's empowerment, might be designated the Marie-Antoinette syndrome. This syndrome entails three characteristics: (1) the demonization and cloning of the woman's influence; (2) the accessibility of the woman's genitalia as the very organ of influence; and (3) a seizing of the woman's body by way of sexual appropriation. My intention in comparing the two women is to demonstrate how ineluctably the body is invested in the political domain, how the entire symbolic system of politics is articulated by using the body—here, the bodies of two women at the site of power, women destined to exhibit a variety of political signs. Interpreting the reception of these signs is a way of probing more deeply the political culture in which these characters evolve.

In each of the two cases under discussion, the woman's influence on her husband is judged nefarious and dangerous. When the right-wing press (whose criticisms of candidate Bill Clinton's wife gave the impression of a concerted attack upon recent political gains by women) stopped attacking Hillary Clinton head-on as a failed maternal image and a domineering wife, the same commentators kept her under surveillance in her new function as First Lady, seeking every opportunity to judge and condemn her—above all for her ignominious failure in her duties as keeper of the East Wing, the "home" quarters of the White House.

At every turn Hillary Clinton is called on the carpet for anticipated departures from the traditional function of the president's wife: the fact that she staked out an office in the section of the White House reserved for political administration, her nomination as head of the task force on health care reforms, and above all, the way in which she managed to reproduce herself like a feminist virus in the ranks of women appointed to high-level positions; besides Donna Shalala, consider the unfortunate nominees for attorney general, Zoë Baird and Kimba Wood (a chapter closed by the confirmation of Janet Reno).[1] Like it or not, Hillary Clinton has changed the nature of White House politics forever. Here are some of the things her critics are saying: the administration is made up of Hillary's clones; she has usurped the vice president's position, indeed reducing him to passivity; and in the process she has rendered difficult the administration's accountability by placing herself as spouse in various powerful governmental positions. But most of all, she has lived up to their worst fears: she dominates her weak husband, placing him literally *under the influence;* Hillary is Bill Clinton's narcotic.

Hillary Clinton has thus made common cause with the new dragon ladies. She has taken her place in an infamous genealogy of dangerous women. In an interview on *Nightline* (10 March 1993) regarding the new powers of the First Lady, Peter Flaherty, president of the National Legal and Policy Center and a Republican fundraiser committed to halting the momentum of Mrs. Clinton, was eager to recall one of the more recent incarnations of these treacherous women. Here is what he said: "I think what a lot of Americans are worried about is that we have some kind of Imelda Marcos wielding power behind the scenes with absolutely no accountability." This representation of an uncontrollable lust for power is best expressed in the *Spy* magazine photomontage of Hillary Clinton as dominatrix (see photo insert).

Of all the images offered by television, that of Hillary Clinton whispering in the president's ear may become the most memorable because of the way it was framed and repeated in the news. What did the press intend for this image to convey if not an exaggerated display of the typical aside, of secretive manipulation—private, spousal behavior overflowing onto the public stage? Another scene, perhaps equally memorable, on the occasion of an open house at the White House was seized upon by the media. When it became known that too many people had shown up for the event, Hillary Clinton was shown to "take charge" not only as the lady of the house but also as a hostess desperate to show that she was in control, a wife capable of directing her husband with frank language (witness her "we just screwed all these people" repeated over and over on the news: an obvious instance of *lèse-décorum*). Here again, television focused on asides exchanged by Mr. and Mrs. Clinton. On Rush Limbaugh's program of 16 February 1993, commenting on that event, the analytical treatment of this image went even further, as the camera tried to zoom in as closely as possible to catch whatever may have been said sotto voce. The camera and particularly the sound sought to capture, decode, and deliberately denounce the language of influence, to catch the female in flagrante delicto of political maneuver. Even on the March 1993 broadcast of *Nightline* concerning Hillary Clinton, the guest commentators admitted to her intelligence, her abilities, her discipline and efficacy, but they were unable to accept her advising the president. It is as if an all-out ban targeting women had been declared: a ban on female influence. The wife's influence upon the husband is considered an attack upon the male's integrity and autonomy, his very "essence."[2]

The scandal of Mrs. Clinton's visibility and her alleged usurpation of the vice president's role both inflame a common prejudice sustained by the gendered hierarchy of the government. The structure of the government readily admits a vice president diminished in image if not in actual status, a paralyzed twin of the head of state (the vice president is supposed to confirm the exclusive power of his hierarchical superior and to shore up his chief's visibility; he is the president's spokesman); homosocial bonding among males is always reassuring. What is disturbing is the type of bonding that partakes of heterogeneity, of difference.

There are other similarities between Hillary Clinton and Marie-Antoinette that could also be studied, other stereotypical tendencies applied to woman; I recall them to show how profoundly immovable mentalities are, how stagnant collective representations can remain.[3] Compare the case of the transformations of Marie-Antoinette's name—Messalina, Agrippina, Isabeau de Bavière, and other epithets, which I will discuss later at length—to the use of Hillary Clinton's name by the Republicans, especially Pat Buchanan, and the talk shows during the last campaign. By calling Mrs. Clinton "Hillary," by isolating her first name, these commentators demonized her as a series of monster types: the she-devil, the independent witch, the improper wife. The use of this unique signifier was intended to conjure up all sorts of negative female images. "Hillary" is a proper name turned heteronym—a *caconym* proper. Detached from the referent, it designates a particular in the guise of a universal stereotype. "Hillary" is the "possessed" name of Hillary Clinton. In a way, by calling herself Hillary Rodham Clinton since the inauguration, the First Lady has taken back her name, reinstating not only the affiliated name of the husband but her own name as well. Not only has she reclaimed control over her name but, perhaps with deliberate, playful cunning, she has lengthened it, correcting the nasty diminutive.[4]

Consider also the general question of adornment and the hoopla created around Hillary Clinton's inaugural ball gown. Anne-Marie Schiro's article on what the First Lady wore, appearing in the *New York Times*, provided information about her designers and of course ample commentary about the traditional gown itself. In this case what was most intriguing to the press was how this unconventional First Lady would be clad. In the end, the public and the press were reassured. Hillary Clinton had proven, in the words of the newspaper, "that she was willing to experiment with clothing and hair styles." In other words she could, like any woman, indulge in glamorous temptation, fall for the vice of beautification by artifice. The same newspaper was also happy to provide details of Hillary Clinton's feminine makeover; hence we learn that the day of the inauguration she received a manicure and that a makeup artist touched up her cheeks with Plum 3 and her lips with Rambling Rose.[5] This type of feminine self-enjoyment through beautification and artifice is reassuring because it is well established in the social imaginary.[6] On the other hand, as Susan Faludi observes, what is problematic in the case of Hillary Clinton is the perception of her own enjoyment of her independence, indeed, of her power:

> She is doing something her predecessors didn't dare. She's abandoned the earnest, dutiful demeanor. She doesn't bear the grim visage of the stereotypical female policy wonk, she's no Jeane Kirkpatrick. Nor does

she make any pretense that power and visibility were forced on her. And therein lies her sin: Hillary Clinton is visibly, tangibly having fun. Eleanor Roosevelt loved the public life, but she rarely revealed her exuberance. Before the media, Ms. Clinton throws back her head and laughs, kicks up her heels and breaks into a dance.[7]

If I insist upon comparing Hillary Clinton to Marie-Antoinette, despite the historical distance that separates them, it is because both of them are victims of a backlash against the advancement of women in the public sphere, against their increased visibility and competition with men for participation in social institutions. When people denounced Marie-Antoinette they also denounced the excessive publicity of aristocratic women, their dizzying emancipation. The queen of France had displayed these new behaviors to the utmost. An extended conservative discourse in the Age of Reason denounces the effeminization of culture by noblewomen, their intellectual promiscuity in the salons, their involvement in political debates.[8] Marie-Antoinette was perceived as the most unbridled symbol of this new representation of women. In the case of Hillary Clinton, the threat stems from the degree to which she has appeared as a model of women's political power, of their success in social and professional spheres traditionally reserved for men, of women's dramatic exit from domestic confinement. She embodies a revolution that has taken place and a measure of progress from which nothing could be taken away; and above all, for the first time, she has brought these new gains with her to the most visible position in the nation.

Thus both women became targets to the extent that for women they represent models of liberation and autonomy, full-fledged *personalities* endowed with legitimate desires and ambitions, engines of positive and gratifying images. They no longer bore the marks of vulnerability associated with the feminine domain. It is for these reasons that the immediate phallocratic reaction was to contain their public affirmation and to turn it around as folklore about women, as something like influence (secrets, underhanded manipulations). It is eminently sexist to make the accusation of influence. Influence is perceived as a form of hysterical persuasion, the incessant effort on the part of the woman to meddle in male discourse or performance. But at the same time influence condemns the woman to illegitimacy; it is a sort of ventriloquism, a cover-up, a dissimulation of the enunciator who is revealed only in the utterance of the other, the one vested with authority of discourse and action. Influence, in the end, always exposes woman in her impotence.

Regarding the question of influence and skirting the offenses in the realm of marital and maternal institutions that the queen of France is supposed to represent, I will cut right to the chase. There are countless accusations of Marie-Antoinette dominating Louis XVI. But one will suffice, so telling is the manner in which it is stated. It is the commentary provided by the great historian Michelet concerning the flight from Varennes. Although accusing the king of duplicity, Michelet confesses his readiness to excuse the monarch and blames Marie-Antoinette more than anyone else for the capture of the royal carriage. He writes: "Being excessively afraid of a separation, never losing sight of the king, but remaining constantly by his side, and wishing to depart at the same time, and with all her friends, she rendered his flight almost impossible." And it is definitely the queen who leads to the monarch's arrest: "Even if he had been recognized, he might have passed . . . but the very sight of the queen awakened every fear."[9] Even during the recent celebration of the bicentennial of the French Revolution I was struck that little research was done around the queen. It was as if she were still a subject of scorn, a wicked figure unworthy of celebration.

In 1989, Myriam Revault d'Allonnes published an important book, *D'une mort à l'autre: Précipices de la Révolution,* which addressed the political turmoil of the Terror, the death drive that characterized the Jacobin government, the impossibility of the foundation of the Republic. There Louis XVI's death receives brilliant commentary, but the queen is not named once in the epidemic of deaths analyzed by the author. Surprising also is Joan Landes' position in *Women and the Public Sphere in the Age of the French Revolution,* a much-celebrated book on the status of women in the French Revolution. Marie-Antoinette, however, remains obscured in the analysis, notwithstanding Landes's controversial treatment of freedom enjoyed by aristocratic women in the salons of the ancien régime, in comparison to the confining roles assigned to women by the defenders of liberty.[10]

Two major correctives to this neglect deserve attention: in this country, Lynn Hunt wrote a superb article reflecting upon the status of the body of the king's consort; and in France, Chantal Thomas wrote a book analyzing the various pamphlets written against the queen.[11] I was struck, reading these two authors, by the degree to which the very question of Marie-Antoinette's image represented for them a fundamental obstacle. Both authors manage with difficulty to explain the trajectory of the Revolution's principal heroine—from fantastic idolatry to irrational calumny, from consecration to repudiation, from an icon of seduction to one of depravity. Should this turn of events be seen as a peculiar reversal of lust?

Again, the bicentennial easily focused on the fate of Louis XVI, reenacting in this return to his death the type of sacralization it achieved during the Revolution itself. The view is still that Louis' death was foundational, that it was the generator of a new nation. How are we, then, to read what happened to the queen? Was her death insignificant and inconsequential? Does it make any sense for, or of, the Revolution? In a text that has been virtually forgotten, "The Sociology of the Executioner," Roger Caillois meditates upon the difference between the two royal deaths:

> If the decapitation of Louis XVI is thus presented as token and symbol of the new regime's advent . . . it is understandable that the execution of January 21, 1793, should occupy, in the course of the Revolution, a position approaching a sort of zenith. It truly represents the highest point of a curve and provides the most condensed and complete illustration of the whole crisis, the most vivid summation of it for memory.
>
> On the contrary, the execution of Marie-Antoinette was by no means an affair of state. It did not revive the majesty of a king in the majesty of a people. The "Widow Capet" appeared before the revolutionary Court, not before the Convention, that is before judges and not before representatives of the nation. They went after her private life. It is as much the woman in her as the queen that is condemned. They went out of their way to disgrace her. The crowd insulted her while the cart carried her to the scaffold. A paper recording the execution mentioned that the wretched woman had to "swallow death for a long time." . . . The falling of the royal head, the ignominious execution of the queen, manifested the victory of the powers of damnation. In general, it aroused more horror and reprobation than the death of the king, it provoked a greater shudder, it aroused more violent reactions.[12]

We could pursue this notion further and say that Marie-Antoinette's execution could also be viewed as foundational but at another, symbolic level. Her death is not political (in the sense that the king's death rallied the new nation and helped define it) but rather highly moral. The queen's execution can be interpreted as the Revolution's attempt to rectify the errant sexuality of the nation. The orgy was over, and the queen's lustfulness had been the symbol of this debauchery. In the language of the Revolution, Louis XVI's despotism or tyranny found its equivalent in the queen's lasciviousness, her wicked profligacy. The sexual promiscuity that had ravaged the nation was gone with the queen's head. In the newspaper *Le Père Duchesne,* Hébert's report on the 16 October event—Marie-Antoinette's *dies horribilissimus*—describes the decapitation, communicating with unreserved *jouissance,* with orgasmic bliss, the dread of going to pieces, the horror of detachment, of unfastening, of coming apart: "At last the feathered tart was beheaded: her accursed head was separated from her neck."[13] The Republic of Virtue was born of the queen's sexual crimes.

Let us, then, begin to trace the trajectory of the ways Marie-Antoinette was imaged during the Revolution, first meditating on what Lynn Hunt has termed the "mysterious body" of the queen. Drawing from the definitive study by Ernst Kantorowicz on the king's two bodies, Hunt clarifies the status of the queen as follows: "Because queens could never rule in France, except indirectly as regents for underage sons, they were not imagined as having the two bodies associated with kings. According to the 'mystic fiction of the "King's Two Bodies'" ... kings in England and France had both a visible, corporeal, mortal body and an invisible, ideal 'body politic,' which never died." Hunt argues that "the queen did not have a mystic body in the sense of the king's two bodies, but her body was mystical in the sense of mysteriously symbolic." The nonmystical body of the queen represented many things: the queen had "in a manner of speaking, many bodies"; but Hunt fails to give specificity to this mystery.[14]

Perhaps Louis Marin's work, *Portrait of the King,* with its departure from Kantorowicz, could be of help to us here and would allow us to give some substance to what Lynn Hunt terms the "mysteriously symbolic" body of the queen. Marin adds to the two bodies first described by Kantorowicz a third one: a "semiotic sacramental body."[15] This is the body as it is represented in the form of portraits and narratives. It is primarily a body of signs, fabricated for representation, offered to the imagination of the subjects. This body is the very site and support of the fantasy of the royal body. An imaginary of the king's sovereignty is expressed through this body, and it signifies political as well as erotic power.

Why not, then, rather conceive also of a semiotic body of Marie-Antoinette, a constructed phantasmatic body? For that we need to start at the beginning, even before Marie-Antoinette arrives in France. Indeed, it could be said that already in Austria Marie-Antoinette is packaged as a doll, carefully prepared for the enjoyment of the French court. Her body is worked upon so that she fits the standard of French elegance. A few anomalies are corrected; the girl is turned into the princess of beauty. Her round forehead is hidden behind a new hairstyle; her crooked teeth, after treatment and consultation with a specialist, become "very beautiful and straight."[16] In the words of Jules Barbey d'Aurevilly, Marie-Antoinette had become "française."[17] With all traces that might betray her native Austria eliminated, Marie-Antoinette undergoes an apprenticeship in artifice. She becomes a miniature mannequin, a collage of prosthetic elegance. Thus stylized, the dauphine is in the process of becoming "Marie-Antoinette," prepped and primped for her performances, already rehearsing for the spectacular numbers awaiting her, which will define her as the queen of France.[18] Maria Theresa, Marie-Antoinette's mother,

> authorized her ambassador at Versailles, Prince Starhemberg, to spend the extravagant sum of four hundred thousand livres for [the dauphine's] trousseau. All the clothes were to be made in Paris, commissioned from the dressmakers who regularly served the French court. It was customary for the dressmakers to send dolls—*poupées de la mode*—dressed in the current styles to clients in distant cities. . . . Scores of these dolls began arriving [in Vienna] as Marie-Antoinette turned thirteen, wearing miniature versions of the robes and gowns proposed for her.

A notable cosmetic detail: "Setting aside her usual strictures . . . the Empress has allowed Antoinette to rouge her cheeks."[19] Thus Marie-Antoinette herself becomes a doll, a perfect replica of these adorned simulacra.[20]

In the words of d'Aurevilly, Marie-Antoinette's lessons in coquetry and her early ornamentation were conceived as a brilliant calculation on the part of the Hapsburg dynasty. It was a way of stabilizing the Bourbon monarchy and putting an end to its reputation for adultery. Marie-Antoinette had to compensate for a long Bourbon line of mistresses who had usurped the queen of France's position; "that is why," d'Aurevilly writes, "they made her beautiful and charming . . . and especially *française*, that is to say airy, as was fashion then."[21] Thus the process of narcissizing Marie-Antoinette began in Austria and continued long after her arrival in France. And Marie-Antoinette was trapped in a compulsive self-beautification project, in the obsessive ornamentation of everything in her surroundings. If there is a style we could call *style Marie-Antoinette* (and as Stefan Zweig remarked, this should be the name for all that is so "wrongfully termed 'Louis Seize'"), it is to be seen in this excess of ornament and decoration, a signature of frivolity she left at the Trianon more than anywhere else.[22] Marie-Antoinette created an architecture with a feminine touch (with an emphasis on fabrics, tapestry, and miniature objects), abandoning the monumentalism and the phallic rigidity of the architecture that had defined the previous monarchs. In this little château the queen wrapped herself in a sort of intimacy with the irrational, a far cry from the rigid, majestic etiquette of Versailles. The Trianon conveys a sort of libertinage of appearances, an indulgence in distractions (for example, in its use of fabrics and mobile mirrors, in the way it constantly transforms space). Walter Benjamin saw this novel organization of space as a phantasmagoria, a retreat where private space supplants the world, withdraws from reality, invents itself as an artistic transfiguration.[23]

What Marie-Antoinette brought to the court and what was to make her an ideal target for attack was precisely this exile from etiquette, this distancing from politics, effecting a radical "demonarchization" of the regime. Because the queen also placed herself at the center of rivalry and imitation, as the equal of other noble women, she was immediately perceived as an agent of contagion; she contaminated by her tastes. She offered herself up for frequent rituals (such as balls, games, and parties) that exposed her as an object to be looked at, an object of desire. She became the court's supermodel, its ruling diva, the queen of glamour.

Thus Marie-Antoinette was progressively perceived as usurping the spectacular role of the king. As Marin remarks convincingly, "The magic of an imagination without limit, which makes marvelous realities of its whims or dreams" belongs solely to the king.[24] What Marie-Antoinette did was to efface the king, to render him invisible, by orienting all circuits of desire toward her body. While the king appeared divested of an image, of political figurability, the queen became the nexus of a theatrical system of communication. The cynosure of every eye, the queen became the condition of visibility of the court, the sole guarantor of representation. And she wielded her power as an *effect* of this representation.

This locus of visibility of the monarch has always been sexual. As Mitchell Greenberg observes,

> The representation of the court is inextricably bound to a politics of spectacle and sexuality, to the imaginary scenario that empowers. For the very essence of a court, of a king, is "parade," an ornamentalism that enhances what is mundanely universal and, with all the attributes of artifice, with all the protocols of rank, of dress, of "dépense," with all the prodigality of financial and sexual largesse, raises it beyond the general and into the empyrean of the unique. In this form of sovereignty, it is nothing so much as the image that defines the sovereign—to himself as well as to his subjects—as (illusorily) Other.[25]

Marie-Antoinette turned the king's *parade* into a giant *masquerade* (to adapt the Lacanian gendering of this illusory pretense of the self).[26] By this I mean that the spectacle of the court ceased to signify politically. All political representation was now replaced with pure spectacle: balls, theater, games.

Thus, by making a spectacle of herself, Marie-Antoinette became a voyeuristic enterprise for a whole nation, the negative heroine of a multitude of pornographic scenarios. For Zweig, the erotic fantasy that Marie-Antoinette became culminated for the revolutionary masses in what he called a veritable "orgasm of fancied lust."[27] One need only sexualize ad infinitum the marvelous representation of the monarch to understand the magnitude of what happened to Marie-Antoinette.

We could say that the queen becomes a scandal, but it is the scandal of representation itself. Marie-Antoinette is an impossible image. The reversal of her charisma does not change the manner in which she commands an absolute control over imaginations. In fact it simply confirms her sweeping hold over the public. Marie-Antoinette fulfils her destiny as *fascinum* by undergoing what Leo Spitzer called *Entlarvung,* "a movement by which a positive quality is converted into a negative quality, a greatness into vileness."[28] The same happens to the king but in a different fashion. Revault d'Allonnes studies this process of "disincarnation" (demystification) of the king, which she views as a displacement of the imagination, an attempt to turn the celebration of the marvelous into an expulsion of monstrosity. How is it possible, Revault d'Allonnes asks, to "transform adoration into horror"? She can only observe that "the transcendence that inhabited the fleshly monarch flips over into a monstrous exception, the divine is converted into bestiality."[29]

What is remarkable in the case of the queen is the expandability of this force of negation, its capacity to multiply, to replicate the images of infamy. One example of this is the Diamond Necklace Affair, staged to embarrass the queen in the very gardens of Versailles. Great pains were taken to simulate a nocturnal apparition of Marie-Antoinette. The actress, a young prostitute named Nicole Le Guay, a supposed look-alike of the queen, was hired as being perfectly suited to impersonate her. The young woman was dressed for the occasion in an informal white linen dress and pink petticoat. As Sarah Maza informs us after brilliantly revisiting this affair, "Le Guay had no idea (or so her lawyer claimed) whom she was impersonating, no notion that this costume, known as a *robe en gaule*, was identical to the one sported by Marie-Antoinette in a recent portrait by Elisabeth Vigée-Lebrun."[30] Maza studies in detail this theme of interchangeable female identities: Jeanne de La Motte, the mastermind of the affair, forged the queen's signature, but her lawyer Doillot claimed that she was in fact signing her "real" name: La Motte brought to Le Guay her own intimate connection to the queen and chose for her protégé the name baronne d'Oliva, an anagram of La Motte's own "royal" name, Valois. All this adds up to a plot with numerous similarities to the plot of the *Marriage of Figaro*, a play in which Marie-Antoinette herself had wished to play the female lead. Maza concludes her treatment of the affair with the perception by Marie-Antoinette's contemporaries of a "ubiquitousness of upperclass female intrigue, at the center of which stood the sovereign herself."[31] This famous affair instituted Marie-Antoinette as a model of parody, already a participant in a chain of imitations that originates with herself. The Diamond Necklace Affair was designed to leave the queen in a state of scandal, with the impossibility of claiming any truth for herself, to drag the queen into the abyss of total imposture.

In the same context of the negative replication of the queen's image, one could interpret the accusation of Marie-Antoinette's lesbianism as the perceived expandability, the contagious perversion, of her narcissism, that is, the cloning of her body of infamy. Unlike the adulterous harems of previous kings, where women were displayed to confirm and uphold the phallic sovereignty of the monarch (they represented a repeated message of the king's prowess), the queen multiplies herself in the court under the guise of her favorites, mistresses, and female friends. When Marie Thérèse de Lamballe, Marie-Antoinette's friend and protégé, is assassinated, her vandalized body (she is raped and cut open from her genitalia to her abdomen) is flaunted in front of the queen. The profanation of her body is performed as a repetition of the lewd acts committed upon her by the queen.

The caricatural iconography of Marie-Antoinette is another example of this expandability. We would do well to follow the lead of historians, such as Linda Orr and Dorinda Outram, who call for a "retraumatization" of the French Revolution, that is, a focusing on the violence perpetrated upon bodies.[32] In this iconography Marie-Antoinette appears in a multitude of metamorphoses, proliferating as a variety of invented bodies. Diderot and d'Alembert appropriately viewed caricature as a sort of "libertinage of the imagination."[33] Here again, as earlier in the logic of impersonation, caricature found in Marie-Antoinette its most perfect subject. Indeed, the queen is conceived as pure disorder, as misfit, as a sexual monster, a divided individual, a figure of impropriety. Thus the caricaturing of Marie-Antoinette uses the eighteenth-century art of grotesques with a vengeance. Barbara Maria Stafford, analyzing the relationship between sexuality and this artistic genre in her book *Body Criticism*, writes that "the grotesque dangerously pictured questionable or equivocal sexual acts and controversial amalgams. Ostentatious structural malformation, and provocative revolt against conventional mores, lay at the heart of its aesthetic operations."[34] Marie-Antoinette finds herself at the center of a prolific *ars combinatoria*, which assembled monsters, hybrid creatures, and a whole procession of deformed beings. She participated in a disconcerting chiasmus of species. The various sexual acts in which she engages, occupying center stage in the pornographic visual literature of the time, belong also to this grotesque enterprise. As a caricature, the queen gives access to a catalogue of pornographic aberrations. She becomes a veritable laboratory of visual experimentations, a distorted icon (see photo insert).

An identical process transforms Marie-Antoinette's name in the literature of the pamphlets, where she is called, as I pointed out earlier, Messalina, Agrippina, Isabeau de Bavière, and so forth. This cascade of calumny finds its target. With each new name, Marie-Antoinette becomes the bearer of a new history, a new narrative for which she will have to stand trial before a tribunal of men. The Revolution continually manipulates the queen's name; through countless curtailments and variations (Toinon, Toinette, Antoinette) runs the common thread of degrading the queen's image, of creating other characters, lascivious clones, in her place. A phantasmatic delirium is staged around these signifiers, these floating, exchangeable signs that can be passed from mouth to mouth. This onomastic invention on the part of the Revolution, its continual scansion of the queen's name with the repetitive force of a ritual, proved the most effective means of creating unanimity around her. In a way, the queen's final appellation—Veuve Capet (Widow Capet)—represents the ultimate endpoint of these processes of identification and substitution. The queen ceases to be the *queen of France*; her name will no longer summon forbidding images of the sacred. No longer exceptional, Marie-Antoinette succumbs to the banality of equality.

If the pamphlets call the queen names and publicize her, they will ultimately call her back to reality, that is, to a definitive exit from the world of fantasies. Marie-Antoinette's long march to the scaffold will take her from a deliberate ignorance of the pamphlets, whereby she keeps a distance between herself and rumors about her, to the point at which she comes to embody these utterances, conforming to the image created of her. Marie-Antoinette becomes the image projected by her persecutors, the incarnation of their hatred; she has absorbed their violence. Chantal Thomas, rightfully nonplussed by this staggering phenomenon, writes: "the words of the pamphlets had become flesh, and this flesh was her very self."[35]

All this ends in what I would call a gradual denarcissization of Marie-Antoinette, in her enforced retreat from the field of visibility, from the glorious theater of gazes. The queen is stricken by a kind of spectatorial and sartorial castration. The revenge of the Revolution upon Marie-Antoinette's body was to turn the terror of her beauty against her by a very slow process of subtraction, leaving her in a kind of specular limbo. All the apparatus of seduction is put out of her reach as the Revolution confiscates her wardrobe; the queen is sentenced to a radical impoverishment of apparel (she will even have to negotiate for a mourning outfit).

The Terror will invent a monstrous image of the queen, an image so frightful that Marie-Antoinette ends up being afraid of herself. This twist is accomplished by turning her initial seduction back upon her, by using the originary terror of her beauty against her with the deadly calculation of inversion. The execution of the queen is a veritable undoing, a sacrifice of the gift of seduction that had been given her. It is an out-and-out dispossession, an exorcism of her power. Likewise, her condemnation as an Austrian and a foreigner is a way of taking back the hospitality that had been extended to her in the beginning.

Jacques-Louis David's sketch of Marie-Antoinette on her way to the guillotine captures perhaps better than any other image this ravaged fabrication of the queen by the men of the Revolution (see photo insert). David's sketch is the final and definitive signature of the process of denarcissization that I have described. What this rendition effects is the disappearance of Marie-Antoinette's figurability, by extracting everything that previously destined her to privileged visibility. The drawing leaves us with an image of a colorless, bloodless, anorexic queen. It is impossible to ignore the intertextual rivalry this image evokes. In a few strokes of ink, David washes out the colors and pigments, strips off the makeup and adornments that envelope the queen in Elisabeth Vigée-Lebrun's official portraits (see photo insert). The painter who has given us the most extravagant glorification of the Revolution—the iconographer and set designer of revolutionary events, the impresario of the Revolution's festivals, the militant of the Terror—effaced the work of his aristocratic rival, the portraits of the queen in all her magnificence. He visited upon the painter the most severe punishment of his ideological judgment. Awarded the pleasure of drawing the queen's ultimate portrait, David signs her off the same way he had signed the Committee of General Security warrants that sent suspects off to the Revolutionary Tribunal, which is to say, to the guillotine. A cadaverous Marie-Antoinette is made to perform her ultimate scandal. David condemns her to a definitive lack *in* representation; on the way to the scaffold, Marie-Antoinette is already dead, drained, effaced, emptied.

However, no act could finish off Marie-Antoinette more decisively than the beheading itself, with the efficacy and the implacability reserved only for reality. The guillotine that awaits the queen will perform the most exemplary punishment of her body of artifice. It will send to Sanson's bucket not simply the head renowned for beauty and arrogance—that coquettish, feathered head, that overpowering metonymy of the queen's constructed artistic persona; the guillotine will also fell the sovereign's fetishized neck. The baron of Tilly pronounced this neck simply "exquisite," and we know that it prompted the setting of the famous diamond necklace, which was commonly known as the most beautiful jewel in the world.[36] In the end that neck, summing up the entire body, will be targeted by the Revolution as the ultimate site of ornamentation. It will become the final ornament to be ravished from the queen. In the words of one pamphlet, giving voice to the guillotine as it awaits its most desired victim, "a pretty head like yours makes a fine ornament for my machine."[37]

Perhaps the only eighteenth-century woman who meets with a similar fate is a fictional one: Laclos' Madame de Merteuil. In *Les Liaisons dangereuses,* to punish his heroine for her libertinage, to mark the fulfillment of what he calls her "destiny," the author mutilates Merteuil by causing her to lose one eye to syphilis.[38] The marquise, monstrously disfigured, is delivered over to the visibility of her crime, forced into the outward representation of her debauchery. The text gives voice to the judgment of the entire community by describing her this way, and insisting on the spiteful but just observation: "the disease has turned her inside out, and . . . her soul is now visible on her face."[39] Merteuil's cyclopean gaze, which makes her the focal point of the vigilant social panopticon, should be understood not only in terms of Christian theology but as a figural dislocation of the offending organ: the eye is a displaced pudendum.

Merteuil's punishment is a judgment pronounced upon her body; she is walking evidence of her crime. Nonetheless, her legibility to others remains traumatic by the very monstrosity of the evidence, the excess of her wickedness in the face of representation. In the view of the social body she is literally unrepresentable. At the same time, Madame de Merteuil's fate inaugurates the modern form of punishment. In Michel Foucault's terms, we might say that she begins a new chapter of "political anatomy."[40] While here as earlier the body is the target of punishment, now the profound criminal depths of its interior are also reached. The soul, as the seat of intentions, will, and inclinations, is smitten along with the body.[41] The soul is thus no longer an illusion but rather the realized palimpsest of the body; henceforth it follows "the unbroken nervure of the flesh" before the tribunal of the law.[42] This intellection of the flesh is what condemns the marquise; she falls victim to the conception of fleshly sensuality as a demonism of flesh animated by spirit.

Stephen Frears, adapting Laclos' novel to the screen, and wishing to stress the fin de siècle scenario of the text, had originally intended to put Madame de Merteuil under the blade of the guillotine. In the end, he does not submit his character to such interpretive harm; the beheading of Glenn Close was filmed, but this particular sequence did not make it to the final copy.[43] Instead the director simply dismisses the marquise in a double episode of denarcissization: first she ransacks her boudoir, smashing mirrors, perfume bottles, and ornaments in a metaphorical gesture of self-mutilation, driving home the accusation of her corruption of the body politic; later the marquise unmasks herself in front of her vanity table. Her features are inflated and deformed by the camera. We see that she has fully internalized the community's punitive gaze.

What can we learn from the way in which these three women are condemned? We must imagine a history of the emancipation of women without its inversion in a terrible backlash, without the swarming of all the negative mythologies—a sad expression of pure regression. Indeed, the phallocratic status quo will yield to an intelligent dissolution only when we have found the means of combating base resentment, absurd panic at the new, and above all recourse to the female scapegoat: when we are able to avoid the mythic repetition of a fateful history. The perverse logic of image making that degrades the most courageous female models of liberation can be halted only at this cost, only if we are willing to pay the price in responsibility.

Notes

1. Margaret Carlson, a *Time* magazine reporter, adds "with all the men" (Margaret Carlson, "A Room at the Top," *Time*, 8 February 1993, 31).
2. The incident of the president's so-called Hollywood haircut for $200 by Cristophe provided a perfect occasion for Clinton's detractors to reaffirm his vulnerability to feminine persuasion. Comments were laced with innuendoes concerning the president's masculinity. This was the case on the floor of the House, particularly with Dan Burton (R-Ind.). It was again Hillary Clinton who was to blame for the scandal. The president of the United States was using the First Lady's hair stylist. Beyond the accusations of populism betrayed, there was some sexual anxiety over the haircut. Bill Clinton's "error" was in avoiding the traditional barber, an act tantamount to cross-dressing. William Safire's comments are most symptomatic and telling. He writes that Clinton's "manly informality" had been "blown away by a hair dryer" (William Safire, "Scalpgate's Poetic Justice," *New York Times*, 24 May 1993, A15).
3. This is what Roland Barthes observed apropos of racist attitudes. Compare his *Mythologies* (Paris: Le Seuil, 1957), 67.
4. On the lengthening of Hillary Clinton's name, Lance Morrow writes in *Time* magazine: "The history of 'Hillary Rodham Clinton' goes back in time, like a novel." Morrow studies the name changes as a "poignant" symptom of the way

in which power, feminism, and politics can dangerously disrupt the "customs of naming." The conservative journalist sums up the career of the First Lady as follows: "So during her demure, cookie-baker phase, she was emphatically 'Hillary Clinton,' mute, nodding adorer and helpmate of Bill. She half-concealed herself in 'Hillary Clinton' until the coast was clear. With the Inauguration, the formal, formidable triple name has lumbered into place like a convoy of armored cars" (Lance Morrow, "Essay: The Strange Burden of a Name," *Time,* 8 March 1993, 76).

5. Anne-Marie Schiro, "A Blue Hat Has Critics Wondering," *New York Times,* 22 January 1993, A15. Right-wing commentators have been quick to talk about Hillary Clinton's closet. Once again Rush Limbaugh provides an example. On his program aired 16 February 1993, Limbaugh commented that President Clinton must have gotten his ideas on how to fix the deficit from Hillary's shopping sprees. What looms behind Limbaugh's accusations is the stereotyping of the female as voracious spender, conspicuous consumer, bulimic buyer. Marie-Antoinette herself was labeled Madame Déficit—this was one of the countless names applied to her at the dawn of the Revolution, ascribing to her the blame for the nation's bankruptcy. We should not have to wait long before Mrs. Clinton will be similarly dubbed, especially if her health plan proposal calls for additional taxes or gives the impression of being costly.

6. Reviewing her performance after one hundred days in the White House, *People* magazine also seems reassured by the balancing act of the busy First Lady: "Hillary doesn't skip the occasional indulgence. Maria Colda, a facialist at Georgette Klinger's Manhattan salon, has flown to Washington to deep-clean the First Lady's pores, and stylist Gabriel DeBakey does her hair for gala parties" (Michelle Green, Nina Burleigh, and Jane Sugden, "Her Own Woman," *People,* 10 May 1993, 86).

7. Susan Faludi, "The Power Laugh," *New York Times,* 20 December 1992, E13. I thank Roddey Reid for pointing out this article to me.

8. In this connection, one of the most symptomatic texts is Rousseau's *Lettre à M. d'Alembert sur les spectacles* (1758), translated as *Politics and the Arts: Letter to M. d'Alembert on the Theatre,* trans. Allan Bloom (Ithaca: Cornell University Press, 1968). On the impact of this question upon the Revolution, see Sarah Maza, "L'Image de la souveraine: Fémininité et politique dans les pamphlets de l'affaire du Collier," in Harvey Chisick, Ilana Zinguer, and Ouzi Elyada, eds., *The Press in the French Revolution, Studies on Voltaire and the Eighteenth Century* 287 (Oxford: Voltaire Foundation, 1991), 367–68, and Leah Price, "Vies Privées et Scandaleuses: Marie Antoinette and the Public Eye," *The Eighteenth Century* 33 (summer 1992): 176–89.

9. Jules Michelet, *Historical View of the French Revolution from Its Earliest Indications to the Flight of the King in 1791,* trans. Charles Cocks (London: H. G. Bohn, 1864), 591.

10. See Myriam Revault d'Allonnes, *D'une mort à l'autre: précipices de la Révolution* (Paris: Le Seuil 1989); and Joan B. Landes, *Women and the Public Sphere in the Age of the French Revolution* (Ithaca: Cornell University Press, 1988).

11. See Lynn Hunt, "The Many Bodies of Marie-Antoinette: Political Pornography and the Problem of the Feminine in the French Revolution," in this volume;

and Chantal Thomas, *The Wicked Queen: The Origins of the Myth of Marie Antoinette,* trans. Julie Rose (New York: Zone Books, 1999). The bicentennial of the Terror seems to have repaired the situation of the ill-fated queen. Without judging their ideological profile, I will mention two publications: André Castelot, *Le Procès de Marie Antoinette* (Paris: Perrin, 1993), and Pierre Sipriot, *Les Soixante derniers jours de Marie-Antoinette* (Paris: Plon, 1993). Consider also the gala spectacle by Robert Hossein, *Je m'appelais Marie-Antoinette,* which is drawing crowds in Paris.

12. Roger Caillois, "The Sociology of the Executioner," in Denis Hollier, ed., *The College of Sociology (1937–39),* trans. Betsy Wing (Minneapolis: University of Minnesota Press, 1988), 246–47.

13. Quoted by Daniel Arasse, *La Guillotine et l'imaginaire de la Terreur* (Paris: Flammarion, 1987), 129.

14. Hunt, "Many Bodies," 119, 120–21, 119.

15. Louis Marin, *Portrait of the King,* trans. Martha M. Houle (Minneapolis: University of Minnesota Press, 1988), 14.

16. Quoted in Jean Chalon, *Chère Marie-Antoinette* (Paris: n.p., Perrin, 1988), 21.

17. Jules Barbey d'Aurevilly, *Les Historiens politiques et littéraires* (Paris: n.p., 1861), 290.

18. On the construction of gender as "style" or performance, see Judith Butler, *Gender Trouble: Feminism and the Subversion of Identity* (New York: Routledge, 1990), 138–41.

19. Carolly Erickson, *To the Scaffold: The Life of Marie Antoinette* (New York: W. Morrow, 1991), 38, 45.

20. On the way in which the story of Marie-Antoinette can be read as a series of costumed events, see Pierre Saint-Amand, "Adorning Marie Antoinette," trans. Zakiya Hanafi, *Eighteenth-Century Life* 15 (November 1991): 19–34.

21. D'Aurevilly, *Les Historiens politiques et littéraires,* 290.

22. Stefan Zweig, *Marie Antoinette: The Portrait of an Average Woman,* trans. Eden and Cedar Paul (Garden City, N.Y.: Garden City Publishing, 1933), 106.

23. The Varennes episode could also be analyzed in terms of this aesthetic economy. The carriage commanded by Marie-Antoinette for the famous getaway is a flash of elegance: "The bodywork of the carriage was painted in deep green, decorated with black molding. The axle and wheels were lemon yellow, the springs and the ornamental hinges were painted in glossy steel shades," and the inside of the vehicle was trimmed with damask. (Rachel Laurent, "Marie-Antoinette: Le Caprice et le style," *Art Press* [1988]: 116). The carriage is a mobile miniature version of the Trianon, a portable chateau: "She ordered a berlin of exceptional size, practically 'a small traveling house,' according to a contemporary. It was ingeniously fitted out with a sort of larder, . . . a cooking stove . . . even a dining table that could be raised up out of the floor. The seat cushions were removable; underneath were commodes" (Erickson, *To the Scaffold,* 274).

24. Marin, *Portrait of the King,* 193.

25. Mitchell Greenberg, *Subjectivity and Subjugation in Seventeenth-Century Drama and Prose* (Cambridge: Cambridge University Press, 1992), 179.

26. Compare Jacques Lacan, *The Four Fundamental Concepts of Psycho-Analysis,* ed. Jacques-Alain Miller, trans. Alan Sheridan (New York: W. W. Norton, 1978), 193.

27. Zweig, *Marie Antoinette*, 98.

28. Quoted in Claude Reichler, *L'Age libertin* (Paris: Minuit, 1987), 134.

29. Revault d'Allonnes, *D'une mort à l'autre*, 39, 44.

30. Maza, "The Diamond Necklace Affair Revisited (1785–1786): The Case of the Missing Queen," in this volume, 87–88.

31. Ibid., 90.

32. See Dorinda Outram, *The Body and the French Revolution: Sex, Class, and Political Culture* (New Haven: Yale University Press, 1989), 157; and Linda Orr, "The Romantic Historiography of the Revolution and French Society," in *Consortium on Revolutionary Europe 1750–1850: Proceedings* (1984): 242–47.

33. *Encyclopédie, ou dictionnaire raisonné des sciences, des arts, et des métiers*, ed. Denis Diderot and Jean le Rond d'Alembert, 18 vols. (1751–72; Lausanne, 1779), s.v. "Caricature."

34. Barbara Maria Stafford, *Body Criticism: Imaging the Unseen in Enlightenment Art and Medicine* (Cambridge, Mass.: MIT Press, 1991), 274.

35. Thomas, *Wicked Queen*, 72.

36. Quoted in André Castelot, *Marie-Antoinette* (Paris: Hachette, 1967), 114.

37. Quoted in Simon Schama, *Citizens: A Chronicle of the French Revolution* (New York: Knopf, 1989), 904.

38. Choderlos de Laclos, *Les Liaisons dangereuses*, trans. P. W. K. Stone (Harmondsworth: Penguin, 1961), 391. A dramatic echo to Merteuil's original and determined project of libertinage: "Conquest is our destiny" (28).

39. Ibid., 392.

40. Michael Foucault, *Discipline and Punish: The Birth of the Prison*, trans. Alan Sheridan (New York: Pantheon Books, 1977), 30.

41. Foucault quotes from Gabriel Bonnot de Mably's *De la législation* (1789): "Punishment, if I may so put it, should strike the soul rather than the body" (ibid., 16).

42. Foucault, *The History of Sexuality: An Introduction*, trans. Robert Hurley (New York: Vintage Books, 1980), 20.

43. See "Glenn Close Interviewed by Robert Maccubbin," *Eighteenth-Century Life* 14 (May 1990): 70.

Eating Cake: The (Ab)uses of Marie-Antoinette

Susan S. Lanser

On 18 April 2001, Harvard University students took over a campus building to protest the failure of the world's richest university to provide its service workers a living wage.[1] What escalated into a widely supported protest occurred barely a month after the appointment of Lawrence Summers as Harvard's twenty-seventh president. Cartoon drawings sprang up in Harvard Yard that portrayed Summers as Marie-Antoinette, mouthing the infamous and misattributed "Let them eat cake." As an emblem of conspicuous consumption and crass insouciance, the queen had crossed the gender line. Figured in her lifetime as a usurper *of* male prerogative, Marie-Antoinette figured here *as* male prerogative.

This surface shift in the queen's—or the president's—gender sits atop deeper parallels not only between Lawrence Summers and Marie-Antoinette but between Harvard and Versailles, two excessively wealthy, landed, class-stratified, standard-setting, male-run institutions inaugurated in the same decade, bastions of ancien régime power nonetheless physically accessible to the public, modestly open to the upwardly mobile, and arguably enabling the very critique of themselves to which Versailles once seemed, and Harvard may still seem, impervious. That it was Lawrence Summers and not outgoing president Neil Rudenstine who got figured as Marie-Antoinette is also apt, for as an appointee not yet in office Summers manifestly did not create and could not yet have altered the unjust wage system that preceded him. The displacement of collective wrath onto Summers by way of Marie-Antoinette thus unwittingly recognized the structural impotence of both. On the other hand, Summers would soon succeed to power, replacing Rudenstine as Marie-Antoinette was alleged to have displaced Louis XVI. In this sense, Marie-Antoinette crossed the gender line in her own life, standing in for the king, for the monarchy, and for France as Summers was standing in that April for Rudenstine, for Harvard and, as former secretary of the Treasury, arguably for the United States.

Through their use of Marie-Antoinette to abuse Lawrence Summers, then, the caricatures in Harvard Yard attacked, as the signifier of a class system, a signified whose power then lay only at the system's edge. This gesture points to the dislocated but pervasive place of Marie-Antoinette in the symbolic order not only of Revolutionary France but of modern America. Indeed, the on-line *Harvard College Handbook for Parents* also offers up Marie-Antoinette and her notorious cake: in a section titled "Some Important Differences from High School," the *Handbook* announces that Harvard examinations are not about "regurgitating memorized facts" but about "relating facts to ideas":

> [S]tudents must think for themselves and express their thoughts clearly. It is all very well to know that Marie-Antoinette lived between 1755 and 1793 and was generous with cake. Although interesting in themselves, these *facts* will not be of much help in responding critically to the exam question, "The French Revolution took its ideas and its form from the political thought of Thomas Jefferson—discuss."[2]

One might wonder why, of all possible historical data, the baseless "fact" of the cake stands in for Fact itself, even as one regrets the missed opportunity to identify the cake eating as cross-cultural folklore attached to French royalty well before Marie-Antoinette's time.[3] The *Handbook* misses another opportunity when it implies that the woman Marie-Antoinette is irrelevant both to the Revolution and to "the political thought" of the presumably more important man Thomas Jefferson. For Jefferson writes his own history of the Revolution upon the body of the queen, charging her with an "absolute ascendancy" over the king's "weak mind" that quashed his enlightened leadership:

> Her inordinate gambling and dissipations, with those of the Count d'Artois and others of her clique, had been a sensible item in the exhaustion of the treasury, which called into action the reforming hand of the na-

tion; and her opposition to it[,] her inflexible perverseness, and daunt-less spirit, led herself to the Guillotine, & drew the king on with her, and plunged the world into crimes and calamities which will forever stain the pages of modern history. *I have ever believed that had there been no queen, there would have been no revolution. No force would have been provoked nor exercised.* The king would have gone hand in hand with the wisdom of his sounder counsellors, who, guided by the increased lights of the age, wished only, with the same pace, to advance the principles of their social institution.

Writing against the backdrop of the Napoleonic Wars, Jefferson goes on to envision his own nostalgic scenario of rational reform that depends critically on the queen's eviction:

> I should have shut up the Queen in a Convent, putting harm out of her power, and placed the king in his station, investing him with limited powers, which I verily believe he would have honestly exercised, according to the measure of his understanding. In this way no void would have been created, courting the usurpation of a military adventurer, nor occasion given for those enormities which demoralized the nations of the world, and destroyed, and is yet to destroy millions and millions of its inhabitants.[4]

Jefferson's verbal excesses against a queen whom he figures *as* excess, like the deployment of Marie-Antoinette to signal Harvard's failings of wage and successes of education, begin to delineate the (ab)uses of the queen both in her day and in our own: in charting the queen's abuses, Marie-Antoinette's critics have also clearly used her for multifarious purposes. This usage joins the eighteenth-century representations to their modern aftermath, suggesting the complicated—at once marginal and central—place of Marie-Antoinette both in the history of the French Revolution and in the popular imaginary that it has spawned.

In this sense it is not so surprising that, of all possible historical factoids, it is Marie-Antoinette's cake eating that the writer of the *Harvard College Handbook* settled on, and after a fashion that renders the queen significant only in her insignificance. For the "Marie-Antoinette obsession" that Terry Castle so perceptively identifies as a sapphic phenomenon forms part of a much larger cultural configuration that is possibly most pervasive in the English-speaking West. Insofar as Internet search engines can chart obsessions, Marie-Antoinette, with "hits" ranging from 24,181 on the Francophone Voilà to 180,000 on (U.S.) Google and 266,932 on (British) Lycos, Marie-Antoinette trebles the numbers for Robespierre and Danton.

Whole Web sites are devoted to reclaiming or promoting her. People who know almost nothing about the French Revolution are familiar with the queen, especially in association with the cake she did not ask anyone to eat.

The Internet is only the latest locus of Marie-Antoinette's incarnation in an extensive range and volume of texts and artifacts. Children can play with Marie-Antoinette paper dolls or read Kathryn Lasky's "diary" of the "Princess of Versailles." Aficionados can delve into novels as old as Alexandre Dumas *père*'s *Le Collier de la reine* [*The Queen's Necklace*] (1849); as odd as Nat Wilder's 1910 *A Royal Tragedy: When Kings and Savages Ruled*; as new as Alan Jolis' *Love and Terror* (1998). Film buffs can view not only the 1938 Norma Shearer/MGM extravaganza of which Laura Mason writes here but a 1995 Arts & Entertainment documentary biography and the recent *Affair of the Necklace,* retelling that fateful story from Jeanne de La Motte's point of view. We can glean historical information from two centuries of biography spanned by the memoirs of Marie-Antoinette's own lady-in-waiting Jeanne Louise Henriette Campan (1822) and the lavishly illustrated 2001 *Marie-Antoinette: The Journey* by the renowned historian of British royalty Antonia Fraser. The wealthiest fans can purchase at record-breaking prices objects once owned by the queen: a console table that went for $2.97 million in 1988, a jewel casket on a tulipwood stand auctioned for $4.93 million in 1991.[5] As Alan Kurzweil puts it, like Marilyn Monroe, Marie-Antoinette has "managed to stimulate staggering displays of scholarship, passion, and oddball devotion. She is by now a cult object, and her cult, like so many, comes complete with shrines and fakes, private altars, con men, collectors, and contradiction."[6]

And yet Marie-Antoinette's place in contemporary histories of the French Revolution is as limited as her popular presence is ubiquitous. With the exception perhaps of Simon Schama's popular and controversial *Citizens: A Chronicle of the French Revolution* (1989), the queen hardly appears in the myriad scholarly histories of the Revolution published during the last half century, not even in the superb CD-accompanied *Liberty, Equality, Fraternity: Exploring the French Revolution,* coauthored by Lynn Hunt, in whose *Family Romance of the French Revolution* the queen figures centrally. I know of no modern historian who would concur with Thomas Jefferson's claim that "had there been no queen, there would have been no revolution"; modern historians indeed have striven to uncover the

complicated knot of factors that engendered the Revolution, propelled its terrors and triumphs, shaped its failures and fantasies. But
the scholarly testimony of the essays here gathered suggests that in
this process of accounting for the Revolution from multiple vantage
points, Marie-Antoinette may now be as overlooked as she was once
over-emphasized.

This volume, however, signals a crucial difference between past
and possible placements of the queen in Revolutionary history.
While accounts such as Jefferson's focused on the queen's own alleged abuses, these essays show us that what also needs to be confronted are others' uses of the queen. What may figure most importantly for a deeper understanding of the Revolution is not so much
Marie-Antoinette the historical figure as Marie-Antoinette the symbolic site: the Marie-Antoinette who was renamed as *l'Autrichienne,*
as Madame Déficit, as Messalina, as Toinette, as Hébert's "excrescence
on the nation's body." In short, historians of the Revolution have yet
to build upon the important scholarship so well represented in this
volume in a way that rethinks the place of the queen in French Revolutionary historiography *tout court.* The most valuable afterword to
this volume, indeed, would be this kind of integrative history.

Marie-Antoinette: Writings on the Body of a Queen lays the
groundwork for such a project by exploring and explaining the
manifestations of the queen during her lifetime and beyond. In this
afterword I want to build upon these gathered essays to ask what the
past and present investments in Marie-Antoinette might be reveal-
ing and what they might be covering up. I will wonder too whether
there is a particularly Anglophone obsession with the queen that,
perhaps following from the marked contrast between Burkean hagiography and Jeffersonian demonization, takes somewhat diver-
gent British and U.S. forms. In considering what kinds of conflicts
have been and continue to be written on Marie-Antoinette's body, I
am especially interested in U.S. responses that enable Lawrence
Summers shallowly to represent the queen as hard-hearted and
Hillary Clinton deeply to refigure her as perverse female influence.
As astute historical inquiries and contemporary engagements with a
historical legacy, the readings gathered here open such questions in
ways that parsing the volume's title may fruitfully illuminate.

If *Marie-Antoinette: Writings on the Body of a Queen* is obviously
about Marie-Antoinette, it is less obviously but more centrally about

her *representation*—that is, about Marie-Antoinette's displacement
into text. As they strive to discover the historical personage buried in
representation these essays also make clear how little we can know of
that "real" person and how complex and polarized a field of inquiry
each reinscription of the queen's story confronts. The fourteen-
year-old archduchess was already being fashioned for political purposes even before she crossed the literal and symbolic waters of the
Rhine "packaged as a doll, carefully prepared for the enjoyment of
the French court," to quote Pierre Saint-Amand. Even in her lifetime, the volume of discourse about her far exceeded the "authentic"
material in her own voice and hand or the observations of reliable
and relatively disinterested witnesses.

Indeed, the young dauphine was from the beginning a literal
personification of interest. Charged with representing Austria's interests in France, Marie-Antoinette quickly became an overloaded
"site of contestation" (to evoke a key phrase of Dena Goodman's introduction). Any two or three complications of her situation would
arguably have sufficed to place the young queen in internal conflict
or external jeopardy. If she had been only Austrian, her position
would have been precarious enough, without her being also the
daughter of the most powerful woman in Western Europe sent to do
her mother's work. If the interests of the House of Lorraine, so well
documented here by Thomas Kaiser, had not been placed upon her
by blood and politics, and if Lorraine did not already prefigure her
own suspect position, the young archduchess might not have occasioned controversy almost as soon as she reached France. If she had
not become queen of the only country with a form of Salic Law,
which bluntly reduced her to a maker of sons such that, in Mary
Sheriff's words, "power passed through the queen's body, but was
not part of her"; if Louis XVI had had mistresses, as did his predecessors, so that the queen was not the solitary site of "pernicious" female influence; if the misbehaviors of previous French kings had
not already compromised the monarchy in the nation's eyes; if Louis
XVI had been able much earlier to consummate his marriage, satisfy
his wife, and sire offspring; if the king had not been indecisive and
the queen not forceful, frivolous, or bold; if there had not been rival
factions within the court; if Marie-Antoinette had been the first or
second and not the eighth surviving daughter of the empress and
thus better educated to assume a royal role; if she had been older,
wiser, or even more docile in ways that might have mitigated her

foreign profile; if she had not tried to be a private subject but had realized that, to quote Sheriff, "a queen could not do as she pleased"; if she had not created a separate female household surrounded with "untamed" English gardens at the Trianon; indeed, if she had not lived at the threshold of modernity in a way that, as several of the contributors to this volume argue, drew upon her the period's conflicts, confusions, and anxieties about women in general: if all of these "if onlys" had not conspired to overdetermine both Marie-Antoinette's personal fate and the fate of her representation, then there might not have arisen so quickly and firmly what Jacques Revel calls "a dark legend about Marie Antoinette which would follow her for the rest of her life."[7]

Built upon a few facts and many, more and less plausible fictions, this legend, says Revel, "created a paper queen" that "gradually replaced the 'real' queen."[8] Thus the queen *became* her representations, and it is in this light that we can best account for the otherwise astonishing fact that she is so well known for words she almost surely never said and deeds she almost surely never did: the dismissive "Qu'ils mangent de la brioche," the diamond necklace she never acquired in a plot for which she was blamed although she was its victim, the sexual-political orgies of every sort, the charge of incest with and by her son. Since what she is believed to have done is that of which she is most probably innocent, discovering what Marie-Antoinette actually did do may well elude inquiry; no one yet, for example, has been able to establish whether she had a consummated relationship with Axel Fersen, whom she doubtless loved. The skewed record renders suspect any iteration of the queen's true history, and it is thus fitting that the present volume declines to "tell her life story" or even to "make sense" of it (Goodman).

If the historical record remains elusive, much clearer are the mechanisms by which representation overtook and overwrote Marie-Antoinette in her own lifetime. Figured as the queen of excess through an excess of representation, Marie-Antoinette is also the figure of excessively partisan renderings, whether as the tragic victim of individualist romance or as the monstrous villain of populist history. In the absence of significant new evidence about the "real" Marie-Antoinette, devotees and critics alike have continued to rewrite her story, struggling not simply for greater accuracy but for the promotion of a point of view. Thus, as Jacques Revel reminds us, the question Germaine de Staël raised in her 1793 *Reflections on the Queen's Trial* is posed again and again: "Was she good? Was she wicked?" and in this way "the queen's case is endlessly reargued."[9] The repeated inquest took on formal incarnation during the 1989 bicentennial, when a dramatic enactment of Marie-Antoinette's biography was staged in Paris and at each performance "every member of the audience was asked to vote on her fate via remote-control switches, and every night they voted overwhelmingly for her acquittal and for the condemnation of her accusers."[10] Such representations keep the queen, as it were, alive—almost literally so for the Association Unité Capétienne, dedicated to preserving France's royal heritage, which uses Jean Chalon's biography *Chère Marie-Antoinette* to declare that "the heart of the 'Autrichienne' has not stopped beating. Assassinated on October 16, 1793, on the eve of her thirty-eighth birthday, Marie-Antoinette is still among us, embodying victims past, present, and future. She is the exemplary victim of slander. And one must be on the victim's side."[11]

Because Marie-Antoinette is a charged site for replaying not only her own life but the significance of the Revolution—"Was it good? Was it evil?"—writings about the queen are also charged. In a particularly vivid illustration of history as intertextuality, every writing about Marie-Antoinette enters a partisan field crowded with fact and fancy and must make its place alongside representations of the queen that it implicitly finds incorrect or inadequate. In this sense, every new writing on Marie-Antoinette is an afterword. Such a layering of representation, already gargantuan in her lifetime, sits in ironic contrast to the republican value on transparency that Lynn Hunt recalls: figuring Marie-Antoinette as a site of lies and secrets rather than of the open heart, the Revolution drowns the queen in further fictions. Many modern representations continue more or less overtly to take sides: the Web site of Leah Marie Brown, for example, rejects "heinous" portraits of the queen (as "selfish, greedy, frivolous, and ignorant," guilty of "lesbianism, treason, incest, and adultery") by rendering Marie-Antoinette a kind of *Good Housekeeping* paragon: "in reality . . . a generous friend, loyal wife, and caring mother . . . stylish, fun-loving, emotional, brave, and considerate."[12]

In sharp contrast to such apologies, the essays in this collection are notable for seeing the queen and her (ab)uses from many sides. Goodman's title brilliantly recognizes that this voluminous body of writing on Marie-Antoinette writes *on* her in a very real sense: that

the queen's body is the site upon which the volume of representation rests, and that in writing *on* her body, history has also written
over it just as Revolutionary pamphlets erased her proper name.
From the start, as several essays here remind us, Marie-Antoinette
had been fashioned literally and figuratively for presentation at
court and re-presentation in portraiture. As queen, she was also read
for "signs of interior intentions and motives" (Hunt), scrutinized to
see whether her soul, like that of Laclos' Merteuil, might at last be
"visible on her face" (Saint-Amand). Not only novels and pornogra-
phies but biographies too have appropriated her voice, put saving or
damning words into her mouth, declared what she felt and thought
or might have said. Hidden within each of these moments is a double temporality and often a double geography: just as each letter exchanged between Marie-Antoinette and Maria Teresa "joins two
points in time," as Larry Wolff tells us, so too each writing about the
queen unites her time and place to the time and place of reinscription in ways that do not always acknowledge, and may even attempt
to obliterate, this duality.

It is thus an important strength of this volume that it confronts
representations of the queen both in her own time and place and af-
terwards, showing conjunctions and disjunctions between the two.
In this process, the essays help us understand why it was specifically
the queen's *body*, and not simply the idea of the queen, on which so
much representation was inscribed. Chantal Thomas reminds us
that "traditionally, the queen's body belongs to the public": it was
stripped naked and re-dressed when she made the symbolic journey
across the Rhine from Austria to France; its most private organs
were exposed to strangers in the uncontrollable vulnerability of
childbirth. Thus Marie-Antoinette the *site* was also always Marie-
Antoinette the *sight,* an object of court surveillance and public gaze.
Her own mother warned her that "all eyes will be fixed on you" in
what Larry Wolff refers to as a "sort of inverted Panopticon." Yet as
Mary Sheriff's comparison between portraits of kings and queens
makes evident, Marie-Antoinette is also a site that cannot *be* represented; no portrait can render her at once a person and a king's wife.
It is thus arguably the queen's own resistance to public ownership
that fostered the re-presentation of her body as monstrous and
pornographic at a time when, as Thomas notes, "aristocrat" and
"libertine" were synonymous and equally insulting terms. If the Trianon sequestered her, the pamphlets intervened by exposing her in

printed images that configured her sexuality as political crime. This public appropriation, as Lynn Hunt shows, was most egregious on the occasion of the trial, when accusations against the now deposed and widowed queen reached a nadir in both substance (the charge of incest on a child's suborned evidence) and rhetoric (Hébert's desire to grind up the queen's body for the people's *pâté*) that makes vivid the ways in which, to paraphrase Barbara Babcock in another context, the woman who is now socially marginal can still be so symbolically powerful.[13]

The Revolution also writes on the queen's body because it is in her sex—in both senses of the word—that Marie-Antoinette signifies. On this question the present volume is particularly illuminating and richly informative. Sarah Maza suggests that the harsh treatment of Marie-Antoinette is part of a "reaction against the presence of women in the public sphere," in a project tied to the emergence of "contractual theories of government." The Diamond Necklace Affair is then understood as "the last political drama of female sexuality under the Old Regime, a prelude to, and harbinger of, the fall of public woman." Elizabeth Colwill notes that "in the Revolutionary pamphlets, the nymphomaniacal queen appears both frighteningly feminine and threateningly virile," and that this contradictory representation marks a historical moment characterized by "competing models of sexual difference." One form of this tension, as Colwill shows and as I have written elsewhere, is that charges of tribadism become a political weapon, a flash point for anxieties about upper-class women and politics.[14] A similar set of contradictions surrounds Marie-Antoinette's portraits: the queen could be painted (even with her mother's approval) *en amazone* that is, *en homme*—while the public was outraged by portraits such as Vigée-Lebrun's *en chemise* that created the queen most vividly *en femme*. Serving, as Sheriff notes, primarily as property designed to produce an heir to a throne she cannot inherit; caught, as Woolf shows us, in the agendas of Austria and France; positioned, as Lynn Hunt writes, "on the cusp between public and private," Marie-Antoinette "was emblematic of the much larger problem of the relations between women and the public sphere in the eighteenth-century."

Jacques Revel has argued that it is not simply the queen but "the female sex" that is the target of attacks against her, "in an age that burned incense to mothers but did not always know what to make of citoyennes."[15] In such a climate, a queen epitomizes the tensions be-

tween patriarchy and democracy that no eighteenth-century government was willing to confront, let alone to resolve. Even the sexual
politics of Jean-Jacques Rousseau, so influential in France during
the queen's lifetime, place a woman such as Marie-Antoinette in a
delicate position, for Rousseau cedes to woman a role of influence
on man. Louise de Keralio's application to Marie-Antoinette of the
adage that "when the woman becomes queen, she changes her sex"
must propel an image different from the "sex change" of a regnant
monarch such as Elizabeth I or the empress of Austria. For if the
queen *consort* changes sex, then she displaces and, as it were, becomes the king. This is precisely the shift that the French feared—once
again, a shift overdetermined (in their minds) by Marie-Antoinette's
Austrianness, her mother's rulership, and her purported wilfulness vis-
à-vis Louis' perceived "feminine" weaknesses. It is thus not in a vacuum
of sexual politics that the counterrevolutionary Edmund Burke, who
had no use for women in the public sphere except as objects of
chivalry, reinvents the queen as an angel hovering "just above the hori-
zon, decorating and cheering the elevated sphere she just began to
move in,—glittering like the morning-star, full of life, and splendor,
and joy."[16] Such rhapsody recuperates the queen's ascendancy by raising her into irrelevance as a kind of heavenly ornament.

Several scholars have noted the close timing of the queen's execution with the closing of the Revolutionary republican women's
clubs in reaffirmation of what Hunt describes as a brotherly "family
romance." They see the murder of the queen as evidence that the
Revolution needed a female scapegoat who would embody the excesses at once of women and of royalty. Saint-Amand proposes that
the representations of the queen as sexual transgressor helped to
clean up the revolutionary body politic: "The Republic of Virtue," he
argues, "was born of the queen's sexual crimes." At the bottom of
these sexual crimes is simply the crime of sex itself—of being a
woman, of being too much woman, of being insufficiently woman,
all of which sometimes amounts to the same thing.

Saint-Amand's and Laura Mason's respective explorations of
women in the twentieth-century United States suggest that "political
conceptions of women are still subject to the same fears and anxieties"
in "the very same language" that beset the queen (Saint-Amand).
Saint-Amand gives the name "Marie-Antoinette syndrome" to this
"fear of women in power" that dogged Hillary Clinton, and he dis-
tinguishes its three attributes as "(1) the demonization and cloning

of the woman's influence; (2) the accessibility of the woman's genitalia as the organ of influence, and (3) a seizing of the woman's body
as a way of sexual appropriation." It is worth asking whether Marie-
Antoinette's shadow might even be causing some of the anxiety
surrounding powerful wives of modern leaders or, conversely,
whether this anxiety reinforces the continued vilification of Marie-
Antoinette. Given the date of MGM's turning Norma Shearer into a
queen whose value as queen depended on her being a good wife and
mother who "would have remained happily in the shadows where
she belonged" had she " found fulfillment in a patriarchal marriage,"
it is tempting to wonder whether the film might be speaking to
Eleanor Roosevelt in particular as well as to American women in
general.

   Marie-Antoinette's positioning through transgressions of gender
has also generated gender identifications that have made unusual
bedfellows of supporters, whether among British women elegizing
the resanctified queen at the time of her trial, among lesbians reclaiming the queen as a stylish figure of same-sex passion in the
nineteenth and early twentieth centuries, or in the new attention to
the queen in feminist scholarship. I want to suggest, however, that
Marie-Antoinette also represents a feminist dilemma that may help
to account for both the fascination and the care that characterize
most current scholarship about the queen. For if, as Goodman
writes, the queen is a "set of sites of contestation," *which* contesta-
tions get put into play may depend on which categories we wish to
deploy, and the queen's double position as female body and body of
the counterrevolution may render her among feminists a figure at
once to reclaim and to reject. Only the most essentializing gender
politics can overlook the queen's collusion with the absolutist agendas
of her rank; only the most ungendered class politics can ignore her
differential treatment on the basis of her sex. It is this doubleness
that leads Terry Castle to ask whether "the lesbian rehabilitation of
Marie-Antoinette" is "an apolitical, aestheticized, even reactionary
subcultural phenomenon." She notes that "since the turn of the century, the queen's numerous acolytes have shown little interest in her
actual political beliefs (except, embarrassingly, to defend them) or
her scabrous role in some of the events leading up to the French
Revolution. Of the feckless, manipulative, often ruthless figure who
comes across in more objective histories, those who romanticize her

love of women have had virtually nothing to say." The Web site for "Cosmetically Correct: THE group for Boston-area Gay and Bi Femmes" bears out Castle's fears. Positioning itself against the lesbian-feminist left, the site proclaims Marie-Antoinette "a self-styled politically incorrect girl watcher who would NEVER be caught dead sporting a pair of ugly brown sandals and a knapsack! When not looking over her shoulder for the ghastly spectre of the guillotine or being fitted for a new ball gown, Marie can be found doing her part to alleviate the suffering of stray cats, leading the crusade against Grapes-of-Wrath chic, or perusing the latest issue of 'Vogue' to see how Ms. Hutton is aging."[17]

Especially in the face of this kind of anachronistic and facile appropriation, it is worth interrogating the reasons for the unabated inscription, both popular and scholarly, upon the body of this queen. Doubtless the politicized nature of Marie-Antoinette discourse generates its own perpetuity, as interpretation begets counterinterpretation in the intensely partisan world of French Revolutionary inquiry. Doubtless too, the relative vacuum that is Marie-Antoinette "herself" stimulates a longing to know that exceeds possibility, stirring endless desire to discover the key, the secret, the "real" that is no longer, if it ever was, available. And doubtless the Marie-Antoinette obsession is part and parcel of the European and Euroamerican preoccupation with royalty in general—and preferably royalty in the form of (feminine) glamour rather than (masculine) power.

In the light of this collective fancy, the attraction of Marie-Antoinette may have something to do with her exceptional position as a fallen queen torn from the world's most magnificent palace and stripped not only of every trapping of her office but of office itself. It is worth speculating that in the British imagination this story would easily take on elegiac or tragic form, not only because there is already a long tradition of British writings deeply sympathetic to the queen, but because of the troubled position of British royalty today: when Antonia Fraser ends her preface to *Marie-Antoinette: The Journey* with "Vive la Reine!" one is tempted to wonder whether a living, British queen is also being cheered. It is worth speculating that in the United States, on the other hand, the story of a queen brought down by "the people" would have a different and more triumphant resonance, allowing the simultaneous enactment of Europhilic fascination with and populist repudiation of royalty. As an especially glamorous queen whose very glamour was an affront to the people, Marie-Antoinette is ideally suited at once to foster romantic longings for aristocracy and to dispense with them.

Such a reenactment suggests a deeper kind of repetition—indeed, a repetition compulsion—beneath Marie-Antoinette's weighty presence in the popular imagination in the United States and England, possibly even more than in France. Chantal Thomas argues that "at bottom, Marie-Antoinette created unanimity": that the monstrous queen figured in the repetitive scheme of the pamphlets constituted a rallying point around which diverse factions could unite. Shlomith Rimmon-Kenan comments that repetition "may lead to a working through, a resolving and overcoming" but it may, conversely, also "imprison and lock the narrative," and that either way, "narrating somebody else's story is hence always also narrating one's own."[18] Rimmon-Kenan's formulation is useful for distinguishing between productive and static repetitions of the queen. Deep explorations of Marie-Antoinette and her representations, like those that appear in this collection, allow us to understand and address both the queen's (ab)uses and the displacements of monstrosity onto other powerful women, as Pierre Saint-Amand does in linking the queen with the First Lady, as Laura Mason does when she exposes the Depression-era fears of women's independence, as Lynn Hunt does when she reveals "the unselfconscious presumptions of the revolutionary political imagination" to be at base masculinist and misogynist. Each essay in this volume indeed halts repetition by opening a new question or by writing an old question in a new way.

On the other hand, the more superficial uses of the queen and the more obsessive investments of her aficionados risk imprisoning and shutting down our understanding of Marie-Antoinette's life both in flesh and in discourse. When the not-yet-inaugurated Lawrence Summers stands in for the excesses of Harvard by way of Marie-Antoinette, blame does not simply fall on the "wrong" individual; what is also "wrong" is the individualizing itself. I mean that the displacement into the personal that is effected by publicly invading the privacy of persons who are connected to, but not quite agents of, the state doubly removes us not only from the critique of those actually in power but, even farther, from the critique of the state and the structures that underwrite it. The woman thus both distracts us from and becomes the displaced site of accountability for the problems she cannot solve. If the original goal of displacement onto the queen might have been to save the monarch, such a displacement also saves the (man-made and man-run) state, just as the displacement onto Hillary may have saved Bill Clinton and at a certain point the presidency itself, while also derailing the Clinton administration's most radical political goals.

It is this kind of imprisoning repetition, I suggest, that resides in the insistent association of Marie-Antoinette with the apocryphal cake. If, as I have suggested, the Marie-Antoinette of British fancy is the angelic, tragically beheaded Burkean queen, arguably a displacement for Britain's own complicated royal history, then the Marie-Antoinette of U.S. popular imagination is, in the end, the trivialized and degraded queen of cake who points to, and then keeps us from interrogating, the class system covered over by the ideology of a classless meritocracy. Such a diminution is featured in this SkyTel display on an ad for a Motorola pager:

> MARIE ANTOINETTE—
> PEASANTS ARE RESTLESS.
> DO NOT MENTION "CAKE."
> TRUST ME.

Below the display, the text informs us that "missing a message can make anyone want to revolt."[19] It is tempting to retort that it is because we miss the message of revolution that we continue instead to evoke the eating of cake in late-capitalist advertisements. It is also fitting, and possibly related to the use of the cake-eating image in Harvard Yard, that the motto of Harvard's continuing Living Wage Campaign is "Because Workers Can't Eat Prestige."

That the popular imagination continues to proclaim Marie-Antoinette's lack of concern for "the masses" not only implies the superiority of American government because it has no monarch, but also subtly reinforces a masculine image of leadership. It is worth underscoring something Pierre Saint-Amand mentions only in passing: it was Hillary Clinton's role as a reformer of health care, one of those standard European benefits that the United States alone condemns as "socialist," which prompted much of the early invective against her. The Marie-Antoinette of the cake is similarly positioned to embody and to displace class politics in pointedly gendered ways.

It is thus no accident, I suggest, that the cake-eating fiction lingers in the popular imagination even (or especially) of the country's most elite university. Its persistence is a sign not simply of ignorance but of a cultural need both for the proverb and for the body of the queen on whom the proverb is inscribed. One of the thousands of Web sites that discuss Marie-Antoinette inadvertently puts the contradiction well: "There was a story in France that when Louis' wife, Marie Antoinette, heard that the people had no bread, she said, 'Let them eat cake.' Marie Antoinette never said that, but it shows how little she knew (and some say cared) about life for the common people of France."[20] In other words, it is precisely what Marie-Antoinette *didn't* say that tells the people who she was. Thus we, the people, get to eat our cake and have it too, reviling the signifiers of class and sex while leaving the system of class and sex intact: Marie-Antoinette creates unanimity.

This volume stands against such simplifying projects by helping us to know how Marie-Antoinette has served the purposes of displacement in her own setting and in ours. It shows us the ways in which dynamics of class, gender, nation, politics, and culture are situated, interwoven, and intersectional. Most poignantly, it teaches us the ways in which the body of a queen helped to consolidate a gendered revolution that, perhaps partly from its fears of women's power, jettisoned its finest dreams: of full citizenship and the equitable distribution of resources for all. For as Adrienne Rich reminds us:

> The decision to feed the world
> is the real decision. No revolution
> has chosen it. For that choice requires
> that women shall be free.[21]

Notes

1. Harvard's Living Wage Campaign, which continues, has been featured in several periodicals along with discussions of Harvard's wealth; see, for example, Joanna Berkman, "Harvard's Hoard," *New York Times Magazine*, 24 June 2001, 39–41.

2. Emphasis mine. The 2001–2 *Harvard College Handbook for Parents* can be found on-line at http://www.fas.harvard.edu/~fdo/publications/0102/parents.html. It is gratifying to see a more appropriate if fleeting mention of Marie-Antoinette on another Harvard Web page, this one on "How to Read an Assignment" by William Rice of the Harvard Writing Center, which offers very thoughtful advice for addressing a hypothetical question on the Revolution's gender politics. See http://www.fas.harvard.edu/~wricntr/documents/Assignment.html.

3. "Let Them Eat Cake" appears in Antti Aarne and Stith Thompson, *The Types of the Folktale* (Helsinki: Folklore Fellows Communication No. 184, 1973) as Tale Type 1446, "The queen has been told that the peasants have no bread" (p. 424). Examples from Estonia, Germany, Russia, and India are named. As Terry Castle

notes, Rousseau attributes the saying to "a great princess," allegedly the Spanish Marie-Thérèse, wife of Louis XIV, in Book 6 of his *Confessions,* published before Marie-Antoinette arrived in France. Antonia Fraser, in *Marie-Antoinette: The Journey* (New York: Random House, 2001) records its attribution to Louis XVI's aunt Madame Victoire (135). The statement (whether or not made by Marie-Antoinette) has also been interpreted as support for the poor by virtue of the French law requiring bakers to sell fancier loaves (such as brioches) at the price of plain bread whenever ordinary bread sold out.

4. Thomas Jefferson, "Autobiography," in *Writings of Thomas Jefferson,* ed. Merrill D. Peterson (New York: Viking Press, 1984), 92–93, emphasis mine.

5. Alan Kurzweil, "Cult of the Queen," *Arts and Antiques* 10 (October 1993): 70.

6. Ibid.

7. Jacques Revel, "Marie Antoinette" in François Furet and Mona Ozouf, eds., *A Critical Dictionary of the French Revolution,* trans. Arthur Goldhammer (Cambridge, Mass.: Harvard University Press, 1989), 254.

8. Jacques Revel, "Marie-Antoinette in Her Fictions: The Staging of Hatred," in Bernadette Fort, ed., *Fictions of the French Revolution* (Evanston, Ill.: Northwestern University Press, 1991), 114.

9. Revel, "Marie Antoinette," 252.

10. Alan Jolis, "Epilogue," *Love and Terror* (New York: Atlantic Monthly Press, 1998), 328.

11. See http://www.capetiens.com/classique5.htm. Translation mine. It is not clear from the Web site whether these words are Chalon's.

12. See http://www.knology.net/~leahmarie/antoinette1.html.

13. Barbara Babcock, "Introduction," in Babcock, ed., *The Reversible World: Symbolic Inversions in Art and Society* (Ithaca: Cornell University Press, 1978), 14.

14. See Susan S. Lanser, "'*Au sein de vos pareilles*': Sapphic Separatism in Late Eighteenth-Century France," in Jeffrey Merrick and Michael Sibalis, eds., *Homosexuality in French History and Culture* (New York/London: Hayworth Press, 2001), 105–16. This volume was copublished as the *Journal of Homosexuality* 41, 3–4 (2001).

15. Revel, "Marie Antoinette," 262.

16. Edmund Burke, *Reflections on the Revolution in France* (1790), ed. L. G. Mitchell (Oxford: Oxford University Press, 1993), 75.

17. The gateway for this site is http://homepages.msn.com/FlirtationWalk/amber 02128/.

18. Shlomith Rimmon-Kenan, "Narration as Repetition: The Case of Günter Grass's *Cat and Mouse,*" in Shlomith Rimmon-Kenan, ed., *Discourse in Psychoanalysis and Literature* (New York: Methuen, 1987), 176–87.

19. The advertisement appeared in *Hemispheres: The In-Flight Magazine for United Airlines,* September 1998, 7.

20. See http://www.mrdowling.com/705-frenchrevolution.html.

21. Adrienne Rich, "Hunger (for Audre Lorde)," in *The Dream of a Common Language: Poems 1974–77* (New York: Norton, 1978), 13. It is striking that the first sentence of this passage ("The decision to feed the world is the real decision") appears on the Web sites of several organizations dedicated to ending poverty, but always without the second part, which insists on the connection with women's liberation.

NOTES ON CONTRIBUTORS

TERRY CASTLE is Walter A. Haas Professor in the Humanities at Stanford University. A specialist on eighteenth-century English literature, feminist theory, and gay and lesbian studies, her publications include *Clarissa's Ciphers: Meaning and Disruption in Richardson's 'Clarissa'* (1982); *Masquerade and Civilization: The Carnivalesque in Eighteenth-Century English Culture and Fiction* (1986); *The Apparitional Lesbian: Female Homosexuality and Modern Culture* (1993); *The Female Thermometer: Eighteenth-Century Culture and the Invention of the Uncanny* (1995), and *Noel Coward and Radclyffe Hall: Kindred Spirits* (1996). Her contribution to this volume won the Crompton-Noll Prize of the Lesbian and Gay Caucus of the Modern Language Association.

ELIZABETH COLWILL is Associate Professor of History at San Diego State University. She is the author of numerous articles on female authorship, sexuality, and the political culture of the Revolutionary epoch. Currently, she is working on a book manuscript on the shifting meanings of gender and race in the French and Haitian Revolutions.

DENA GOODMAN is Professor of History and Women's Studies at the University of Michigan. Her publications include *Criticism in Action: Enlightenment Experiments in Political Writing* (1989) and *The Republic of Letters: A Cultural History of the French Enlightenment* (1994). With Elizabeth C. Goldsmith she coedited *Going Public: Women and Publishing in Early Modern France* (1995).

LYNN HUNT is Eugen Weber Professor of Modern European History at the University of California at Los Angeles. She is the author of *Politics, Culture and Class in the French Revolution* (1984) and *The Family Romance of the French Revolution* (1992). She has edited several volumes including *Eroticism and the Body Politic* (1991) and *The Invention of Pornography: Obscenity and the Origins of Modernity, 1500–1800* (1993).

THOMAS E. KAISER is Professor of History at the University of Arkansas at Little Rock. He has published studies of many aspects of eighteenth-century French political culture, including royal propaganda, public opinion, and the impact of royal mistresses on perceptions of the monarchy. Currently, he is finishing a textbook on early modern Europe and preparing a monograph on the history of French Austrophobia and its role in the vilification of Marie-Antoinette.

SUSAN S. LANSER is Professor of English and Comparative Literature and Chair of Women's Studies at Brandeis University. Her publications include *The Narrative Act* (1981) and *Fictions of Authority: Women Writers and Narrative Voice* (1992). Lanser has coedited *Women Critics 1660–1820* (1995) as well as the Broadview edition of Helen Maria Williams' *Letters Written in France* (2002). Her current project is a book tentatively titled "Sapphic Subjects and the Engendering of Enlightenment."

LAURA MASON is Associate Professor of History at the University of Georgia. Her first book, *Singing the French Revolution: Popular Culture and Revolutionary Politics* (1996), investigated popular singing practices during the Revolutionary decade; her current project, *The Equals of Vendôme: Politics, Justice, and the End of the French Revolution*, examines the political climate surrounding the trial of Gracchus Babeuf and the Equals during the Directory. Mason has reviewed films for *American Historical Review* and published an essay on biography and film entitled "Looking at Life," in *Rethinking History* (1997).

SARAH MAZA is Jane Long Professor and Chair of the History Department at Northwestern University. The author of *Private Lives and Public Affairs: The Causes Célèbres of Prerevolutionary France* (1993), her most recent book, entitled *The Myth of the Bourgeoisie: An Essay on the French Social Imaginary, 1750–1850*, will be published in 2003.

PIERRE SAINT-AMAND is Francis Wayland Professor and Chair of French Studies at Brown University. He has written on various aspects of the eighteenth century. His publications in English include *The Libertine's Progress: Seduction in the Eighteenth-Century French Novel* (1994) and *The Laws of Hostility: Politics, Violence, and the Enlightenment* (1996). In French, he recently edited *Thérèse philosophe* for the Pléiade edition of *Romanciers libertins du XVIIIe siècle*.

MARY D. SHERIFF is Daniel W. Patterson Distinguished Term Professor at the University of North Carolina at Chapel Hill. She is the author of *Fragonard: Art and Eroticism* (1990) and *The Exceptional Woman: Elisabeth Vigée-Lebrun and the Cultural Politics of Art* (1996). She is also the editor of *The Cambridge Companion to Watteau* (forthcoming). Her latest work, *Moved by Love: Inspired Artists and Deviant Women in Eighteenth-Century France*, is due to be published in 2004.

CHANTAL THOMAS is Director of Research at the Centre National de la Recherche Scientifique (Paris), specializing in eighteenth-century literature. She has written numerous books of criticism and personal essays, including *Casanova: Un voyage libertin* (1985); *Thomas Bernhard* (1990); *Sade* (1994); *La vie réelle des petites filles* (1995); and *Coping with Freedom* (2001). Thomas has treated the subject of Marie-Antoinette in *La Reine scélerate*, which appeared in English as *The Wicked Queen* (1999), and most recently her first novel *Les Adieux à la reine* (2002) which won the Prix Femina, given each year to the best work of fiction by a French woman.

LARRY WOLFF is Professor of History at Boston College. He is the author of *The Vatican and Poland in the Age of the Partitions* (1988), *Postcards from the End of the World: Child Abuse in Freud's Vienna* (1988), and *Inventing Eastern Europe: The Map of Civilization on the Mind of the Enlightenment* (1994). His most recent book is *Venice and the Slavs: The Discovery of Dalmatia in the Age of Enlightenment* (2001).

Index